Corporate Fraud and Internal Control

A Framework for Prevention

RICHARD E. CASCARINO

WILEY

John Wiley & Sons, Inc.

Library of Congress Cataloging-in-Publication Data

Cascarino, Richard.
 Corporate fraud and internal control : a framework for prevention/Richard E. Cascarino.
  p. cm.—(The Wiley corporate F&A series)
 Includes bibliographical references and index.
 ISBN 978-1-118-30156-2 (cloth); ISBN 978-1-118-41980-9 (ebk);
 ISBN 978-1-118-42172-7 (ebk);ISBN (eMobi) 978-1-118-43402-4 (ebk)
 1. Fraud–Prevention. 2. Auditing, Internal. I. Title.
 HV6691.C38 2013
 658.4'73–dc23

                2012022692

4

Printed in the United States of America

10 9 8 7 6 5 4 3 2 1

Contents

Preface

DATING BACK TO 3500 BC, records of various civilizations indicate by patterns of checks and ticks that record verification took place. In ancient Egyptian, Greek, Chinese, and Roman civilizations, rulers sought to confirm official records by comparing two sets of such records. The lowest-ranking magistrate in ancient Rome was a *quaestor*, or investigator. This elected official traditionally worked within the treasury to supervise the financial affairs of the empire.

Accuracy of records was tested, typically by two officials working together. One official read from the one record sheet and the other checked against the other record sheet. The term "auditor" is derived from the Latin *auditus*, meaning a hearing.

With the fall of the Roman Empire, auditing and internal control disappeared in Europe. It was not until the Middle Ages that the growth of centralized control once again demanded proof of the adequacy and correctness of record keeping and the prevention of the defrauding of the king.

In the Orient, however, audit can trace its ancestry back to the Western Zhou Dynasty some 3000 years ago, in which it continued in various forms until the Song Dynasty in 992AD when a "royal audit court" was established. Audit in China took the form of Inspectorates until the Revolution of 1911 when an Audit Court was established, a Chamber of Audit set up, and Audit Law was issued. Auditing continued until the founding of the People's Republic of China in 1949 when audit was conducted by internal supervision within the Departments of Public Finance.

In 1982, the Constitution of the People's Republic of China was promulgated resulting in the 1983 formation of the National Audit Office of the People's Republic of China.

Today, capital markets, which have been rocked by recent corporate scandals and frauds on an international scale, are demanding that financial organizations, publicly listed companies, multinational companies, and the public sector implement sound corporate governance. Large-scale fraud has severely eroded investor confidence; in many cases, investors are simply waiting for the next large fraud to be announced.

In the past, many organizations, companies, and government bodies have operated in a purely reactive mode to the problem of fraud. That is, only after a fraud had taken place were decisions made regarding how to combat it. With the increasing impact of corporate governance legislation and the changes in society of recent years, the need to fight fraud in a proactive manner has become paramount.

Companies now must accept their corporate responsibility to protect assets and employees from the temptations and impacts of fraud.

At the individual level, fraud is impacting every citizen, either directly through being defrauded or indirectly through the impact of higher taxation or shopping bills. Individual fraud is also creating an atmosphere in which individuals feel cheated and defrauded, and that they have the right to retaliate by cheating and defrauding others.

Police services are under increasing pressure to combat all types of crime, particularly violent crime. As a result, often white-collar crime, corruption, and fraud are treated as the "poor relation" at the low end of the resources chain and receive priority only in egregious cases when they become front-page news in the newspapers.

As a result, organizations have no choice but to develop plans and strategies to deter, detect, and, where required, prove fraud utilizing their own in-house control mechanisms and systems of internal control.

This book addresses the roles of the board and its management and audit committees in implementing a system of internal controls that adequately defends against fraudulent and corrupt practices both within the organization and against it. The book itself consists of 12 chapters.

Chapter 1, "Nature of Fraud," introduces fraud and irregularities, covering the elements of the crimes of theft and fraud as well as the nature and cost of fraud. It includes the basics of fraud and financial irregularities and defines fraud and prejudice resulting from fraud. It also presents general safeguards to make fraud in commerce more difficult, and ways to seek redress from fraud perpetrators.

Chapter 2, "Elements of the Crimes of Theft and Fraud," explores how fraud and conventional theft differ legally. It also helps identify the principal control elements required to reduce the likelihood of a fraud occurring and its impact, should it occur, and to increase the probability of early detection in the event of an occurrence.

Chapter 3, "Frauds Against the Individual," identifies specific types of fraud against the individual that, left unchecked, may increase the probability of a loyal employee turning against the employer in desperation. It also identifies corporate responsibility in educating employees against potential fraud attacks against them personally.

Chapter 4, "Frauds Against the Organization," helps readers recognize specific types of fraud against the organization, their red flags, and the failure or lack of internal controls that expose organizations to such attacks. It also differentiates between internal frauds carried out from inside the organization against the interests of the organization, and external frauds carried out against the organization from an external source with or without the cooperation of current employees.

Chapter 5, "Fighting Corruption," identifies areas of vulnerability within the organization that expose it to managerial-level frauds and internal corruption. It also identifies areas and indicators where organizations may be—unwittingly or deliberately—the perpetrators of such corruption against third parties.

Chapter 6, "Role of Ethics in Fighting Fraud," explores the nature and role of ethics within the organization to combat fraud and helps readers evaluate the current state of ethical structures within an organization. The chapter helps readers design a code of conduct that will reduce the likelihood of fraud occurrences and increase the probability of early detection.

Chapter 7, "Controlling Fraud," defines the roles of corporate governance and the structures organizations utilize to prevent fraud. The chapter helps readers evaluate the system of internal control the organization relies on to minimize fraud and makes practical recommendations for improvement where required. The chapter emphasizes the role internal audit must play in controlling fraud.

Chapter 8, "Fraud Risk Management," identifies appropriate techniques to establish the corporate fraud risk profile and clarifies the roles of internal, external, and forensic audit in the fight against fraud. It helps readers design and implement effective whistleblowing both within and external to the organization as a fraud preventive and detective measure.

Chapter 9, "Investigating Fraud," assists the reader in identifying the red flags and indicators of fraud that should trigger a fraud investigation. It also identifies the forensic techniques available and the resources and training required to implement an appropriate fraud investigation. In addition, it covers the requirements for establishing an internal investigation function and determination of the appropriateness and the appropriate measures for tracing and recovering lost assets.

Chapter 10, "Computer Fraud and Countermeasures," helps readers identify areas of vulnerability to fraudulent use of information systems and processing of fraudulent transactions. It also helps facilitate the design and implementation of appropriate measures to defend the digital assets of the organization.

Chapter 11, "Legal Issues Surrounding Fraud," assists readers to evaluate the current legislative framework for the country or countries in which the organizations are operating and evaluate the effectiveness of deterrent mechanisms for fraud, including international electronic fraud.

Chapter 12, "Industry-Related Fraud Opportunities," identifies fraud opportunities specific to certain industries as well as government institutions. Its aim is to assist in the design of effective control mechanisms against specific risks to achieve optimal control effectiveness at minimized cost.

In addition, appendices are provided to give examples of antifraud opportunities, policies, and checklists as well as the basis for legal jurisdictions for fraud prevention and prosecution. An educational version of IDEA Data Analysis software is also provided via a web site download.

CHAPTER ONE

Nature of Fraud

Fraud is like cancer. Most of us know someone who has it. We know people who will eventually have it. It has become common but we can take steps to protect ourselves through healthy choices and regular checkups using the latest tools and technology. But if people ignore the problem and live dangerously, then there's a much greater chance of becoming a victim.

—Toby Bishop, CEO, Association of Certified Fraud Examiners

After studying this chapter, you should be able to:

- Briefly outline the definitions and concepts underlying fraud and irregularities

- Describe the basic types of fraud
- Understand the profiles and motivators of fraud
- Define the responsibilities for fraud detection and prevention

More and more incidents of private and public fraud are being reported daily in the media, and increasingly prosecutions for this offense are being conducted in the various courts. This chapter examines the phenomenon in order to obtain a full appreciation of what exactly fraud is.

FRAUD AND IRREGULARITIES: DEFINITIONS AND CONCEPTS

Throughout history, the development of negotiable instruments, from cowrie shells to plastic cards, have led to the creation of a set of rules and conventions for trade and the promotion of smooth and orderly commercial interactions among individuals and countries. The breaking of these rules and conventions helps white-collar criminals make a living—in some cases a fortune—while evading discovery. In many countries, the courts and judicial system do not afford economic crimes the priority of crimes involving violence.

Fraud itself is a legal concept existing within the criminal laws of virtually every civilized country, although slight variations exist. In most countries, fraud may be deemed to occur when these individual elements exist:

- An untrue representation about a material factor event is intentionally made by an individual or organization.
- Such representation may or may not be believed by the person or organization to which the representation was made.
- The victim could suffer the possibility of harm or prejudice as a result of the misrepresentation.

For example, within South African law, fraud may be conveniently defined as being "the unlawful and intentional making of a misrepresentation which causes actual prejudice or which is potentially prejudicial to another."[1] Actual proprietary prejudice is not necessarily required for fraud. Even nonproprietary or potential prejudice may be sufficient. Thus, fraud is not a crime against property only; it also can be regarded as a crime against the interests of the community in general.

The Arkansas Department of Finance and Administration defines occupational fraud in this way:

> Occupational fraud and abuses can be defined as the use of one's occupation for personal enrichment through the deliberate misuse or misapplication of government resources or assets. Occupational fraud and abuses include misappropriation of assets in the form of cash theft, fraudulent disbursements, theft or personal use of inventory or other non-cash assets. Fraud can also take the form of bribery and corruption when kickbacks, gifts, or gratuities are offered to government employees from contractors or vendors to influence decisions of government agents or employees.[2]

A clear distinction must be drawn between the intention to deceive and an intention to defraud since a causal link is required between the misrepresentation and the actual prejudice.

Courts have traditionally worked on the basis that fraud is punished not because of the actual harm it causes but because of the potential harm or prejudice inherent in the misrepresentation, so that even if the potential victim should not believe the misrepresentation or not have acted on it the intent and possibility of harm means that a fraud has still occurred. Put more simply the intent and possibility of harm means that a fraud had been committed even if no loss occurred.

A crime that is commonly confused with fraud is *theft by false pretenses*. Fraud is always committed when a theft by false pretenses occurs, but the converse is not necessarily true since, in addition to misrepresentation and actual or potential prejudice, theft by false pretenses requires an appropriation of property capable of being stolen.

The misrepresentation leading to fraud can also be committed by means of an admission whereby the perpetrator fails to disclose a material fact that, unless revealed, could induce the victim to act to his or her prejudice if there was, in fact, a legal duty to disclose.

Once this broader definition of fraud is realized, it can be understood that occurrences of fraud are much more prevalent than we believe based on the large-scale frauds that hit the newspapers. Fraudulent misrepresentation is an everyday occurrence in our lives; it ranges from bending the truth in providing an excuse for an employer to utilizing company assets for personal benefit on the pretext that it was in the company's interest. Each of these acts falls under the heading of criminal fraud in its most literal sense and potentially could result in a criminal conviction. Due to this broad definition, a level of white noise results, whereby fraudulent acts of a petty nature become tolerated and norms and ethical standards decline. As a result, fraud becomes acceptable if the end justifies the means. The economic stresses in today's society internationally create pressures and aspirations to attain a standard of living higher than many individuals are capable of achieving on merit. This situation, in turn, increases the likelihood of such persons achieving those aspirations by deceit.

No definitive preventive control can stop all fraud in its tracks since fraud is developed based on the ingenuity of defrauders. Some new, not-yet-anticipated variation on a theme always occurs.

Victims of Fraud

One common misconception is that frauds are carried out only by individuals against organizations. In many cases, when fraud is carried out by an individual acting on behalf of an organization, the fraudulent activity could be looked on as: *any business activity in which deceitful practices are resorted to by an organization or representative of an organization with the intent to cause economic injury that would deprive another of property or other entitlements.*

Although it is tempting to make the assumption that frauds may be confined to one class of victim—for example, the cost of insurance fraud being borne by the insurance industry—in reality, in most cases, the ultimate bearer of the cost of fraud is the general public. By the same token, government losses to taxation fraud ultimately are passed on to the taxpayers in general. Losses from corporate fraud, either from embezzlement or financial manipulation, are normally ultimately borne by customers.

In the event of fraud covered by government regulation, recourse for losses may be sought from the regulatory body. Nevertheless, ultimately they get passed on once again to the consumer or public.

In complicated cases such as payment card frauds, the ultimate loser may appear to be the cardholder (rarely and only if negligence can be shown), the merchant who accepted the fraudulent card, the merchant-acquiring bank that processes the transaction of the cardholder, and the card issuer. Once again, in reality, costs generally are passed on through higher insurance premiums, higher fees for banking services, higher interest rates, higher credit card fees, or reduced dividends to shareholders.

The net effect is that the public ends up bearing the brunt of losses from fraud. Thus, the public perception of fraud as a "victimless" crime can therefore be seen as a false supposition and true only in that the cost may be spread over a large population. Thus, it may be seen that there are two forms of victims of fraud.

The *primary* victims are those who suffer the initial harm of fraud, whether these victims are individuals, corporations, or governmental bodies. The *secondary* victims are those who sustained the ultimate economic impact of losses attributable to fraud.

Nature of Fraud

Although many executives have an image in mind of what fraud is, the image may differ from executive to executive and may, indeed, differ widely in respect of the true nature of fraud. In order to adopt a comprehensive policy toward the minimization of fraud within the organization, a full fraud risk assessment is required to identify those opportunities specific to a given set of operations. Only once the fraud risks are understood can a system of internal controls be designed to address those specific risks. Even then, fraud can never be truly eliminated, but the internal controls can provide reasonable assurance that both instances of fraud and also waste and general misuse of resources can be reduced.

Much of the corporate fraud that takes place results from poor bookkeeping practices combined with poorly trained and inattentive staff. When this situation is combined with the inadequate internal and interdepartmental communications commonly found within organizations, the opportunities for undetected business scams grows exponentially. Making staff members aware of fraud opportunities and their responsibility in preventing and detecting fraud combined with a conduit through which to report fraud is fundamental in establishing good corporate control.

In order for fraud to occur, three elements must be in place. This trio is known as the fraud triangle (see Exhibit 1.1) and is used both in fraud prevention and fraud detection. Its origin is attributed to the criminologist Donald R. Cressey, who formulated this hypothesis regarding trust-violating behavior to explain why people commit fraud.

Pressure or Motivation

In general, the motivating factor leading individuals to commit fraud can be defined as a form of pressure. This pressure can take the form of significant financial need (or perceived need) and may include anything from medical expenses to a simple case of expensive tastes. For this pressure to translate into

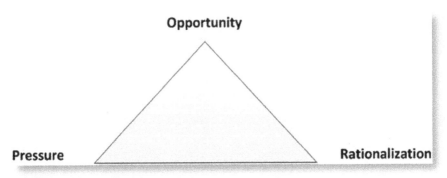

EXHIBIT 1.1 Fraud Triangle

a fraud-enabling pressure, generally some secrecy is involved; the potential perpetrator believes that the motivator must be kept secret and solved privately. Motivation can also be nonfinancial, such as the need to cover up for a third party's poor performance in the workplace or to produce good results and work.

Rationalization

Rationalization is the process by which fraudsters can reconcile their behavior in committing the fraud with their own internal belief system regarding honesty and trust. For those who are generally dishonest, rationalization is easy; for others, however, rationalization involves the prioritization of the pressure source against their own moral code. For example, placing the needs of a family member ahead of the need to remain loyal to an employer. In this way they can convince themselves that, despite their moral standards, the fraud is OK. Rationalizations may include these and others:

- The money is needed for the benefit of a family member or loved one.
- The money is not being stolen, simply borrowed and will be returned in due time.
- The employee feels unfairly done by, so there is a degree of entitlement to the theft.
- There is no other recourse, no alternative source of aid; it is a choice between steal or lose everything.
- The person has a lower set of ethical values and does not believe that stealing in such a fashion is wrong.
- The employee holds a poor opinion of the ethical standards implemented within the organization; therefore, he or she is only doing what everyone else does.

Once an apprehended fraudster attempted to justify his theft by pointing out that he only stole $5,000 while the company had claimed $10,000 on its insurance policy; therefore, he had done nothing wrong since the company had made 100 percent profit on his theft.

Opportunity

Opportunity involves the capability of people to commit the fraud in what they believe will be an undetectable manner. The opportunity may come about due to the individual's job-related access to the assets to be stolen combined with knowledge that management oversight is weak in this area, and other internal controls will be ineffective in either preventing or detecting the fraud. Most fraud opportunities are created by poor management oversight or weak preventive controls. An absence of detective controls increases the probability that fraud will occur.

Within the fraud triangle, organizations have limited opportunities to recognize pressure and rationalization, but they can significantly reduce opportunities by the design and implementation of business procedures, processes, and controls that will limit employees' ability to commit a fraud, and will increase the probability of detection should an opportunity be seized.

Detection involves not only being alert for anomalies in business records and areas where internal controls may be ineffectual but also for red flags in employee behavior traits and changes in behavior patterns.

Red Flags

Red flags are early warning indicators that the risk of fraud in a particular area either is higher than is normally tolerable or has increased over a period. Once again, these red flags can be categorized as pressure sources, changes in behavior, and general personality traits.

Pressure Sources

Pressure sources in individuals that supervisors should be alert for include:

- Medical problems for the employee or a family member
- Substance abuse
- Family member's loss of a job
- Lifestyle exceeding income capacity
- Divorce
- Financial pressures from a variety of sources

Changes in Behavior

Changes in behavior that could alert supervisors to the possibility of fraudulent practices include:

- Sudden increase in the visibility of material possessions
- Apparent increase in absenteeism
- Decreases in productivity and increases in signs of dissatisfaction at work
- Mood changes and irritability increase
- Borrowing money from coworkers
- Refusing promotion
- Refusing to take vacation time
- Working unnecessary overtime
- Carrying large amounts of cash
- Rewriting records for neatness sake

General Personality Traits

Studies in organizations where high levels of fraud occurred indicate that certain specific personality traits may be indicative of potential fraudsters. These include:

- Work performance levels considerably higher than the norm
- Dominating and controlling attitudes
- Living beyond their means
- Disliking their work being reviewed
- Maintaining close relationships with vendors or customers
- Exhibiting a strong desire to display material wealth

It should be noted that none of these red flags proves that a fraud has taken place or will take place. They are simply indicators that should alert supervisors or management to a higher potential fraud risk, particularly when combined with known weakness in internal controls within an area where an employee has sole authority and responsibility.

Frauds can take many forms and come from a variety of sources, both within and outside of an organization. Within an organization, fraud can be perpetrated by any level of staff or management. Outside of the organization, fraud can be perpetrated by customers or clients, suppliers—indeed, by persons without any contractual connection to the organization. A particular fraud could be directed against the organization itself or against assets it holds on behalf of clients.

Typically, the primary objective of fraudsters is to obtain something of value. The secondary, although essential, objective is to conceal their actions in order to avoid detection. In order to obtain value, typical fraudsters commonly seek to:

- Remove funds or other assets
- Understate payments due to the organization
- Overstate claims on the organization and receive payment
- Misrepresent applications for credit on insurance

Types of Fraud

Frauds can be split into two broad categories: frauds against the individual and frauds against the organization. These two categories are not necessarily mutually exclusive, and some frauds involve a combination of techniques. These fraud categories will be covered in depth in Chapters 3 and 4.

Frauds against the Individual
- Consumer frauds
- Telephone frauds
- Online auction fraud
- Charity frauds
- Misrepresentation of material facts
- Concealment of material facts
- Advance fees (4–1–9) frauds
- "Middleman" frauds
- Bait and switch
- Larceny
- Extortion
- Counterfeit goods and intellectual property
- Affinity frauds
- Pyramid schemes
- Ponzi schemes
- Career opportunities
- Cash recovery frauds

Frauds against the Organization
- Check fraud
- Obtaining fraudulent loans
- Unsolicited orders
- Embezzlement
- Bribery
- Corruption
- Conflicts of interest
- Theft of trade secrets
- Breach of fiduciary duty
- False claims
- False conveyancing
- Tunneling
- Conspiracy
- Lapping
- Kiting
- Fraudulent affiliations
- Counterfeit money
- Benefit frauds
- Insurance fraud
- Payment card frauds
- Pension frauds
- Tax fraud
- Insider trading and market abuse
- Procurement fraud
- Falsification of time sheets
- Falsification of expense claims
- Forgery
- Creation of fictitious employees (ghost employees) and collecting the payments
- Failing to terminate existing employees and collecting the payments
- Billing for services not rendered

 ## COST OF FRAUD

A major difficulty in estimating the cost of fraud is the fact that fraud often goes undiscovered and therefore unreported. For this reason, the available statistics may fail to reflect actual losses. In the past, such undetected fraud was subject to guesstimates with no indication of the reliability for the figures produced. Recently targeted measurement has given greater reliability to the estimated values for such fraud.

Fraud losses impact virtually every business enterprise and governmental function. Despite advances in fraud detection technologies, fraud losses have grown exponentially, imposing major cost increases in many industries. The impact on individual industries is explored more thoroughly in Chapter 12. In addition to direct losses, fraud may be seen as part of the economic externalities. An economic externality occurs when one business implements actions, or refrains from taking action, and in doing so passes on costs to another business.

For example, where an employee is dismissed for fraud-related offenses but no prosecution takes place, the ex-employee is free to seek employment with another organization and repeat the offense. Prieston and Dreyer in their book *Mortgage Fraud, The Impact of Mortgage Fraud on Your Company's Bottom Line,* sum this situation up: "While fraud does exist in retail organizations, it is typically related to a particular loan officer and is more often than not quickly discovered. The employee is usually terminated from his [or her] position and moves on to new company until the same thing happens all over."[3]

For many organizations, this migration of the fraud risk to a third party is seen to be "not my problem" as long as the perpetrator no longer works for their business. Indeed, some organizations see such a movement as to their advantage since the likelihood is that the perpetrator will stay in a similar industry and may well end up working for a competitor and imposing economic disadvantage on that organization. Such organizations typically refrain from publicizing in any form either the fact of the fraud or the method by which it was carried out. As a result, fraudsters can utilize the same techniques without an increase in the likelihood of detection.

According to the Association of Certified Fraud Examiners Report to the Nations on Occupational Fraud & Abuse,[4] a typical organization will, in all probability, lose some 5 percent of its annual revenue to fraud. When this percentage is applied to the estimated gross world product (GWP) for 2009, this figure translates to a potential total fraud loss of more than $2.68 trillion (now $3.2 trillion based on the 2010 GWP). Other key findings included:

- The median loss caused by the occupational fraud cases in the study was $160,000. Nearly one quarter of the frauds involved losses of at least $1 million.
- The frauds lasted a median of 18 months before being detected.

- Fraud perpetrators often display warning signs that they are engaging in illicit activity. The most common behavioral red flags displayed by the perpetrators in our study were living beyond their means (43 percent of cases) and experiencing financial difficulties (36 percent of cases).
- Occupational frauds are much more likely to be detected by tip than by any other means.

In 2006, the International Fraud and Corruption Report[5] examined the nature and costs of fraud in six countries: Australia, Canada, France, Germany, Ireland, and the United States.

Although the research was conducted in the United Kingdom, that country was excluded from the report due to difficulties with measuring losses to fraud since there was no legal definition of fraud as an offense in its own right.

The research was based on 2004 figures. Germany led the way in the cost of fraud in terms of the percentage of gross domestic product at 9 percent; in the United States, the cost amounted to 6 percent of GDP, although the actual cost of fraud in the United States at that time amounted to $660 billion.

In 2010, the National Fraud Authority (NFA) in the United Kingdom published its first Annual Fraud Indicator, estimating fraud losses in that country to be at least £30.5 billion per annum. The NFA readily acknowledged that the figure was underestimated as some significant areas of fraud were excluded. By the time of publication of the 2011 report,[6] many of these areas were included, resulting in a more comprehensive indication of the extent of fraud lost in the United Kingdom. According to the 2011 estimate, the cost of fraud was around £38.4 billion per annum. The public sector accounted for some 55 percent of fraud losses with tax fraud forming the largest component of that sector; its losses ran at an estimated £15 billion per annum.

The private sector losses were £12 billion per annum. The financial services industry saw the highest losses in this sector at £3.6 billion, while charities accounted for a further £1.3 billion. Direct losses suffered by individuals as a result of fraud were estimated to cost £4 billion, primarily as a result of schemes involving mass marketing, rentals, and online ticket fraud.

Another 2011 report in the United Kingdom[7] indicated that the financial cost of fraud and error can be accurately measured like any other business cost. According to the report, a typical 12-year average loss to fraud was more than 5 percent of total costs with fraud losses rising in the first two years after the start of the recession to over 6 percent. Fraud was "the last great unreduced business cost," but implementation of appropriate control mechanisms could reduce such costs by up to 40 percent within 12 months. The report draws a distinction between the traditional costing areas of an organization, in which costs can be forecast and budgeted and control mechanisms typically are designed and implemented in advance in order to improve efficiency. It is accepted that, within these areas, costs are a necessary part of doing business. Fraud, however, is frequently a "denied" cost. People believe that fraud happens to other organizations, not to their own; therefore, companies often do not implement preventive controls until after a significant fraud occurs. In reality, fraud is an unnecessary cost in that the business would continue at the same level of effectiveness should fraud not be present but at considerably higher levels of efficiency.

Where appropriate fraud preventive measures have been implemented, the results have been impressive. For example, government departments in the United States reporting loss reductions in several programs of up to 35 percent over a five-year period.[8] In the United Kingdom, the National Health Service reported loss reductions of up to 60 percent between 1999 and 2006.[9]

However, organizations that do not effectively manage fraud risks can incur a much larger costs. The longer the fraud continues, the greater the loss that is incurred.

In addition to the initial losses, cost of fraud includes the cost of insuring against loss of assets due to employee dishonesty as well as loss of reputation. Cost of investigation to substantiate such insured losses may also be expensive and can, in some cases, exceed the original cost of the fraud sustained. Some insurance policies cover investigation costs, but others do not or cover them only for proven fraud that is covered by the specific policy.

In the event of a claim, typically only losses that can be proven and quantified can be claimed successfully. Therefore, determining the cost of the loss is a critical component of successful asset recovery.

Intangible losses, such as the impact on corporate morale, may not be insured unless previously agreed to within the terms of the policy.

Internal fraud involving employee dishonesty cannot be completely eliminated but can be deterred with an effective internal control structure. One of the main deterrents to insider fraud is the degree of certainty that any attempt will be detected early and that the perpetrator will be caught. This deterrent appears to have more impact than the punishment the apprehended fraudster may expect. For that reason, it is critical that organizations encourage the reporting of fraudulent activities or suspected wrongdoing by maintaining a strong culture of ethics and integrity, while at the same time giving employees a method and the confidence to carry out such reporting without fear of retribution.

Costs of Corruption

In addition to straight losses caused by conventional fraud, another class of loss is that brought about by corruption such that "insiders" profit at the expense of "outsiders." Previously, corruption was seen as a by-product of lack of regulation in the commercial world and of corrupt political systems. In practice, however, heavily regulated economies suffer corruption at about the same rate as poorly regulated economies.

Various forms of corruption exist, from low-level bribes to junior public officials that have little financial impact on the economy as a whole but are very hard to prevent, through systematic corruption affecting whole areas of government and organizations, where dishonesty is the norm and honesty is seen to be irrational. Once again, as with other forms of fraud, it frequently is seen as someone else's problem. Complacency and attitudes that "such things only happen in the developing world" and "that sort of thing doesn't happen here" open the door to the bending of the rules as well as actively seeking exceptions to rules and regulations. Corruption includes the purchasing of intangibles, such as access to decision makers, direct influence, or political appointment, and can be seen in virtually every country in the world.

One of the major problems in dealing with large-scale corruption is deciding just what the term *corruption* means. Corruption includes not only *bribery* (payments made in order to gain an advantage over competitors or a rival, typically including the abuse of power) but also embezzlement (misappropriation of funds from the organization or government department) as well as direct *fraud* (theft through misrepresentation as previously defined).

Corruption is dealt with in more detail in Chapter 5.

In the United States, the Improper Payments Information Act of 2002 required public agencies to publish a "statistically valid estimate" of the extent of fraud and error in their programs and activities. In 2010, this act was reinforced by the passage of the Improper Payments Elimination and Recovery Act, which required increased reviews, audits, and reports for certain high-cost programs with high rates of improper payments.

Under these acts, the government pursues perpetrators of allegedly fraudulent acts and holds individual officers and directors accountable for compliance breaches of procurement policies and procedures. Regulators now require that the governance boards of organizations have a working knowledge of the regulatory scheme under which their organizations operate and with the compliance programs enforced within their own particular organization.

Corruption is covered in more detail in Chapter 7.

NOTES

1. *The Law of South Africa*, Vol. 6, pp. 330–331. (1994) Butterworths: Durban.
2. www.dfa.arkansas.gov/offices/accounting/internalaudit/Pages/Relationship-betweenInternalControlsandFraud.aspx.
3. Arthur J. Prieston and Jaqueline A. Dreyer, *Mortgage Fraud, The Impact of Mortgage Fraud on Your Company's Bottom Line* (Mortgage Bankers Association of America, 2001, Washington, DC).
4. ACFE, 2010 *Report to the Nations on Occupational Fraud and Abuse*, www.acfe.com/uploadedFiles/ACFE_Website/Content/documents/rttn-2010.pdf.
5. NHS Counter Fraud and Security Management Service, International Fraud and Corruption Report (2006). NHS Counter Fraud and Security Management Service, London.
6. National Fraud Authority, Annual Fraud Indicator, 2011, www.homeoffice.gov.uk/publications/agencies-public-bodies/nfa/annual-fraud-indicator/annual-fraud-indicator-2011?view = Binary.
7. Jim Gee, Mark Button, and Graham Brooks, *The Financial Cost of Fraud — what Data from Around the World Shows* (PKF [UK] LLP and the Centre for Counter Fraud Studies at University of Portsmouth, 2011), Portsmouth.
8. Maggie Mahar, *Taking On The "Epidemic" of Health Care Fraud*, www.health-beatblog.com/2011/08/-taking-on-the-epidemic-of-health-care-fraud.html.
9. NHS Press Release NHS PATIENT FRAUD REDUCED BY MORE THAN HALF SINCE 1998: www.nhsbsa.nhs.uk/Archive/pr.patient.fraud._11.08.06.pdf.

CHAPTER TWO

Elements of the Crimes
of Theft and Fraud

There are three things in the world that deserve
no mercy, hypocrisy, fraud, and tyranny.

—Frederick W. Robertson, English preacher (1816–1853)

After studying this chapter, the reader should be able to:

- Briefly describe the elements necessary to meet the legal requirements to differentiate between fraud and conventional theft.
- Identify the principal control elements to reduce the likelihood of a fraud occurring and its impact should it occur, and to increase the probability of early detection in the event of an occurrence.

Common law, also known as precedent or case law, originated in the United Kingdom during the reign of Henry II (1133–1189), and is based on the concept that the decision previously made sets a precedent and should be followed in subsequent cases.

In the United States, individual states may have variations on the concept of common law. For example, Louisiana uses a system unlike any other state; it is based on the French Napoleonic code. California drew originally from its Spanish origins a system of Spanish civil law, which was changed in the mid-1800s into a codified system based on common law. The federal government operates on a variant whereby federal courts may interpret common law while Congress is free to legislatively overrule the court's decision.

The common law offense of theft is one of the most prevalent offenses committed in today's society. Theft can be motivated by simple greed, as when individuals or organizations have a desire to enrich themselves at the expense of others, or from desperation, based on a perception of a hopeless economic situation. It has become common practice for large organizations to include as a normal part of the budget an amount to be written off for the crime of theft. Some estimates indicate the average dishonest manager will be in a position to steal 12 times that of an average hourly worker.

In order to be classed as theft, normally there would have been a *contrectatio*, which is Latin for "handling," whereby the perpetrator must have actually *handled* the object stolen, normally to remove it from the lawful possession of the owner. In today's environment, however, where theft can take place electronically with no physical handling of the assets removed, this definition may have to change.

According to Professor C R Snyman of the University of South Africa, the term *appropriation* is more appropriate to describe the act of theft. The elements of theft would then consist of an act of appropriation of a certain type of property via unlawful means with an intention to appropriate.[1]

The act of appropriation itself has two elements: The thief deprives the lawful owner or possessor of his or her property and then the thief him- or herself exercises the rights of an owner in respect of the property.[2] This approach does not require that the subject of the theft be physically handled and is more appropriate in instances involving electronic data.

Theft of electronic data emerged as a new form of theft with the advent of information technology. No longer does theft require the physical movement of hardware components or physical computers; electronic information, software programs, and confidential data are all available for misappropriation. In these cases the items stolen remain physically intact. Intangible assets, such as electronic funds, can be stolen via electronic means, and online banking, at both the corporate level and via home Internet banking, has created considerably more opportunities for the misappropriation of funds.

Employees may also "steal" computer time or services, particularly in their use of the Internet access available within many organizations. This theft is without considering the impact on the organization of the downloading of inappropriate material.

Copying of proprietary data from a computer system (*data leakage*) may appear to be theft but does not comply with the common law principles of the offense (to deprive the rightful owner of the use of his or her asset). In the case of copying of computer data, the original data still exist and are available to the rightful owner. The advent of technology has turned this crime more into a breach of copyright than straightforward theft. The international response to data leakage has been erratic, to say the least. Individual countries and states define theft as potentially including *theft of computer services* (Delaware Code); *anything whether animate or inanimate* (Canadian Criminal Code); *property including electronic impulses; electronically produced data; confidential, copyrighted, or proprietary information; private identification codes on numbers which permit access to a computer by authorized computer users or generate billings to consumers for purchase of goods or services* (State of Illinois Code).

Over the years, many different legal definitions of fraud have been promulgated, including fraud as a criminal act, fraud as a tort for civil action and fraud as defined by professional organizations in an attempt to give their members evaluation criteria to judge the sufficiency of evidence gathered. All of these definitions agree in general that in order to be defined as fraud, certain criteria must be met. These criteria include the ones listed next:

- A *misrepresentation*, perversion, or distortion of the truce has been made either in the form of spoken or written words or even in the conduct of the accused—for example, nodding of the head. In order to be classified as a misrepresentation, the perpetrator must be aware that he or she cannot meet the expectations created by the misrepresentation. For example, issuing of a check knowing that there are no funds to cover or being insolvent without informing creditors could constitute fraud.
- The misrepresentation has resulted in an actual or potential *prejudice* to the victim or to a third party. The acid test is normally whether the misrepresentation was such that a "reasonable" person acting in a "normal" manner might be deceived.
- Another class of prejudice, known as *nonproprietary prejudice*, does not necessarily involve direct prejudice to a third party. For example, the production of a forged driver's license when charged with the traffic offense or writing an examination on behalf of another person could be classified

as a nonproprietary prejudice. Likewise, the making of false allegations against the dignity or reputation of a third party could result in a nonproprietary prejudice. Under such circumstances, a fraud may be deemed to have been committed even though there is no causal link and even if the misrepresentation was unsuccessful. It has long been accepted that there can be no such thing as attempted fraud. The actual fraud took place when the attempt was made, whether it was successful or not.

▪ In order for fraud to exist, there must be *intention* to defraud. Negligence regarding the truth of a statement is not the same as intent. The perpetrator must be aware of the fact that the representation is false and must make it with the intention that it be acted on by the victim in a manner prejudicial to him- or herself as a result of the misrepresentation. The intention must relate both to the misrepresentation and to the actual or potential prejudice. Intending to deceive does not necessarily mean intending to defraud, but intending to defraud always includes the intention to deceive. In order to establish that a fraud has taken place, intention to acquire advantage does not have to be proved. If it is proved that the accused had an intention to defraud, the motive is immaterial. Fraud even can be deemed to have taken place when an attempt has been made to defraud an individual, even if the attempt was unsuccessful and the potential victim was unaware that an attempt actually had been made. For example, if a letter including a fraudulent misrepresentation is intercepted in the mail prior to reception by the intended victim, it may still be judged that a fraud has in fact taken place.

 ## DOCUMENT FRAUD

Despite the advent of computerized systems, much of the fraud encountered would be impossible without the use of fraudulent documents. Documentary evidence to substantiate payments, qualifications, nationalities, and even currency still is necessary. A negotiable document is anything that can be exchanged for monetary value including:

▪ Checks
▪ Money orders
▪ Titles
▪ Deeds of ownership
▪ Certificates of qualifications

- Identity documents
- Licenses and registrations
- Medical prescription forms
- Traveler's checks

College degrees from fictitious universities can be purchased for as little as $450 for an associate's degree to as high as $2,000 for a three-way combination of bachelor's, master's, and PhD.

Computerized systems have made it easier to commit document fraud with the use of scanners, color printers, and color photocopiers that produce copies indistinguishable from the originals.

In days gone by, document fraud was carried out using the basic techniques of erasure and cut and paste. These techniques have been in use for over 100 years and have resulted in the development of security techniques designed to make straightforward document changes more difficult to commit and easier to detect. Use of high-quality security paper with chemical detectors and void pantographs made it more difficult to alter a document without changing its physical characteristics, thus making alterations easy to detect. Document issuers were required to take all possible measures to protect documents from forgery, alteration, or duplication. These activities came under the rubric of "due diligence" on the part of the documentation issuer.

In today's computer environment, the ease of duplication of documents requires that security features in negotiable documents be considerably enhanced. Such features now include techniques such as:

- *Safety paper.* Due to the ease of scanning, original documentation must be printed onto paper with built-in safety features, such as toner grip. Toner grip is a coating applied to paper that provides greater anchoring of toner when laser printing. In addition the use of fluorescent fibers integrated into the paper which, while invisible under normal light conditions, are detectable under ultraviolet light, but will not duplicate on copiers or scanners making fakes obvious.
- *Fourdrinier watermarks.* These watermarks are faint designs that are pressed into the paper during the manufacturing process. Such watermarks may be seen from either side of the paper; artificial watermarks, however, are visible only on the side on which the artificial mark is applied. Artificial watermarks can be simulated via computer; Fourdrinier cannot.
- *Artificial watermark fluorescent patterns.* This form of watermark is printed like an ink and is visible on the face or back of a document at a 45-degree

angle. These patterns provide a major verification and also can be authenticated under ultraviolet light. The need for this form of watermark resulted from the easy availability of normal artificial watermark stock paper at retail stores and on the Internet.

■ *Microline typeface.* This technique uses a very small typeface in place of a solid rule signature line. It can be used to display, for example, the company name, which is visible only under magnification. This feature is nonreproducible via scanner or photocopier, where the line would simply be reproduced as a solid line.

 ## CORROBORATING DOCUMENTS

In addition to negotiable documents, business relies heavily on documents of various forms to corroborate identities, credentials, or even terms and conditions on contracts. Warranties on goods are also commonly distributed in documentary form. Such documents include:

■ Driver's licenses
■ Identification cards
■ Immigration documents
■ Passports

In all of these cases, the creation of fraudulent documents is a mechanism with which to facilitate the intent of the fraud. The fraudulent document is not itself the intent; it merely provides the perpetrator with the capability of adopting a new identity or gaining access to a restricted area or even border crossing. Once access has been achieved, the perpetrator can continue to the actual fraud itself, whether it is obtaining funds by false pretenses, illegal entry to a country, fraudulent claim of benefits, or impersonation of legitimate ownership of an asset.

 ## PROCUREMENT FRAUD

In the procurement process, a variety of fraud techniques are found, including price fixing, bid rigging, supply of defective products, products substitution, defective pricing, and cost/labor mischarging.

In 2006, the United States created the National Procurement Task Force with the intention of promoting the prevention, error detection, and prosecution of procurement fraud as well as enhancing prosecution of fraud involving corrupt contractors to the government. Thirty different government agencies are involved with the task force and, since its inception, more than 400 procurement fraud cases have resulted.

An alternate form of procurement fraud involves collaboration between an employee working with an outside vendor in order to defraud the employer through the authorization of bogus or inflated invoices, payment for services or products not delivered, or work that is never done. Payments may take the form of cash, vacations, home improvement, or even a financial stake in the vendor company. In some cases, the outside vendor may in fact be a shell company set up by the employee specifically to defraud the employer.

Price Fixing

The procurement process is by its nature a competitive activity that can operate effectively only when competitors price independently and honestly. Price fixing is an anticompetitive activity involving an agreement among competitors to fix prices, thus colluding to inflate prices and cheat customers. Typically, increased costs then get passed on to the public. Technically, price fixing is an agreement among competitors to fix, raise, or simply maintain a price at which the goods and services are sold. The agreement need not necessarily require competitors to charge exactly the same price, but may involve limiting price differentials, use of standard formulas for computing prices, or control over discounts granted.

Price fixing is most commonly found in markets that are crowded and mature with a declining demand and a distinct absence of product differentiation.

In the United States, the 1890 Sherman Act prohibits such agreements and criminal prosecutions by the Antitrust Division of the U.S. Department of Justice are frequent. Violation of the Sherman Act is classified as a felony and punishable by a fine of up to $100 million for corporations and up to $1 million or ten years imprisonment or both for individuals. In extreme cases, even these limits may be exceeded.

Price fixing is commonly identified by certain telltale signs. Discounts may be eliminated in markets where discounts traditionally were given. Prices may stay the same for long periods of time. Prices may increase at a rate disproportionate to cost increases.

These indicators may arouse suspicions of collusion but cannot be taken as proof. They merely serve to draw attention to the requirement for further investigation in order to determine whether collusion is in fact taking place.

Bid Rigging

Bid rigging is also an anticompetitive activity that involves competitors agreeing in advance which organization will submit the winning bid during a competitive bidding process. Not all potential bidders need to participate in order to accomplish bid rigging. Variations on this type of fraud include *complementary bidding*, in which certain competitors agreed to submit bids that they know will be unacceptable to the buyer either because of the price or because of the terms of contract. This form of bid rigging is among the most frequently occurring and is designed to give the appearance of genuine competitive bidding.

A variation on this is *bid rotation*, in which competitors all submit bids but take turns in being the low bidder and therefore the winner of the contract. This form of bid rigging is easier to detect as the rotation typically follows a set pattern, which, if monitoring is taking place, soon becomes apparent.

In an attempt to lessen the predictability of bid rotation, a technique known as *bid suppression* may be used. In this scheme, one or more of the competitors that normally would be expected to bid will either refrain from bidding or withdraw a previously submitted bid, normally during the short list phase of selection, so that the designated winner will be chosen.

In the case of competitive bidding for large contracts, subcontracting agreements may be used as part of a bid rigging scheme. Competitors who agree not to bid or not to submit an acceptable bid may receive a subcontract from the winning bidder at a higher rate than the one they would have submitted.

Red flags for bid fixing may include:

- One or more bidding companies continuing to submit unsuccessful bids with a single company winning most of the contracts
- A group of companies consistently bidding for the same contracts with a rotation of the lowest bidder
- Sudden reduction in bid prices whenever a new bidder enters the market
- Consistent subcontracting by winning bidders to one or more unsuccessful competitors in the bidding process
- The sudden withdrawal of a successful bid and the subsequent subcontracting to the new bid winner

Once again, red flags are not definitive proof, only an indicator that further investigation may be required.

Supply of Defective Products and Product Substitution

In defective product and product substitution schemes, contractors provide a product or service that is different from the one specified in the contract. This could be achieved by using unapproved, refurbished, or inferior parts in a manufacturing process, or parts sourced from a nonauthorized supplier. Certificates indicating the "genuine" nature of components are readily attainable using standard document fraud techniques. The result could range from a product that is technically deficient and cannot fulfill its intended purpose to a personal service contract that remains unfulfilled.

Defective Pricing

Defective pricing involves contractors inflating their costs in order to increase profits or limit their losses. This is normally seen in "cost plus" contracts in which the price quoted is the supplier's cost plus a certain percentage. This is commonly the result of intentionally using old or inaccurate cost data. In the United States, the Truth in Negotiations Act (1962) requires contractors to submit cost or pricing data prior to negotiations and to certify that the data are accurate, current, and complete as of the close of the negotiations.

Indicators that may suggest the possibility of defective pricing include:

- The certification of false or misleading information (i.e., information that is not complete, accurate, and current as certified)
- Estimates used as a basis for negotiation higher than supporting documentation

The submission of defective pricing data is not classified as a specific indicator of fraudulent behavior by the contractor, and recovery under the contract clause is not based on fraudulent intent. Contractors who knowingly submit defective information during negotiations are, however, guilty of fraudulent intent.

Cost/Labor Mischarging

Cost/labor mischarging frauds involve a contractor or supplier fraudulently inflating the cost of labor or materials on cost-plus contracts. As in all contracts, material costs are vulnerable to fraud since material is susceptible to physical theft. A common mechanism for such fraud is the diversion of materials from the contractual use to another commercial use with the cost being charged to the original contract. Labor mischarging typically occurs when the contractor charges for work which was not actually performed. This could take the form of undocumented labor time or fraudulent use of fictitious time cards. Labor costs are particularly sensitive since supporting third-party documentation in the form of invoices or purchase orders may not exist to substantiate the costs. Reliance is therefore placed on the integrity and accuracy of the contractors' labor accounting system.

Red flags in this area may include:

- Large movements in labor costs
- Reclassification of costs from indirect to direct or vice versa
- Distinctive patterns of charging for labor or materials
- Overall laxity in the system of internal controls

 ## BRIBERY AND CORRUPTION

Bribery and corruption encompass a broad range of activities including the giving or receiving of a bribe or gratuity as well as engaging in activities involving a conflict of interest. A bribe is generally defined as something of value given to a person in a position of authority with the intention of influencing decisions or activities. In many cases involving bribery of government officials, there is no requirement to prove the intention to influence.

In some cases, perpetrators may engage in a corruption practice without the knowledge or approval of the company for which they carry out the task. Frequently, however, the corruption entails a deliberate, approved, and prearranged act. In such cases, companies frequently call on third parties to act on their behalf, particularly in reference to international business transactions. The involvement of intermediaries providing real services may be perfectly legitimate, but they can also be used as a cover to conceal bribery and corruption. Use of joint ventures to mask bribery with cash amounts being siphoned off as "dividends" to corrupt officials is particularly tricky to identify. In high-value bribes, the recipient may be a family member or relative of the bribed employee. Shares in the joint venture may be owned by family members.

Conflict of interest includes situations where employees engage in activities that could be deemed to create a conflict between the employees' personal interests and their duty to loyally serve the best interests of their employer. When an individual or corporation is in a position to exploit his or its own professional or official capacity in some way for personal, family, or corporate benefit, such self-dealing would be classed as a conflict of interest.

Perhaps the most publicized form of corruption is *bribery*. Bribery entails a straightforward offer of something of value to influence the decision maker. This could take the form of favors, money, gratuities, and other forms of kickback. It may be rationalized as "the only way to get decisions made" or even "that's the way business is done here." Bribery may be done at the commercial or political level in order to, for example, gain access to high-value state contracts or to avoid legislative oversight.

An insidious form of corruption is the practice of *nepotism* in which a person in authority favors friends or relatives in the granting of contracts or employment. Again, a common rationalization is "I gave him the job because I know the quality of his work." While this may be true in some circumstances, in many cases, the person awarded the work may be underqualified or even unqualified to carry it out.

Nepotism is a specific case of *conflict of interest*. Where there is a known conflict between a decision maker's self-interest and the interests of the employer, the employee's duty is to put the interests of the employer first. As an example, an executive working for a large company in Africa purchased a piece of land, knowing that his company intended to acquire it for expansion purposes. The executive paid an equivalent of $150,000 for the land in the name of a company he created especially for the transaction. One week later, the "company" sold the land to his employer for $1,500,000. When this was discovered during the course of a routine audit, the company decided not to prosecute because of the embarrassment factor.

Embezzlement is another common form of corruption and abuse of power. It occurs when dishonest employees or public officials steal money or resources for their own personal use and includes the use of company assets, such as cars or property, for unauthorized purposes.

An extreme form of corruption within an organization is *extortion*, in which a person in authority coerces another in order to achieve payment or favors for action taken. This could involve getting to the head of a waiting list or simply providing preferential treatment. It differs from bribery in that the payoff is actively sought by the insider rather than offered by the outsider.

INDUSTRIAL ESPIONAGE

Trade secrets within organizations may be vulnerable not only to unscrupulous competitors but also to disgruntled employees. In today's economic climate where a fluid workforce has become the norm and corporate loyalty has declined, internal theft of secrets has become a more lucrative target to employees who lack commitment or loyalty to the organization. Industrial espionage may take the low-tech form of simple Dumpster diving or may involve a more sophisticated attack on the integrity and confidentiality of the organization's computer systems. Once again, companies place a great deal of emphasis on the prevention of penetration of systems by outsiders but in many cases pay little heed to the legitimate access of insiders. The Federal Bureau of Investigation (FBI) estimates that every year billions of dollars are lost to foreign and domestic competitors who deliberately target economic intelligence in U.S. industries and technologies.[3] Major methods of conducting such espionage includes:

- Targeting and recruiting insiders
- Bribery, cyberintrusions, wiretapping, theft, and Dumpster diving to gain economic intelligence
- Engaging in apparently innocent business relationships in order to gather economic intelligence, including trade secrets

Fraud defense requires a heightened awareness within organizations of the potential for espionage from rivals and competitors in a variety of markets, including overseas.

In the business world, inside information can make the difference between profit and loss and between success and failure. Trade secrets stolen from an organization can eliminate its competitive edge. Today's economy is heavily dependent on the information age. During the Industrial Revolution, power accrued to individuals and organizations that could manipulate physical objects more efficiently and effectively than their competitors. In the Information Revolution, power accrues to those individuals and organizations that can leverage information more effectively than the competition. Almost any information derived from a competitor can be of value to an unscrupulous individual or organization. Contracts and agreements, price lists and discounts, research documents and market analysis, or even personnel records may have a high value depending on the use to which they are put.

In the past, obtaining such information required illegal physical access to corporate premises. With the rapid implementation of technology throughout organizations, failure to invest in appropriate security mechanisms and internal controls may be a shortcut to corporate suicide. The advent of open systems architectures and cloud computing is an open invitation to information theft. Implementations of appropriate control mechanisms combined with effective education of personnel on the need for information security and their role in its provision is essential to maintaining the integrity and confidentiality of information.

Computer hacking may still take a physical form, where an intruder enters the corporate premises, perhaps disguised or even employed as a member of the cleaning staff, with the ability to search for unsecured workstations, and passwords left lying about, gain access to communication boxes and wiring closets, or install keystroke loggers, software, or hardware drives. Such access gives the intruder an ideal opportunity to go Dumpster diving, as previously mentioned. Memos, letterheads, and calendar information commonly found in trash cans provide intruders with small amounts of usable information with which to start the corporate hack.

Perhaps the easiest method of gaining illicit access to corporate information systems is via *social engineering*. From casual conversations with corporate employees or even their friends or relatives, hackers may gain all of the information required either directly to derive a password or, alternatively, to send a communication ostensibly from someone the employee knows, requesting a password for some urgent administrative work. A variation of social engineering is a technique known as *shoulder surfing*, which is as simple as standing behind someone and watching them enter the password. Indeed, I have stood in front of a bank teller and watched her enter her password, reading the keystrokes upside down. When I asked her why she chose that particular word for password, she could not understand how I knew what it was. Again, this is a clear case of insufficient employee education.

The massive increase in wireless networks has opened up the door to eavesdropping on communications from inside or even outside an office building. Hacker tools abound, allowing eavesdroppers to identify unprotected networks or networks with low levels of encryption that are readily susceptible to the use of *wireless sniffers*.

In 2000, a study by the Brookings Institute estimated that the value to U.S. companies of intangible assets was "at least 50%, and possibly as much as 85%."[4] In 2011, Symantec estimated that industrial espionage costs U.S. businesses alone more than $250 billion per annum.[5] The Symantec research was undertaken by forensic psychologists Eric D. Shaw and Harvey V. Stock in order to identify those factors leading to insider theft of intellectual property. Their research indicated two basic classes of thief. The first is the "entitled, disgruntled thief" who has been partly involved in the development of the information stolen and who, when leaving the organization, takes a copy with him or her to the new employer. The second category of thief is the "Machiavellian leader" who intends specifically to use the information either as an object for sale or in development of a competing product. Persons in the second category, Shaw and Stock felt, would plan the theft carefully without necessarily showing any disgruntled behavior, thus alerting nobody within the employing firm as to their intention to steal company-confidential information.

In addition to the conventional insider turned thief, corporate spies and hackers may enter from an outside source, such as the Internet or from the organization's trading partners, either customer or vendor, with direct computer connections into the corporate network. Corporations also may be at risk from gun-for-hire contractors known as *kites*. A kite, working for a third party, may collect information from a competitor. Should the kiting activities be discovered, the person's third-party employers have plausible deniability that they were in any way involved. Any traceable involvement typically would be covered by a contract stating that the consultant would abide by all ethical rules in providing information to the third party.

In many of these cases, the ultimate theft is an opportunistic crime. The insider or the outsider has been given the opportunity to access the corporate information that is underprotected or even unprotected. Absence of adequate internal controls due to undertraining, trust in employees, lack of supervision, failure to take disciplinary action when grounds for such action is found, and lack of an adequate auditing presence are all forms of leaving the door open for the theft.

 ## CHECK FRAUD AND MONEY LAUNDERING

Purchases made with fraudulent checks are common form of corporate fraud. Payment is made in the full knowledge that the check will be dishonored by the receiving financial institution and the organization that accepted such payment will suffer a direct loss.

Despite the advent of electronic trading, check fraud remains one of the largest challenges facing businesses and financial institutions today. Indeed, advances in information technology make it increasingly easy for check manipulation to occur. Simple counterfeiting through the use of desktop publishing and color printers or copiers puts check fraud within the reach of the most amateur criminals. Check forgery, counterfeiting, and alteration all have become easier to accomplish unless appropriate steps are taken to implement proper controls and to reduce both the likelihood and impact of check fraud. Check fraud is covered in more detail in Chapter 4.

Money laundering, at its most basic, is the act of making money derived from one source look as if it comes from another source. At its most common, it involves trying to make money obtained by illegal means appear as if it originated from a legal source. Given the volumes of money derived from illegal activities, such as drug trafficking and the funding of terrorism, the laundering of large quantities of cash has become critical.

Basic money laundering is a three-stage process.

1. *Placement* involves the introduction of the illegally gained cash into a legitimate financial institution. Most countries have legislation requiring banks to report high-value cash transactions. This means that the money has to be broken down into smaller amounts and spread around so that the sheer size of the cash deposit is not a giveaway.
2. *Layering* involves the movement of the funds using a variety of financial transactions to make the trail hard to follow. It includes such transactions as wire transfers between different accounts, in different countries, in different names, and purchase of high-value items, such as diamonds, houses, or aircraft, to change the form of the money.
3. *Integration* involves the reintroduction of the money into the mainstream economy as legitimate assets apparently coming from legal transactions. It may take the form of investments in a legitimate business in exchange for a share of the profits or perhaps sale of the high-value asset.

Because of the movement of financial transactions through the global financial systems, major international efforts continue to be made to fight money laundering. In the United States, the Bank Secrecy Act (1971) requires the filing of currency transaction reports in order to create a money trail to facilitate the tracking of untaxed funds. By 2007, the U.S. Departments of Treasury, Justice, and Homeland Security developed the national anti–money laundering strategy.

The United Nations Office on Drugs and Crime assists members to adopt legislation to prevent money laundering from financing terrorism. It furnishes members with the necessary expertise and knowledge to implement legislation while, at the same time, increasing the ability of local justice officials to investigate and prosecute complex financial crimes. It also facilitates the exchange of information among member states.

Anti–money laundering controls are covered in detail in Chapter 12.

 ## NOTES

1. C. R. Snyman, Criminal Law, 4th ed. (Butterworths, 2002), p. 469, Durban.
2. Ibid., p. 477.
3. Federal Bureau of Investigation, "Economic Espionage," www.fbi.gov /about-us/investigate/counterintelligence/economic-espionage.
4. Margaret Blair, "New Ways Needed to Assess New Economy," Los Angeles Times, November 13, 2000, http://articles.latimes.com/2000/nov/13/local /me-51109.
5. "Insider Data Theft: When Good Employees Go Bad," www.symantec.com /connect/blogs/insider-data-theft-when-good-employees-go-bad.

CHAPTER THREE

Frauds Against the Individual

Rather fail with honor than succeed by fraud.

—*Sophocles (496–406 B.C.)*

After studying this chapter, you should be able to:

- Identify specific types of fraud against the individual that, left unchecked, increase the probability of a loyal employee turning against the employer in desperation.
- Recognize red flags indicating these types of fraud.
- Identify appropriate controls to reduce the likelihood of such frauds occurring and to increase the probability of early detection if they occur.
- Identify the corporate responsibility in educating employees against potential fraud attacks against them personally.

Incidents of private and public fraud are being reported daily in the media, and more and more prosecutions for this offense are being conducted in the various courts. This chapter examines the phenomenon of fraud in order to obtain a full appreciation of what it exactly is.

ONLINE AUCTION FRAUD

With the increasing popularity of Internet auctions, online auction fraud has become a significant risk factor to individuals. It includes fraud due to the misrepresentation of a product advertised for sale through an Internet auction site, the nondelivery of an item purchased through an Internet auction site, and nonpayment for goods purchased through an Internet auction site. At any given time, several million items are for sale via online auction houses with many thousands of people using such auctions as their main source of income. Most such transactions are legitimate with the terms and conditions fulfilled in full. eBay currently estimates that the rate of confirmed fraud is 1 in 40,000. That said, the U.S. Federal Trade Commission reports that almost 50 percent of online fraud is auction fraud by both sellers and purchasers. Typical among such frauds are:

- Failure to send purchased items
- Failure to pay
- Misrepresentation of the item for sale
- Switching the purchased item and returning a defective equivalent
- Sale of stolen goods
- Sale of pirated or counterfeited goods
- Charging excessive shipping costs
- Selling nonexistent goods in order to extract credit card details

Controls to Prevent Online Auction Fraud

Perhaps the most obvious control is to understand the risks prior to participating. Items purchased via an online auction may not be as represented in descriptions or photographs. It is the responsibility of the buyer to ensure that the item offered is exactly what he or she desires. Sellers, particularly of high-value items, can be checked out in advance.

If it is a corporate seller, the Better Business Bureau may be able to provide assistance.

At a minimum, an online search may uncover multiple clients who have had painful experiences with the seller.

Be wary of short-term auctions. Auctions lasting only one to three days may be a red flag that the auction is fraudulent. The fraudster can obtain the money quickly and disappear before a whistle can be blown.

Where possible, contact sellers prior to bidding to find out as much as possible about sellers themselves, their terms and conditions, warranties, and shipping costs.

When paying, avoid sending a check or money order whenever possible. Payment with a credit card may give you some recourse should the merchandise be misrepresented or undelivered. Credit card payment offers a far higher probability of being able to track the identity and location of the seller.

Refuse to hand over personal information, such as identity or Social Security numbers, driver's license numbers, or bank account details. Legitimate sellers do not require this information.

If you are the seller and payment is to be made electronically, have payment made into a nondisbursing account. (Nondisbursing accounts can receive payments in but cannot be used for payments out.) Your bank can transfer the funds from a nondisbursing account into your normal account. Under no circumstances provide your normal bank account details. Doing so would be a gift to an online fraudster.

If the item or deal appears to be too good to be true, it probably is not true. With notable exceptions, if the price seems absurdly low, it may be that the item does not, in fact, exist. It may be better to lose a bargain than to pay a very low price for nothing at all.

 ## CONSUMER FRAUDS

This category includes a variety of scams, including rogue dialing, lottery/prize scams, and other communications-based frauds. In addition, consumer frauds would include claims for products and services including "guaranteed" alternative health care products or sex aids. These form the modern basis of the old-fashioned snake oil and patent medicine frauds (guaranteed to cure the rheumatism, palsy, dropsy, and female complaints). They can also include frauds involving the purchase of high-value merchandise and its collection before full payment is received. Commonly, these frauds include the receipt of a false banker's draft or checks and electronic payments that are then not honored.

Rogue dialers make use of malicious coding commonly hidden in spam e-mail or Web pop-ups. The coding installs itself and is activated when the computer connects to its normal Internet service provider (ISP). Operating in stealth mode, the program then disconnects the computer from the normal ISP and establishes contact using a premium rate phone number instead. The user gets Internet connectivity and believes the access is normal until their next phone bill arrives.

Controls to Identify Rogue Dialers

Where the connection is made via dialup, the simplest method is to check every time a connection is made for the number dialed as the correct one. If connection is made via broadband, it is important to ensure that any dial-up modems are disconnected. Dial-up access is frequently used as a backup mechanism in case the broadband connection fails, particularly in developing countries. For a more sophisticated user, the Windows Task Manager can be used to view the list of programs running and, perhaps, identify rogue programs running in the background. Software to remove and the deter malware such as rogue dialers is readily available free of charge on the Internet, but, again, care must be taken regarding the source of the software to ensure that it has not itself been infected with malware.

Lottery/Prize Scams

In lottery scams, you are notified that you have won a prize for competition that would have required a payment had you entered, such as national lotteries. Without purchasing a ticket no entry in the lottery would occur. Put another way, "Congratulations you have won" is a meaningless phrase since you did not buy a ticket and therefore you could not have won. In many countries, lotteries, other than those conducted by states and certain licensed charitable organizations, are illegal. A variation on this theme is the *sweepstakes* scam. "You have already won" without having to enter and no payment required is the typical theme. After a series of "innocent" e-mails or phone calls, you have to pay certain fees and taxes. If any payment is required in order to collect winnings, there is no sweepstakes involved, only a lottery. Such enticements commonly use the names of legitimate charities, organizations, or even governments.

The intent of these scams is to have gullible recipients either pay money in advance (taxes or transfer fees) or at least provide details of bank accounts in order to receive the purported winnings. Needless to say, the winnings will not arrive and the bank accounts will be emptied.

Controls to Identify Lottery/Prize Scams

The primary controls to prevent such scams are user awareness and skepticism. Legitimate lotteries are run by governments or authorized charitable organizations. A legitimate lottery cannot be won by a person who has not entered, normally by purchasing a ticket.

Payment of taxes is *not* required in advance. In countries where lottery winnings are taxed, payment is made after the winnings are received. Lottery companies do not notify the winners. Winners have to notify the lottery that they wish to claim a prize.

If the lottery "won" is an overseas lottery, a clue as to its falseness may be the fact that it is against national law in many countries to participate in any overseas lottery, usually due to exchange control legislation. Where the approaches are made telephonically, just say no, request your number be removed from their lists, and give no further information. If callers wish to confirm your name or any other details, ignore them. They would have had that information before they called you if they were legitimate.

 ## TELEPHONE FRAUDS

In a typical telephone fraud, targeted victims receive a communication in the form of a letter, e-mail, mobile text message, or similar informing them that they have won a major prize. This prize can be claimed by phoning a specific telephone number. The victim is kept waiting on the line for several minutes, which are chargeable as the number dialed was a premium rate telephone number. Should the prize actually exist, it will come out to be a cheap give-away item. More commonly, victims hang up after waiting on the line, by which time the damage is done and the telephone fees have been incurred. Variations on this theme include calls reporting to be from the victim's credit card company or from a parcel delivery company. Once again, the number given is a fake, high-cost premium rate telephone number having nothing to do with the organization from whom the call apparently originated.

Other common telephone frauds include:

- Membership of *buying clubs*, where a "free" offer may trigger bills for other products that will be delivered regularly.
- *Gifting club* membership. These frequently purport to be local charitable or church groups with associated joining fees. In reality, many are simply pyramid schemes requiring constant recruitment to survive. Ultimately, the pyramid collapses and joining fees are lost.
- *Government grants schemes*, where their contactor claims to represent some form of government agency informing you that you are eligible to receive

a free grant with no requirement for repayment. All that is required is your bank account details to pay the money into. In some cases, a refundable "processing fee" may be requested. In neither case will any grant be forthcoming.

▪ *Reloading phone scams* attempt the double scam by approaching a person who has already been the victim of a fraud and may be susceptible to a second fraud. Callers may claim to represent a company or government agency that can recover the money you lost on the first fraud. Calls will follow indicating progress until finally your money has been recovered and can be returned to you contingent on you paying a "processing fee." The assumption is if you were gullible once, you will be gullible again.

Controls to Identify Telephone Frauds

Once again, the primary controls to prevent such scams are user awareness and skepticism.

If the communication comes in the form of a mass-mailing letter or e-mail, it is unlikely that you have won a significant prize. If you do not remember entering the contest when a telemarketer calls, be suspicious.

If "free" offers are made, check whether they relate to a membership or some form of extended service contract.

Remember that, in today's Internet world, area codes mean nothing. A number may look like your local area code, but the caller could be anywhere in the world.

Beware of callers who attempt to associate themselves with the brand name of a high-profile company with which you do not do business. In the United States, it is illegal for promoters to pretend a nonexistent association with another organization. Other countries apply different rules, but the principle is the same.

Beware of toll-free 800 numbers that direct you to a pay-per-call 900 number for which the fees may be extremely high.

Always check the legitimacy of any government agency that appears to have contacted you and offered you money. "National" or "Federal" in the name of an organization means nothing.

 ## CHARITY FRAUDS

Many legitimate charities rely on donations from the public to survive. They request these legitimate donations via online advertising, direct mail, e-mails, and telemarketing. Unfortunately, fraudsters use the same techniques and also claim to represent charitable organizations.

In today's world, it is unfortunately true that no sooner than a disaster is declared fraudsters latch on with charity appeals, frequently driven by the Internet. Not only do these scams deprive donors of their money, they also strip legitimate charities of funds they would have received had there been no misrepresentation by a third party. In addition, these frauds have the side effect of making potential donors more cautious and therefore less likely to donate in times of need. This is a variation from conventional consumer fraud because donors do not expect to receive a product. For this reason, it may be classified as fraud only if it can be proven that donors were deceived regarding intended use of the donation and the legitimacy of the charity involved.

Controls to Identify Charity Frauds

The primary controls to prevent charity frauds are recognition of the warning signs of a potential fraud. Examples of warning signs include:

- Thanks tendered for a pledge of which you have no recollection
- Requests that donations be made in cash
- High-pressure appeals to your charitable instincts

Always check exactly who is seeking the donation. If a local charity appears to be involved, check with it independently whether it is aware of the solicitation.

Legitimate charity fundraisers will not object to providing the contact details for the charity.

If in doubt, check your local or national register of charities and confirm with them independently.

If in doubt, say no. You can always make your contribution directly to the charity of your choice.

MISREPRESENTATION OF MATERIAL FACTS

In the misrepresentation of material facts type of fraud, the perpetrator makes false statements, claims, or intentional misstatements of one or more material facts in order to convince someone to hand over an asset. To prove misrepresentation of material facts, the victim must prove intent, which in many cases is not easy. Typically, proving intent involves proving the individual elements of misrepresentation, including:

- The making of a material false statement
- Prior knowledge of the falsity of the statement by the accused
- The degree of reliance placed on the statement by the intended victim
- Damages or losses incurred by the intended victim

The requirement for such proof has the implication that any statement made by a person who does not honestly believe it to be true may be deemed a fraudulent misrepresentation, should the matter come to court. Even unrealistic assumptions where perpetrators had reasonable grounds to believe they were unrealistic could be classified as misrepresentation. Generally in fraud cases, the misrepresentation must relate to an "existing fact." Accusations of fraud based on promises to do something in the future would not normally be classified as misrepresentation unless victims can prove that the statement was made with the present intention not to comply with the future promise.

A second class of misrepresentation is *negligent misrepresentation*, which occurs when a perpetrator makes a statement without necessarily having reasonable ground for a belief in the truth of misrepresented fact. Such grounds may be offered as a defense when the other elements of misrepresentation can be easily proven.

Omission of a material fact (concealment) may or may not be classified as fraudulent misrepresentation, depending on whether the accused had a duty to disclose the facts in question.

In all events, seeking redress will require victims to demonstrate that, in the absence of the fraud, the losses, damage, or injury would not have been incurred.

 ## CONCEALMENT OF MATERIAL FACTS

Concealment of material facts means that the fraudster must have had knowledge of a material fact, have had a duty to disclose, and have concealed it with intent to mislead or deceive the other party. Once again, proving intent may be difficult. The primary issue to be determined is whether the supposed fraudster had a duty of disclosure to the victim due to their relationship or the nature of the transaction. Should such a duty to disclose exist, liabilities must be proven in the same manner as any other misrepresentation.

Controls to Identify Misrepresentation or Concealment

Misrepresentation and concealment of material facts cannot be prevented. They can however be detected if sufficient care is taken. There is an old saying in dealing with material facts: "Never believe what the first person tells you, particularly if it's what you want to hear."

In examining any proposal made, the safe questions would be: "What if this wasn't true?" and "What could stop this from happening the way I want?" With these questions in mind, intended victims should be able to exercise due caution regarding the impact of a misstatement and the ways in which concealment could negatively impact the proposed transaction.

 ## ADVANCE FEES (4-1-9) FRAUDS

Advance fees frauds involve the offering of services that require an up-front payment in order to cover costs. The advance fee is taken and the fraudster disappears. Many such frauds have involved offering the transfer of funds from another country with currency restrictions. The victim is offered a commission to be the recipient of funds with no risk to him- or herself. The fraudster may offer official-looking documentation confirming that such funds are available and will be paid.

All that is required is the payment of an amount to cover initial expenses (always much smaller than the commission to be paid). Unfortunately, the fraudster does not have such funds available; therefore, the victim, in order to obtain the commission, is requested to cover the initial expenses. Once the money has been handed over, the fraudster will disappear together with all traces of the "officials" who confirmed that the money was available.

Generally speaking, national authorities in the country from which the message appears to have originated do not view complaints by victims who have been defrauded sympathetically. Victims thought they were conspiring to evade the law in the originating country or to bypass taxation procedures. In some cases, the fraud may seek the advance fees in order to pay bribes to government officials, which would also be illegal.

The 4-1-9 fraud is named after the section of the Nigerian penal code that addresses fraud schemes, and these schemes are often very creative.

They also are known as the Nigerian letter, but these frauds originate in many countries.

Controls to Avoid 4-1-9 Frauds

The 4-1-9 frauds are well enough known now for most law-abiding individuals to recognize them as hoaxes. Nevertheless, there are still enough potential victims to make continuing these schemes worth the while of fraudsters. Some victims have even been lured overseas, where they have been kidnapped by fraudsters and suffered a loss of large sums of money. In one case in South Africa, the pastor of a small church had been informed that a congregation in the United States was routing funds amounting to $1 million to the church. It had been intended for a congregation in Nigeria but that church had closed, and it had therefore been decided to route the money to his congregation. Unfortunately, the money was now in Nigeria. To release the funds, taxes amounting to 50,000 South African rand were required in Nigeria. The fraud was uncovered when the pastor approached his bank to mortgage the church in order to raise the funds to send to Nigeria. He was crushed to learn that he had been a victim of an attempt to perpetrate a fraud and that there were no funds and no U.S. congregation.

Any individual claiming to represent any form of government, lawyers representing unknown dead relatives, and officials who have large sums of money that need to be moved out of a particular country should be viewed as potential fraudsters and reported to the appropriate authorities.

"MIDDLEMAN" FRAUDS

Similar to the 4-1-9 fraud, middleman frauds offer the opportunity to become the middleman for a person or organization looking to expand into your region and seeking a local representative for a variety of reasons. No capital outlay is involved; all the individual has to do is receive payments and forward them to a third party while retaining a commission percentage. The payment received is fraudulent, although victims do not find out until after they pay the third party out of their own funds.

It is possible that you may be requested to act as a middleman recruiting investors to place their money in the hands of the fraudster on the basis of their trust in you. Should you be realize that you have become the middleman in such a fraud, the best thing to do is to approach the authorities immediately with every piece of evidence you have showing how you were fooled into bringing others into the scheme. At this stage, all you have going for you is your credibility so hide nothing and invent nothing.

A business area where a middleman may inadvertently be the beneficiary of a third party's fraudulent schemes is discussed in Chapter 4 under the heading "Click Fraud."

In a variation on this theme, I was approached in South Africa by a man claiming to represent a company in Zambia that wished to bring students to South Africa for me to train. We met and a fee for the service was negotiated. At this point I was informed that it was impossible to get the funds out of Zambia; however, it was possible to get (smuggle) emeralds out of the country. The man had done this before, selling the emeralds in South Africa and paying South African fees out of the proceeds. Unfortunately, the buyer would deal only with a white person, and the previous middleman had moved to Australia. Would I be willing to act as middleman for a commission of 20 percent of the proceeds, over and above the fee for the training?

Because of the nature of my work, I could recognize this readily as a middleman scam, so I said that I would have to consult with my partner (nonexistent) and contacted the South African Police Services fraud squad. I met the fraudster again with my "partner," a senior inspector in the fraud squad, and had him repeat the offer. From there on it was a police affair.

▦ BAIT AND SWITCH

Bait and switch is a form of fraud in which the fraudster lures in customers by advertising goods at an unprofitably low price and then reveals that the advertised product is not available but that an alternative (more expensive) product is. The goal of the bait and switch is to persuade some people to purchase the substitute item as a means of recovering money already expended in an attempt to obtain the bait or to offset the disappointment of not obtaining the bait. In order to demonstrate that a fraud has occurred, it must be proven that the fraud was intentional and was part of a greater selling scheme. An example of this would be a retailer who continues to advertise a low-cost product in order to attract customers knowing that he is out of stock or has never had stock of the low-cost bait. When the retailer has advertised that the low-cost item is available in limited quantities or for a limited time, no fraud has taken place.

Similarly, if the low-cost item is available and the purchaser is sold a more expensive product without any untruths regarding the advertised product that the customer *could* have chosen to buy, no misrepresentation took place and no fraud occurred.

Bait and switch can also apply, for example, to warranties that are denied because they "don't cover this specific item," hidden fees added to the bill, or additional parts that are required to make the discounted item actually work.

Controls to Prevent Bait-and-Switch Fraud

Once again, prevention of bait-and-switch frauds lies in the hands of the consumer. Where items of a known quality are offered at a price considerably below the normal market price, consumers should be wary of the possibility of a bait and switch. Where the quality is unknown, the offer may be quite legitimate but for an undesirable product. It falls to consumers to examine the quality and be satisfied that the product offered for a given price is a product they desire to buy. When a fraudulent bait-and-switch offer is detected, prosecution requires high levels of documentation and corroborating evidence. Generally, it is not cost effective for the victim of such a fraud to go to extreme lengths to gather such evidence, even if consumers feel that a loss has been incurred. Nevertheless, they can report such activities to the appropriate authorities and vote with their feet by choosing another retailer. In the United States, such reports can be made electronically via the Internet to the Better Business Bureau, which tracks such customer complaints.

 LARCENY

Larceny was originally categorized as a crime in order to differentiate it from robbery. It was originally defined as the taking of property in nonviolent face-to-face encounters. Normally, in this category, the perpetrator must have taken or converted the property of another without the consent of the owner with the intent to permanently deprive the owner of its possession. Within the fraud context, *larceny by trick* includes the taking of property *with* the owner's consent when that consent was obtained fraudulently or by deceit. In some countries and in some states in the United States, larceny has been incorporated into the overall crime category of theft; in others it remains a separate category. It may also be differentiated based on value resulting in the crime of *grand larceny*.

EXTORTION

Obtaining something from an individual or organization through coercion or the use of actual or threatened force or fear, including the fear of an official's office or of economic loss, is classified as extortion and is a criminal offense. As noted earlier, extortion is differentiated from bribery based on how the crime takes place. Bribery involves the offering *to* an individual or organization a benefit or reward in return for favors granted. Extortion involves the obtaining of benefit or reward *from* an individual or organization through the use of threats. The threats could range from denying favors to the individual of the organization, through disclosure of embarrassing or personal information to threats of physical abuse against the victim.

Worldwide, extortion is seen to be a more heinous crime than bribery due to the intentional abuse of the trust placed in the extortionist, and typically attracts a heavier prison sentence if proven.

COUNTERFEIT GOODS AND INTELLECTUAL PROPERTY

Intellectual property, as a part of property law, is a major component of innovation, and it is believed that intellectual property protection is one of the major factors in generating growth in the world economy. One of the major controls in combating trade in counterfeit goods and intellectual property is the use of patents and similar mechanisms, which enable inventors, authors, and artists to derive some of the benefits of the innovations. Protection mechanisms include the use of a *copyright*, which grants the author of original works exclusive rights for a fixed period of time. *Trademarks* involve the use of signs to distinguish the source of goods and services in combination so that they are eligible for registration as a trademark. *Patents* are used to grant exclusive rights to inventions for a fixed period of time. Such inventions can be either in the form of processes or products, but they must be seen to be new rather than simply a modification of someone else's patented idea, and they must be capable of industrial application, that is, an invention which can be made or used in some kind of industry.

Counterfeit goods is a term used to refer to any goods that are copies made without the consent of the legal holder of entitlement and without authorization by the legal holder. *Pirated* copyright goods is another term describing the same offense.

AFFINITY FRAUDS

The term *affinity fraud* refers to investment scams where the perpetrator capitalizes on members of a specific group, praying on the members of cohesive groups, such as religious or ethnic communities, the elderly, or professional groups. The word *affinity* itself raises connotations of similarity and relationships. The fraudsters who promote affinity scams may indeed be members of the group or frequently enlist respected leaders—community or religious—from within the group to disseminate information about the scheme, by lending their name to the scheme, thereby convincing others that a fraudulent investment is legitimate and of significant benefit to all involved. Commonly, those leaders themselves become unwitting victims of the fraudster's ruse.

Victims of such frauds often fail to notify authorities or seek legal redress, particularly where respected religious or community leaders have been used to convince others to join the scheme. Under these circumstances, many victims refused to believe that the scheme was, in fact, fraudulent from the outset. Either remedy is sought within the group, or losses are written off in order to avoid public embarrassment.

Many affinity frauds involve *Ponzi schemes*, where money from new investors is used to make payments to earlier investors in order to create the illusion that the investment is successful. This ploy is used to trick new investors to invest in the scheme by creating a belief that investors are making profits. Once the market reaches a saturation point, the scheme commonly collapses, and investors discover that most or all of their money is gone together with the fraudsters.

Bernard Madoff, currently serving a 150-year prison sentence for running perhaps the best-known recent Ponzi scheme, amounting to some $65 billion, is believed to have specifically targeted the so-called "Jewish circuit of affluent members of the Jewish community" in recruiting victims.

Controls to Identify Affinity Frauds

Any investment includes a degree of risk. To avoid affinity frauds, potential investors must carefully examine risk elements prior to purchase. Investment schemes that come with personal recommendations from trusted members of the community are no less risky than any other investments. Opportunities coming by word of mouth may be particularly suspicious.

Potential investors should be very wary of investment schemes offering extremely high profits with guaranteed returns. Very few investments return extremely high profits, and those which do typically involve extremely high risk.

Such schemes are normally offered with extremely tight decision dead-lines. Targeted victims are pressured in order to deny them the opportunity to think rationally about how likely it is that someone is willing to give them high-profit, low-risk returns simply because they like them.

Affinity frauds are being marketed via the Internet through targeted e-mails offering a "one-time opportunity, act now or regret it forever." Any such offers should be reported to the appropriate authorities within the country. In the United States, the complaint center of the Securities and Exchange Commission can be found at www.sec.gov/complaint.shtml.

PYRAMID SCHEMES

A pyramid scheme generally is an operation whereby people participating in the scheme are entitled to receive more money than they invested by reason of recruiting others. The money is made through recruitment, while the product or service has no real value. Such schemes have brought financial misery to thousands and have even resulted in suicides.

Many pyramid schemes attempt to appear legitimate by claiming that members will receive benefits, such as commissions on goods sold or discounted travel services. These are attempts to make the scheme look like a simple multilevel marketing program. In reality, the aim of the scheme is to encourage members to recruit new victims to invest their own money in the scheme.

In some Internet versions of pyramid schemes, participants are given the opportunity to obtain a valuable free gift by purchasing a low-volume item from a web site. The member at the top of the list will receive a free gift only when a set number of new members have signed up. The schemes are known as matrix schemes. Once again, the victims are those who purchase their way in, never reach the top of the chain, and therefore accrue no benefits. There are many more such victims than the number of participants who actually gain some minor benefits.

The seductive aspect of the pyramid scheme is that those involved early do, in fact, make substantial profits for their initial investment. In my student days, I was involved in a postal version of such a scheme that involved an investment of £3. (At that time such schemes were not illegal in the United Kingdom.) Should the pyramid complete, I stood to gain a return of £726. In reality, a postal strike stopped the pyramid dead in its tracks after six weeks. By that time I had already received a return of £26 (a considerable amount for a student in those days). When the postal strike ended one month later, I was approached by several people who had invested their £3 and wished to get the scheme moving again by selling to me at a lower level in the pyramid. Neither I nor anyone else I knew rejoined, and many thousands of people were out of pocket to the tune of £3.

Controls to Identify Pyramid Schemes

When offered investment opportunities, consumers should beware of the technique known as *inventory loading*. Inventory loading occurs when the investment opportunity appears safe because investors receive its worth in products for sale—products that ultimately may turn out to be low-quality and inflated-cost items. Often investors will get their money back "if only 50 percent of the goods are sold." In reality, the likelihood of selling more than 10 percent is very low, particularly when the market becomes saturated with other members trying to sell the same items to the same market. Where such inventory loading occurs across the pyramid, those at the top will make substantial gains on the products they have sold to the investors.

Another common indicator of a pyramid scheme is a lack of provable end-consumer sales. The sales figures quoted in promoting such schemes ultimately appear as sales from members of one level of the pyramid to members at the next level down. This ties in to the financial incentives to members in the pyramid to recruit other members. Revenue from sales becomes unimportant, as more money can be made simply in recruitment. Sales to nonpyramid members may be so low as to be nonexistent, ultimately leaving all members with unsalable goods.

 PONZI SCHEMES

These schemes are named after Charles Ponzi, who, in the 1920s, offered the Italian American community of South Boston an investment opportunity guaranteeing a 50 percent return on money in 45 to 90 days. Ponzi's claim was that he could a pay this rate of return by turning a 400 percent profit by trading and redeeming postal reply coupons that exploited fluctuations in currency exchange rates. Once the scheme was running, Ponzi discovered that, although he could make profits, they were at a very low level and hardly worth the effort. As a result, he stopped redeeming any coupons but continued to gather money from investors. When he paid the original investors a 50 percent return out of subsequent investors' money, word got around and investments poured in. When the scheme finally went bankrupt, he owed investors in excess of $6 million, an enormous sum in those days.

A Ponzi scheme, therefore, is one in which no legitimate investment exists and the money from later investors is used to pay off earlier obligations providing an appearance of legitimacy. In effect, investors' returns come not from earnings but from the principal contributed by subsequent investors. Such schemes, like pyramid schemes, are based on a premise of continuous recruiting and thrive while their reputations are intact. When confidence and credibility fail, no new investors can be found. Since there was no actual investment in the first place, all investors typically lose their money, other than what can be recovered in lawsuits.

Controls to Identify Ponzi Frauds

Once again, the best controls are the alertness and skepticism by potential investors. Many Ponzi schemes attract investors by personal recommendations from those who can demonstrate high returns already earned. Any scheme that is performing substantially better than the rest of the investment market should be suspect.

Some investors, even though they suspect a potential fraud, continue with the investment in the hope of being one of the early investors who makes money at the expense of later ones. When the scheme collapses and they lose their money, they generally claim complete ignorance of the nature of the scheme and say how badly they have been deceived.

▦ CAREER OPPORTUNITIES

In today's economic environment with higher-than-normal levels of unemployment, frauds involving the securing of agency fees in return for career enhancement opportunities have mushroomed. Fees are paid up front with the agencies delivering few, if any, careers systems. There are legitimate placement agencies that, for a fee, represents career seekers and attempt to place them in an appropriate position. Sometimes it is difficult to differentiate between legitimate agencies and fraudsters apparently offering the same service.

Some agencies may present themselves as authorized agents of companies seeking staff. Many recruitment agencies do legitimately seek staff on behalf of organizations. They do not, however, seek payment from applicants; their fee is paid by the company that employed them to recruit on their behalf.

A similar type of fraud is the work-at-home fraud, which offers a "business opportunity" to make a lot of money in a short period of time with no qualifications or skills required. Again, an advance fee is taken with either no work resulting or no payment for work undertaken. If in doubt as to the legitimacy of such "opportunities," potential applicants can always ask for more information before providing their details. Applicants may write:

> Hi, I could indeed be interested but would need more information as I would not wish to waste your time. Could you please tell me:
>
> ▪ Where this job is physically located?
> ▪ What is the salary offered?
> ▪ Is this the full package or are there additional benefits; if so, what are they?
> ▪ How long has the organization been in business?
> ▪ If relocation is necessary, will the company reimburse these costs?

Should the advertiser fail to answer these questions or return a "Your question has been passed on . . ." reply, it is probably a scam.

Identifying Career Opportunity Frauds

Fraudsters have become adept at generating Web sites that look legitimate or may even be copies of legitimate sites. If an opportunity looks tempting, check out the agency with search engines. WHOIS databases such as WHOIS.com or WHOIS.net which can look up the identity and ownership of web sites may give an indication as to the genuineness of the agency, how long it has been in business, and who the domain name is registered to. A site such as godaddy.com will provide information on who registered the domain, who its administrator is, where the domain is hosted, when it was created, and when the name will expire.

Be wary of providing personal information. Recruitment agencies will not need driver's license numbers, ID documents, Social Security numbers, bank account records, or utility bills. Certain financial institutions may seek a Social Security number so that a background check can be carried out. In some states, no employer other than the U.S. Federal government is permitted to request a Social Security number until you are an employee.

Most organizations legitimately recruiting do not progress to this stage until an offer of employment is made. The individual can always write on an application document "SSN will be provided upon job offer." A potential employer who is unwilling to settle for that may well be an employer to avoid.

 ## CASH RECOVERY FRAUDS

Adding insult to injury, cash recovery schemes specifically target previous victims of fraudulent practices. The individual is contacted by an apparently legitimate company that claims that it can recover money that has been lost and apprehend the perpetrator. In some cases, the organization will ask for "administration" fees or will point out that no fees are payable in advance and only a small percentage of the recovered money will be taken as a commission. Obviously, the company will require the victims' bank details in order to pay the recovered money into the bank. This information is then used to empty victims' bank accounts.

As with all frauds against individuals, credulity and a healthy sense of skepticism form the basis for all defense mechanisms. When asked for advance fees, try instructing the company to take the money from the funds they claim they have recovered. Representatives may tell you that the money is under the control of a court and can be paid only to you personally. Be careful not to agree, particularly in writing, to pay them a fee after you have been paid. The money may already be on its way to you with no intervention from the fraudster who simply seeks to benefit from your refund.

CHAPTER FOUR

Frauds Against the Organization

> Whoever commits a fraud is guilty not only of
> the particular injury to him who he deceives,
> but of the diminution of that confidence which
> constitutes not only the ease but the existence of
> society.
>
> —*Samuel Johnson, English poet and writer (1709–1784)*

After studying this chapter, you should be able to:

- Recognize specific types of fraud against the organization, their red flags, and the failure or lack of internal controls that exposed the organization to such attacks.
- Differentiate between internal frauds carried out from inside the organization against the interests of the organization and external frauds carried out against the organization from an external source with or without the cooperation of existing employees.

- Identify appropriate controls to reduce the likelihood of such frauds occurring and increase the probability of early detection.

BANKRUPTCY FRAUD

In bankruptcy fraud, the fraudster files a notice of bankruptcy. All creditors receive a copy of the notice. The fraudster then approaches creditors individually, telling each in turn that they are a favorite and that he or she wants to see them get paid something out of what remains. The creditor frequently settles for a low percentage of the amount owed. After a settlement with one creditor is reached, the fraudster moves on to the next creditor, and the next, until all creditors have settled for a small fraction of the amounts owed. The fraudster then withdraws the petition for bankruptcy, having extinguished most of the debt for a fraction of the original amounts.

CHECK FRAUD

Purchases made with fraudulent checks are a common form of corporate fraud. In such frauds, payment is made with the full knowledge that the check will be dishonored by the receiving financial institution, and the organization that accepted such payment will suffer a direct loss.

Check fraud is discussed in more detail in Chapter 12.

OBTAINING FRAUDULENT LOANS

Obtaining loans with no intention of repaying them is a common fraud technique primarily against financial institutions. It includes raising money in order to lease nonexistent properties or stealing goods by means of fake references from other financial institutions or trading partners.

All such references should be viewed with a healthy degree of skepticism. Fake references can be difficult to detect since they tend to be highly complementary to the person or organization seeking finance, as genuine references would be. When contacting those who provided references for confirmation, one must ensure that the person whose giving the reference actually works for the company and has the authority to give such a reference.

Fraudsters commonly provide false contact telephone numbers for a direct line or a specific person to provide the reference sought. Such direct references should be viewed with suspicion. Where trade references are given by other companies, care should be taken to check the existence of such businesses since trade references have, in the past, been provided by nonexistent companies.

The most common form of loan fraud, and the most expensive, is mortgage fraud. The victims primarily are financial institutions, although such frauds can be perpetrated against individuals. Mortgage fraud typically involves borrowing money against an asset in which it value is insufficient to cover the debt or with stated income insufficient to repay the debt.

In its 2010 Mortgage Fraud Report 2006, the Federal Bureau of Investigation (FBI) defines mortgage fraud as "the intentional misstatement, misrepresentation, or omission by an applicant or other interested parties, relied on by a lender or underwriter to provide funding for, to purchase, or to insure a mortgage loan." [1]

Generally, mortgage loan origination fraud can be categorized into fraud for profit and fraud for property.

Fraud for profit is generally seen to be more problematic for financial institutions as it typically involves multiple loans as well as schemes to gain illicit proceeds from property sales. This form of mortgage fraud frequently involves an insider at the lending institution who is in a position to cover up the fact that a single property has had multiple mortgage bonds issued against it. In some cases, it has been shown that there was, in fact, no borrower and no actual property. Falsification of loan documents and misrepresentations of property values are common in such schemes.

A variation on fraud for profit involves illegal *property flipping* schemes. Such schemes involve fraudsters acquiring the property at a price. The fraudsters then have the property fraudulently valued at many times the actual price. The property is then sold to a third-party shill or straw buyer (someone who permits their name and personal details to be used for the purpose of obtaining a mortgage loan with no intention of taking possession) at the fraudulently valued price, with the mortgage being taken out for 80 percent of that value. The straw buyer then disappears, leaving the financial institution with a large mortgage on a low-value house. Generally, such mortgages are government insured, leaving taxpayers to take the loss.

Fraud for property schemes normally involve minor misrepresentations by applicants regarding their income, ability to pay, or value of other outstanding debts. This form of fraud may result in property repossessions with the attendant financial losses to the institution as well as potential loss of reputation; however, the individual loss per case is generally lower than in cases of fraud for profit.

Occupancy fraud occurs when borrowers state that they intend to live in the property whereas, in fact, it is intended to be acquired for investment purposes. Although many borrowers would not see this as fraud, interest charged on investment properties is normally higher than for residential properties since the default rates are higher. Financial institutions consider such misrepresentation of purpose as intentional fraud.

Use of a *silent second mortgage* involves the borrower being given an independent loan by a second lender without the knowledge or approval of the primary lender. This additional loan can significantly increase the risk of default since a borrower's equity in the property may be considerably less than the primary lender believes.

Title/escrow/settlement frauds and no satisfaction of mortgage include refinancing with the stated intent to pay off mortgage loans, and diverting the funds to other purposes. Other such schemes may include intermediaries such as brokers or attorneys diverting funds from the purchaser's intention, such as paying contractors or insurance, and pocketing the money.

Short sale frauds is a preforeclosure sale in which the lender agrees to sell the property for a value less than the amount owed. Fraud typically occurs when the purchaser obtains the property at the lower price and immediately resells it for a higher price. Such frauds may involve collaboration among the purchaser, appraiser, attorneys, and nonattorneys.

Unfortunately, in today's economic climate, many owners find themselves in a negative equity situation. In some cases an owner's solution is simply to walk away. In other cases the borrower applied for a loan to purchase a second property. After the new property has been purchased, the borrower will allow the first home to go into foreclosure. This fraud is known as a *buy and bail*.

With the large amounts of money involved in property purchases, residential or commercial, fraud schemes are snowballing. In the United States, Freddie Mac reported that short-sale transactions were up 700 percent between 2008 and 2010, as reported in the FBI 2010 Mortgage Fraud Report.

Other fraudulent loan schemes may include obtaining commercial loans in the name of the organization by a form of corporate identity theft involving forged loan documentation.

Internal Controls to Prevent Loan Fraud

Document analysis remains the most effective form of fraud prevention regarding loan frauds. In mortgage frauds, a common red flag may be the use of a standard contract with limited amendments, which is not typical of true negotiation. These contracts, known as boilerplate contracts, are not in them-selves fraudulent but may indicate fraudulent intent.

Where mortgage payments are made by an entity other than the borrower, or where signatures on documents are inconsistent throughout, document analysis should readily detect such anomalies.

Major documents in mortgage loan applications include:

- An itemized list of all charges imposed on a borrower and seller for the real estate transaction. In the United States, this form is known as a HUD-1 and is required in all transactions involving federally related mortgage loans. This document includes all settlement charges and agency commissions, indicating whether these costs go to the buyer's or seller's account.
- The good-faith estimate form. It is supplied to the purchaser by the lender or mortgage broker to inform the purchaser of all costs and whether some-one else will service the loan after closure. Again, this form is a require-ment in the United States.
- A verification of employment form. This form is sent directly to the employer for confirmation of employment and earnings.
- Current pay slips.
- Wage and tax statements from the employer for previous years.
- Previous tax returns.
- Bank statements.
- Assets statements.
- Identification documentation.

The intention is to ensure that borrowers are who they claim to be, are gainfully employed, can afford to pay for the loan, are not already in significant debt, and fully understand the terms and conditions of the loan.

 ## UNSOLICITED ORDERS

When a company receives an order from an unexpected source, it is commonly looked on as an unexpected free gift. Unfortunately, the free gift may prove expensive if the order is fraudulent. For example, customers who approach an organization directly with unsolicited orders may be a source of concern in an organization that carries out most of its business through a conventional sales force. Sudden, unexpected, urgent orders can be used to create a willingness in a company to cut corners in the checks and balances normally carried out in its rush to obtain a large new customer. Such urgency, particularly where it involves the granting of credit, may be an unacceptable risk.

Even if the customer is known, many fraudsters establish their credibility by placing small orders, which are paid for on time. Once credibility is established, larger orders are placed with no intention of ever paying for them. Such a technique is known commonly as a long-firm fraud. Within a long firm, the basic intention is to run the company as an apparently legitimate business, gradually extending the amount of cash advances (advance fees) from customers at the same time as the amount of credit from suppliers is increased. When the pot is large enough, the fraudsters vanish with both the customers' money and suppliers' goods.

An alternative version of the unsolicited order scam comes when the organization is offered a free trial of a product, which then becomes a regular order delivered and billed.

Internal Controls to Detect Unsolicited Order Fraud

Red flags to be aware of include:

- Customer presses for "urgent" delivery with rush shipment on credit.
- Hard data on the customer's company is hard to obtain.
- Customer is totally familiar with your credit policy (e.g., the order is just below the level to trigger more detailed credit checks).
- Customer keeps pressing how advantageous the sale is to *you.*

Controls would include:

- Avoid granting instant credit to unknown customers.
- Where credit references are given, check the value of the order on which the reference is based.
- If a new customer wishes to remove the goods immediately, ensure cash is paid in advance.
- If a new customer uses you as a credit reference, double check any references you were given and be careful of future orders.

 ## EMBEZZLEMENT

Embezzlement entails the fraudulent conversion of personal property by the person in possession of that property where the possession was obtained as a result of trust placed in the embezzler. Embezzlement did not derive from common law. Instead, it is a statutory crime—that is, a crime that is defined by statute. A statute generally describes the offender as being a person entrusted with, or in possession of, another's property. In such cases, the property itself subject to embezzlement will be spelled out in the statute. In the United States, this definition can vary from state to state. Some states may define property as anything that can be the subject of larceny while other states use a more all-inclusive definition and recover both real and personal property with public funds and property identifying a separate offense.

Commonly, statutes defined the elements of the embezzlement as including:

- The property embezzled must belong to a person other than the accused.
- The accused must have an intent to defraud at the time of conversion.
- The accused must have been in a position of trust such that the property was held by him or her for some legitimate purpose.
- The property must have been converted at some point after the accused had original and lawful possession of it.

Conversion, itself, is simply an act that interferes with a true owner's right of possession of his or her own property. Conversion in an embezzlement involves the accused assuming the right of ownership in an unauthorized manner and without the consent of the true owner.

Internal Controls to Detect Embezzlement

Given that embezzlement normally involves a person within the organization in a position of power, primary controls are those that increase the difficulty of a single insider being able to divert assets to his or her own ownership. Such controls would include:

- Division of duties between accounts receivable and accounts payable
- Unusual patterns in check cancellation such as dual endorsements
- Independent receipt of bank statements from the employee handling receipts of payments
- Background and credit checks on all employees in a position to handle assets
- Ensuring ongoing monitoring of all potential problem areas, such as purchasing, receiving, cash disbursements, inventory, data processing, and bookkeeping

BRIBERY

Bribery has been defined as "the giving, receiving, offering or soliciting of any 'thing of value' in order to influence a person in the performance of, or failure to perform, his/her duties."[2] Such bribery may include soliciting the commission of any other type of fraud or the influencing of an official to carry out any act that violates the lawful duty of that official. Under such circumstances, bribery is defrauding the employer of that official of the right to honest and loyal services by an employee. Such bribery may include giving, receiving, offering, or soliciting of a "thing of value" because of an official act that has already taken place.

In the case of commercial bribery, the offense is the same but the intent is to affect some business decision without the organization's knowledge or consent.

Bribery in itself is not only illegal in most countries, but it can cause companies' own reputations and staff morale to decline due to the culture of corruption.

Different countries may have different applications of the law regarding bribery. In South Africa, the common law crime of bribery applied only to persons in the public sector; that law has now been replaced by a general corruption offense involving the receipt and offering of unauthorized gratification by or to a person within an employment relationship.

In the United Kingdom, bribery is included as part of the Antiterrorism, Crime, and Security Act of 2001. A company can be held criminally liable if it is deemed to have aided or abetted any act of bribery by an overseas subsidiary. In 2011, the Bribery Act came into effect and included in its definitions bribing another person, being bribed, bribing a foreign public official, as well as failure by a commercial organization to prevent bribery by associated persons.[3] It includes a separate offense of consent or connivance by a senior officer in committing any of the general offenses of bribery. It recognizes that while corporate hospitality and promotional and other business expenditures can be used to bribe; thus, such behavior is not criminalized if it is "proportional" and intended for "legitimate commercial purposes." The act also prohibits the practice of paying sums of money to induce foreign officials to perform routine functions that would normally be seen as part of their duties. Such payments are classified under the act as "facilitation payments."

 CORRUPTION

In every country in the world, corruption and bribery extends in its application from the corrupt public officials to the corrupt activities that can and do occur in today's corporate boardrooms involving such activities as payoffs or bribery.

Public corruption—the misuse of public office for personal gain—can occur either through straightforward embezzlement of public money or when public systems break down, forcing citizens to deliver bribes or make other compromises in order to receive the services they are entitled to.

Corruption in the private sector can be as minor as a payoff to get to the head of the queue or as major as organized crime corrupting employees of organizations for gain. Countries worldwide are striving to reduce rates of corruption by increasing the probability of corruption being detected and proven in court and by imposing stiff penalties if corruption is proven.

For example, South Africa has adopted a multiagency approach to fighting corruption. In April 2004, the Prevention and Combating of Corrupt Activities Act came into effect to replace the former Corruption Act. It has had a dramatic effect on the way business is conducted in South Africa. The act aims at preventing and combating corruption and related activities committed in South Africa and abroad by creating a general, all-encompassing offense of corruption. It also criminalizes a variety of specific activities that are either corrupt or relating to corruption. Corruption is dealt with in more detail in Chapter 5.

CONFLICTS OF INTEREST

Conflict of interest is a crime that is similar to bribery. When an organization or person, acting on behalf of another organization or individual, has, or even appears to have, a self-interest in the activity or a hidden bias and such bias is not made known to the represented party, a conflict of interest has occurred. Conflicts of interest may occur in business, academia, law, government, or even medicine.

The key element in defining conflict-of-interest situations is the failure of fiduciary responsibility. In the medical field, this failure can impact the health and well-being of patients if practitioners or medical organizations allow private gain to influence the selection of treatment options to the detriment of patient care. Conflicts of interest exist when the public expects that the person in a position of trust will place the interests of the clients ahead of their own financial gain or other personal interests but where their own and the clients' interests may pull in different directions. This is not to say that all such conflicts will result in decisions being made against the clients' interest, but only that the potential for such occurrences increases.

In the integrated reality of modern business, it is inevitable that conflicts of interest will occur; they do not inevitably lead to fraud. At the board level, individuals represent the best interests of the stakeholders. At times these interests may conflict, as when the interests of the shareholders, of the employees, of customers, and of suppliers may all pull in different directions. In addition, the interests of the individual board members may also be conflicted. On the other side of the coin, employees may find that their duty of loyalty to their employers conflicts with their own best interests. Suppliers' loyalty to their customers may conflict with their loyalty to their own organization. Consultants may find that their loyalty to their client conflicts with their own consultancy or even their professional organization. In an arm's-length relationship between individuals or organizations with no previous association, it is to be expected that each party will put their own interests first and expect the other party to do the same. Where a fiduciary relationship exists, a key element for a successful ongoing relationship is trust that the other party will represent the best interests of the individual or organization that is paying a fee for that trust. The lawyer's clients expect their interests to be held ahead of the lawyer's potential future business with the opposition. Patients expect a doctor to place their interests ahead of those of a pharmaceutical company or the doctor's own research project.

In many countries, within the public sector, laws exist that prohibit conflicts of interest in government employees and those doing business with the government. In the private sector, conflicts of interest may not be a criminal offense, although the results may be deemed to be unjust enrichment and therefore a criminal offense.

Internal Controls to Prevent Conflicts of Interest

All these daily conflicts can be managed by a combination of oversight and disclosure. However, should such a conflict of interest result in a loss to the represented party, a fraud may be deemed to have taken place.

 BREACH OF FIDUCIARY DUTY

When a person is employed by, or has a duty to, an organization or another individual and acts in a manner not in the best financial interests of that organization or individual, a breach of fiduciary duty has occurred. "A fiduciary relation exists between two persons when one of them is under duty to act or to give advice for the benefit of another upon matters within the scope of the relation."[4]

A breach of fiduciary duty is not a criminal offense but is a civil matter. As such, the burden of proof required for conviction is not as onerous as for criminal fraud, although it is normally unnecessary to prove wrongful intent.

Most business relationships, although they involve trust and confidence in the parties to the relationships, are not fiduciary relationships in the legal sense. In order for a claim to be made in regard to such a relationship, the defrauded party must prove that it was an accustomed belief that another would act in its best interest—for example, where the defrauded party is guided by the judgment and advice of another.

▓ THEFT OF TRADE SECRETS

A trade secret is taken to be a collection of information that is not public knowledge and by the use of which an organization seeks to gain an economic advantage over customers or competitors. This information may be a formula, process, pricing structure, or other information that the organization deems to be confidential or classified. In all cases, for information to be classified as a trade secret, the individual or organization must be able to show that it has taken reasonable steps to maintain its secrecy. Failure to do so will be taken as an admission that the information was not secret and that therefore no wrong was done in its acquisition.

Companies typically seek to protect such information against unlawful disclosure by their employees or business partners through the use of nondisclosure contracts and noncompete agreements. Unlike a patent (discussed in Chapter 3), which is for a limited period of time and eventually expires, "confidential" information is taken to be permanently confidential. Also unlike a patent, there is nothing to stop a third party from independently using the information once it is obtained. In other words, the trade secret is legally protected only while it remains a secret. Once disclosed, it is, by definition, no longer secret.

Once again, there is a disparity in the legal treatment across international and, in some cases, national borders. In the United States, trademarks and patents are protected under federal law. Until 1997, trade secrets were generally protected under state laws, but not all states were in agreement despite the existence of the U.S. Uniform Trade Secrets Act. Generally, the perpetrator must have possessed information valuable to the business that was intended to be treated confidentially and must have breached the confidential relationship by improper means. Such a breach of confidentiality is a particular problem in any industry where formulas are critical to business survival and competitiveness.

Similarly, secrecy often surrounds the development of new software and operating systems to be released globally or developed for in-house use, marketing strategies, or costing information.

The publishing of trade secret information over the Internet presented organizations with new problems. In the late 1990s, there was very little legal recourse and, despite attempts to seek damages, the secret is now lost and no longer protected. Copyright may be protected but secrets, once revealed, are gone forever.

Since 1997, the U.S. Economic Espionage Act has made theft or misappropriation of trade secrets a federal offense with both the perpetrator and the receiver of the stolen secrets liable under the act. The act included financial information and computer software and codes, and defined the information as deriving independent economic value from not being generally known or readily available by proper means to the public whether the value is actual or only potential.

Where such information is not patented or trademarked, lawful methods may exist to uncover confidential information. Techniques such as reverse engineering (taking a competitor's product apart to see how it is put together) may not be illegal if no trademark or patent is infringed. Similarly, headhunting the competition's best workers is not illegal as long as no theft of proprietary information goes along with hiring those workers.

If an organization uses improper means, such as industrial espionage, to secure trade secrets, the individual or organization that secured the information probably will be held to be guilty of other crimes relating to its acquisition rather than its use.

In order to seek redress, a claimant must be able to show that the information removed could be classified as a trade secret, that reasonable steps were taken to preserve its secrecy, and that a confidential relationship was breached to acquire the information improperly.

Internal Controls to Prevent Theft of Trade Secrets or to Seek Redress for such Theft

As previously stated, the organization must have implemented physical security to prevent the physical theft of confidential information. Such security procedures could include:

- Fence parameters
- Visitor control systems
- Security personnel

- "Authorized Personnel Only" signs at access points
- Sign-in/sign-out procedures for trade secret materials
- Use of identity badges
- Written security policies
- Confidentiality and nondisclosure agreements

In addition, control over logical access to digital information must be maintained, including controls such as:

- Unique user IDs and passwords
- Use of firewall protection
- Segregation of confidential information
- Use and scrutiny of access logs
- Restrictions on the use of external computer programs or storage media

Human resource controls are also required, including:

- Conducting background checks on new employees
- Reminding employees of confidentiality agreements during exit interviews

If the organization can prove a loss as a result of unauthorized disclosure, it can seek redress in both criminal and civil courts.

FALSE CLAIMS

A false claim fraud occurs when a person knowingly and intentionally makes a false or fictitious representation as a material fact, which results in financial loss to the victim to whom the false representation was made. As a subcategory, insurance fraud impacts both the insurance organization and future insured persons or organizations in that fraud costs are ultimately paid for by the insured through higher premiums.

The U.S. Department of Justice reported in its December 19, 2011, briefing that, in fiscal year 2011, it recovered $5.5 billion with more than $3 billion being recovered under the civil False Claims Act. Fraudulent claims investigations were led by health care fraud, mortgage frauds, government grant frauds, and contracting frauds, with health care fraud alone accounting for $2.4 billion of the recoveries. These frauds are in addition to insurance frauds, tax frauds, credit card fraud, and the like.

The common types of fraud against the government are:

- Health care fraud
- Pharmaceutical-related fraud
- Construction and procurement frauds
- Defense fraud
- Disaster relief fund
- Overseas reconstruction fund
- Research fraud

Health Care Fraud

The cost of health care is increasing exponentially in the developed world due to an aging population. In the developing world, improvements in health service delivery have also caused rocketing costs. Some of this cost is government funded and some is funded by private insurance policies. Although there are legitimate reasons for cost increases in the health sector, one of the major reasons is high levels of fraud committed against both private and public health care programs. Such frauds include but are not limited to:

- Charges made for nonexistent patients or patients who underwent no treatment but nevertheless were charged.
- Charges made for services not rendered including diagnostic tests of pharmaceuticals not supplied.
- "Unbundling" of services, which attract large discounts when performed together, as they normally are. Individual billing can result in considerably increased charges.
- Conducting unnecessary medical procedures including diagnostic tests, treatments, and supply of medical devices.

Pharmaceutical-Related Fraud

With the high value of drugs supplied to health care providers, the temptations exist for certain less-than-scrupulous pharmaceutical companies to use marketing schemes, pricing schemes, and even illegal kickbacks to increase profits. In some cases, drugs may be marketed to physicians for uses for which the drugs have not been approved. This *off-label* use may, in some jurisdictions, be illegal for physicians or for pharmaceutical manufacturers.

A common fraudulent scheme is the use of financial incentives to hospitals and doctors to promote their prescription of particular drugs to patients. Common among these bribery types are:

- Vacation schemes provided as incentives
- Direct payments to hospitals and doctors
- Payments for attending conferences
- Excessive payments for membership on "advisory boards"
- Supply of "free samples" of drugs, which may then be sold to patients
- Tickets to sporting events
- Funding of phony drug trials

Some insurance companies also offer inducements in order to have their products given priority when prior insurance approval is required.

Price inflation is a technique used to increase the price charged to government agencies, which are large pharmaceutical users, by charging higher prices to low-volume users so that the average price, on which government prices are based, appears greater than it should be.

Construction and Procurement Frauds

In capital projects involving large cash flows, the opportunity for fraud through a variety of techniques escalates. Frauds in this area include:

- Bid rigging
- Overcharging for materials
- Overcharging for manpower
- Use of substandard materials
- Poor-quality workmanship
- Payment of bribes and kickbacks
- Shortcutting contracted standards

Supply of capital goods as well as consumables and services are all subject to the inflating of costs, substandard delivery, and failing to meet contractual obligations.

Defense Fraud

Another area open to false claim frauds on a large scale is the supply of products and services to the defense industry. Again, the substitution of inferior or refurbished products can considerably improve the profit margin in areas where contracts commonly go to the lowest bidder and low profit margins are common. Since defense products are commonly high volume, it is impractical to do full quality checks on all items supplied, and substandard goods can slip through.

Many such contracts are awarded on a cost-plus basis. When similar products are sold elsewhere, it is possible to load their costs into the cost-plus contracts, thus improving the profit margin on both contracts. The "cost-plus" contract appears to have additional costs, which will result in increased revenue, and the other products lose nonrecoverable costs to the "cost-plus" contract, thus increasing their profitability. In a similar manner, where contractors use a combination of fixed-price and cost-plus contracts, shifting costs from fixed-price contracts to cost-plus ones increases the profit margin on the fixed-price contract while also increasing the amount that can be charged on the cost-plus contract. This technique is known as *cross-charging*.

Disaster Relief Fraud

Just as individuals can be defrauded over contributions to disaster relief funds, so too do some individuals and organizations seek to defraud legitimate relief funds by submitting fraudulent claims, as happened in many cases against funds set up for restitution in the Gulf oil disaster and with Hurricane Katrina funds.

In addition to claims for benefits, fictitious suppliers of goods and services in disaster relief areas have attempted to place false claims against these funds.

Overseas Reconstruction Fraud

As with other heavily funded governmental or charity relief efforts, the potential for wide-scale fraud, including overcharging, charging for nondelivered services, bribery, and corruption, is enormous. In a submission to the Commission on Wartime Contracting in Iraq and Afghanistan, the Defense Contract Audit Agency reported $3.2 billion of questionable claims primarily related to subcontractor activities and $1.5 billion of unsupported claims. The commission estimated that fraud and waste in both areas averaged $12 million per day over the last ten years.[5]

Research Fraud

Governments and private industry commonly fund research and development projects within industry and academia. Typical fraudulent claims in this area include:

- Submitting false grant applications to qualify for the funds available under grants
- Overclaiming costs, time, and other associated expenses
- Using grant money for unauthorized purposes
- Falsification of progress reports
- Falsifying results of research

In many cases, such frauds remain undetected until the funder is alerted by a whistleblower.

This is not a definitive list but merely some of the major types of claims fraud perpetrated on government departments and private sponsors worldwide.

Internal Controls to Prevent Claims Fraud

In all these cases, common factors facilitating fraud and abuse include nonexistent, inadequate, or confusing documentation coupled with a lack of oversight of the disposal of funds. Where operational systems are doing with large-volume legitimate claims, they inevitably are targets for fraudsters. The sheer volume of legitimate claims makes it possible to make false claims in the knowledge that detection will be unlikely. Even where detected, missing audit trails make proving the case against fraudsters extremely difficult.

Prevention of such frauds involves the use of proper of authorization documentation, insistence on adequate record keeping, and independent verification of the accuracy and completeness of such records. The quality of record keeping should be such that independent scrutiny is facilitated rather than impeded and should be a contractual clause in any contracts awarded.

FALSE CONVEYANCING

A fraudulent conveyance commonly arises in debtor/creditor relations, with particular reference to debtors who make themselves "insolvent" for legal purposes. The common mechanism involves a debtor who donates assets, usually to an "insider"—who may be an individual, a relative, or a partnership in which the debtor is a general partner or a corporation in which the debtor is an officer, director, or person in control—and leaves him- or herself nothing to pay the creditors. The same technique applies if the debtor is a corporation, officer, director, or person in control, or relative of such person, or a partnership in which the debtor is a general partner. If prosecuted successfully, the plaintiff may be entitled to recover the property transferred or its value from the transferee who has received a gift of the debtor's assets.

Fraudulent conveyancing can occur in connection with leveraged buyouts, where the management or owners of a failing organization will cause the organization to borrow on its assets and use the loan proceeds to purchase the management or owners' stock at highly inflated prices. The creditors of the corporation then have little or no unencumbered assets left on which to collect their debts. There are two ways to prove a fraudulent conveyance: One is when it can be proved that a debtor makes a transfer with intent to defraud, hinder, or delay his or her creditors. The second is when it can be proved when a debtor transfers property without receiving "reasonably equivalent value" in exchange for the transfer if the debtor is insolvent at the time of the transfer or becomes insolvent as a result of the transfer.

 ## TUNNELING

A critical challenge in corporate governance is controlling shareholders from extracting private benefits. Tunneling is a financial scheme instigated by the company's own management or major shareholders that may or may not be illegal.

Legal tunneling may include transfer pricing favoring the controlling shareholders, transfer of assets from a firm to the shareholder at below-market prices, loan guarantees using the firm's assets as collateral, or simply expropriation of corporate opportunities from a firm by the controlling shareholder.

Illegal tunneling consists of fraudulently pumping out valuable property and assets into the fraudster's own private firm. It also covers the crime of siphoning the organization's equity into third-party hands. Expropriation of the firm's value by insiders may take the form of:

- *Cash flow tunneling*, in which the defrauded organization is encouraged or even forced to buy assets or consumables from organizations associated with board directors at inflated prices. In some cases, this may involve acquisition of assets that are unnecessary to the business of the defrauded company. Such transactions may include outright theft as well as fraud.
- *Asset tunneling*, which can involve the sale of assets from the organization to individuals or organizations associated with the fraudster at below-market values or sale-and-leaseback agreements that are financially detrimental to the organization.

▪ *Equity tunneling*, which can involve both equity dilution and freeze-out. Equity tunneling may involve dilutive share issues, insider trading, and holding on to acquisitions until ultimately minority shareholders can be frozen out. In either case the original owners lose a substantial part of their owners' equity.

Fraud occurs where the perpetrators have a duty of care requiring a board member to act as a reasonable, prudent, or rational person would in that position. In addition, fiduciary duty requires insiders not to profit at the expense of shareholders or the organization.

In general, such transactions benefiting insiders may be allowable unless there is a clear indication that the transaction has no legitimate purpose or that its sole intent is expropriation. In most countries, courts interpret duty of care using the business judgment rule, which places the onus on the plaintiff to prove willful negligence on the part of the perpetrator.

Where such transactions are deemed part of corporate policy, the business judgment rule often overrides normal fiduciary duty. Obviously, if the accused perpetrator is a majority shareholder, he or she can dictate corporate policy. A controlling shareholder is in a position to dilute the shareholdings of minorities through closed subscriptions to new shares.

In some cases where equity funding has been provided, the minority shareholder may have control of the board. In such a case, it is possible for the minority shareholder to provide additional funding in the form of a loan and for the board later to vote to convert the debt to equity, with the original minority shareholder thus assuming the role of majority shareholder. At this point, they are in a position to set corporate policy as they choose.

In economies where shareholder protection is not good, ownership structures frequently are either state or family controlled. In Asia, for example, corporate control is improved by cross-holdings among firms and structures that segregate the ownership and control rights within corporate structures.

In countries where the law is based on common law principles, tunneling is less common because of the law's broad principle of fairness to minority shareholders. In these areas, minority shareholders' burden of proof in attemping to prove deliberate fraud is in a more favorable position. The greater levels of protection for minority shareholders may be one reason why countries with advanced civil law are popular as investment centers.

A 2000 article in the *Journal of Financial Economics* suggested that countries whose legal systems restrict tunneling more effectively suffered less in the financial crisis of 1997 to 1998.[6]

Where ownership vests in large numbers of shareholders, the use of independent board and committee members becomes one of the primary control mechanisms. In some cases, this method can be a highly effective control mechanism.

Warren Buffett is quoted as saying, "These people [independent directors], decent and intelligent though they were, simply did not know enough about business and/or care enough about shareholders to question foolish acquisitions or egregious compensation."[7]

CONSPIRACY

In many countries, the law indicates that, to be a crime, conspiracy occurs only where there is intent that a crime be performed, there is an agreement among two or more persons to engage in that crime, and where one of the conspirators commits an overt act to further the conspiracy. There is no general requirement that the plan was actually put into effect, but an overt act could include any step that may indicate that the execution phase of the conspiracy has begun. The step may not, in its own right, be illegal but must be carried out with an intent to achieve the purpose of the conspiracy. It is the act itself that creates the link to all participants in the conspiracy and not just the individual who conducted the act.

In the case of corporate conspiracy, in order to comply with the court requirement that the corporation had knowledge of the agreement made and the relevant circumstances, it must be possible to prove the corporation's knowledge of the conspiracy, either through and employee or agent.

Conspiracy may be charged in a variety of criminal acts, including trespass, creating a public nuisance, outraging public decency in the United Kingdom, or murder, as well as in the committing of a fraud. It is generally taken as a crime in its own right where the person who conspires to commit fraud and ultimately commits the fraud may be charged both with fraud and conspiracy. The conspiracy was taken to have occurred as soon as an agreement was made with criminal intent. The intent could refer to either the purpose of the agreement or the means by which it is carried out.

LAPPING

Lapping involves the use of funds received in payments to conceal a theft of cash. The fraudster initially steals funds offered in payment of a debt.

To conceal the initial theft, the fraudster uses a subsequent payment by a second party to make good the shortage resulting from the original theft. Payment from a third customer is used to cover the second shortage and the process continues. Commonly, lapping is used initially to cover up a loss or shortfall in a single account. Failure to transfer monies in to cover the loss would result in its discovery so, as a short-term measure, money is transferred from a different account. Obviously, this leaves a shortfall in that account, which also must be covered up. This type of fraud is commonly seen in conjunction with kiting if losses accumulate and a cover-up becomes extensive.

 KITING

Kiting is made possible when a financial institution permits the withdrawal of funds from an account based on check deposits that have not yet cleared. Under such circumstances, the funds may be in transit or they may, in fact, be non-existent. Using two bank accounts, fraudsters typically write a check on one bank account and then deposit it into their second bank account. Just before the check is processed to the first bank for payment, the fraudster then deposits a check written off the second bank account, which also has insufficient funds. Kiting is possible due to the delay created by the collection of funds by one bank from the other, which creates an artificial balance.

By continuously kiting checks from bank account to bank account drawn against nonexistent balances, the fraud continues. Money may then be obtained from legitimate sources of goods purchased by writing checks against the nonexistent balances.

Internal Controls to Prevent and Detect Lapping and Kiting

At the corporate level, kiting may involve enormous sums of money. Interbank transfers, whether electronic or by check, are particularly susceptible. Red flags on check processing may include overissue of checks, use of bogus checks, use of postdated checks, or delayed presentation of checks issued. Careful checking of check processing and bank reconciliations together with verification of electronic transfers assist greatly in early detection of such frauds, which are illegal in many countries.

FRAUDULENT AFFILIATIONS

In order to establish credibility, a fraudulent company may claim an association with a well-known and legitimate company, say by pretending to be a branch or subsidiary of an existing and well-known organization. Company names that are similar to well-established brand names should be treated with suspicion. Impressive trade names implying stature or international status may also be misleading. Claims of overseas offices or foreign ownership, which is difficult to confirm, are also popular.

With the intense competition that businesses have faced in recent years, there is pressure on all parties to move quickly, get the big order, or get new customers. This pressure leads to the cutting of corners and elimination of controls, which make it easier for fraudsters to exploit the organization's vulnerability.

Frauds frequently come to light as a result of an allegation from a third party regarding misconduct on the part of the organization or an officer. In many cases, such allegations are anonymous. Companies often are tempted to ignore them since to do otherwise would require an uncomfortable decision. Other frauds are detected when significant changes to profitability, market share, or cash flow occur. Some frauds are revealed purely by accident when an individual is looking for something else.

COUNTERFEIT MONEY

In terms of the classic concept of getting something for nothing, counterfeiting is the ultimate, "printing your own money". In the days before the proliferation of affordable, high-quality home computing, counterfeiting required a substantial investment in equipment as well as a high level of engraving skill. To combat home electronic counterfeiting opportunities, bank note issuers around the world have introduced more and more sophisticated counterfeit-proof bills with features such as laid lines, microprinting, thread detail, and others already discussed. Many of these features can be scanned successfully; however, the best computer printers lose some of the detail when the bills are examined under a magnifying glass. In addition, bank note issuers choose colors that are difficult to match, and the back/front alignment is difficult to achieve. Some manufacturers of color laser printers and color copiers embed a concealed serial number and manufacturing code that prints on every document produced. Thus, a counterfeit bill can be traced directly back to the specific printer.

Nevertheless, with a good enough printer and adequate care, fraudsters can end up with bills that could pass naked-eye inspection; because the bills are not printed on the proper paper, however, simply handling the note would make the counterfeit obvious. Fraudsters have attempted to create counterfeit bills to be used in vending machines where no human handling is required. To prevent this fraud, note issuers use some magnetic inks; the vending machines can detect lack of this ink.

Unlike the paper we normally use in business, which is cellulose based, the paper used for money is made from fibers of cotton and linen, known as rag paper. The pens used to detect counterfeit bills contain iodine, which changes color when it contacts cellulose. In addition, paper used for money feels considerably thinner than normal paper and has tiny colored fibers mixed in, which is very difficult to reproduce on an inkjet printer. Rag paper can be purchased, but it will not feel like the rag paper used in bank notes.

Some fraudsters have attempted to obtain the correct paper by taking low-denomination notes, bleaching the printing, and reprinting them as higher-denomination notes. Attempting this may show up other anticounterfeiting controls, such as plastic security strips, color-shifting ink, and watermarks.

Counterfeiting typically results in a direct loss to the organization or individual given the counterfeit money. It is also generally seen as a crime against the state and is punished severely. In the United States, it is classed as a felony and is generally handled by the U.S. Secret Service, an organization that was originally formed specifically to address the counterfeiting of currency. The penalties for counterfeiting around the world are severe because of the impact that it has on national economies when the currency becomes suspect.

BENEFIT FRAUDS

Benefit frauds take a variety of forms designed to defraud the government by claiming Social Security or other benefits to which the claimant is not entitled. Frauds in this category range from the false claiming of unemployment benefit, through housing benefit frauds, to simple failures to notify changes to benefit status by claimants. This type of fraud is particularly prevalent in the United Kingdom because of the system of government benefits paid to individuals as part of the U.K. welfare state. However, any country in which benefits are paid to the economically disadvantaged is susceptible to this type of fraud.

In the United States, the current economic situation has significantly increased the size of government benefit programs, including unemployment insurance and food stamps. Estimates of the size of these frauds vary significantly, although it is believed that, in the United States alone, improper unemployment insurance payments have amounted to over $17 billion in a single year, 2010, according to the Department of Labor.

INSURANCE FRAUD

In terms of value lost, insurance fraud is the second largest white-collar crime in the United States. This category includes the falsification of claims against insurance companies by individuals as well as by organizations. These frauds may take the form of inflated claims or fictitious claims as extreme as arson for gain, and include the provision of false information on insurance applications in order to get coverage on nonexistent or overvalued assets. Fraud occurs when a person knowingly lies in order to obtain some benefit or advantage to which he or she is not entitled.

Insurance fraud encompasses a variety of fraudulent claims including claims on:

- Property insurance
- Fire insurance
- Automobile insurance
- Life insurance

In addition, it encompasses medical and health care insurance frauds, as previously mentioned. In the United States, insurance fraud laws are taken as a state issue, and not all states have specific insurance fraud laws.

Property Insurance

Perhaps the most common form of property insurance fraud from an individual perspective is the making of false claims for theft of insured property. It is not, however, exclusive to individuals. False claims on corporate property insurance also occur on a large scale. It can range from the padding of claims that the actual theft has taken place (soft fraud) to paid-for arson (hard fraud) so that unprofitable operations may be claimed on insurance policies.

In the event of a natural disaster such as an earthquake, flood, or tornado, it is common for insurance companies to be flooded with exaggerated claims in which companies that have suffered genuine losses also seek to dispose of obsolete merchandise or unprofitable business subsidiaries as disaster damage in order to have a legitimate claim on the insurance policy.

Property claims also include those made against airlines and other transportation carriers for baggage or cargo lost or damaged in transit. Although most of these claims are genuine, a proportion is fraudulent.

It is a common part of many "conspiracy theories" to attribute disasters to insurance frauds. One of these documents perhaps one of the most outrageous property insurance frauds in history, if it is true. A claim was made by Robert Gardiner in 1998 that the *Titanic* was not the ship that sank on April 14, 1912.[8] Gardener suggests that the sister ship of the *Titanic*, the *Olympic*, was swapped and made to look like the *Titanic*, including being fitted with all of the *Titanic's* equipment, cutlery, tableware, and the like as part of an insurance fraud, and that the *Olympic*, disguised as the *Titanic*, was scuttled while the original *Titanic* went on to serve as the *Olympic* for 25 years. The motivation, Gardener suggested, was that the *Olympic*, following a collision with a cruiser HM *Hawke* in 1911, was so severely damaged as to have been an economic write-off on which the insurers (Lloyds of London) refused to pay since the *Olympic* was found to be at fault.

Under this theory, the intention was that the *Titanic* would be scuttled to sink slowly within the range of rescue ships but that it all went wrong when one of the rescue ships (riding with no lights) was hit by the *Titanic* with the resultant high-speed sinking.

This theory has largely been debunked, notably in the work done by Mark Chirnside.[9] If it was true, the loss of 1,500 lives plus the insurance loss would rank this as one of the most infamous frauds of all time.

Fire Insurance

Losses arising from fire are one of the highest-cost categories for insurance companies. In the United States, statistics from insurance companies indicate that the largest single cost of fire losses in nonresidential commercial buildings is arson, accounting for one third of residential fires.[10] Fire insurance fraud includes inflated claims of loss from genuine fires as well as losses as a result of deliberate arson.

Automobile Insurance

The highest number of fraudulent insurance claims in the United States concern automobile insurance, including motorcycles, trucks, snowmobiles, and the like. These frauds encompass an array of schemes, including:

- The insurance of phantom vehicles through forged title or registration papers in order that a report of theft can be made and a fraudulent insurance claim made.
- Owner destruction of defective vehicles followed by a claim for theft.
- Export fraud involving the illegal exportation of an insured vehicle followed by a claim for theft.
- Thirty-day specials where an owner of a vehicle requiring extensive repairs will report it stolen and conceal it for 30 days until the claim has been settled. Thereupon, the vehicle may be "discovered" and the insurance company now owns a nonroadworthy vehicle.

Automobile insurance fraud can be committed unintentionally by individuals or organizations seeking to lower their insurance premiums. Providing false information regarding accidents, traffic violations, or normal miles driven may also be seen as a fraud in the event of a claim.

Life Insurance

A major temptation for life insurance fraudsters is the size of the potential payout and not always to the family of the insured.

Most life insurance companies operate a two-year incontestability clause. This means that, for the first two years of a policy, a life insurance policy may be rescinded if it can be demonstrated that applicants intentionally deceived the company when they completed the application. After that time, the companies do not attempt to rescind the policy based on information given the time the policy was taken out.

A faked death is a common source of life insurance fraud. In some cases, the insured have been known to fake their own deaths in order that their "survivors" may make a claim; in others, policies are taken out on "relatives" who have no relationship to the fraudster and whose death is then faked using forged death certificates and other documentation. In addition to the insurance company being defrauded, the innocent "corpse" may find him- or herself accused of insurance fraud as well as unable to get future life insurance.

A rising source of life insurance fraud is known as stranger-owned life insurance. In this scam, an outsider owns a policy on someone else's life. Using the two-year incontestability clause, an insurance company may rebut a claim if the policy has been sold on in the first two years; however, a scammer may offer to purchase an insurance policy for the insured or it may be used as collateral for a loan from the scammer. If the insured dies before the loan is paid, the family receives a benefit and uses some of it to repay the loan for the purchase of the life insurance. If the insured does not die during that time, he or she may elect to pay back the loan with interest and keep the policy, sell the policy to repay the loan, or simply transfer the policy to the lender. If the policy ownership is sold or transferred to the lender, it ends up the beneficiary, and the insured may find him- or herself uninsurable in the future.

Whole-life insurance policy commissions may considerably exceed the commissions for other types of insurance. An unscrupulous agent may sell what the buyer believes is one type of insurance and switch it to the more lucrative whole-life policy. This is a variation on the bait-and-switch fraud discussed in Chapter 3.

Annuity plans offered by insurance companies can be subject to a fraud known as churning. In this fraud, scammers attempt to get older annuity holders to replace the current annuity with a new one with the advantage of an immediate cash bonus. As far as the new annuity itself is concerned, purchasers may find themselves locked into an annuity that cannot be accessed for up to 15 years without paying a large penalty for early withdrawal. The cash bonus may or may not be forthcoming.

A variation on this scam is a practice of twisting, which is based on the fact that sale of large annuities mean lucrative commissions for some agents. Larger annuities may be approved by the insurance company by the inflation of the applicant's net worth by the agent, and smaller annuities get replaced with a large one. Unfortunately, the large annuity frequently comes with restrictions on when the payout will be made, and it may leave the applicant in a situation where the annuity payment is unaffordable and the money cannot be accessed without paying large surrender fees.

Failure to comply with terms and conditions specified in any insurance policy can result in the denial of a claim with or without the inference of fraud. For example, cancellation insurance estimated to be worth $17.5 million was taken out by AEG Live with Lloyds of London prior to the Michael Jackson "This Is It" tour. Subsequent to his death, Lloyds argued that the policy would not have been issued had they been aware of his alleged addiction and use of prescription drugs. The dispute is ongoing at this time.

Not all insurance fraud takes place against insurance companies. In some cases, insurance companies have been known to seek false evidence in order to avoid paying a legitimate claim. Insurance fraud is covered in more detail in Chapter 12.

PAYMENT CARD FRAUDS

Payment card frauds are perpetrated against the issuers as well as merchant acquirers of debit, credit, and charge cards. A common source of this category of fraud is the e-tail market, where items are purchased remotely using stolen or counterfeited cards with delivery to an address that is not the cardholder's billing address. Even fraudulent use of automated teller machine cards can result in losses to the organization as well as disputes with cardholders as to their involvement in the fraudulent use of the card.

Payment card fraud is one of the simplest forms of identity theft. When items are paid for with a credit card, most receipts blank out the credit card number but some still print the full credit card number. With the card holder's signature, that is all that is required to perpetrate a card fraud. Many of these receipts get thrown away and end up in the hands of fraudsters.

Despite all the efforts of financial institutions, people are still not on their guard against credit card fraud. Many people do not even sign their cards or check statements of account. People lend their cards to friends, leave receipts or cards lying around, and give out their account number over the phone or via the Internet to almost anyone who asks.

Even for those who are careful to protect their credit card information, use of these cards is not without danger. The Internet is rife with breaches of security on service provider sites resulting in the disclosure of client information, including credit card details.

Card frauds come in a variety of forms. Individuals can be affected by application fraud, when someone falsifies an application in order to acquire a credit card using someone else's identity. "Intercept" frauds involve the theft of a legitimate card before it reaches its final destination. In addition, stolen and lost cards make up a significant portion of such frauds.

More sophisticated credit card fraud schemes involve techniques such as skimming, where the information on the card, either on the smart chip or the magnetic strip on the back, is copied from one card to another.

A new Internet phenomenon is the "triangulation" fraud, which is a variation on the lapping and kiting frauds already covered. In this fraud, the merchant offers a product for sale via a Web site. When a customer seeks to buy the product, the merchant requires payment only after delivery. The merchant then uses a fraudulent credit card to purchase the item via the Web for delivery. Once the item has been delivered, the merchant receives the purchaser's credit card details to lap over for the next fraudulent offer. This scam continues, kiting in value, until eventually the Web site closes and the fraudster opens a new one.

For those who seek to make a business selling fake credit cards, blank cards, magnetic stripe encoders, and card embossers are readily available via the Internet, as are credit card generators, which are emulation software packages that can be used to create valid credit card numbers and expiry dates for cards drawn on the bank of the fraudsters' choice.

From a corporate perspective, the corporation's own credit card holders are vulnerable to all of the fraudulent schemes discussed. In addition, however, the organization is itself vulnerable to fraudulent use of credit cards against it. When a bricks-and-mortar merchant (as opposed to an electronic trader) accepts a credit card and the charge on the card is authorized, the merchant will get paid even if a stolen card was used (assuming the merchant conforms to the credit card issuers' regulations).

In "card not present" transactions, such as Internet, mail order, or telephone sales, the merchant normally assumes liability for charge-backs on credit cards after fraudulent use, even if the financial institution has authorized a transaction. Also, the merchant may face increased charges from the credit card processor or even loss of the card company account.

Such frauds and ways to prevent them are discussed in more detail in Chapter 12.

PENSION FRAUDS

Pension frauds come in two forms: frauds against a person who is drawing a pension and frauds by the organization supposedly collecting contributions toward pensions. The latter includes fraud on the part of the employer who is deducting the pension contributions but not investing them, or fraud on the part of the organization or fund with which the pension funds are invested.

Alternatively, the organization may simply fail to make its own contribution toward the fund, resulting in the final pension being underfunded.

There are two basic kinds of employer-sponsored pension plans:

1. Defined benefits plans, in which the employer makes periodic payments to the employee once the employee retires based on length of service with

the company. In this type of plan, the employer assumes all of the investment risk.

2. Defined contribution plans, which require the employer to contribute a given amount to an employee's retirement account on a regular basis for a set period. Placement of the funds is at the discretion of the employee, who then assumes all of the investment risk.

Common frauds involving pension schemes include:

- Insurance company misrepresentation of allowable tax deductions and exemptions.
- Pension plan dipping by employers to gain cash needed to run the business. Such frauds can also occur in the diversion of legislated deductions from employees, such as tax payments.
- Pension plan overpayments by employers and/or employees because of misrepresentation by insurance companies. In one of the more serious forms of this type of scam, in the United States, employers utilizing 412(i) pensions and 419 welfare benefit plans can be informed that specific type of plans can pay up to ten times more than traditional plans with ready withdrawal on a pretax basis. The promoters and agents receive substantial commission on the plan sales, while the employer may be guilty of participating in an abusive tax shelter since the Internal Revenue Service made 412(i) plans reportable transactions.
- In some cases, investment firms pay commissions to "placement agents" or "introducing agents" when a contract is awarded. This commission becomes a problem only when the person receiving the commission is also an advisor to or trustee of the pension plan or related in some other way to either. In such cases, the commission, known as a pay to play, is a bribe, although it is not necessarily illegal.

From the other perspective of false pension claims, fraud can take the form of the claim of pensions by relatives or others for retirees who may be long deceased. One of my clients did an analysis of its retirees and discovered that in one particular location, the life expectancy of retirees appeared to be four years longer than the national average because of pension fraud at a local office. Pensioners had died and the company had not been notified. As a result, pensions were continuing to be paid and the proceeds were split between the surviving relatives and a pensions office employee.

Simple theft of pension checks in transit has led to moves to electronic payment and use of e-governance to secure pension payments.

 TAX FRAUD

Tax fraud has been the subject of many books and is too specific for a book of this nature. Nevertheless, organizations need to be aware of the many forms such fraud can take.

Tax fraud involves the failure to pay direct, indirect, or excise taxes. It encompasses the full range of individuals failing to declare income tax revenue authority through large-value tax evasion schemes perpetrated by large corporations. Included among such fraud schemes are:

- Concealing or transferring of assets and income
- Operating with two sets of financial accounts
- Falsifying personal expenses as business expenses
- Claiming false deductions
- Recording false amounts in accounts and records

Tax fraud also includes the false claiming of tax credits and the false claiming of tax rebates via schemes such as value added tax (VAT). In the latter case, tax receipts may be offset against taxes paid, leaving an opening for a business to overclaim the amount of taxes paid to reduce its tax burden.

In several countries where the conversion from a sales tax to VAT took place, it was ruled that organizations who owned goods that had already been tax-paid in the warehouse under the previous tax regime of sales tax could reclaim the tax already paid as if it was VAT, which had been paid. This resulted in attempts at large-scale fraud; fictitious invoices to organizations indicated that large amounts of sales tax had already been paid. The idea was that this fictitious tax would be offset against incoming VAT charged to customers.

Excise tax frauds generally relate to the failure to pay excise duties on such items as alcohol and tobacco. This fraud again ranges from small-scale smuggling (where duties are evaded) to frauds involving underinvoicing items attracting ad valorem duty and misdeclaration of quantities for items attracting specific duties (where duties are underpaid).

Local taxes are not immune from fraudulent schemes in relation to nonpayment.

INSIDER TRADING AND MARKET ABUSE

Insider trading is often assumed to be against the law but can, in fact, be perfectly legal. It is not illegal for corporate insiders to buy and sell shares in their own companies as long as such transactions are reported to the appropriate body. In the United States, officers of companies trading in their own securities must report this to the Securities and Exchange Commission (SEC). The SEC has, in the past, ruled that possession of nonpublic information prior to a trade is enough to be considered insider trading unless the insider can demonstrate that the trades are conducted as part of a preexisting contract.

Illegal insider trading is taken to encompass trading in a security in breach of a duty of trust and confidence. It is the possession of nonpublic information regarding the security, which makes it a breach of fiduciary trust and therefore illegal. It also includes the passing of such information to third parties and the trading in the security by those parties. The use of such information would be classified as insider trading in cases of:

- Trading in the securities of an organization by directors, corporate officers, and employees who are in possession of significant corporate information of a confidential nature.
- Family members, business associates, and friends of such individuals who receive such confidential information and go on to trade the securities.
- Government employees who gain such information because of the nature of their employment in the government and go on to abuse such information.
- Employees of providers of special services to organizations in connection with the information who go on to trade the securities based on that knowledge. These could include employees of banks, brokerage firms, law firms, and other specialized service providers.
- Any other individual who took advantage of confidential information obtained from an employer.

These offenses may not result in direct losses to any particular organization but indirectly affect the overall integrity of the market and therefore investors' confidence.

CLICK FRAUD

Click fraud is a specific type of Internet crime. It is intended to defraud advertisers who use a type of World Wide Web advertising known as pay per click

(PPC). An operator of a Web site, or webmaster, displays on its Web site links to advertisers' sites in exchange for a charge for each time a visitor to the site clicks on that particular link. Each time a valid Web user clicks on the link, the advertising network, a company that connects advertisers to web sites that want to host advertisements, reimburses part of the fees paid to it by the advertiser and the webmaster, while retaining part of the click fee.

Fraud can occur when clicks are made on the links by an automated script purporting to be a legitimate user of the Web site. These clicks generate a charge per click with no genuine advantage to the advertiser. The advertiser suffers the loss while both the webmaster's site and the advertising network gain financially.

In large-scale click attacks, patterns may be readily discernible with one computer site or a few associated sites generating large volumes of clicks in a short time. Combining the scripts with *bots* (small-scale programs running scripts from a variety of computers scattered across the Web), a *botnet* unknown to computer owners can create multiple *zombie* computers on innocent machines and generate high-volume clicks from an apparent variety of users; however, a pattern may become obvious due to the routing through the webmaster's machine. If the webmaster was, in fact, the advertising network, this pattern would not be apparent.

Variations on the click fraud can be carried out not to benefit a webmaster but merely to financially damage an advertiser. In this case, it is not necessary to route through a single Web site as all Web sites where the advertising took place could be attacked with resultant excessive costs to the advertiser.

Internal Controls for Detecting Click Fraud

Where sophisticated techniques have been used to hide patterns of fraudulent clicks, proving fraud is problematic. When advertising networks detect probable fraud patterns, often their best solution is not to charge the advertiser. This, however, can cause problems with webmasters that are legitimately carrying the advertising and that may get caught up in the nonpayment. In 2006, an evaluation of Google's click fraud detection mechanisms by Alexander Tuzhilin concluded that fraudulent click detection filters employed worked reasonably.[11] The overall architecture was described as: anomaly based (seeking deviations from the norm), rule based, and classifier based using data mining classifiers. Since then, advertising networks have expended a great deal of time and effort refining their click detection methodologies.

COUNTERFEIT GOODS AND INTELLECTUAL PROPERTY

Counterfeiting may be defined as manufacturing, producing, or making any goods without the authority of the owner of the intellectual property right in the protected goods, or applying to such goods the subject matter of that intellectual property right, or a tolerable imitation thereof, so that the goods are calculated to be confused with or to be taken as being the protected goods of the owner of the right (Counterfeit Goods Act of South Africa of 1988).

The key element of the fraud is that the potential purchaser must believe the article to be genuine. These items can range from faked car parts through drugs, such as Viagra or antibiotics, to "genuine" Microsoft software products. Such counterfeits not only represent a loss to the original intellectual property holder but also a blow to its reputation when the fake product fails to deliver.

In 2008, the Organization for Economic Co-operation and Development (OECD) produced a report titled *The Economic Impact of Counterfeiting and Piracy*.[12] It conducted analyses based on international trade data which indicated that up to $200 billion of internationally traded products could have been counterfeited or pirated in 2005. Since this figure was for internationally traded products only, the impact of internal domestically produced and consumed counterfeit products were not included. In 2009, the figure was updated $250 billion.[13] This figure exceeds the gross domestic product (GDP) of many countries. Despite being able to derive figures for actual counterfeiting, the OECD concluded that it was "difficult, if not impossible, to quantify the net effect of counterfeiting piracy on the economy as a whole."

In 2010, the U.S. Government Accountability Office (GAO) found that previous internal government estimates of economic losses resulting from counterfeiting could not be substantiated due to the lack of underlying studies.[14] The three most commonly cited estimates of U.S. industry losses to counterfeiting were traced to a 2002 FBI press release, a 2002 Customs and Border Protection press release, and a Federal Trade Commission estimate of losses due to counterfeit goods in the U.S. automotive parts industry. The study found that for none of these estimates could the source be identified. Nevertheless, these figures continue to be used as evidence of volumes and values of counterfeiting.

In this study, the GAO differentiated among the protection schemes for intellectual properties including copyright, trademarks, and patents:

▪ *Copyrights* were defined in the study as "a set of exclusive rights subsisting in original works of authorship . . . for a fixed period of time."

- *Trademarks* were defined as "any sign or any combination of signs capable of distinguishing the source of goods or services [that] is capable of constituting a trademark."
- *Patents* referred to "exclusive rights granted to inventions for fixed period of time whether products or process is, in all fields of technology, provided they are new, not obvious (involve an inventive step), and have utility (are capable of industrial application)."

These definitions are critical in defining fraud as it applies to intellectual properties.

A further study in 2010 by the World Intellectual Property Organization's Advisory Committee on Enforcement concluded that many previous studies had severe shortcomings both in terms of the data employed and the methodologies used for analysis.[15]

In 2011, a report commissioned by the Business Action to Stop Counterfeiting and Piracy (BASCAP) attempted to build on the work done in the OECD reports by including the value of domestically produced and consumed counterfeit and pirated products; the volume of pirated digital products being distributed via the Internet; and the broader effect on an economy-wide basis. Its estimate on a worldwide basis indicated totals ranging from $455 billion to $650 billion with a forecast for 2015 of $1,220 billion to $1,770 billion. The BASCAP also attempted to evaluate the impact on government tax revenues, welfare spending, cost of crime, and other broader economic impacts as well as employment losses, although these were restricted to a group of 20 economies.

 ## PROCUREMENT FRAUD

Corruption within the purchasing process, including abuse of insider information in the processing of tenders as well as collaboration with price-fixing rings, is a major headache to many organizations and government departments where large-scale procurement takes place. A subset of these frauds is the billing of firms for fraudulent claims of order placement, such as advertising in a business directory.

This form of fraud has already been covered in detail in Chapter 2.

Other common forms of fraud include:

- Falsification of time sheets
- Falsification of expense claims

- Forgery
- Creation of fictitious employees (ghost employees) and collecting the payments
- Failing to terminate existing employees and collecting the payments
- Billing for services not rendered

NOTES

1. www.fbi.gov/stats-services/publications/mortgage-fraud-2010/2010-mortgage-fraud-report.
2. Asian Organization of Supreme Audit Institutions, Understanding Fraud and Corruption, www.asosai.org/asosai_old/guidelines/guide_un_st_fru_corruption.htm.
3. U.K. National Archives, Bribery Act 2010, www.legislation.gov.uk/ukpga/2010/23/contents.
4. Paul v. North, 191 Kan. 163, 380 P.2d 421, 426 (1963). The Restatement (Second) of Torts 874 cmt. a (1979).
5. Commission on Wartime Contracting (CWC), Transforming Wartime Contracting Controlling Costs Reducing Risks, 2011, www.wartimecontracting.gov/docs/CWC_FinalReport-lowres.pdf.
6. Simon Johnson, Peter Boone, Alasdair Breach, and Eric Friedman, "Corporate Governance in the Asian Financial Crisis," Journal of Financial Economics 58, no. 1–2 (2000).
7. Warren E. Buffett, Shareholder Letters, Berkshire Hathaway Inc., 2003, www.berkshirehathaway.com/letters/letters.
8. Robin Gardener, Titanic:. The Ship That Never Sank? (Surrey, UK: Ian Allan Publishing, 1998).
9. Mark Chirnside, Olympic and Titanic — An Analysis of the Robin Gardener Conspiracy Theory, 2005, www.markchirnside.co.uk/Conspiracy_Dissertation.pdf.
10. Robert Corry, Underwriting Against Arson, 2012, www.interfire.org/features/underwrite.asp.
11. Alexander Tuzhilin, The Lane's Gifts v. Google Report, July 2006, http://googleblog.blogspot.com/pdf/Tuzhilin_Report.pdf.
12. Organization for Economic Co-operation and Development, The Economic Impact of Counterfeiting and Piracy (Paris: Author, 2008).
13. Organization for Economic Co-operation and Development, Magnitude of Counterfeiting and Piracy of Tangible Products: An Update (Paris: Author, 2009).

14. Government Accountability Office, "Observations on Efforts to Quantify the Economic Effects of Counterfeit and Pirated Goods," GAO-10-423, April 2010.
15. Carsten Fink, Keith Maskus, and Yi Qian, "The Economic Effects Of Counterfeiting And Piracy: A Literature Review" World Intellectual Property Organization, 2010, www.wipo.int/edocs/mdocs/enforcement/en/wipo_ace_6/wipo_ace_6_7.pdf.

CHAPTER FIVE

Fighting Corruption

But when you have bad governance,... these resources are destroyed: The forests are deforested, there is illegal logging, there is soil erosion. I got pulled deeper and deeper and saw how these issues become linked to governance, to corruption, to dictatorship.

—*Wangari Maathai, Kenyan activist (b. 1940)*

After studying this chapter, the reader should be able to:

- Identify areas of vulnerability within the organization that expose it to managerial level frauds and internal corruption.
- Identify areas and indicators where the organizations may be unwittingly or deliberately the perpetrators of such corruption against third parties.

Corruption is defined in the Oxford English Dictionary as "dishonest or fraudulent conduct by those in power, typically involving bribery" and "the action or effect of making someone or something morally depraved." From this highly conceptual definition, it is apparent that corruption comes in a multiplicity of forms with perhaps the most common being bribes used to influence the award of public contracts, affect judicial decisions, derive various benefits from the public sector, and even lower tax liability.

As a result, the term *corruption* can signify different things to different people and its interpretation is partially based on culture. That which is classified as "corruption" within one society or even within one organization may be seen as the customary and accepted way of doing business within others. It is this disparity that makes the role of ethics (see Chapter 6) so critical in establishing clear guidelines for fighting corruption.

Corruption comes about as a result of a variety of factors including, among others, historical, political, economic, and social factors. Corruption may be seen in small bribes of public officials in the course of daily execution of their duties up to and including large-scale bribing of bureaucrats and even politicians. Where such bribery becomes systemic, the cost to economies and to corporations and individual taxpayers may be enormous. Government expenditures are encouraged by the corrupters to be wasteful and inefficient because doing business that way may realize more profits for the corrupter as well as the corrupted. Where large-scale corruption occurs, it typically bleeds resources from the needy and from the provision of essential government services.

Additionally, widespread corruption has the effect of segregating that part of society that cannot afford to pay bribes and kickbacks. It may also alienate potential investors and donors who otherwise would have invested in jobs, infrastructure, and other opportunities to boost flagging or developing economies and bring respite to the worst off.

In addition to bribery, corruption can take the form of theft, abuse of public assets, diversion of public monies to private interests, as well as disclosure of privileged information and abuse of authorities' and executives' discretion. All of these can, if appropriately manipulated, lead to increased income to the corruptors.

In 2010, Transparency International's Global Corruption Barometer indicated that six out of ten respondents reported that corruption levels in their respective country had increased over time with the biggest increases perceived by respondents in North America and the European Union.[1] Overall, eight out of ten respondents judged that political parties are corrupt or extremely corrupt, making political parties the most corrupt category of institution worldwide, closely followed by public officials and civil servants. One in two respondents considered that their government's actions to stop corruption were ineffective.

In terms of petty bribery, the police topped the list as the institution most often reported as the recipient of bribes. The least-bribed officials are the tax authorities.

Here we look specifically at three major areas in which corruption flourishes if it is inadequately controlled:

1. Bribery in the placing of contracts
2. Nepotism and favoritism
3. Abuse of authority

All of these feed on and contribute to diminishing ethical standards and decreasing public faith in governance and organizational integrity.

Competition for large-scale contracts is generally fierce and adversarial, attributes that may be seen as positive factors in encouraging price competitiveness and efficiency. Unfortunately, they also have the potential to cultivate an environment in which corruption becomes embedded and the norm in doing business. Overall, corruption can undermine trust in institutions and governments while destroying jobs and even damaging economies with impacts that can last tens of years. Some of the largest-scale contracts are those in the public sector. The impact of bribery within those contracts can have a major detrimental impact on national economies and a nation's tolerance for corruption.

 ## BRIBERY IN CONTRACTS

Bribery in contracts can and does happen from the smallest contract, such as an employment contract, to the largest contracts involving multinational conglomerates. At the lowest end, bribery can become the norm of doing business where lunches on the company become vacations at company expense, use of corporate assets in return for favors, and eventually straightforward payoffs for bending the rules in favor of the individual or organization seeking to win the contract.

On a larger scale, payoffs to be awarded large or long-term contracts can be colossal and, in addition to monetary reward, can take the form of political favoritism. No sector can claim to be completely free of bribery. However, certain sectors are looked on as particular targets for procurement bribes due to the values of the contracts awarded as well as the complexities that make detection of backhanders such as bribes considerably more difficult.

Where a contract is awarded internationally, the opportunities for siphoning off "commissions" combined with opportunities for tax evasion and money laundering make such procurement a prime target for organized criminals.

Certain organizations may be seen to be higher risk depending on the sector, country, and type of contract they seek. In the United Kingdom, the Financial Times Stock Exchange (FTSE) is seen to be a world leader in the creation and management of equity, bond, and alternative asset class indices. The group works with partners and clients worldwide. As part of its measurement criteria, the FTSE4 Good Policy Committee oversaw the development of the FTSE4 Good Criteria for Countering Bribery.[2] The criteria attempted to identify those organizations having the highest levels of exposure to risk of engaging in bribery by measuring them in terms of:

- Sector
- Country
- Public contracts

Companies found to be high risk in all of these sectors were then identified as ones with a high overall risk in the area of bribery.

Fighting bribery in public procurement involves three main control opportunities, namely identification and investigation of bribes, use of clear and unambiguous rules and regulations, and an increased ethical climate:

1. Detection mechanisms involving the use of organizations and individuals with specific skills to identify, investigate, and prosecute bribery and corruption are required. In a modern, computer-driven business environment, many controls can be implemented electronically to facilitate early detection of patterns that may indicate the presence of bribery or corruption. Knowing that bribery or corruption is happening can, in some cases, be counterproductive if it becomes known that wrongdoing was detected but nothing was done about it. This can have the effect of encouraging others to follow the same corrupt lines in the belief that someone else got away with it, so can I. To reduce the probability of bribery and corruption, both early detection and swift and undesirable punishment are required.

2. To prevent and/or detect such corruption early, rules and regulations must be clear and unambiguous and properly enforced. Having the wrong rules and laws in place may encourage fraud and corruption; likewise,

ineffectively policing and enforcing even the right laws can have an equally negative impact. Compliance with such rules must become the norm rather than the exception. All involved must have a heightened sense of ethical behavior and a strong resistance to wrongdoing. These attitudes will assist in the generation of a culture of alertness and awareness.

3. An across-the-board awareness of the negative impacts of bribery has to be cultivated within and around the organizations or government functions concerned. Management, staff, customers, and suppliers must believe that accepting a bribe is against the best interest of the organization and the individual; all must be willing to take the appropriate steps to report any known occurrences and assist in their investigation. As this attitude becomes embedded in the culture of the organizations or national bodies, people begin to see that bribery and corruption are unacceptable not because they will be caught and punished but because they are against the interests of all. Transparency, involving both clarity of the procedural base and the verification that rules were followed, assists in the development of this ethical climate.

How Does Bribery Occur?

In order to understand how bribery occurs in the placement of contracts, it is necessary to understand the mechanisms behind contract placement. In this way, the strengths and weaknesses of the control frameworks intended to defeat corruption can be determined.

Rules regarding the rewarding of contracts may be strong, weak, or even nonexistent. The overall objective for procurement rules is to ensure the acquisition of the most appropriate quality and quantity of goods and services for the lowest overall cost. This does not necessarily mean the lowest price. Prices quoted on contracts can be easily reduced by substituting inferior products and services to give the impression of best value for money while, at the same time, making the value derived from the service contract almost nonexistent.

Implementing tendering procedures designed to favor specific organizations and preclude competitive bids from nonfavored companies is another form of abuse. Sole-supplier contracts or preferred tenderer contracts have high potential for bribery. This does not mean that all such contract agreements are indicators of bribery or even are undesirable. Sole-supplier contracts may be offered because of previous experience with a particular supplier that has proven of the quality of work or items supplied and the integrity of the supplier throughout the duration of the contract. The same applies to preferred tenderer contracts.

To understand the bribery opportunities, the tendering process itself must be understood.

Generically, the tendering process can be seen as an 11-stage process:

1. Procurement planning
2. Product design
3. Advertising
4. Invitation to bid
5. Prequalification of bidders
6. Technical evaluation
7. Financial evaluation
8. Postqualification
9. Contract award
10. Contract implementation
11. Verification and follow-up

Procurement Planning

Effective procurement planning is designed to achieve optimum efficiency and economy in the acquisition of products and services. In this process, the specific roles and responsibilities of all individuals with a job function which involves attainment of significant parts of a given project are integrated to ensure comprehensive coverage.

The planning process begins with the recognition of a specific business need calling for the acquisition of resources not currently in place. The plan itself must address:

- What is needed
- When it is needed
- How it will be obtained
- Who will obtain it
- How much it will cost

The duration of the planning phase of procurement is heavily dependent on the risks inherent in the proposed acquisition in terms of criticality as well as complexity and cost. Where the acquisition is deemed to be of low cost, easily defined with clear measurement criteria, and where there are several alternative suppliers of the goods or services, the procurement may well be treated as a commodity purchase with reduced emphasis on strategic planning.

Where a commodity or service is of low cost but nevertheless has a multiplicity of potential solutions, a request for information (RFI) is normally used to clarify the scope of the service required as well as the organizations that can supply the requirement.

Where the goods and services are of high value but the scope and objectives are clear from the start, a more formal, structured procurement approach is normal. This would involve issuing a request for proposal (RFP) that outlines the requirements in terms of deliverables, time scale, and measurement criteria.

In the case of a higher-risk, high-value, low-clarity acquisition where potential solutions may be uncertain, it is common that the RFI be carried out as a first step leading to an RFP.

Properly structured acquisition procedures developed as a result of a successful plan may be expected to improve schedule success since the roles and responsibilities of the key members in the procurement process are clearly defined and quantifiable.

A thorough understanding of the business needs at the planning stage facilitates more effective selection of procurement types to be employed and achieves more robust implementation process and management of a contract execution because of improved communication frameworks.

Where the procurement process has been clearly laid out based on mutually understood and quantifiable deliverables, the whole framework from that point on becomes more resistant to opportunities for bribery and corruption and the concomitant risk of quality breakdowns and failure at later stages in the tendering process.

Tasks to be achieved in the planning process include:

- Development of an integrated procurement plan methodology
- Assignment of roles and responsibilities for the duration of the tendering process
- Clarification of the business objectives to be achieved and the scope of the work to be tendered for
- Development of clear measuring criteria and an evaluation methodology to be maintained throughout the tendering process
- Ensuring a clear understanding of potential service and goods suppliers of the outcomes, tasks, time scales, and deliverables required

Product Design

The first stage of the procurement plan is normally product design. Based on information derived during the planning process, either as a result of the RFI or based on already clearly understood objectives and criteria, a clearly laid out business requirements specification (BRS) must be developed. This BRS ensures that all parties to the tendering process have demonstrable understanding of all requirements and that no later claims of misinterpretation or misunderstanding will arise.

Product design is normally spelled out in the RFP. Internal control over the contents of the RFP is critical since it is at this stage that opportunities for misunderstandings requiring financial adjustments to the proposal can be enabled, inadvertently or deliberately. Where bribery has taken place already, the formulation of the RFP can be tailored specifically target the products or services available from a single supplier. The RPF itself should be closely examined and agreed to by all internal parties, including operational management, legal services, and internal audit. There is little point in having strong internal control to ensure compliance with the contract based on an RPF that already has corruption and inside dealing built in.

At this stage, prior to submission of their business and financial proposals, interested tenderers must clarify any doubts they may have in the interpretation of the RFP. Once a tender has been submitted in response to the RFP, it can be amended only with the agreement of all parties.

Advertising

It is generally accepted that value for money can best be achieved through transparency and foreseeable contract conditions achieved through open advertising in the acquisition process as opposed to a process in which insider knowledge can influence the bidding process. In today's business environment of electronic acquisition and e-procurement, many of the internal controls designed to ensure fairness in the tendering process may be ineffective or nonexistent. Instead of requiring closed bids to be publicly opened at a set time, many RFPs require bids to be made via e-mail.

Where this process is properly controlled, it can be as effective as the closed bid scenario; however, the process is open to electronic sniffing (eavesdropping on communication lines) at the sender's or the receiver's end or in transit, breaching the confidentiality of the bidding process and exposing the organization to rigged bids.

Very few organizations require submitted bids to be encrypted and to remain encrypted until a set time when they will be decrypted publicly. Attempts may be made to have all bids submitted to an impartial third party but, once again, this measure secures only the recipient end of the communication. This vulnerability opens the doors to corruption and submission of bids using insider information as well as the perception of corruption, which can be as damaging as actual corruption in the long run.

Invitation to Bid

In noncompetitive procurement processes, either via sole-supplier contracts or the restriction, for the sake of efficiency, to a preselected list of bidders for a given contract, the process becomes more vulnerable to bribery and corruption. Nevertheless, use of noncompetitive procurement processes should not be seen as proof of corruption. As mentioned, a supplier's history with the organization may make it desirable to include that supplier in any list of prospective bidders. By the same token, where a supplier is the sole source or the sole *reputable* source of specific expertise or goods and services, it is good business practice to operate with the sole-supplier contract.

Nonetheless, the existence of such contracts creates the opportunity for bribes and inducements in order to become the sole bidder or at least make it to the bidding short list.

When sole-source contracts are unavoidable, a procedure for prequalification in the bidding process can substantially increase the integrity of the bids by facilitating transparent monitoring of the selection process. Such a method decreases the risk of corruption and increases the potential for value for money acquisition through competitive bidding.

Prequalification of Bidders

Where open competitive bidding is inappropriate and restrictive competitive bidding has been selected as the best alternative, prequalification of bidders reduces the opportunity for insiders to award a tender to a selected supplier. Such prequalification normally involves supervisory oversight and the examination of a proposed supplier's reputation, track record for quality of work, and financial stability.

In addition to making a tainted bid less likely, prequalification facilitates organizations that were not selected to tender becoming an effective tertiary oversight group with the potential to call attention to perceived corruption in the bidding process. Such nonselected organizations are in a position to challenge their exclusion before bids are accepted raising the probability of unbiased selection.

Prequalification controls, while helpful as detective controls, do not in themselves prevent or even guarantee detection of corrupt tendering practices.

Technical Evaluation

The first stage of the evaluation process normally is technical evaluation. This evaluation is done on the basis that if the goods or services supplied cannot achieve the business objective, it generally matters little how cheaply the goods or services were acquired. This stage is perhaps the one that offers the greatest opportunity for introducing bias in favor of or against a specific supplier.

Whether A is better than B may boil down to the opinion of an expert. The independence of the expert is critical in ensuring the integrity of the process. Supervisory review may be ineffectual due to the technical nature of the evaluation criteria, and many organizations, having paid for the "expert," see no value for money in rejecting his or her opinion.

In order that this charge not be leveled at large-value projects, delay is often used to give the impression of careful consideration of all facts and alternatives. Selection by committee may be introduced to avoid a single-expert bias. Unfortunately, many committees are assembled based on rank rather than expertise, and high-ranking laypersons tend to be influenced by the committee member they perceive to be the expert, thus defeating the object of the exercise while at the same time adding delay, cost increases, and confusion. In the end, the evaluation remains in the hands and at the discretion of the expert.

Financial Evaluation

Once it has been decided that the bidder's proposal is technically sound, the process moves on to financial evaluation. Depending on technical complexity and difficulty of execution, contracts may be awarded on a lowest-bidder basis, as long as the minimum technical performance criteria are achieved, or to the best technical evaluation, as long as a minimum financial performance criteria are achieved.

This phase can be a very difficult one in which to prevent corruption creeping in. In a long-term project or a project involving the development of a unique product, it may be very difficult to determine labor and material costs, both direct and indirect, over the life of the project. It is this complexity that has led many government contracts to adopt the cost-plus contract, wherein a supplier of goods or services contracts to provide them on the basis of cost recovery plus an agreed percentage profit. This enables the supplier to include an unknown degree of flexibility in a proposal. It reassures the client that the supplier's profit percentage will not be excessive.

This technique, of course, assumes that the costs will be fairly and accurately recorded and only costs directly attributable to the contract will be included. At the financial tendering phase, the bidder has the opportunity to pad contract costs because of the size of the unknown factors. Generally, however, this is not the opportunity to defraud the client. Padding the costs will result in higher tender bid, which may be rejected on a competitive basis. More commonly, costs are underestimated, resulting in an apparently lower bid that nevertheless has the flexibility to be increased should more costs suddenly appear.

The financial proposal must be evaluated in depth to determine the likelihood that the work can be done for the given costs and to ensure that the contract does not include inadvertent loopholes.

Postqualification

Postqualification is the process of validating and verifying all bidder statements and documents to ensure their compliance with the technical, financial, and legal requirements of the bid. This process takes place after bidders have been qualified for submission of a tender bid.

The technical requirements require verification of the stated experience and competence of the bidder as well as the authenticity and adequacy of any bid security.

Postqualification of the financial bid would involve ensuring the accuracy and validity of financial proposals together with the adequacy of the funding required for the bidder to maintain an adequate cash flow to sustain operations throughout the project.

Legal verification would ensure the existence, currency, and validity of all permits and licenses required together with all documentation submitted as part of the bid's eligibility requirements. This step may involve ascertaining whether the bidder has any outstanding tax disputes, legal disputes, blacklisting, or other pertinent encumbrances with the potential to make the bid ineligible unless significant bribes had already been paid.

Contract Award

It is during the contract award stage of procurement that determination is made of the winner of the contract bid. This is the final stage of which bribery and corruption can occur in the placing of the contract. When objective criteria have been used with appropriate weightings in place, the selection procedure should have taken place in a fair and verifiable manner. As long as no bias or external influence intrudes at this stage, the contract may be deemed to have been awarded in a corruption-free manner.

Contract Implementation

The implementation phase of procurement is, once again, an area where the opportunities for bribery are rife. Such opportunities could include:

- Amending work orders
- Substitution of inferior quality materials
- Charging for work which did not occur
- Inflating material usage or time spent
- Supplying contracted services that do not meet specifications
- Overlooking defects in items or services procured
- Incomplete servicing of the contract
- Missing of deadlines
- Simple overcharging

Strong internal controls, primarily on the detection side, are required to ensure the execution matches the agreements previously made in the procurement process.

It should not, however, be assumed that all such corruption takes place at the instigation of the service supplier. This phase provides officials with the opportunity to indulge in solicitation of bribes or even, with the addition of physical threats, extortion in order to benefit from payments due for services rendered. Taken to the extreme, insertion by corrupt officials of delays into contracts where profit margins are already low can create significant cash flow problems for organizations that have stayed within the letter and the intent of the contractual agreement.

Verification and Follow-up

The verification and follow-up phase of the procurement process normally is carried out by a third party, such as the organization's internal auditors, with the intent of ensuring that no unacceptable practices occurred during the design, placement, and completion of the contracts. Other parties, such as the organization's legal advice team, may also be involved to ensure all terms of contracts were met and no inadvertent breaches of legislative requirements occurred, and the external auditors to ensure the financial soundness of the records of items or services procured and costs incurred are kept.

The more complex the contract, the greater the number of rules, procedures, and red tape to be gone through, and the larger the opportunity for undetected corruption and bribery.

Designing a compliance program for enforcing anticorruption activities and supervision includes elements of:

- Implementation of a senior-level leadership/oversight monitoring mechanism
- Building a corporate corruption risk profile to identify vulnerable phases in projects where corrupt actions could occur in order to facilitate monitoring
- Development of written standards and policies as a guide to operational managers and staff, particularly in areas where human discretion would normally be expected in decision making
- Development and issuance of guidelines for reporting of concerns regarding compliance with the anticorruption standards and policies
- Provision of basic training on recognition of unacceptable business practices and the reporting mechanisms available
- Clearly established procedures to minimize opportunities for bribery and corruption to occur and to ensure that should such activities occur, detection would be swift and punishment severe
- Development of compliance audit work programs to ensure that control continues to be exercised in all phases of the procurement process
- Development of investigation procedures and identification of investigatory resources required should red flags indicate the potential existence of bribery and corruption within the execution of the procurement process
- Development of a response plan in conjunction with internal and external legal advice and the consultation of the human resources division to handle any unauthorized or illegal activities detected

Internal control structures are required to ensure that the decision-making process and the overall structures of the procurement process itself are appropriate. Particular attention should be paid to authority levels and segregation of duties in decision making, and the internal controls must ensure adequacy of supervision from start to finish. A full audit trail indicating decisions made, on whose authority, and independently verified by whom will be required throughout the process but most especially during the verification and follow-up process.

The intent of the verification and follow-up is not only to ensure that no unauthorized activities took place during this procurement exercise but that lessons learned will be applied so that the next procurement will run even more smoothly.

Where suspicions arise regarding improprieties in the acquisition process, the organization may elect to hire forensic auditors if there may be legal repercussions and if the evidence sought may have to be produced in court.

RED FLAGS AT ENRON AND WORLDCOM

Perhaps two of the best-known recent cases leading to business collapses took place at Enron and WorldCom. The businesses shared common traits that, in retrospect, indicate underlying problems at both:

■ *Lack of director independence.* This situation is common in organizations where directors have a financial relationship either as primary stockholders or have received personal loans from the organization. Other indicators include company directors who have personal conflicts by serving on the boards of other associated companies, directors who are also employees, and directors who are a key supplier or customer.

■ *Poorly structured compensation schemes.* A chronic problem in many corporate failures is the inclusion of short-term rewards, such as sizable annual bonuses or short-term stock options, as substantial parts of the compensation package. This situation can lead to the adoption of business practices detrimental to the survival prospects of the organization.

■ *Adoption of inappropriate (and sometimes illegal) accounting practices.* In WorldCom, this involved transferring specific current costs into capital accounts, thus fraudulently concealing operating expenses and enabling the company to report higher earnings. In a similar manner, Enron operated a multiplicity of special-purpose vehicles that facilitated off-balance-sheet accounting, thus concealing liabilities.

■ *Multiple and conflicting use of audit firms.* Utilizing different arms of the same firms to undertake nonaccounting services, such as consulting and outsourcing of internal audit services, placed the audit firms in a situation where a large part of their income was derived from conflicting interests.

NEPOTISM AND FAVORITISM

Nepotism is a particular variety of favoritism in which preference is given to relatives in employment, salary levels, placement of contracts, awarding of honors, or other abuse of power regardless of the relatives' merit.

Nepotism involves family members, including distant relations, in an organization working within the same chain of command. Where nepotism occurs, detrimental effects can be noted in the areas of:

- Workplace safety
- Security
- Quality of supervision
- Effective internal discipline
- Workplace morale

In many family-owned organizations, relatives are frequently rotated into executive positions, in some cases without appropriate preparation. This can be a very effective talent-sourcing mechanism in that family members may have been indoctrinated into the corporate culture from birth and may be placed where natural talent has been shown. Despite some success stories, however, a problem can be created among upper managers and directors who believe that career progression is reserved for family members.

Nepotism can also cause problems where relatives believe that their promotion was unmerited (whether true or not) and become demoralized and feel pressured to maintain a level of performance that would not normally be sought in other employees.

In other organizations, nepotism is virtually impossible to avoid. For example, geographical isolation may ensure that one organization is the major employer in the region and the workforce is drawn from that specific region. Inevitably multiple members of a family work for the same organization. This situation can, in fact, be very effectively managed by encouraging the family unit to adopt an internal culture of loyalty to the employer, and internal family relationships hold individuals accountable for inefficiencies and ineffectiveness. Even within effectively managed organizations, problems may occur should, for any reason, the organization need to terminate the services of a family member.

From a legal perspective, nepotism can conflict with antidiscriminatory legislation as can antinepotism policies. Where preference in employment has been given to family members, outsiders may claim discrimination under laws in many countries. By the same token, individuals who marry coworkers may find themselves in a position where one or another is required to leave the employment or transfer to another department. In some countries, the law could see this as unfair dismissal or, in the case of a transfer, as constructive dismissal, where the employee's terms and conditions of employment have changed to the extent that the job is no longer the one they were employed to do and the company has made their working conditions unacceptable. It can then be deemed that the organization artificialy "constructed" a situation where the employee had no choice but to resign. In such circumstances, some organizations ensure that if anyone must lose his or her position, it will be the female partner. This, again, may be in breach of laws precluding discrimination against women.

Other companies have found themselves in breach of labor law where an existing employee has been terminated in order to make room for a family member to enter the job market.

Nepotism Policy

In order to reduce the impact that nepotism or the perception of nepotism can cause in the workplace, many organizations adopt a specific policy regarding potential conflicts of interest. Certain organizations strictly prohibit the employment of employees' relatives; others permit the employment of relatives who are suitably qualified for a given position as long as no actual conflicts of interest are created.

For example, individuals who are related by marriage or blood or are members of the same household may be permitted to work within the organization, and even within the same department, as long as there is no direct reporting or supervision between the relatives. Care is normally taken to ensure that related employees have no fiscal or human resources relationship within the workplace.

Other Forms of Favoritism

Nepotism is not the only form of favoritism that can lead to undesirable results. *Cronyism* can also have a negative impact on organizational performance.

Cronyism is a more general form of favoritism involving partiality in business decisions toward friends and associates; the old phase "It's not what you know, it's who you know" is an example of cronyism. Cronyism has many names, including the Americanism "good ol' boy network" and the United Kingdom's "old school tie." In all cases it is characterized by the conferring of favors on members of a network of insiders and may take the form of favoritism in hiring and awarding of contracts. Where large-value contracts are placed, accusations of cronyism are rife, particularly if a single supplier is believed to have been singled out for preferential treatment.

As with nepotism, cronyism ultimately may result in a reduced dynamism in the business environment. Where competition is believed to be ineffectual, the business may incur an overall rise in costs. Quality of work may suffer as there is no impetus to do better so as to achieve future contracts since the presumption is that they will be awarded not on merit but on friendship. In addition, cronyism within an organization can lead to conflict when multiple groups develop. As can be seen in many popular television programs where groups of individuals are placed into a competitive environment, informal relationships develop and can lead to a degradation of the work ethic as competing teams seek to gain advantage over the other side.

In 1996, a study by Prendergast and Topel indicated that favoritism and biased performance appraisal within organizations may derive from personal preferences toward individual employees.[3] In addition, a bias toward individuals can result in a distortion of incentives and a degradation in job performance.

A more recent study on the impact of social connections and incentives in the workplace indicates that the payment of supervisory bonuses linked to the subordinates' output causes a fundamental realignment toward supporting workers with high abilities.[4] This does not eliminate favoritism, but it does move the bias in a direction that benefits the organization.

Controlling Favoritism

Controlling favoritism starts with a recognition that favoritism exists within the workplace. Many supervisory-level staff favor one employee over another without even realizing it. Controls that can help avoid favoritism include:

- Avoiding family relationships in the workplace where possible or, at minimum, ensuring no supervisor–subordinate relationship exists.
- Ensuring that all advancements, compensation, and awards are based solely on performance using an objective and public method for evaluating such performance.
- Being alert to office gossip, which may indicate the perception of favoritism. Misconceptions must be corrected as soon as possible.
- Ensuring that the workplace environment encourages all employees to discuss any concerns with at least two independent people at the supervisory level.
- Conducting performance appraisals separately and at a different time from salary reviews.
- Introducing incentives that will realign supervisory interest with that of the organization. Even comparatively low levels of incentives can have a disproportionately positive impact on overall performance.

ABUSE OF AUTHORITY

Abuse of authority can be defined as an arbitrary or capricious exercise of power by an official or employee resulting in an adverse impact on the rights of another individual, or resulting in advantage or personal gain to the abuser. In many countries, abuse of power and authority within the public service is seen as a disciplinable offense causing damage to the interest of the state, the public interest, or the rights and interests of citizens of the country as spelled out in law.

Abuse of authority generally is characterized by intent. It should not be confused with decisions and outcomes caused by incompetence rather than abuse of authority.

In the workplace, abuse of authority may take the form of intimidation, threat, or humiliation. Like the other abuses, it can significantly reduce the growth and profitability of an organization by negatively impacting worker efficiency and, at the same time, creating a high employee turnover and a reduced ability to recruit fresh talent. Red flags for abuse of authority include:

- Inappropriate criticism
- Humiliation in front of other employees
- The making of derogatory comments to other employees
- Provision of negative evaluations to other perspective employers, should the employees seek a more positive work environment elsewhere
- The silent treatment
- Micromanagement
- Assigning menial work to senior staff
- Withholding information
- Workplace bullying

Abuse of authority is not typically an isolated case of a single employee whose negative behavior can be offset by the introduction of an appropriate corporate regulation saying such behavior is "not allowed." Such a directive is a good first step, but a fundamental change in corporate culture is required to eliminate such abuse.

Corporate culture is an accumulation of the ways in which the members of any organization operate collectively in their attitudes and actions. Corporate culture is a factor of the communications among members and has as its foundation the structures, communication networks, and processes within the organization as well as the stories, traditions, rites and rituals, and vocabulary used.

Stories related by members of an organization give clear indications of the cultural value and organizational history. These tales become part of the traditions of the organization and are generally expressed in the rites and rituals of the company. The monthly board meeting, the weekly production meeting, and the daily department meeting all are rituals conveying the attitudes and expectations of the organization and its members. Where negative attitudes exist at the highest levels, they will percolate down to all operational levels. If the organization develops a culture where abuse of authority is tolerated, then abuse of authority will become the norm.

In their book *The Bully-Free Workplace*, Gary and Ruth Namie discuss the organizational factors that both encourage and sustain bullying and the negative impacts on organization missions as well as individual productivity.[5] They lay out a detailed plan to stop the destructive impact of such behavior on the organization by creating explicit policies against bullying.

DEVELOPING AN OVERALL ANTICORRUPTION CULTURE

The most effective method of combating the insidious intrusion of corruption within an organization involves the intentional design and implementation of a culture that neither facilitates nor tolerates corruption in any form.

An anticorruption culture will be based on the observance of shared norms throughout the organization. These norms typically have, at their foundation, management's declared ethical stand and intolerance of corrupt behavior in any form. When management makes a clear statement as to the unacceptability of corruption, levels within the organization drop substantially in a comparatively short period.

A full-blown corruption risk assessment is required to identify any weak areas where corruption could lie unnoticed. This assessment should be done at the operational management level to promote the awareness of managers' responsibility to detect and eliminate corruption if any form within their area of authority.

Organizational responsibility for prevention and detection of corruption has to be clearly established and communicated to all employees. Each person must know his or her role in the overall plan and how to report any wrongdoing they may detect.

In many cases where corruption has occurred, subsequent investigation has indicated that the activities were known to others within the organization but were not reported. The most common reason given for nonreporting is that the individual does not know whom to report it to and is unsure whether he or she should report it. There can be no doubt about this. A clear and well-communicated internal reporting structure is required with employees who report misdeeds fully protected from any retaliation.

Another common reason given for nonreporting is that nothing would or could be done. To maintain the information flow as part of the culture of intolerance for wrongdoing, a feedback mechanism is essential to communicate to all involved that a report was made (the reporter can remain anonymous), an investigation took place, and appropriate action was instituted.

All concerned also must understand that internal reporting of wrongdoing is not whistleblowing but the duty of all employees. External reporting should take place within a clearly defined authority structure authorizing specified internal individuals to ensure that all external agencies that may have a statutory right to be informed are indeed informed. At the same time, legitimate authority within the organization must do this external reporting. Unauthorized disclosure, particularly if an investigation is still under way, may jeopardize the ongoing legitimate business of the organization as well as its reputation. Where such information is disclosed in an unauthorized manner and investigations subsequently determine that no misdeed took place, the organization may be highly exposed to lawsuits for defamation of character, slander, or libel.

For these structures and procedures to become embedded as part of the corporate culture, all parties involved must be fully aware and accepting of the no-tolerance policy. This embedding will involve an ongoing staff awareness program across the organization at every level; all employees must understand that the rules apply equally and fairly to all. Exceptions undermine the ethical culture of the organization and severely reduce the effectiveness of an anticorruption culture.

NOTES

1. Transparency International, Global Corruption Barometer 2010 Report, www.transparency.de/fileadmin/pdfs/Wissen/Korruptionsindices/GCB_2010.pdf.
2. FTSE Good Policy Committee, Countering Bribery Criteria, London, 2006, www.ftse.com/Indices/FTSE4Good_Index_Series/Downloads/FTSE4Good_Countering_Bribery_Criteria.pdf.

3. C. Prendergast and R. Topel, "Favoritism in Organizations," Journal of Political Economy 104 (1996).
4. O. Bandiera, I. Barankay, and I. Rasul, "Social Connections and Incentives in the Workplace: Evidence from Personnel Data," Econometrica 77 (2009).
5. Gary Namie and Ruth Namie, The Bully-Free Workplace (Hoboken, NJ: John Wiley & Sons, 2011).

CHAPTER SIX

Role of Ethics in Fighting Fraud

> Virtue lies in our power, and similarly so does vice,
> because when it is in our power to act, it is also
> in our power not to act.... So, if it is in our power
> to do a thing when it is right, it will also be in our
> power not to do it when it is wrong.
>
> —*Aristotle, philosopher and polymath (384–322 B.C.)*

After studying this chapter, the reader should be able to:

- Identify the nature and role that ethics play in the organization to combat fraud, and evaluate the current state of the existing ethical structures within an organization.
- Design a code of conduct that will reduce the likelihood of fraud occurrences and increase the probability of early detection.

Ethics are frequently confused with individual moral principles but, in fact, go far beyond them. Ethics address issues from both practical and idealistic perspectives and, as a result of this dual focus, the ideal in many cases conflicts with the practical. For this reason, ethics have been described as being "above the law but below the ideal."[1] Merely obeying the law is not, in itself, ethical since ethics are concerned with making decisions regarding what is right in situations where there are options or where there is little guidance from the law itself.

 ## HOW MORAL DECISIONS ARE MADE

Lawrence Kohlberg developed a theory related to moral reasoning being the basis for ethical behavior. Kohlberg identified six stages that individuals go through in developing the capability for moral reasoning. [2]

Level I: Preconventional morality, which is common in children. At this level, rules are made external to the individual who does not as yet identify with the values behind the rules themselves. Morality of an action is judged by its direct consequences.

- Stage 1. *Obedience and punishment orientation.* As children, we learn that there is a fixed set of rules laid down by powerful authorities that we must unquestioningly obey. Failure to obey will result in punishment.
- Stage 2. *Individualism and exchange.* At this stage of development, children start to realize that there may be different perspectives on a given ethical challenge and that individuals see things relative to themselves and make their decisions accordingly.

Level II: Conventional morality, which is typical of adolescents and adults. Morality of actions is judged by comparison to society's views and expectations.

- Stage 3. *Good interpersonal relationships.* At this stage of development, adolescents believe that to maintain good interpersonal relationships, individuals should live up to the expectations of family and community and behave in a manner acceptable to them. *Community* in this sense could include the community at large, a community of peers of the adolescent, gang membership, or the scouts.
- Stage 4. *Maintaining the social order.* This stage involves a shift in emphasis from the need to be accepted by family and community to the need to maintain the rules by which the family and community operate.

Level III: Postconventional morality. At this level, also known as the principled level, individuals begin to develop their own set of principles, which may be inconsistent with those of society or the family.

- Stage 5. *Social contract and individual rights.* Individuals operating from stage 5 believe that there are certain fundamentals that make a society work—namely basic *rights* and *democratic* procedures—and that individuals should operate within the rules of society but have a democratic opportunity to change those rules.
- Stage 6. *Universal principles.* Individuals operating at stage 6 believe, like those at stage 5, that there is a need to protect certain individual rights while settling disputes through democratic processes. However, individuals at stage 6 recognize that democratic processes, working for the good of the majority, do not necessarily work for the good of all. Martin Luther King, Jr., for example, believed laws were valid only insofar as they were grounded in justice and that there was an obligation to disobey unjust laws. The recognition of the democratic process, however, made it obligatory that he accept the penalties for his actions.

Given the variability of the individual's development with regard to moral conduct, it can be seen that ethics in the business environment must go beyond the complexities of moral decisions.

As applied in a business context, ethics are intended to provide organizations with the tools to deal with moral complexities since many business decisions have an ethical component.

An understanding of business ethics is fundamental to the development of an ethical climate in which fraud is neither condoned nor tolerated and where ethical considerations govern all interactions among organizational members, the public, employees, customers, suppliers, governmental authorities, and the community within which the organization operates.

NATURE AND ROLE OF ETHICS

In considering the impact of ethics on the probability of fraud occurring within an organization and the likelihood of its early detection, it is useful to recognize that the overall areas of economic activity within which management will make decisions are commonly dominated by tensions between legal and ethical choices. Rossouw, in his studies on business ethics in Africa, identifies three main areas where such conflicts could arise.[3]

1. *The macro or systemic dimension,* consisting of the policy framework created by the state, which determines the basis for economic exchanges both nationally and internationally.
2. *The meso or institutional dimension,* consisting of the relations among economic organizations, such as public entities, private sector entities, private individuals, and those outside the organizations.
3. *The micro or intraorganizational dimension,* consisting of the economic actions and decisions of individuals within an organization.

Rossouw demonstrates the interrelationship among these three dimensions where, for example, a private institution may decide to participate in a community upliftment program or to support previously disadvantaged communities and must demonstrate its commitment to corporate social responsibility. Within the same organization, the implementation of affirmative action policies may give rise to conflicts over staff appointments as demographic quotas dominate recruitment policies.

Business executives daily face the challenges of making ethical decisions within complex competitive business environments while addressing multiple goals and objectives, cultural contradictions, and a constantly moving regulatory environment. At the same time, pressure continues to rise to ensure sustainability, accountability and transparency, and personal actions and decisions. Ethical tensions are heightened where public scrutiny of the organization's activities occurs.

Given the dynamic and constantly changing environment of both regulatory legislation and competitive assaults, an organization may find that a decision that is both ethical and legal at one moment has become unethical, illegal, or both.

To understand the complexities of making "ethical" decisions, that is useful to learn the history of ethical theories and the foundations that underlie them.

Ethics are frequently confused with individual moral principles but in fact go far beyond them. Ethics are designed to address issues from both practical and idealistic standpoints. As a result, the ideal is commonly in conflict with the practical. In his book *A Critical Introduction to Ethics*, Wheelright defined three fundamentals underlying the impact of ethics and decision making[4]:

1. Ethics involve questions requiring reflective choice.
2. Ethics are concerned with the consequences of decisions.
3. Ethics involve guidance as to what is right and wrong.

The most fundamental schism in ethical theory is the division between cognitivism, which claims that it is possible to know moral wrong from right objectively, and noncognitivism, which claims that we cannot know moral wrong from right because all such judgments are subjective and influenced by cultural preferences. In other words, noncognitivism claims that moral right and wrong is whatever is declared so by a particular cultural group. This view that morality is culturally relative is known as *moral relativism* and is supported by the differences in existing cultural views seen around the world.

Over the years, ethical theory has evolved into a variety of classes or principles:

- The *imperative principle* reflects a belief that there are effectively no choices. Nothing is negotiable, and strict compliance with the code of ethics is required at all times. Under the imperative principle, there is no such thing as a lesser of two evils. This form of ethical judgment is a standard used within many religions and is frequently applied, for example, by pro-life advocates who view the taking of life a wrong under any circumstances without exception. This class of ethical theory can cause problems in business decision making when two or more provisions appear to be in direct opposition to each other or where the ethical principle produces results out of proportion to the actual business situation.
- The *utilitarian principle* holds that actions should bring the most good to the most people. This is the ethical principle underpinning social ethics in countries where the good of the majority is the basis on which decisions are made. This principle can result in society endorsing individual and ethical acts in order to bring about the greater good.
- *Act utilitarianism* is a subclass of utilitarianism that requires that all acts must lead to the greatest good for the greatest number. From this perspective, it holds that if existing rules do not provide the greatest good for the greatest number, they should be broken. This ethical base is common in revolutionary politics as well as corporate politics.
- *Rule utilitarianism* takes an opposing stand and proposes firm and publicly advocated moral rules to which all acts must conform. Again, under this principle, there are no special cases. This class of utilitarianism is the standard for many fundamentalist religions.
- *Deontological ethics* draw their base from the consequences of acts. Under this class of ethics, the concept of duty is paramount and actions commonly result from this concept. Ethical principles in this class of

theory are deemed to be independent of each person's conscience.[5] This can be a potentially dangerous ethical stance; anything can be justified under it in the name of duty, and individual consciences may condone acts that could ultimately lead to societal disintegration. The "duty" ethical argument is common in repressive organizations where lying, cheating, and stealing from customers is tolerated as long the organization benefits.

▪ *Classical ethics* as related to business ethics have, over the years, been propounded by Plato, Aristotle, and Adam Smith among others. Under classical theory, there is no direct relationship between business and society's goals and objectives. Adam Smith[6] stated that, provided there is competition to satisfy customers' desires, the common good is best served by the pursuit of individual self-interest. In that manner, human welfare will be maximized without being part of the intention of those self-interested individuals. Smith also, however, warned that people in business will do anything to avoid such competition thriving.

▪ *Ethical Moralists.* Over the years, the classical view has been modified to represent business as attempting to achieve egotistical goals by following established rules for the benefit of all. Within this ethical class, business is seen to have distinct social responsibilities. This view is typically held by *ethical moralists* who believe that business should have societal goals outside of its normal business forms of survival and making profits giving rise to Kant's view of business as a good citizen.

Business ethics involve the application of ethical rules and principles within a commercial context. Such ethics normally exceed the boundaries laid down by law. From an ethical perspective, a law frequently represents a minimum standard for organizations to comply with. Ethical dilemmas within the business environment typically occur when a choice has to be made between two or more options that offer a variety of potential results on organizational profitability and competitiveness and stakeholder wishes and aspirations.

Perhaps the most significant ethical issues facing business today may be seen as *legal and ethical.* Although ideally management should aspire to make decisions that are both ethical and legal, many business decisions may be viewed as: legal but not ethical, ethical but not legal or even illegal, and unethical. For example:

▪ *Legal but not ethical.* The organization may have been behaving in an unethical manner although there is, at present, no law forbidding the behavior. In certain jurisdictions, the dumping of toxic waste may be seen to be unethical, but there may be no current legislation forbidding it.

▪ *Ethical but not legal.* The organization may be addressing issues from the highest ethical standpoint but still may be in noncompliance with specific statutory legislation. For example, certain companies that refused to fully comply with apartheid legislation in South Africa acted against the law although many saw their behavior as attaining a high ethical standard.

▪ *Illegal and unethical.* Organizations or even individuals may place self-interest ahead of both ethical and legal considerations.

Employee Ethics

As employees, individuals themselves have three specific ethical obligations to comply with:

1. *The duty of obedience.* Employees have a duty to obey all reasonable directions as long as doing so involves no requirement to perform illegal or unethical acts.
2. *The duty of loyalty.* Acts should not be performed against the interests of employers when the person is acting as an employee. This is occasionally disputed with some organizations insisting the duty of loyalty applies 24 hours per day while others argue that it applies only when the person acts as an employee
3. *The duty of confidentiality.* The intent of this duty is to ensure that information acquired as a result of the operations of the organization is not used contrary to the interests of the organization or to further the interests of either the employee or any other person or organization. This duty is generally taken to cover information obtained during the course of the employee's activities on behalf of the employer but does not apply if the information is freely available or general knowledge.

The issues involved in implementing good corporate governance are laid down in a variety of internationally accepted recommendations, but companies take individual approaches to the implementation of good governance principles. Sound corporate governance practices call for corporate ethics to be spelled out in codes of ethics in order to deal with any failure of management and employees to comply with laws and regulations affecting an organization. Such codes typically include lists of unacceptable practices and the penalties to be incurred.

General business ethics codes may require, among other things, that all products sold should meet safety standards, all guarantees should be met, untrue and misleading advertising are prohibited, and labor laws are complied with. As far as employees are concerned, to ensure compliance with the three duties listed earlier, such codes normally include statements that employees should not:

- Divert business opportunities from the company
- Publicly denigrate the company, its services, or products
- Manipulate corporate incentive schemes to their own benefit
- Make use of corporate assets in an illegal or unauthorized way
- Make false or deceptive statements about corporate affairs to the company's detriment

Codes of Conduct

In terms of fighting fraud, one of the most powerful controls is the implementation of a formal *corporate code of conduct*. Such codes do not, in themselves, enforce ethical behavior; rather, they should be seen as *directive* controls expressing the requirements of the organization in situations where ethical decisions must be made. While directive controls do not compel obedience, they serve as a mechanism for expelling a member of a population for non-compliance. For example, a breach of the corporate code of conduct could be grounds for dismissal. Such codes are most effective when they are combined with detective controls designed to identify breaches of the code.

Most corporate governance policy-making committees around the world, including the Treadway Commission in the United States, the Cadbury Commission in the United Kingdom, and the King Commission in South Africa, endorse and require the use of corporate codes of conduct. Having such a code, however, solves only part of the problem. To be effective, enforcement mechanisms must ensure compliance at all levels. Such enforcement has the effect of setting an ethical climate at the top of the organization where it can then "waterfall" down through the levels until ultimately ethics become part of the corporate culture. Open channels of communication between management and employees can help promote, for example, the reporting of fraud.

Codes of conduct tend to take two forms:

1. *Lists of improper behaviors with the consequences should such behaviors occur.* Such codes are easy to enforce but extremely difficult to keep comprehensive and current since business circumstances are constantly changing.

2. *Positive statements of honest intentions.* Such statements tend to be all-embracing and open to interpretation to suit the interpreter's particular interests. In addition, such statements are almost impossible to enforce due to their flexibility.

Most effective codes of conduct combine positive generalizations with specific prohibitions. They normally include the basic rules of acceptable and unacceptable behavior and define corporate requirements regarding such variables as:

- Confidentiality
- Conflicts of interest
- Standards of corporate practice
- Acceptance of gifts

Despite management's best efforts, ethical dilemmas will arise in the course of conducting business due to conflicting values among various stakeholders. Because legal, political, and economic systems differ across the world, inevitably ethical dilemmas will be different. In multinational operations, different ethical solutions may be required. Management must attempt to resolve such conflicts while staying within the law(s) under which the organization operates.

MANAGING ETHICAL RISK

In order to achieve the best results for the organization, ethical risk must be properly managed. As can be seen in Exhibit 6.1, like all management activities, ethical risk must be measured through a conscious risk evaluation process, leading to active engagement by management, with appropriate rewards designed for demonstrably measurable achievements by individuals who will then be rewarded.

Legislation in countries around the world has required the introduction of ethics management programs that have the same general characteristics:

- Establishment of a code of ethics/code of conduct
- Assignment of senior executives to monitor compliance
- Implementation of training and communication programs regarding the code
- Exercise of due care in delegation of authority

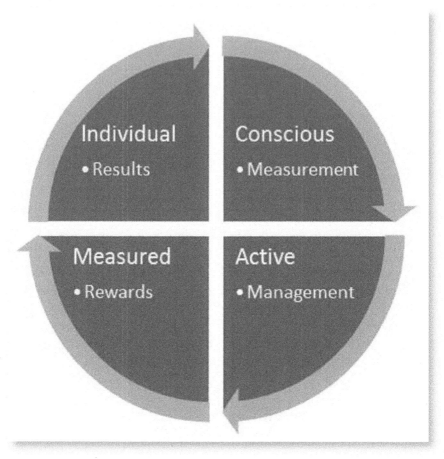

EXHIBIT 6.1 Managing Ethical Risk

- Consistent and unbiased enforcement of the code
- Provision of safe reporting mechanisms with adequate monitoring and independent review
- Appropriate response to offenses under the code
- Integration of ethics into the corporate culture

Such integration will not happen overnight and requires significant effort on the part of the organization. Nevertheless, the impact across all facets of operations, but particularly including reduction in fraud and corruption within the organization, generally make the exercise highly beneficial and cost effective.

Reviewing the Code of Ethics/Code of Conduct

From an internal control perspective, the code of ethics/conduct will require a periodic review, commonly by internal audit. This review should:

■ Ensure that well-established ethical standards exist for acceptable business behavior and establish a climate encouraging good internal control
■ Review steps taken by the board to establish a formal code of conduct
■ Evaluate whether the board stresses the importance of the code
■ Review the program for monitoring compliance with the code of conduct
■ Review the methodology for keeping the code of conduct up-to-date
■ Obtain updates from management regarding compliance

The primary objective of such a review is to ensure the code is appropriate and properly embedded throughout the organization. This three-step process involves identifying whether the code of conduct in use is appropriate to the nature of the business, corporate culture, and environment within which the organization is doing business. Appropriateness may include the use of a formal vendor code of conduct, compliance with which would be compulsory for all vendors seeking to do business with the organization. The second step is to determine whether the code has been appropriately disseminated throughout the organization and is understood by employees and external stakeholders. The final stage involves a compliance audit to ensure that the code has been appropriately implemented and is monitored on an ongoing basis. At each stage, recommendations may be required regarding code appropriateness, the effectiveness of the communication of code values, and the manner in which it is being implemented and monitored.

Typically such reviews involve:

■ Comparison of the code itself to other accepted role models within the industry, if available. If other examples are not available, the code should be evaluated against the accepted value system of the organization.
■ Interviews with senior managers, clients, suppliers, and other stakeholders as appropriate to ensure their understanding of their duties and responsibilities under the code.
■ An evaluation of the appropriateness and effectiveness of the monitoring mechanisms designed to achieve compliance with code.
■ Evaluating the degree of compliance and commitment required under the code from third parties, such as suppliers.

In cases where a vendor code of conduct is required, which often occurs when dealing with overseas vendors where different value systems may operate, a right to audit must exist in vendor contracts and vendors must agree to abide by the corporate vendor code of conduct. As with audits of the organization's own code of conduct, audits of overseas vendors would focus on the management procedures utilized to ensure continual monitoring and compliance with the corporate vendor code of conduct.

Some organizations go so far as to utilize a vendor code of conduct as part of the pre-screening process for aspirant suppliers. Such an approach is condoned by the U.S. Department of State as being in line with its attempts to ensure corporate social responsibility as part of good governance, prevention of corruption, and the advancement of human rights.

Where such audits take place, violations have been seen to commonly include:

- Use of underage workers in geographically remote facilities
- Sexual harassment of employees
- Intimidation of employees
- Remuneration at levels below minimum wage levels
- Use of undocumented labor
- Exposure of workers to illegal or unsafe working conditions
- Bribery of company employees by outside vendors

As with any other compliance audit, the appropriate recommendations for violations should be made and followed up with to ensure compliance. Recommendations could go as far as dismissal of employees, termination of contracts with vendors for noncompliance with agreements, or even prosecution of individuals where the violations breach not only the code of conduct but also the law.

 REPORTING OF FRAUD

In 2010, a survey carried out by the British Retail Consortium[7] revealed that, despite the growing importance of fraud, only about one third of all incidents were reported to the police. Reasons given for nonreporting were varied but included:

- Small or no loss or damage suffered
- No confidence in police response

- Too time consuming
- It was only an attempted fraud

In 2008, a KPMG survey in Singapore[8] found only 49 percent of frauds being reported to the authorities. In 2006, a KPMG survey in South Africa on fraud[9] within medical schemes also reported that only 12 percent of respondents would "always" report to the police although 86 percent said they would "sometimes" report to police. Again, the main reasons for nonreporting were:

- Cost implications of investigation
- Lack of confidence in the ability of the police
- Desire not to tie up their own resources for years with criminal cases
- Lack of confidence in the justice system
- No chance of financial recovery

In 2011, a report by Roderic Broadhurst indicated the highest reasons for nonreporting were[10]:

- Not worth reporting/not serious enough
- The police would not have been able to do anything/slight chance of success
- Lack of time/too much trouble
- Lack of proof/evidence/witnesses

Interestingly, in none of these reports was fear of negative publicity given as a reason for nonreporting. Cost implications and lack of confidence in police response and ability to do anything appeared to be the dominating factors.

The 2011 KPMG report, however, confirmed that on a global basis, where there was no regulation or law requiring public disclosure, 77 percent of fraud investigations undertaken have no public disclosure and detailed internal communications regarding the fraud declined to only 13 percent of survey respondents.[11] Reasons given included fear of damage to a reputation, loss of investor confidence, and regulatory sanctions.

Individual Reporting of Fraud

Often investigators who investigate a fraud are informed that several witnesses were aware of the fraud but had not reported it.

In 1997, a study was carried out in the United States specifically on the degree to which Americans tolerate insurance fraud.[12] In 2007, a follow-up study[13] evaluated the differences over time.

In 1997, it was concluded that the bulk of the population could be broken into four basic groups:

1. *Moralists.* No tolerance for fraud with a strong support for punishment. This was the largest group at 30 percent of those surveyed.
2. *Realists.* Also a low tolerance for fraud but with an understanding why, in some instances, some people might justify the fraud they commit. This group came in at 21 percent of those surveyed.
3. *Conformists.* This group was fairly tolerant of fraud and believed that everyone was doing it. They saw it as "no big deal" if people took advantage of an opportunity to defraud when presented. Of those surveyed, 25 percent were in this group.
4. *Critics.* This group was the most tolerant of insurance fraud and other white-collar crimes, believing that insurers have only themselves to blame. Although the smallest group, the critics had little regard for large institutions, including government and business. This group accounted for 20 percent of those surveyed.

When the survey was repeated in 2007, the tolerance for insurance fraud had increased in two groups and decreased for the *realists*, who remained static at 21 percent, and the *Moralists*, who had decreased from 30 percent to 26 percent of the population surveyed. *Conformists*, those tolerant of fraud, had increased from 25 percent to 27 percent, but the biggest movement was in the *critics* group, those most tolerant of fraud, which had increased from 20 percent to 26 percent and were equal in size to the *moralists*.

This meant that some 53 percent of the population surveyed was at least tolerant of insurance fraud.

The surveys also reviewed the participants' perception of other types of fraud, including credit card fraud and tax evasion. Although the groups considered these frauds to be far less acceptable than insurance fraud, the number of people who thought that such behavior was unethical did decline. Across the board, survey members were more inclined to consider outside factors and extenuating circumstances in determining whether behavior was unacceptable.

Individuals who were aware of fraud but had not reported it gave several reasons for their failure to act; chief among them was that while they suspected fraud, they had no proof. The second highest category consisted of those who thought it was none of their business followed by those who knew the perpetrator as a friend or neighbor. Not knowing where to report it was still a significant factor in the decision not to report. Other reasons given were concerns over personal safety, not believing the behavior was wrong, and "extenuating circumstances."

Encouraging Reporting and Whistleblowing

In order to increase the number of individuals who are willing to report fraudulent and other improper activities in the workplace, organizations can do a lot to impact the reasons given for nonreporting. The belief that a person needs a lot of evidence on which to base a report may owe its existence to television programs in which amateur sleuths are ignored by police and have to investigate crimes themselves.

Knowing the caseload and pressure that police services are under, individuals may feel that their report will lack credibility unless they can produce convincing evidence. Nevertheless, internal reporting does not require individuals to have substantial evidence in order to alert company authorities to suspected wrongdoing. Suspected frauds are most commonly reported to department heads, internal auditors, general managers, and financial directors. Where reporters suspect that any of these individuals may be involved in the fraud or may have a relationship with the accused person, an alternate and anonymous means of reporting must be available.

One effective way of facilitating fraud reporting is the introduction of a fraud hotline. On such hotlines, organizations or individuals, either external to the company or internal, can report suspected wrongdoing with or without evidence and with or without identifying themselves. Companies that have introduced such reporting mechanisms indicate that up to 60 percent of reported wrongdoing cannot be substantiated or is simply malicious. Nonetheless, in most cases, the remaining tip has proven to have more than justified the cost of the hotline.

Where hotlines have proven ineffectual, a common reason is poor publicity regarding their use. Either no one knew how to use the hotline, or, when it was used in the past, no action was taken or seen to be taken, and no feedback was given on actions taken and their effectiveness. Reporters must understand that they will not face retribution from the organization, whether their report is substantiated or not. They should also understand that no employee will be held accountable for refusing to carry out a directive that is in violation of the law or constitutes fraud.

Any fear of reprisal will result in the collapse of the reporting system. The organization must encourage all employees to submit all good-faith concerns and complaints without fear of retaliation of any kind and without regard for the position of the person or persons responsible for the complaint or concern.

Should the reporter prefer to discuss the matter confidentially with an actual person, an opportunity must exist and be communicated accordingly. Many organizations use the audit committee as a resource in such reporting. Individuals involved with any subsequent investigation must use extreme care to ensure that, when requested, reporters' confidentiality is fully maintained.

NOTES

1. Walter G. Kell and Richard E. Ziegler, *Modern Auditing* (Boston: Warren Gordon & Lamont, 1980), p. 769.
2. Lawrence Kohlberg, Charles Levine, and Alexandra Hewer, *Moral Stages: A Current Formulation and a Response to Critics* (Basel/NY: Karger, 1983).
3. Rossouw, D., *Business Ethics in Africa*, 2nd ed. (Cape Town: Oxford University Press South Africa, 2002).
4. P. Wheelwright, *A Critical Introduction to Ethics*, 3rd ed. (New York: Odyssey Press, 1959).
5. Immanuel Kant, *Fundamental Principles of the Metaphysics of Morals*, 9th ed. (New York: Longmans, Green, 1923).
6. Adam Smith, *The Wealth of Nations* (Bantam Classics, 2003, Random House NYC)
7. British Retail Consortium, *Retail Crime Survey*, www.brc.org.uk/Downloads/2010_BRC_Retail_Crime_Survey.pdf.
8. KPMG, *Fraud: Prevent, Detect, Respond:* www.kpmg.com/SG/en/IssuesAndInsights/ArticlesPublications/Documents/forensics_FraudSurvey2008.pdf.
9. KPMG, *Profile of a Fraudster Survey 2007*, www.kpmg.co.uk/pubs/ProfileofaFraudsterSurvey%28web%29.pdf
10. Roderic G. Broadhurst, *Business and the Risk of Crime in China: The 2005–2006 China International Crime Against Business Survey* (Oakland, CA: Griffin Press, 2011).
11. KPMG, *Who Is the Typical Fraudster: KPMG Analysis of Global Patterns of Fraud*, 2011. www.kpmg.com/global/en/issuesandinsights/articlespublications/pages/global-fraud-patterns.aspx.
12. Coalition Against Insurance Fraud, *Four Faces: Why Americans Do and Do Not Tolerate Insurance Fraud* (Washington, DC: Author, 2009).
13. Coalition Against Insurance Fraud, *Four Faces: Why Americans Do and Do Not Tolerate Insurance Fraud a Study on Public Attitudes from 1997 tp 2007*, www.insurancefraud.org/downloads/Four_Faces_07.pdf.

CHAPTER SEVEN

Controlling Fraud

The mistake you make, don't you see, is in thinking one can live in a corrupt society without being corrupt oneself. After all, what do you achieve by refusing to make money? You're trying to behave as though one could stand right outside our economic system. But one can't. One's got to change the system, or one changes nothing. One can't put things right in a hole-and-corner way, if you take my meaning.

—*George Orwell, English novelist and journalist (1903–1950)*

After studying this chapter, the reader should be able to:

- Define the roles of corporate governance and the structures utilized by the organization to prevent fraud.

- Evaluate the system of internal control relied on by the organization to minimize fraud and make practical recommendations for improvement where required.
- Understand the internal audit role in controlling fraud.

Controlling fraud goes beyond giving the appearance of tackling the problem by tinkering with some of the fundamental causes. Not only has it become essential in both commerce as well as governments to reduce fraud to the lowest achievable level, but it also is necessary to implement the appropriate control structures to maintain fraud at that level into the future. Ensuring the integrity of systems and personnel enables the organization to focus on its primary business objectives regardless of the nature of the industry or governmental function.

CORPORATE GOVERNANCE AND FRAUD PREVENTION

In their 2003 investigation into the collapse of Enron, Swartz and Watkins concluded that since evidence shows that the worst incidences of fraud are committed by insiders, with executives who are assigned to manage and control organizations figuring prominently among insiders, fraud is a crucial control problem that cannot be alleviated without effective corporate governance.[1]

Perhaps one of the difficulties in obtaining a clear definition of corporate governance is the fact that a clear definition of a corporation is lacking. In 1819, Chief Justice John Marshall, in issuing judgment in the case of *Trustees of Dartmouth College v. Woodward*, ruled that:

> A corporation is an artificial being, invisible, intangible, and existing only in contemplation of law. Being the mere creature of law, it possesses only those properties which the charter of creation confers upon it, either expressly, or as incidental to its very existence.[2]

Writing in 2001, John Adams quotes Henry Bosch, the former chairman of the National Companies and Securities Commission, as stating:

> There is a wide gap between the maximum possible and the minimum excusable, and the whole spectrum is observable in Australian corporate governance; the best of our boards are performing well, but there is a long tail of boards in which a little thought is given to governance,

and in which more attention is given to personal gain than fiduciary duty.[3]

Nevertheless, definitions of corporate governance abound, and there is no universally accepted definition despite the fact that recently there has been a growing recognition of the critical role of corporate governance in the deterrence of fraud. Corporate governance as a whole relates to the rules, processes, and laws under which businesses are operated, regulated, and controlled and includes such players as the board of directors and the audit committee as well as internal audit. The European Community alone offers these definitions:

> Corporate governance is the system by which companies are directed and controlled.
>
> **—Cadbury report (United Kingdom)**

> Corporate governance describes the legal and factual regulatory framework for managing and supervising the company.
>
> **—Berlin Initiative Code (Germany)**

> Corporate governance, in the sense of the set of rules according to which firms are managed and controlled, is the result of norms, traditions, and patterns of behavior developed by each economic and legal system.
>
> **—Preda report (Italy)**

With such a variety of definitions, it is not surprising that fundamental models of corporate governance around the world offer different approaches to the same problems.

- The Anglo–U.S. corporate governance system offers a theoretical system of checks and balances shared among managers, shareholders, and the board of directors. The board of directors is seen to be the source and focus of proper accountability to management and shareholders. Managers are seen as responsible for the daily operations of companies. Shareholders hold the power at the annual shareholders' meeting to elect the board of directors and vote.
- The German corporate governance system is typified by a supervisory board consisting of outsiders, shareholders, and employees as well as a

management board consisting solely of insiders. This system is used commonly throughout Europe.

- The Japanese corporate governance system consists of a large board of directors primarily made up of insiders but may include government, management, banks, and *keiretsu* (a group of closely related Japanese companies that own each other's shares and bonds and give each other preferential treatment as business partners. Each *keiretsu* is formed around a large bank.).

With this variety of structures in place, formulating a single definition of good governance is problematic. The variety also makes formulation of universal rules regarding fraud prevention more difficult. Nevertheless, it is possible to find common traits and objectives in many of the models.

Corporate governance is generally associated with the quality of financial reporting and reduction in instances of fraud. Following the incidence of major accounting scandals, such as Enron and WorldCom, as well as the increase in the number of earnings restatements, it was recognized that major reform was needed in the roles and responsibilities for oversight of management by external auditing, the audit committee and the board of directors. In 2002, the United States enacted the Sarbanes-Oxley Act (SOX) with the intention of significantly expanding the responsibilities of auditors, management, audit committees, and boards of directors. Since then, many organizations worldwide aim for full compliance with SOX as part of the way they do business with the United States.

Even the nature of the external audit profession has changed of recent years. Three of the largest audit firms either divested or publicly announced plans to divest their consulting businesses T in the wake of the dissolution of Arthur Andersen in 2002, formerly one of the Big 5 accounting firms following the Enron scandal.

Aligned to these changes, in 2003, the New York Stock Exchange, NASDAQ, and the American Stock Exchange adopted additional sets of corporate governance rules applying to most listed companies. Included among those provisions and in line with SOX, it was ruled that the board of directors of a publicly traded company be composed of a majority of independent directors and that the board's audit committee consist entirely of independent directors with the least one member having financial expertise. In addition, restrictions were placed on the types of services that outside auditors could provide to their audit clients. These reforms were not universally welcomed; suggestions were made that, while the overall U.S. governance system had performed well despite some spectacular lapses, the danger now facing business on a whole was over-regulation.[4]

Some believe that the spread of boards with independent directors increases the ability of those boards to monitor managers with the result that a lower incidence of accounting fraud is being perpetrated and uncovered.

Corporate Culture versus Legislation

When SOX was first introduced, one of its primary objectives was the prevention and detection of corporate accounting fraud. Unfortunately, as with many other regulatory efforts to limit the impact of fraud, fraudsters appear to be staying one step ahead.

In the 2011 PwC Global Economic Crime Survey, respondents reported a 13 percent increase in economic crime over the previous two years.[5] KPMG reported board-level fraud perpetrators accounting for some 18 percent of frauds, up from 11 percent in 2007, and fraud at the chief executive officer (CEO) level running at 26 percent in 2011, again up from 11 percent in 2007.[6] This is confirmed in the 2011 E&Y Global Fraud Survey with respondents in western Europe recording twice as many significant frauds as previously.[7]

In part, this increase may be due to the efforts made within organizations affected by SOX to map processes and evaluate control effectiveness in order to facilitate the signing of the appropriate management representations. What appears to have been missed is the principal reason why SOX was created in the first place: to prevent fraudulent behavior by dishonest board executives.

Organizational culture can be a strong influencer on employee attitudes and can determine whether employees feel pressured or encouraged to overstep the boundaries laid down in codes of conduct and commit fraud.

The corporate culture itself is the embodiment of the attitudes, values, and experiences that guide what employees believe. Depending on the nature of the organization and the attitudes of individual managers, one of three attitudes to the corporate culture may be seen to develop.

1. *Doesn't apply in this organization or this part of the organization.* This attitude frequently develops in organizations operating in older industries where working practices and attitudes have continued unchanged for years and the primary focus is task oriented with operating efficiency and cost control at the forefront.
2. *Yes, it's important, but we don't have the time/resources/skills to do anything about it.* This attitude has grown over recent years, partly due to the economic downturn resulting in organizations attempting to maintain or increase outputs with fewer resources. This attitude may result

in short-term improvements in operational efficiencies but can, in the longer term, cause the best-qualified and most experienced staff to move to organizations with more convivial approaches.

3. *It's not only important, it is critical.* Such organizations recognize the impact of the corporate culture whether they seek it or not and whether they value it or not. Every organization has a corporate culture that works to or for its own benefit.

Healthy corporate cultures are typified by reductions over time in turnover and absenteeism, greater innovation, improved efficiency, and reductions in waste, abuse, and fraud.

An organization's culture generally is believed to be made up of five basic components:

1. *Shared values.* Whether for good or bad, the fundamental cornerstones of the corporate culture are the values shared between the organization and its employees. The values themselves include the beliefs and aspirations of individuals and the company.

2. *Corporate and individual goals.* If the organization wishes to influence the behavior of its employees in a manner favorable to the company, corporate goals must be clearly stated so employees can individually align with them.

3. *Communications.* Continuous communication ensures that employees are aware at all times of the environment within which the organization is operating. When hard times are encountered, clear communication encourages employee buy-in to corporate responses with clear ownership of the actions decided on and responsibility assigned. It also facilitates communication upward to make management aware of problems before they can escalate with negative impacts on worker morale.

4. *Consistency of approach.* Corporate cultures thrive when their organizations can consistently apply their value systems. Goals and objectives may fluctuate in reaction to market forces, but, when all involved understand what the changes are and why they are being adopted, the culture can support the process rather than being a barrier.

5. *Celebration of achievement.* Where individuals or divisions have performed beyond expectation, the creation and communication of "corporate heroes" is an effective way of spreading the values and helping others aspire to the same levels of performance. In addition, such an approach makes it considerably safer for employees to try and fail than simply to not try.

Improving the corporate culture to reduce the likelihood of fraud involves a series of steps listed next that must all be implemented.

- *Improved communication.* Effecting a paradigm shift in corporate culture relies heavily on effective communication throughout the organization. The message has to be understood by all concerned and accepted on a personal basis with buy-in to the value system underlying the corporate intent.
- *Information gathering.* The effectiveness of management decisions relies on the fundamental information regarding the environment within which those decisions must be implemented. To be successful in both formulating decisions and designing the structures required to ensure that effective implementation occurs, management must understand the organizational tone as seen by employees, customers, and suppliers in terms of their values and beliefs as well as their perceptions of the company itself. This can take the form of questionnaires, surveys, or any other information-gathering technique favored by the organization. Without such an understanding, management's decisions may be reduced to guesswork and wishful thinking regarding the outcomes.
- *Setting the tone at the top.* Employees often model the attitudes and actions of executive role models. If employees believe that the tone at the top is corrupt, the same tone will cascade down through the organization. From the top to the bottom, behavior must be seen to be fair, unbiased, and beyond reproach.
- *Strengthening of the internal control environment.* Internal controls across the organization must be reviewed and strengthened with a particular emphasis on fraud prevention in order to both prevent and detect fraud. Many internal control structures are poorly designed in that their overall monitoring depends heavily on one or two key individuals. This method may be effective as long as those individuals perform the duties with honesty and integrity. Should the individuals not do so, often there are no backup controls that would detect such failure. Standard business controls will continue to be required, including:

- Background checks on employees
- Segregation of duties
- Adequate supervision
- Limitations of authority
- Access control to assets including propriatory information as a corporate asset

▪ Fraud risk assessment
▪ Use of advanced data analysis techniques

In addition to these controls, detective controls over the fraud monitoring mechanisms are needed to give early warning of failures in the key control elements. Where such fraud control elements flow through the hands of one individual, there must be a method of determining whether the controls remain effective and the information must be fed back to a third party.

▪ *Improved feedback mechanisms.* Many frauds are detected through feedback and tips. Making feedback mechanisms available and known can considerably improve the probability of receiving such information early in the fraud process while losses are still controllable. Such feedback mechanisms include hotlines, exit interviews, and customer and supplier surveys.

Organization striving to improve corporate culture often ask: "How much effort is enough?" and "What is the ideal culture?" There is no easy way of determining what culture is most appropriate to a particular environment. Studies of "excellent" companies indicate that those that progress well have some common traits:

▪ Customer focus
▪ Simple organization structures
▪ Lean staff
▪ Involved management
▪ Entrepreneurially structured
▪ Action takers
▪ Clear focus

Although encouragement of such cultures does not ultimately prevent fraud, fraud seems to occur less often in organizations exhibiting these traits. At present, there is insufficient data to determine a causal impact between the improved cultural climates and the reduction of fraud with any great degree of reliability.

AUDIT COMMITTEE'S ROLE IN FIGHTING FRAUD

Overall, the major purpose of the board's audit committee is the oversight of the financial reporting of an organization. In the United States, since the 2002 Statement on Auditing Standards No. 99, *Considerations of Fraud in a Financial*

Statement Audit (SAS 99) auditors have been required to question management's awareness and understanding of fraud.[8] As a result, audit committees now must have greater financial expertise, act with a greater level of conservatism, and be cognizant of the need for improved reporting accuracy. In 2009, a research paper on the audit committee oversight process reported that audit committees believe that members take a more active role in monitoring the financial reporting process and that they have increased the frequency and length of their meetings.[9] The paper also reports an improved governance environment with a willingness to call management to account. Despite this, many definitions of corporate governance omit the role of the audit committee, in part because often the audit committee is viewed as a subcommittee of the full board.

The audit committee as a whole should consist of members with the appropriate skills and experience to carry out the committee's assigned role. Expertise in these areas is required:

- The particular sector or industry within which the organization functions
- Financial expertise
- Professional skepticism
- Understanding of best practice in risk management
- Sound knowledge of governance, assurance, and internal control
- Skills in business specialties dictated by the needs of the business, such as banking, insurance, information technology, taxation, or legal matters

The most critical role in the audit committee is that of the chairperson. The chair must have expertise and experience in governance and the ability to bring together within the committee the skills and knowledge required for the committee to operate effectively while retaining its independence.

The effective audit committee chairperson will ensure:

- The agenda is appropriate and covers all risky areas, including fraud.
- Regular communications exist with the head of internal audit outside of normal audit committee meetings.
- Regular communications exist with the CEO outside of normal audit committee meetings.
- Closed sessions occur periodically with only full audit committee members in attendance.
- Internal and external auditors are able to meet privately with the audit committee.

- The committee receives adequate funding and has the authority to engage the service of financial experts, legal counsel, and any specialists required to fulfill its responsibility.

The roles and responsibilities of the audit committee normally are laid out in a formal, written charter that lists the accountability, duties, membership, roll, authority, and responsibilities of the committee. This charter needs to be reviewed, renewed, and confirmed each year with the governing body. An effectiveness audit should be carried out on the work of the audit committee at least every three years. This audit may involve the use of outside consultants as a conflict of interest may occur if internal audit carries this review out.

Unfortunately, not all audit committees are created equal, and some continue to perform at a level that fails to achieve the corporate governance needs. Most audit committees meet between six and eight times per year; however, many audit committees of corporate boards meet only two or three times per year. In such cases, it is difficult for such a small group of outsiders to detect fraud in large, complex organizations. In addition, the audit committee typically has an agenda beyond overseeing the financial reporting of the organization. Everything from the business strategy of the corporation, oversight of the internal audit function, and even the hiring and firing of the CEO may be part of its oversight functions, which reduces its ability to detect accounting irregularities or fraud.

The SOX mandate that at least one member of the audit committee have financial expertise can result in one member of the committee at most having such experience; other committee members may reduce their oversight and rely just on the expert.

Governance of the audit committee itself is one of the most significant areas of potential fault in corporate governance. To be effective, the audit committee needs to operate under a formal charter that spells out its constitution, priorities, areas of responsibility, frequency of meeting, agenda, and reporting responsibilities.

In the past, membership of the audit committee has also caused difficulties due to conflicts of interest. Independence may be presumed to be impeded where an audit committee member is:

- A present or former executive of the company or an associated company
- A significant, controlling, or dominant shareholder
- An executive or board member of an entity that is a significant shareholder

- A significant supplier of goods or services to the organization including those in advisory, audit, or consultancy capacities
- Associated financially or through close family relationships with a significant shareholder
- Associated through family ties with any executive of the organization

Given the critical role the audit committee plays in ensuring the development, monitoring, and enforcement of an environment where fraud is unlikely to occur and will be detected early, should it occur, the audit committee must be seen to be above suspicion and to deal equitably with all suspected of fraud or other misdemeanors. Any relationship that may interfere with the exercise of objective judgment should preclude that individual's membership on an audit committee.

The audit committee should, at a minimum, review the fraud strategy and plan implemented by the organization on an annual basis. The overall impact of the strategy and specifically the impact in those areas identified as high fraud risk need to be drawn to the attention of the board and executive management so appropriate internal controls can be implemented.

Procedures should be established for the receipt, retention, and handling in a confidential manner of any anonymous submissions from any stakeholder regarding questionable business procedures or areas of potential misconduct.

In KPMG's 2010 international survey of audit committee members, audit committees from around the world agreed that their key focus areas were[10]:

- Financial statement issues—such as fair value, asset impairment, and disclosures
- The impact of public policy initiatives on the company's reporting, compliance, risk, and control processes
- Liquidity, access to capital, and cash flow
- Maintaining internal controls
- The ability of the company to manage risk—and particularly to identify risks that are "around the next corner"

Interestingly, the emphasis on risk management within this survey primarily links strategy and risk, with the maintenance of internal control and the role of internal audit being more focused on operational and strategic risks rather than fraud as a risk.

When asked to select the three greatest concerns of the audit committee in 2010, only 6 percent of the 1,200 audit committee members selected included fraud in their lists. Certain factors that contribute to fraud prevention, including the ethical culture, internal controls, and antibribery laws were highly rated but only maintaining internal control was specified by 28 percent of respondents.

Risk management in general rated the highest area for attention with financial statement issues a close second. It is understandable with the sheer volume of legislation being promulgated that compliance with the legislation would form a key element of audit committee priorities, but with the growth of fraud, particularly at the executive level, it is surprising that fraud scored so low by comparison.

When asked to evaluate their own effectiveness, many respondents rated the committee as "effective" but admitted that its effectiveness could be improved. Primary areas for improvement included:

- Focusing meeting agendas on important items rather than checklists
- Drawing better-quality information from a wider variety of sources with a greater internal transparency
- Having a better understanding of the company's strategies and risks

Grant Thornton, in 2011, published an audit committee guide specifically addressing managing fraud risk.[11] The volume emphasized the U.S. audit committee's role in adequate supervision and reporting and for responding to:

- Fraud in a financial statement audit
- Actual, precede, or potential conflicts of interest
- Anonymous tips and complaints
- Through interaction with general counsel, compliance matters such as those related to the Foreign Corrupt Practices Act (FCPA)

This supports the position taken by the Institute of Internal Auditors (IIA), the American Institute of Certified Public Accountants (AICPA), and the Association of Certified Fraud Examiners (ACFE) in their document *Managing the Business Risk of Fraud: A Practical* Guide, which was written to provide guidance to the board as well as to senior managers and internal auditors.[12] This document is covered in more detail in Chapter 8.

As part of good governance, the audit committee is obliged to give the board of directors assurance regarding the prevention and detection of any possible fraud or illegal acts as well as the remedial action taken by management. The audit committee normally is expected to include a statement on fraud risk within the audit committee charter. In order to ensure the adequacy of the fraud risk management interventions, it is essential that the audit committee understands the business fraud risks and the internal control structures designed to address those risks within the organization. Based on this understanding, audit committee members are then in a position to evaluate the adequacy of the policies and procedures in place to detect fraud and other illegal activities. With the complexity of business transactions and the changing regulations, the committee needs to keep pace with the organization's efforts to ensure compliance such that any unauthorized financial movements would be detected early and investigated thoroughly.

A regular part of the audit committee's agenda should be the evaluation of the audit's assessment of fraud risk and the appropriateness of the audit plan to examine the internal controls designed to mitigate these risks. The committee requires assurance that the areas of highest fraud risk have been identified and are being addressed and that the planned audit scope can be relied on to detect fraud, should it occur. In addition, depending on the country, the audit committee itself may have to comply with legal obligations in regard to corporate fraud.

At the end of each audit committee meeting, the members must be satisfied that all fraud risk areas are known, that adequate internal control structures have been designed and implemented, and that the structures are not only adequate but also effective in prevention and early detection of fraudulent activities. Any changes in accounting principles or material audit adjustments should act as red flags to alert committee members to the need for further investigation.

Audit Committees in the Public Sector

As in the private sector, effective audit committees in the public sector can make a significant difference to the system of internal control in financial reporting as well as the integrity and efficiency of the audit process. This sector includes government departments as well as public entities, such as state-owned enterprises, local governments, and entities such as armed services. Unlike private companies, where the top of the governance tree typically is the board of directors and perhaps an executive committee, in the public sector, the chief executive is commonly at the top, perhaps with an oversight committee and ultimate reporting at governmental level. In many government departments, no controlling board exists, and the chief executive reports directly to the government.

This structure can change the role of the audit committee somewhat as in the public sector, the organization's objectives are less likely to be creating profitability for shareholders and more likely to concern service delivery.

Regardless, public entities still must demonstrate to stakeholders that the systems and processes in use are adequate to carry out their accountability and governance responsibilities.

In addition to their awareness of fraud risk within the government sector, audit committees are commonly established with a variety of priorities, including:

- Implementation of "best practices"
- Improving the capability of audit
- Minimizing fraud potential
- Improving internal control
- Ensuring efficient use of resources
- Acting as an advisory body to the CEO, introducing fresh perspectives and a private sector experience and expertise

The committee's responsibilities vary depending on the complexity, size, and requirements of the particular public entity. As with the private sector, public sector audit committees require independence, clear communications, and accountability. Due to the value of assets under control in most government entities, weaknesses in internal controls can dramatically increase fraud probabilities. Audit committees operating in the public sector should be even more aware of fraud risks and the need for effective monitoring.

In most countries, there exist specific auditing standards for the government sector. Part of the audit committee's brief is to ensure that the system of internal controls is both adequate and operating effectively to reduce fraud risks to acceptable levels. Included within these responsibilities is the need to determine:

- Whether there are any material weaknesses in the overall system of internal control governing fraud prevention, detection, and reporting
- Whether the internal control system can provide reasonable assurance that any instances of fraud and corruption would be detected within an acceptable time frame and reported accordingly
- Where fraud, the likelihood of fraud, or the potential for fraud are detected, the appropriate and timely action is taken to reduce the impact or likelihood of fraudulent activities
- Whether the controls governing the use of electronic data processing are adequate to ensure the integrity, confidentiality, and fraud resistance of systems, communications, and record keeping

As in the private sector, the effective functioning of the public audit committee depends on the competence of committee members combined with their ability to act independently. Most members of public sector audit committees are external appointments to ensure the objectivity of the audit committees as a whole. It is possible that, where a governing body exists, the chairperson of that body may be a member of the audit committee as long as there is no impairment of the committee's role of giving unbiased and frank advice. It is common to invite senior staff members in to audit committee meetings at audit committee's discretion, but there should be no right of access. Audit committees must retain the ability to hold closed meetings at which only committee members are present.

In some jurisdictions, meetings of government committees may be open to the public for reasons of public accountability. Given that audit committees may be seen as government committees, in certain circumstances, meetings may have to be open to the public. Normally, however, there is a proviso that, under certain circumstances, the public may be excluded if, for example, a fraud potential was being discussed or where there is a specific need for free and frank discussions without public oversight.

In some areas of government, the operation may be considered too small or too low risk to warrant the appointment of a full audit committee. In such instances, executive management and the oversight authority must be even more vigilant about fraud opportunities and occurrences, particularly where internal audit does not operate as a permanent function but makes use of consultants on a need-to-have basis. The danger being that such usage of these exists only in reactive mode to allegations of wrongdoing rather than proactive mode to assist in the designed an evaluation of systems of internal control to reduce the likelihood of wrongdoing and increase the detection probability.

INTERNAL CONTROL AND THE PREVENTION OF FRAUD

Many organizations have a designated chief compliance officer to oversee fraud investigations or bring in forensic investigators to carry out such investigations. These actions, essential as they are, are nevertheless reactive responses where fraud is already suspected.

A more desirable, effective approach is the proactive design, in which a system of internal control that limits the possibility of fraud occurring is constructed and implemented. If fraud occurs despite an effective internal control structure, fraudulent activities are detected in a timely manner and remediation and recovery of assets that have been fraudulently removed can occur.

According to another KPMG study, internal controls in 2011 were now considerably weaker than they were in 2007, when the previous survey was done, and management review was less robust.[13] KPMG therefore predicts that currently undetected fraud will become apparent in greater numbers over the next few years.

COSO's Approach

In 1992, the AICPA, IIA, American Accounting Association (AAA), the Institute of Management Accountants (IMA), and the Financial Executives Institute (now known as the Financial Executives International [FEI])— groups collectively referred to as the Committee of Sponsoring Organizations (COSO)— issued a jointly prepared study titled *Internal Control: An Integrated Framework*.[14] This document identifies the fundamental business objectives of any corporate or government entity. These include achievement of desired outcomes, economy and efficiency of operations, safeguarding of assets, reliability of financial and management reports, as well as compliance with laws and regulations.

COSO defines internal control broadly. It is effected by people, designed to provide reasonable assurance regarding the achievement of the three primary objectives of all businesses:

1. Economy and efficiency of operations, including achieving performance goals and safeguarding assets against loss
2. Reliable financial and operational data and reports
3. Compliance with laws and regulations

In order to ensure achievement of these objectives, COSO defines five components that would assist management achieve them:

1. *A sound control environment.* Such an environment requires the correct level of attention and direction from senior management. It is created by ensuring the hiring of managers and employees who possess integrity, ethical values, and are competent. The environment is seen to be a function of management's philosophy and operating style. In order to be effective, it requires the proper assignment of authority and responsibility together with the proper organization and utilization of available resources. Management

must ensure that staff members are trained and developed to the appropriate standard to ensure that staff members can competently exercise control.

2. *A sound risk assessment process.* This process requires that effective methods are implemented so management can be aware of the risks and obstacles in the way of successful achievement of business objectives. Management must establish a set of objectives that integrate all the organization's resources so that all the departments operate in unison toward achieving the overall objectives. The risk assessment itself involves the identification, analysis, and management of the risks and obstacles to the successful achievement of the three primary business objectives, described earlier.

3. *Sound operational control activities.* Control activities involve the establishment, execution, and monitoring of sound policies and procedures. These help to ensure the effective implementation of actions identified by management as being essential to address risks and obstacles to the achievement of business objectives. Activities include authorization, reviews of operating performance, security of assets, and segregation of duties.

4. *Sound information and communications systems.* These systems facilitate the running and control of a business by producing reports containing financial, operational, and compliance-related information. The systems utilize both internally generated data and information on external activities, conditions, and events that management need to be aware of when making decisions and communicating the company's activities to the outside world. In order for this awareness to happen, appropriate information must be identified, captured, and communicated in a way that enables people to carry out their responsibilities. Effective communication must flow down, up, and across the organization. (Top management must send a clear message to all personnel that control responsibilities must be taken seriously.) For communication to flow effectively, all personnel must understand their own roles in the internal control system as well as how their individual activities relate to the work of others. Personnel also must be able to communicate significant information upward and with external parties.

5. *Effective monitoring.* Effective monitoring ensures the effectiveness of the control process. The entire control system has to be monitored in order to assess the quality of the system's performance over time. Deficiencies must be reported, with serious matters reported directly to top management. In addition, there must be separate, independent evaluations of the internal control system. The scope and frequency of these independent evaluations depend mainly on the assessment of risks and obstacles and the proven effectiveness of ongoing monitoring procedures.

Internal Controls

COSO also addresses the problem of the confusion which can arise over the definition of an internal control. A control is taken to be *any action taken by management to increase the likelihood that an organization's objectives and goals will be achieved.* Control results from the planning, organizing, and directing of management in order to ensure that the organization is working toward the stated objectives. COSO also differentiates between corporate objectives and goals which are seen to be strategic, and management objectives which are primarily tactical.

- *Corporate objectives and goals* are expressed in statements of organizational intent, such as "Costs will be reduced by 5 percent over the next year."
- *Management objectives* are tactical expressions of how the corporate objectives are intended to be met. For example: "A cost reduction and quality improvement program together with a drive to reduce shrinkage and internal fraud will be embarked on in order to reduce costs by 5 percent over the next year.
- *Internal controls* are actions taken to ensure that management objectives are properly planned and executed. For example: "A stock count exercise will be carried out on a monthly basis in order to identify areas of shrinkage, and security will be tightened by the addition of an inspection function prior to all finished goods leaving the factory."

It can be seen that the *planning, organizing,* and *directing* roles of successful management encompass the responsibility for internal control.

While it is acknowledged that no internal control system can be 100 percent effective in the prevention of fraud and the elimination of risk, the intention of such a system is to reduce the likelihood of a fraud occurring or the size and impact of such a fraud to the extent that management is prepared to accept the risk.

Controls themselves are generally classified into *preventive controls*, which stop untoward events from happening but, unfortunately, are never 100 percent effective. *Detective controls* are those controls that alert management that an undesirable event has occurred. Such controls are normally time critical in that, although the damage has already been done, the extent of the damage can still be limited. *Corrective controls* come into effect after a problem has been detected and serve to limit the extent of damage, recover from damage, and prevent damage from recurring.

Other types of control exist. *Offset controls* include insurance or outsourcing of critical functions, where the risk has now been transferred to a third party. Outsourcing can be seen as an offsetting preventive control in that the risk has being transferred due to a business decision that was made for other strategic reasons. Insurance normally is seen as an offsetting corrective control that transfers the risk but does not come into effect until the damaging event has actually happened.

A fifth category of control is *directive controls*, which are not in themselves preventive. They are used where human discretion is involved in decision making to indicate the direction that the organization wishes the decision to take. For example, a no-smoking sign is an example of a directive control. It does not, in itself, stop anyone from smoking; it merely indicates to individuals that, in this particular area, smoking is not allowed. Depending on the nature of the risk faced, directive controls can be highly effective in discouraging negative behavior.

Control Objectives

A common mistake in both designing and evaluating systems of internal control is to confuse the number of controls and testing each individual control with achieving an effective system of control. All systems of internal control should start from the same common source. What control objectives are we are seeking to achieve? A lock on a door may seem to be a strong control, but until the control objective is defined there is no way of evaluating the control. Is the objective to keep people in or to keep people out? Until that is known, no decision can be made as to which side of the door the lock should be on. Many managers and even auditors have great difficulty in establishing the control objectives for a given area. Without that knowledge, the appropriate internal control structures cannot be built. What then results is a series of individual control steps that may or may not lead to the desired result.

In any operational area of the business, the overall *business objectives* should be easy to identify. For example, the business objective of procurement may be seen to be acquiring the things the organization requires to carry out its normal business functions. Within those business objectives are the *operating objectives*, which direct the day-to-day activities and may, in themselves, conflict. There may, for example, be a conflict between the need for control and the need for timeliness, or the need for quality improvement and the need for cost reduction. The *control objectives* then become those things that must be done correctly in order to achieve the business and operating objectives.

Examples include acquiring items at the appropriate price, from an authorized vendor, in an appropriate quantity and quantity, and in an authorized manner.

Control objectives can be defined by operational area or by organizational functionality. For example, control objectives for financial management functions could include:

- Maintaining accounting records in accordance with generally accepted accounting principles
- Ensuring that applicable laws, regulations, and internal rules are complied with
- Ensuring that all managerial financial reports are accurate, relevant, and complete and available only to appropriately authorized staff
- Ensuring that budgetary controls exist and are appropriate and enforced
- Ensuring that all employees are aware of their responsibilities to be alert for potential fraud and other misdeeds and to report any such problems

In terms of risk, risk and control objectives are two sides of the same coin. If the control objective is to ensure that budgetary controls exist, are appropriate, and are enforced, the control risk is that budgetary controls do not exist, are inappropriate, or fail to be enforced on a consistent basis.

Once the control objectives have been detailed, the system of internal control can be designed to ensure that individual controls, working together, can raise to a high probability the likelihood of achieving the control objectives. In essence, if the objective is to lock people out, the best place for the lock probably would be on the inside of the door with key access restricted to those inside the room.

Working from the perspective of control objectives makes it a lot easier to determine whether the system of internal controls is designed adequately, assuming all controls function as intended, to reduce the risk to a level that management is prepared to accept it. Should that level of control not be obtained when all existing controls function as intended, additional controls will be required to reduce the residual risk to acceptable levels. In order to achieve this control, frameworks are established that involve these primary ones:

- *Segregation of duties.* These segregation of duties controls are the policies and control procedures to ensure that those who physically handle assets are not the same people who record asset movements, who reconcile those records, or who authorize transactions. Controls should allow for the procedures performed by one person to effectively provide a check on the procedures of another in the transaction process. The critical issue in the segregation of duties is that duties performed by different people should not be incompatible and that individuals are adequately qualified and trained to perform the relevant control procedures.

▪ *Competence and integrity of people.* Underpinning the control system are the people who enforce it. In order for controls to be effective, those who exercise control must be capable of doing so and honest enough to do so consistently.

▪ *Appropriate levels of authority.* A common mistake in control structures is the granting of too much authority within control boundaries. Authority should be granted only on a need-to-have basis. If there is no need for a particular individual to have specific authority, it should not be granted.

▪ *Accountability.* For all decisions, transactions, and actions taken, there must be controls that will allow management to work out who did what with an acceptable degree of confidence.

▪ *Adequate resources.* Controls that are inadequately resourced will generally fail when they come under stress. Adequate resources include manpower, finance, equipment, materials, and methodologies.

▪ *Supervision and review.* Adequate supervision of the appropriate type is essential for sound internal control.

Once management can be assured that, if all controls are functioning, the control objectives will be attained, it can identify the degree of control monitoring needed and identify the key controls that require the most monitoring.

From an audit perspective, this identification facilitates the selection of key controls to be audited with an assurance that if these controls function as intended, there is a high probability that the control objective will be achieved and the overall the business objective will be achieved.

Within a system of internal controls, control types can be categorized into those involving:

▪ Control over physical access to assets
▪ Levels of authority combined with segregation of duties
▪ Control over the recording and reconciliation of movements of assets
▪ Control over logical access to computer systems containing the records of assets and, in some cases, the assets themselves

Physical access to assets is perhaps the easiest form of internal control to communicate to stakeholders. Most people recognize the need to control physical access to their own property and therefore can relate to the corporate position. Unfortunately, many people are negligent over implementing physical access controls to their own property. As a result, in the workplace, implementation of such controls is problematic.

While the locking of desks, doors, and files is obvious, in the workplace situation where workmates tend to trust each other, these basic controls are often ignored. As a result, if you are recognized as an insider, no further access restrictions apply. When the organization has spent time and effort to introduce access control methods such as employee IDs, access control cards, and electronic surveillance equipment, often the assumption is made that control exists merely by the purchase of equipment.

The design of the internal control system and structures may be adequate to reduce the risk to acceptable levels if the controls are implemented appropriately and applied consistently. When they are not well implemented, the organization may be operating at a considerably higher risk level than it believes. One requirements of operational management is to ensure that where the system of internal controls has been evaluated as adequate, the implementation and monitoring ensures consistent application of those controls. One organization I worked for operated with a clean-desk policy. All desks had to be cleared of documents and anything confidential locked away before the staff left for the night. The CEO occasionally walked through the offices at 6:00 A.M., shredded anything that was left lying on a desk, and then the owner of the desk was disciplined. This may seem extreme but it only had to happen once and after that nobody forgot.

Physical access is normally restricted to those who require it to carry out their job functions and access is granted on a need-to-have basis. While not 100 percent effective in preventing either fraud or simple theft, such controls have a deterrent effect as they send a clear indication to all involved that controls are taken seriously and that there are probably other controls that are not so visible that would trap potential fraudsters. Unfortunately, weak physical controls or controls that are known not to be enforced also send a signal: the organization is not serious about maintaining strong internal controls and there are probably other weaknesses in the control structure that fraudsters could exploit.

Those controls with no direct impact on reducing the risk of fraud occurring still may prove beneficial in the investigation of a fraud. Use of closed-circuit television or key-card access control can help establish who was physically in an area when an incident occurred. In the same way, use of identification and authentication techniques assisting in the control over logical access to computer systems has both preventive and detective advantages.

Implementation of a control structure requiring specific levels of authority in order to make decisions, execute commands, or process transactions can be a highly effective fraud prevention tool. These control levels indicate maximum and minimum authority levels for each employee. Any breaches of these controls are seen as red flag indicators. Sensitive duties can therefore be segregated to ensure that incompatible duties cannot be performed by the same person.

One of the more important controls within this area, and one that frequently is neglected, is the use of formal, detailed job descriptions. This control can spell out areas of sensitivity where segregation of duties is a must as well as those areas where duplication of duties is essential, such as double authorization of high-value transactions or two signatures on a check. Other control elements, such as a requirement that employees take consecutive annual leave of specific length during which time access to corporate premises is not allowed, have proven strong detective controls in cases of fraud where an employee must be physically present to abet its concealment. Most job descriptions indicate what is expected of the employee in general terms. Few drive down to the detail of what is permitted and particularly what is not permitted in carrying out the job. Where formal, detailed job descriptions are used, it becomes an easy management monitoring task to note when division of duties are breached. Where they are not used or are overgeneralized, identifying a failure to segregate duties is virtually impossible. It is equally difficult to enforce control mechanisms within computer systems if those controls do not exist in the business area.

It is long been known that those with direct responsibility for control over assets should not be the same people as those controlling the recording of assets and again should be segregated from the responsibility of reconciling records of assets. All this sounds good in theory, but in practice it is not so simple. Many departments and job functions operate with minimum staff levels. It is difficult to enforce segregation of duties if there is only one person available to do all of the tasks. In such circumstances, duties obviously cannot be segregated.

Achievement of the control objective is critical, not the individual control technique used. With this in mind, it is apparent that, instead of trying to force the segregation of duties in an area where it is not possible, what is required is finding another control technique that could achieve the same objectives with different resources. Where segregation of duties is not possible, for example, ongoing supervision with either spot checks or 100 percent scrutiny depending on the severity of the risk may be possible and perhaps more appropriate.

A case in point occurred within an organization transferring the proceeds from the sale of gold bullion through an electronic funds transfer system. The system was based on personal computer and required one individual to enter all transactions. A second individual would then log in and authorize all transactions. A third individual then logged in and transferred the payments to the bank. The bank, on receipt, would fax back an acknowledgment to the organization. The organization processed, on average, 15 transactions per day with an average value of $20 million per transaction. On the face of it, the control looks adequate with three levels of entry, authorization, and pay with a separate verification. In reality, a single person, Betty, entered all transactions. Then she logged out and logged back in with her supervisor's ID and authorized all transactions. Once they were all authorized, Betty logged out, logged back in with a third ID, and paid all transactions to the bank. The bank then sent a fax confirmation to the fax machine sitting beside Betty, who then filed all of the faxes. Every day $300 million in value was processed. The bank account itself had not been reconciled for six months. When I pointed this out to the head of finance, he threw up his hands in horror and assured me that he would ensure that Betty would do a bank reconciliation every night from then on. From a fraud perspective, that was kind of missing the point.

Even if Betty was the only employee available to carry out the transactions, for $300 million of risk per day, it would have been worth the time for the head of finance to authorize those transactions and carry out an end-of-day reconciliation personally.

Active supervision is essential in organizations where there is difficulty in achieving segregation of duties. In the example just given, allowing the head of finance to authorize the transactions personally would not be ideal. In some circumstances, it could be seen as a red flag for potential fraud.

Good supervision can be a highly effective fraud preventive mechanism as long as a supervisor is fraud-aware and takes an active role in reviewing and double-checking work carried out by subordinates. Supervisors need to be aware of the fraud possibilities within their areas of operations, particularly when unusual events occur. Errors with no apparent cause, reconciliations that should balance but do not, or any circumstance outside the norm should trigger alerts in supervisors' minds. Complaints from customers or suppliers are good sources of external alerts that should never be ignored. Any irregularity reported externally needs to be followed up to determine its accuracy and, if appropriate, the cause.

It is also part of the supervisor's duty to ensure that subordinates remain aware of fraud. Giving feedback about frauds reported via the hotline, fraud newsletters, or even a reminder to staff about risks, red flags, and things to watch for can all help.

Many organizations now keep records of assets in computer systems. For example, creditors' records, debtors' records, asset registers, and pay information are all held on computers, which may or may not belong to the organization. The data may even exist in the "cloud."

In such cases, the assets the organization owns are essentially whatever the computer says it owns. If a fraudster wishes to steal an asset, the easiest way is to simply remove it from the asset register. If it is not on the asset register, it does not belong to the company. Who does it belong to? Possibly whoever has physical access to it (i.e., the fraudster). The amount of money the organization is owed is whenever the computer says it is owed. By adjusting the computer records, the fraudster can remove or amend debt. In the same way, by adjusting creditors' records, fraudsters can create debt that the company will then pay. Manipulation of payroll records can result in payments for fictitious overtime to payment for fictitious employees (ghost employees). At one point, the auditor general for one African country estimated that 30 percent of the total government payroll consisted of ghost employees. Computer fraud is covered in depth in Chapter 10.

All controls operate within the framework of a *control environment*, a term that describes the overall infrastructure within which other control elements will function. Primary among these are the:

- *Organizational infrastructure.* The organizational infrastructure defines the individual manager's responsibilities, sets limits of authority, and facilitates the proper segregation of duties. If the organizational structure is problematic and individuals are granted the excessive power or duties are poorly segregated, the effectiveness of the individual controls may be weakened substantially.
- *Control framework.* This framework includes the policies and procedures describing the scope and activities of a function, including its relationships with other parts of the organization as well as the degree to which external influences, such as laws and regulations, impact it. The competitive environment within which the organization operates and union agreements also impact functions.

The nature of the control framework may be either complex or extremely simple. Large organizations have a tendency toward highly structured control frameworks; smaller organizations frequently use personal contacts among employees to communicate rather than formal structures.

As previously mentioned, major areas of control include:

- Segregation of duties
- Competence and integrity of employees
- Appropriateness of the levels of authority
- Accountability
- Adequacy of resources
- Supervision and monitoring

The effective combination and integration of these controls can lead to significant reductions in the probability of fraud and increases in the probability of detection.

Internal Control and Detection

In its 2010 *Report to the Nations on Occupational Fraud and Abuse* in 2010, the ACFE indicated that tip are the most common detection method for fraudulent activities, accounting for almost three times as many frauds reported as any other form of detection.[15] Management review and internal audit combined achieved only 75 percent of the effectiveness of tips in fraud detection. Most of these tip came from other employees, but customers, vendors, and anonymous tips combined accounted for over 40 percent of information received. Based on these figures and other research covered in the study, it is apparent that the effectiveness of hotlines can be considerably increased by publicizing them not only to employees but to customers, vendors, and the world at large. The report also indicates that, in organizations where hotlines were used, losses suffered were considerably lower than in organizations not employing them.

Despite the effectiveness of hotlines as a detective control, the survey indicated that fewer than half of the organizations suffering from fraud had a hotline in place at the time the fraud occurred. Many of those suffering from a fraud already had preventive and detective control mechanisms in place; 66 percent had internal audit or fraud examination departments, 70 percent had a formal code of conduct in place, and more than 75 percent had external audits carried out on the financial statements. The low effectiveness of these controls in detecting fraud events does not, however, indicate their lack of effectiveness in preventing fraud.

In smaller organizations (typically fewer than 100 employees) with fewer resources applied to antifraud internal control structures, fraud incidence was considerably higher than in larger organizations with formal antifraud controls in place. Even comparatively low-cost and low-effort controls, such as codes of conduct, management review of controls, and use of hotlines, have significant impacts. Smaller organizations often lack methods to both prevent and detect fraud.

In terms of losses suffered, comparing losses in organizations where controls were implemented against those organizations without the controls, the internal controls having the most impact on reducing the values of losses were seen to be hotlines, employee support programs, surprise audits, and fraud training for staff members at all levels.

Controls having the least impact on reducing the value of frauds when implemented included rewards for whistleblowers, external audit and management certification of financial statements, independent audit committees, and internal audit/fraud examination departments. These findings were in stark contrast to the opinions of those surveyed, who rated internal audit and management reviews as the most important controls in detecting or limiting fraud.

Where fraud had occurred, respondents indicated that the biggest single element allowing it to take place was a lack of internal controls, such as segregation of duties. Next in rank were frauds in which the perpetrator overrode existing internal controls in order to conceal or commit the fraud. Respondents felt lack of reporting mechanisms such as hotlines to be the lowest control weakness contributing to the fraud. In large-value frauds, the most commonly cited factor was a poor tone at the top.

According to the survey, over 80 percent of fraudsters were employees or managers; fewer than 20 percent were owners/executives. In terms of value, however, fraud by owners/executives came in at almost four times the value of managerial frauds and almost ten times the value of employee-level frauds. In all cases, male perpetrators outnumbered females by a factor of 2 to 1. Most frauds appeared to be carried out by individuals in the age range of 31 to 45, although, the highest-value frauds were carried out by individuals over the age of 60.

In terms of numbers of frauds, accounting, operations, sales, and upper management were the departments holding the greatest number of fraudsters, while the highest-value frauds were perpetrated by individuals within executive/upper management, the board of directors, legal, purchasing, and finance. Interestingly, internal audit came in as the lowest department in terms of both number of fraudsters and values of fraud.

The ACFE makes a significant contribution to identifying the inherent risk of fraud and areas where internal control can be implemented most effectively.

FIGHTING SHRINKAGE

Shrinkage is the loss of products somewhere between the point of purchase from a supplier or internal manufacture and the point of sale. The term *shrinkage* is commonly used to define losses in the retail sector, but it can be applied equally to manufacturing, construction, or any other processing operation. For the purposes of this book, however, I restrict my discussion to retail shrinkage.

In the retail environment in the United States alone, according to the preliminary findings of the 2011 National Retail Security Survey, shrinkage losses were $37.1 billion in 2010, up some 10 percent over the previous year and amounting to 1.58 percent of total sales.[16]

According to the preliminary findings, losses can be broken down as shown:

- Employee theft: $16.2 billion (43.7 percent)
- Shoplifting: $12.1 billion (32.6 percent)
- Other losses including administrative error: $4.8 billion (12.9 percent)
- Vendor fraud: $2 billion (5.4 percent)
- Unknown causes: $2 billion (5.4 percent)

Companies also reported that 18.7 percent of employee thefts involved collusion between internal and external sources.

Although these statistics place employee theft as the number-one cause for shrinkage in the retail environment, shoplifting gets more press coverage and publicity simply because of its visibility. From a fraud perspective, however, employees engaging in product trafficking is a far more serious threat, particularly when combined with vendor fraud, which often requires employee collusion.

Employee fraud in the retail environment is perpetrated through a variety of techniques. Nevertheless, certain existing controls can be used to detect retail employee theft and fraud:

- Review cash register transactions, looking for small cash refunds, returns, excessive drawer openings. In older cash registers, this would involve examination of the copy rolls, but in modern registers, this information is digitized and is subject to continuous monitoring using appropriate computer software.
- Use technology to increase the frequency of inventory counting.

- Interrogation of returned transactions and the voided/deleted/canceled sales report.
- Monitor inventory adjustment reports daily basis.
- Alarm the back door and monitor it with closed circuit television.
- Perform periodic spot checks of all garbage.
- Institute inventory management automation.
- Rotate staff members responsible for incoming goods.

None of these checks is foolproof, but each goes a small way to help employees realize that what they do is under scrutiny. The concept that "Big Brother Is Watching You" can go a long way toward reducing the likelihood of attempted fraud and theft.

With the advances in technology, social networking, and mobile commerce, the potential for shrinkage through electronic shoplifting is enormous. In the United States, the biggest shopping day for pre-Christmas sales, known as Black Friday, occurs on the Friday after Thanksgiving. On that day in 2011, almost 10 percent of consumers used a mobile device to make a purchase, while 14 percent used a mobile device to visit a retailer site according to the IBM Coremetrics Benchmark Report [17] site. Retailers are finding that antifraud measures implemented for e-commerce that can detect the shoppers' locations may not be effective controls in the m-commerce (mobile-commerce) world as the web address of a mobile device changes continuously. This topic is addressed in more detail in Chapter 10.

 ## INTERNAL AUDIT ROLE

In 2009, the IIA produced a practice guide titled *Internal Auditing and Fraud* to clarify the internal auditor's role in preventing and monitoring fraud risks and how such risks should be addressed in conducting audits and investigations.[18]

This guide is intended as specific clarification certain of the IIA *International Standards for the Professional Practice of Internal Auditing*, namely:

- IIA Standard 1200: Proficiency and Due Professional Care
- IIA Standard 1220: Due Professional Care
- IIA Standard 2060: Reporting to Senior Management and the Board
- IIA Standard 2120: Risk Management
- IIA Standard 2210: Engagement Objectives

Internal Auditing and Fraud emphasizes the six-point fraud management program consisting of:

1. Company ethics policy
2. Fraud awareness
3. Fraud risk assessment
4. Ongoing reviews
5. Prevention and detection
6. Investigation

The guide highlights the roles of internal audit in assisting management by determining the adequacy of internal controls and whether the organization fosters an adequate internal control environment.

The guide also points out a variety of approaches that could be considered while conducting internal audit activities. These approaches include:

▪ Auditing management controls over fraud
▪ Auditing to detect likely fraud
▪ Considering fraud as a part of every audit
▪ Conducting consulting assignments to help management identify and assess risk and determine the adequacy of the control environment

The guide addresses the roles of all parties involved within the organization in fraud prevention and detection but focuses specifically on the role of the internal auditor. It suggests that, in relation to fraud, the internal audit role can include:

▪ Either the initial or the full investigation of suspected fraud
▪ Root cause analysis and control improvement recommendations
▪ Monitoring of a reporting/whistleblower hotline
▪ Provision of ethics training sessions

The guide also states that where internal audit is assigned such duties, it has a duty to ensure that persons with the appropriate skills and competencies to carry out those tasks are available. It is not expected that internal auditors have the same knowledge base as fraud or forensic investigators specifically tasked to detect investigate fraud; during the course of normal audit work, however, the tests carried out by internal audit should improve the chances that fraud indicators will be detected.

The IIA suggests that during audit engagements, internal auditors should always consider fraud risks in assessing the design of the internal control structure and document those risks in their working papers. To do this effectively, internal auditors must be sufficiently knowledgeable to be able to identify fraud red flags when apparent. They must understand potential fraud schemes and scenarios likely within the scope of the activities being audited. Where control deficiencies are noted, the internal auditor then is responsible for designing and implementing additional tests to determine whether a fraud has in fact occurred.

Whether any red flags were detected or not, internal auditors must evaluate management's response to fraud risks and ensure that the fraud risk management program continues to be implemented effectively. In all cases, internal auditors must maintain an appropriate degree of professional skepticism since they are in a position, while focusing on internal controls effectiveness, to uncover common frauds that may exist. The next table lists typical fraud schemes and forms of detection.

Type of Fraud	Form of Detection
Cash Schemes (occur frequently but rarely material)	
	☐ Bank reconciliation
	☐ Cut off bank statements
	☐ Surprise cash counts
	☐ Investigation of customer complaints
	☐ Review of journal entries
	☐ Review of sales/cash trends
Accounts Receivable Schemes	
☐ Lapping	☐ Accounts receivable confirmations
☐ Fictitious receivables	☐ Cut-offs
☐ Charge-offs	☐ Trend analysis on written-off accounts
☐ Personal borrowing	☐ Matching deposit dates
Inventory Fraud Schemes	
☐ Theft	☐ Missing documents
☐ Misappropriation	☐ Physical counts
☐ Scrap sales	☐ Analytical review

(continued)

Type of Fraud	Form of Detection
Purchasing Fraud Schemes	**Analytical review for:**
☐ Fictitious invoices	☐ Timing of bids
☐ Overbilling	☐ Pattern of bids
☐ Checks paid to employees	☐ Amount of work
☐ Conflict of interest	☐ Pattern of new vendors
	☐ Matching addresses
	☐ Lack of street addresses on invoices

Payroll Schemes

Type of Fraud	Form of Detection
☐ Ghost employees	☐ Independent payroll distribution
☐ Overtime abuses	☐ Flashing cash around
☐ Withholding taxes	☐ Matching addresses

In addition to normal internal auditing skills, auditors operating in the detection phase must be able to:

- Elicit facts from witnesses in a fair, impartial, and lawful manner
- Act as part accountant, part investigator, and part criminologist
- Deal effectively with people: professionally, thoroughly, and empathetically
- Communicate the results of the audit accurately, completely, and in an unbiased manner

A communication protocol that is already in place is more effective than one that is put in place after a fraud is detected. As with many internal audit findings, deciding in advance who should be informed, how, and when, can obviate knee-jerk reactions that may occur when serious matters are uncovered.

When internal auditors are acting in the role of forensic auditors, they must understand what their role is. The term *forensic auditing* may be defined as the methodology for resolving fraud allegations from inception to disposition with sufficient proof to prove or disprove allegations of fraud. This methodology includes obtaining evidence, taking statements, writing reports, testifying to findings, and detecting and preventing fraud. Among the goals of the forensic auditor are to:

▪ Individually prove each element of fraud, including the intent, disguise of purpose, reliance by the victim, and concealment of the offense.

▪ Obtain a legal confession (a binding confession of guilt) that is legally admissible.

In their normal role as internal auditors, auditors assist management to establish a control environment in which fraud is unlikely to occur but, if it does occur, it will be quickly detected. When acting as forensic auditors, auditors' goal is the resolution of fraud, that is the determination of the how? who, and what of fraud with sufficient proof to prove or disprove allegations, working on the presumption that all cases will eventually end up in some form of litigation with the associated burden of proof.

The internal auditor's role in fraud risk assessment is covered in more detail in Chapter 8.

Control Self-Assessment

Control self-assessment (CSA) uses techniques performed by management to quantify the impact of fraud risks and effectiveness of control structures at an operational level in a way similar to the assessment processes followed by internal audit. Self-assessment tools can be used to improve antifraud processes and so add immense value to an organization. CSA goes beyond the bounds of internal audit by making the organization as a whole responsible for management control and governance of fraud risks through embracing, planning, and operating a CSA process.

Although none of the common control frameworks specifically mentions CSA, there is a general feeling in the auditing community that CSA is a significant tool in implementing enterprise risk management as suggested by COSO (in the United States and generally worldwide), the Criteria of Control Board (CoCo)[19] (in Canada), the Cadbury Committee Report[20] (in the United Kingdom), or the King Committee Report[21] (in South Africa). These frameworks all include monitoring and risk assessment among the fundamentals of internal control.

One of the main reasons for introducing CSA in 1987 was the constraint on internal audit resources due to budget cuts, coupled with the increased demands caused by growing awareness of the need for good corporate governance. Under a CSA model, management accepts full responsibility for internal control, although some CSA implementations involve collaboration between internal audit and management so that they take joint responsibility for evaluating the adequacy and effectiveness of the system of internal control designed to prevent and detect fraud.

Internal auditors operating in a fraud deterrence context may choose to use CSA in several ways:

- As a tool to ascertain the state of the existing control process and evaluate management's understanding of fraud risks in the business process
- To gather information on the history of transactions processed and the actual operation of antifraud controls as a substitute for extended testing by internal audit
- As a complete audit fraud risk assessment in its own right by combining the first two uses

Resources

Budget and staff cuts have caused audit management to realize that changes must be made. CSA puts the main responsibility for the design, operation, and maintenance of internal antifraud control back on management.

Collaboration

As we have seen, in the fraud risk context, CSA can be a collaborative process, with internal audit and management working together to achieve common goals. This technique can also direct internal auditors to areas where CSA is deemed ineffective, which could be viewed as a red flag to potential fraud areas.

Empowerment

CSA facilitates empowerment. The process is owned overall by management. Management accepts responsibility for internal control over fraud and exercises that responsibility. Empowerment is probably the single most significant aspect of CSA for fraud management, even more than collaboration.

Implementing CSA

CSA generates data in sporadically, instead of evenly over the course of an extended audit schedule. CSA practitioners must be prepared to handle large quantities of data in short periods of time and seek indicators that the fraud risk has increased.

There are several methods for implementing CSA ranging from the most mechanistic type of audit using internal control questionnaires (ICQs) to group workshops.

Internal Control Questionnaires

ICQs are sets of questions used by auditors as checklists to determine whether expected controls exist. External auditors documenting their understanding of internal control generally use ICQs. Internal auditors complete ICQs during the preliminary survey phase of the audit using observation and interviews. ICQs help establish the level of theoretical control activity and affect the level of substantive testing that is needed by clarifying the degree of assurance required.

Under CSA, management can be asked to complete a fraud ICQ as a form of self-audit. This ICQ may be used as a risk assessment tool before a forensic audit is conducted. If management is to complete the ICQ independently, it must have a full understanding of internal control concepts as they relate to fraud, the purpose of the instrument, and how to complete it.

Customized Questionnaires

One improvement on the normal ICQ approach is the use of customized structured questionnaires. This process may consist of internal control sign-off on a folder of questions about various control activities designed to prevent and detect fraud. This folder usually contains a description of the control activity and a schedule of when the activity must be performed (e.g., daily, weekly, etc.). Normally, these questionnaires are customized and can be verified by upper management and the internal auditor at any time.

Folders like these often are found in extremely high-risk areas, such as bank cash handling, or in highly regimented control environments, such as treasury transactions.

Those completing the questionnaires must carefully consider the questions and answer honestly. One weakness in the ICQ approach lies in the danger that the individual completing the ICQ may be the fraudster or in collusion with the fraudster.

Control Guides

Control guides are computerized folders containing a description of the expected set of antifraud internal controls for the operations covered. They are still often used by internal auditors who specialize in financial fraud audits although in the CSA version, these control folders become antifraud internal control workbooks used to facilitate discussion regarding operations, risks, and controls. Internal auditors and management discuss the completion of the workbook in order to determine the degree of reliance that internal audit can place on its completion, and internal audit then uses the workbook as part of its preliminary survey. One application is based on a series of interviews with senior management.

Interview Techniques

Many internal audit departments interview senior management about issues, plans, and concerns as part of the annual planning cycle. The CSA approach using interview techniques is a more structured tool than the use of ICQs or control guides. Interviews allow for interaction between the information provider and the information gatherer. Using structured interviews to gather management's input regarding fraud risk for the assessment process ensures that the same questions are addressed in each session.

Workshops

A popular method of conducting CSA is to use the work group session model, which derived from the original research at Gulf Resources (Canada) conducted by Bruce McCuaig, Paul Makosz, and Tim Leech at the end of the 1980s.[22] They developed two distinct versions of the workshop model.

Control Model Workshops
Control model workshops are training seminars that focus on developing managers' and staff knowledge and capability to assess, manage, and report on internal control via using control design models. In the case of assessment of fraud risk, these workshops may mark the first time management and staff have been required to formally consider the possibility of fraud.

The central premise of these workshops is that the facilitator must transfer knowledge to the work group in order for the work group to assess the controls and risks. This approach increases the assessor's understanding of the overall fraud risk and improves the design of internal control systems.

One control framework often used in control model workshops has major categories that include:

- The definition and communication to participants of organizational goals and objectives
- The definition of *commitment controls* (derived from the Canadian Institute of Chartered Accountants 1995 report mentioned earlier[23]), which are soft controls that involve and unite the people in the organization and could include the corporate vision, mission, and purpose statements
- Planning and risk assessment processes
- Competence, training. and continuous learning, involving the acquisition and maintenance of the skills required to attain the organization's goals
- Direct control activities and mechanisms
- Indicator controls, which are performance indicators of control problems
- Monitoring/feedback, which is the process of gathering and using information to adjust the control system

In applying this framework in a fraud context, focal points of control and areas of sole control must also be considered and evaluated. Alternatively, the COSO *Enterprise Risk Management—Integrated Framework* may be used directly.[24]

Interactive Antifraud Workshops

Interactive antifraud workshops are process consultation workshops in which management and staff evaluate the state of antifraud internal controls. In this model, the underlying philosophy is that management owns the concept of internal control and continues to own the problem throughout the workshop. The facilitator then introduces the information regarding the controls during the workshop. Interactive workshops differ from control model workshops in that they require more facilitation skills, especially during the process consultation phase. Interactive workshops have the advantage that they take less time, because they do not emphasize the training element as control model workshops do.

Both workshop approaches use antifraud control frameworks to ensure that the relevant issues are covered comprehensively. Some feel that control model workshops are a substitute for traditional internal audit while interactive workshops are normally considered another tool of the internal auditing function (i.e., they supplement traditional auditing approaches).

Workshops last a day or two, and each is facilitated by members of the internal audit staff. For a workshop to be successful, participants must believe that they can express themselves freely on any subject, including corporate culture and ethical implementation. In addition, all concerned must a strongly committed to the objectives of the process.

Interactive antifraud workshops consist of group analysis of the strengths and weaknesses of the internal control systems relied on by the department with specific reference to fraud prevention and timely detection.

Because of the high potential for concealment, facilitation skills are critical in these sessions. It takes a great deal of effort to discuss and capture strengths and improvements in internal control during interactive workshops. Once teams have identified a risk, they must formulate an action plan.

NOTES

1. M. Swartz and S. Watkins, *Power Failure: The Rise and Fall of Enron* (London: Aurum Press, 2003).
2. *Trustees of Dartmouth College v. Woodward*, 1819, 17 U.S. (Wheat.) 518.
3. John D. Adams, *Collapse Incorporated: Tales, Safeguards and Responsibilities of Corporate Australia* (CCH Sydney, Australia, 2001).
4. Holmstrom, Bengt, and Steven N. Kaplan, *The State of U.S. Corporate Governance: What's Bengt Holmstrom, Steven N. Kaplan Right and What's Wrong?* (Cambridge, MA: National Bureau of Economic Research, 2003).
5. PWC, *Cybercrime: Protecting Against the Growing Threat: Global Economic Crime Survey*, 2011, www.pwc.com/en_GX/gx/economic-crime-survey/assets/GECS_GLOBAL_REPORT.pdf.
6. KPMG, *Analysis of Global Patterns of Fraud: Who Is the Typical Fraudster*, 2011. www.kpmg.com/US/en/IssuesAndInsights/ArticlesPublications/Documents/who-is-the-typical-fraudster.PDF.
7. E&Y, *Driving Ethical Growth–New Markets, New Challenges, 11th Global Fraud Survey*, 2011, www.ey.com/Publication/vwLUAssets/EY-11th_Global_Fraud_Survey/$FILE/EY_11th_GLOBAL_FRAUD_Survey.pdf.
8. AICPA, AU Section 316, *Consideration of Fraud in a Financial Statement Audit*, 2002, www.aicpa.org/Storage/Resources/Standards/Downloadable Documents/AU-00316.PDF.
9. M. Beasley, J. Carcello, D. Hermanson, and T. Neal, "The Audit Committee Oversight Process," *Contemporary Accounting Research* (Spring 2009).
10. KPMG *2010 International Audit Committee Member Survey*, 2010, www.kpmgauditcommitteeinstitute.com.
11. Grant Thornton, *Managing fraud risk: The audit committee perspective*, www.grantthornton.com/staticfiles/GTCom/Audit/Assurancepublications/Audit%20committee%20guides/ACH_Guides_Managing_Fraud_Risk_.pdf.

12. Institute of Internal Auditors, American Institute of Certified Public Accountants, and Association of Certified Fraud Examiners, *Managing the Business Risk of Fraud: A Practical Guide* (2008), www.acfe.com/uploadedFiles/ACFE_Website/Content/documents/managing-business-risk.pdf.

13. KPMG, "Who Is the Typical Fraudster: KPMG Analysis of Global Patterns of Fraud," KPMG Central and Eastern Europe Ltd., 2011, www.kpmg.com/US/en/IssuesAndInsights/ArticlesPublications/Documents/who-is-the-typical-fraudster.PDF.

14. Committee of Sponsoring Organizations of the Treadway Commission (Coso), *Internal Control — Integrated Framework (1992)*, AICPA.

15. Association of Certified Fraud Examiners, *Report to the Nations on Occupational Fraud and Abuse* (Austin, TX: Author, 2010).

16. National Retail Federation, *Preliminary National Retail Security Survey Findings*, 2011, www.nrf.com/modules.php?name = News&op = viewlive&sp_id = 1136.

17. IBM, *IBM Coremetrics Benchmark Report* www-01.ibm.com/software/marketing-solutions/benchmark-reports/index-2011.html.

18. Institute of Internal Auditors, *Internal Auditing and Fraud* (Altamonte Springs, FL: Author, 2009).

19. Canadian Institute of Chartered Accountants, *Guidance on Control* (Toronto: Canadian Institute of Chartered Accountants, 1995,).

20. Cadbury Committee, *Financial Aspects of Corporate Governance* (London: Gee & Co., 1992).

21. King Committee, *King Report on Corporate Governance* (Johannesburg, South Africa, Institute of Directors, 2009).

22. Institute of Internal Auditors, *Professional Practices Pamphlet 98-2 A Perspective on Control Self-Assessment*, www.iiajapan.com/pdf/data/csa/pp98-2.pdf.

23. Canadian Institute of Chartered Accountants, *Guidance on Control.*

24. COSO, *Enterprise Risk Management–Integrated Framework.*

CHAPTER EIGHT

Fraud Risk Management

Take calculated risks. That is quite different from being rash.

—General George S. Patton, American General in World Wars I and II (1885–1945)

After studying this chapter, the reader should be able to:

- Identify appropriate fraud risk management techniques in order to establish the corporate fraud risk profile.
- Clarify the roles of internal, external, and forensic audit in the fight against fraud.
- Design and implement effective whistleblowing both within and external to the organization as a fraud preventive and detective measure.

When people indulge in fraud, they do not do so with the expectation of being caught and punished. They commit fraud because they believe they can get away with it. To implement effective fraud risk management, risks need to be examined from the potential fraudster's perspective. Where conventional risk assessment methodologies start with inherent risk and move toward limiting those risks by the quality of the system of internal controls, fraud-related assessment looks at the controls from the perspective of how can they be bypassed, who can bypass them, whether it be known, by whom, and how.

In a 2010 survey, Ernst & Young reported that one in seven of those organizations they interviewed had never conducted a formal risk assessment and more than one quarter of those who had conducted such an assessment admitted that they had not updated their fraud risk assessment in the previous year.[1] Although board members were increasingly concerned about personal liability, they were insufficiently informed to manage the organization's risks of fraud and corruption.

ESTABLISHING THE CORPORATE FRAUD RISK PROFILE

Fraud-related assessment is a critical element in the governance of any organization. In a public company, it falls under the legal duty of care to shareholders. In many jurisdictions, it comes under the heading of regulatory compliance. Fraud-related assessment falls within the remit of a professional standards obligation for many professions associated with financial management. It is a significant component of the overall enterprise risk management, and it enhances the corporate reputation and strengthens the overall ethical environment.

Ideally, fraud-related assessment is carried out by a team consisting of staff members from accounting and finance, risk management, internal audit, legal and compliance, information technology (IT) personnel, and others drawn from nonfinancial operational functions. Executive-level staff do not participate on the team, although their support is essential for the process and to ensure buy-in at all levels.

The corporate fraud risk profile is different from the conventional corporate risk analysis in that it's carried out with a different emphasis. Three types of risk normally are considered when evaluating corporate risk:

1. *Inherent risk.* Inherent risk is the likelihood of a significant loss occurring before any risk-reducing factors are taken into account. In evaluating inherent risk, the evaluator must consider the types and nature of the risks as well as the factors indicating that a risk actually exists. To achieve

this, a high degree of familiarity with the operational environment of the organization is required.

2. *Control structure risk.* Control structure risk measures the likelihood that the control processes established to limit or manage inherent risk are ineffective. In order to ensure that the controls are evaluated appropriately, the risk evaluator must understand how to measure the effectiveness of individual controls. Doing this involves identifying those controls that provide the most assurance that specific risks are being minimized within the organization. Control effectiveness is strongly affected by the quality of work and the degree of supervisory control.

3. *Residual risk.* Residual risk is the degree of risk remaining after control structure risk has reduced the likelihood and impact of inherent risk. The objective of the exercise is not to eliminate residual risk but to reduce it to a level that management can accept.

To evaluate the effectiveness of risk control measures, a thorough understanding of the business process addressed by those controls is required. This understanding allows the evaluator to prioritize the processes in terms of which of them are delivering less-than-optimum performance could have serious consequences. Based on this assessment, a risk model or risk framework can be structured to describe and quantify the effects and likelihood of possible negative consequences.

A slightly different process must be followed for a corporate *fraud* risk profile. The evaluator will still look at inherent control structure and residual risk but the evaluation of each will be different.

Inherent risk is still classed as the risk before taking into consideration risk-reducing elements, however, the inherent risk in this case is specifically that of fraud. Such frauds could come in the variety of forms, as discussed in Chapters 2 and 3. Specific threats can be grouped into common causative groups; for example, one group might contain multiple individual types of fraud risk that are all caused by a lack of supervisory control; another group of risks may all be caused by inadequate physical access controls.

Grouping risks based on causation makes it possible to identify those control elements that, if properly designed and implemented, can be most effective in reducing the likelihood that a risk will occur or in reducing the impact if it does occur. Such groupings also allow control structures to be designed to ensure that all causative factors are considered when evaluating the relative strength or weakness of the control environment. This evaluation is normally carried out on the assumption that all controls will function as intended on an ongoing basis.

A specific *fraud risk model* will use internal formulas that model a total business risk of fraud in each of the organization's processes. This type of model may be distinguished from the normal business *risk frameworks* used in conventional business risk modeling.

Identifying and quantifying fraud risks will largely depend on the objectives of each part of the organization together with the assets under control. It is an iterative process that must be carried out continuously as the business environment changes.

Techniques to identify fraud risk usually involve both quantitative and qualitative prioritization. Quantitative information, such as value at risk, maybe be comparatively easy to determine. The probability of risk may be more subjective and based on perceptions of previous fraud experience. *Process analysis* is a technique that permits the identification of key dependencies and control nodes within a business entity where fraud could occur. The risk analysis then involves estimating the significance of the risk of fraud in that particular process and assessing the likelihood of frequency of such a fraud occurring.

Many fraud risk assessment methodologies use a scoring system based on probability of fraud occurring within a specific time scale. Unless the organization has historical evidence from which to draw probable frequencies with mathematical accuracy, probability largely is guesswork. Even where such historical information is available, normally the caliber of internal controls at the time the historical frauds took place is not known.

A more effective method is to evaluate the inherent risk, identify the controls intended to mitigate or reduce the probabilities of those risks, and then evaluate the likelihood of a fraud being attempted or successful in today's environment with the controls currently in place.

Fraud-related analysis is far from a foolproof technique. Inherent limitations include a poor judgment in assessing probability of fraud and lack of adequate or accurate information on the potential cost of fraud. In addition, the effectiveness of the internal control structure in offsetting the risk of fraud may fail to consider the probabilities of collusion between insiders and outsiders to bypass the internal controls or the ability of management to override the internal control structures with no independent scrutiny. Nonetheless, meaningful risk analysis can substantially decrease the likelihood of fraud; it alerts management to changes needed to the control procedures and links control objectives to activities required to achieve them.

When looked at from the perspective of the fraudster, risk can be assessed as:

- *High* if it is believed that a fraud would succeed despite the controls that are currently in place and assumed to be effective.
- *Medium* if it is believed that a fraud may be able to succeed but may be detected further down the line.
- *Low* where we have confidence that the current control structure would prevent an occurrence of an undetected fraud.

This perspective changes the concept of fraud risk from the probability of an occurrence within a time period to the ability of the control structure to resist attempted frauds.

The initial phase of the fraud risk assessment involves a clear definition of the intended deliverable as well as the extent and depth of the assessment. One effective model uses a five-stage process:

1. Identify participants in the process by business unit and establish the key risks from their perspective.
2. Conduct a high-level assessment with each of the participants to clarify their fraud risk concerns.
3. Conduct a workshop with participants drawn from a common business unit in order to elicit their prioritization of the risks and their identification of the key control elements.
4. Consolidate individual business unit results and accumulate them toward the overall corporate fraud risks assessment.
5. Based on identified shortcomings, develop a risk response strategy and implementation plan.

Identifying the participants includes educating them so that all participants are clear as to what fraud is and the definition of risk within their own particular business area. They must also be up to date on the control environment currently relied on to detail and detect fraud. This phase of the exercise may come as a shock to some of the participants who have never had to consider their business operations in terms of potential fraud.

The high-level individual assessment can be a useful exercise since participants in an open workshop may be reluctant to admit concerns regarding fraud and the source of fraud in public. In an operation where a strong manager dominates, it may be difficult to get participants to go up against the boss without the assistance of a strong facilitator.

Open workshopping requires noncritical participation by all involved where it is understood up front that anything can be and is on the table. Discussing concerns on a round-robin basis can be an effective way to elicit individuals' true feelings on both fraud sources and presumed effectiveness of existing control structures.

The risk response plan should become apparent when the group identify the controls relied on and the areas of risk concern not addressed by those controls.

The fraud risks can then be summarized into key categories that will form the basis for the risk response plan to be applied across all business units. At the same time, the source of the fraud risks can be identified and prioritized. Major risk categories commonly are drawn from:

- Misappropriation of assets
- Discrepancies in financial reporting
- Corruption and extortion
- Avoidance of government regulation
- Improperly obtained revenue
- Avoidance of expenses
- Money laundering
- Computer fraud and all its forms
- Loss of confidentiality of information

Comparative risk assessment involves a combination of the likelihood of fraud occurring and the impact on the business if it does. Consideration must also be given to the fact that monetary loss may not be the worst impact on the organization. Loss of reputation and loss of customer confidence may be more damaging the long run than a straight monetary loss inflicted by the fraud. Other such impacts could include legal settlements and/or fines, loss of employees, loss of customers, and even a lowered share price.

Fraud risk assessment may be carried out by business function or by business cycle or by some combination thereof. Organizing the risk assessment around a previously risk-evaluated business cycle may be tempting since the process can be simplified into an expansion of the work already done. However, this method may not consider every business cycle or identify every fraud risk.

To be effective, fraud risk analysis has to be done at a detailed level, examining individual business functions in which fraud could occur as well as the types of fraud possible in that area and the stakeholders who may be in a position to perpetrate a fraud.

 ## CASCARINO CUBE

This discussion is a generic approach to fraud risk identification and prioritization. The approach must be tailored to the requirements of an individual organization. It is referred to here as a cube although it is, in actuality, a cuboid with the number of layers dependent on the individual functions, threat sources, and fraud risks to which the organization is exposed (see Exhibit 8.1).

Using a methodology similar to the five-layer process already discussed, the participants from each functional area meet in an open workshop to identify the principal fraud risks and major sources of fraud threats in their particular business function. This process is open-ended and can operate as a modified Delphi group in which each participant identifies one single fraud opportunity in the business area, assuming there were no controls or that none of the controls worked. The process then moves on to the next participant for another

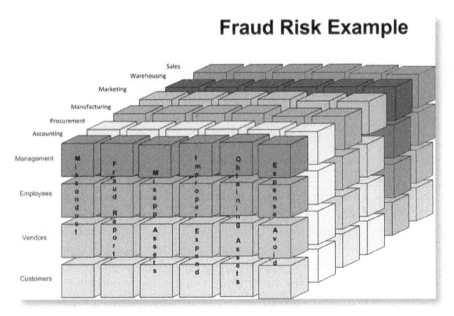

EXHIBIT 8.1 Fraud Risk Example

single fraud opportunity. This process is repeated participant by participant until no one can think of any fraud opportunities other than those identified. At this point the workshop facilitator seeks common themes within the fraud opportunities to summarize into generic fraud risk categories. Each one spelled out as understood by the group. The group then prioritizes these risk categories by combining likelihood and damage potential to arrive at an overall risk ranking.

The process is then repeated to identify the sources of fraud threats and risk-rank them.

When the risk categories and processes are placed on a spreadsheet, the top left-hand corner consists of the greatest threats coming from the most likely sources.

This workshop is repeated for each of the functional areas in order to draw up a three-dimensional cuboid representing the prioritized fraud threats ranked against the sources of those threats for each functional area of the organization.

When the organization's fraud risk profile is prioritized and structured, higher-ranked threats from the most significant threat sources form the upper left-hand corner of each functional slice.

Each functional slice may then be evaluated separately. The preventive, detective, and corrective controls are identified and allocated to the specific cell representing a fraud threat (such as misconduct) from a given fraud threat source.

At this stage, no attempt is made to determine whether the controls that are believed to exist actually do exist and function as intended.

The object of the assessment is to determine whether the various controls intended to mitigate a particular fraud risk from a particular fraud threat source is adequate to reduce the risk to acceptable levels, assuming the controls function as intended. Inadequacy of controls indicate that fraud risk is at too high a level, even if all of the controls work as intended. Such a vulnerability must be addressed, usually by the introduction of additional controls.

Once all mitigating controls have been identified, they can be evaluated in order to determine which controls can give management the most assurance (whether it be from a preventive, detective, or corrective perspective). These are designated the key controls and form management's most critical defenses against those specific fraud risks. From management's perspective, these controls would be subject to the most stringent monitoring in normal operations. From an audit perspective, typically these controls would be selected to be tested for effectiveness.

If, after testing, these controls are found to function as intended, management may be assured that fraud risk is being controlled to the desired level in an adequate and effective manner and that the likelihood of a successful fraud occurring in that area from that source, while not eliminated, has been reduced to a level within a band of tolerance specified in advance.

Where such testing of controls determines that the key controls are not functioning as intended, the cause of failure must be determined and rectified. In the meantime, the other controls in that particular minicube can be evaluated to determine whether they have sufficient cumulative impact to maintain the overall control at the desired level. If they do, the effectiveness of these controls also must be tested.

If the controls do not function as intended, the response plan must be to address why the controls are not functioning. Given that those controls were deemed acceptable, the objective is not to introduce additional controls but to make the "acceptable" but nonfunctioning controls function as intended. This method has the benefit of not introducing extra controls for their own sake but focusing rather on the achievement of the risk control objectives.

This approach has an additional benefit: It becomes easier to see which procedures consume excessive resources without significantly contributing to the overall fraud risk control objectives. Where such a procedure exists but is not a key control in any area within the cube, its appropriateness can be called into question and the impact of eliminating that procedure should be evaluated. In this way progress management can be not only effective but also efficient.

Once key controls have been identified within each of the individual minicubes, they may be traced three dimensionally into other minicubes within other functional areas and threat sources. This then permits a three-dimensional map of the impact of this key control failure could have across all functional areas facing the same sources of risk.

Additionally, as can be seen on the diagram the three-dimensional nature of the cuboid enables management and auditors to examine control adequacy and effectiveness in vertical slices of *functional areas* indicating all fraud risks and threat sources affecting them, horizontal slices of *threat sources* indicating the functional area and fraud risk affected or sliced by *fraud risk* showing all threat sources and functional areas affected.

By maintaining the cube and associated controls as risk levels change with the business, and by keeping the control list current and tested, the overall fraud risk and control architecture can be monitored to ensure that the overall residual fraud risk to the organization remains at acceptable levels.

ROLES OF THE INTERNAL, EXTERNAL, AND FORENSIC AUDITOR

With the tightening of the rules and regulations regarding elimination, detection, and combating fraud in the workplace, the roles of all participants concerned with managing fraud risk have expanded enormously. A greater emphasis now is placed on the successful implementation of fraud preventive and detective methods. Unfortunately, many executives still work on the basis that if the auditors, internal or external, have given an operational area the famous "green tick," indicating their acceptance of the control environment by definition there is no fraud, there is no possibility of fraud, and management can relax. In reality, the auditor role is to approach all audits with professional skepticism, but neither the external nor the internal auditor is in place on a day-to-day basis. Only management can ensure the ongoing efficiency and effectiveness of the system of internal control intended to prevent and detect fraud.

Internal Audit

As spelled out in Chapter 7, the internal audit role is to assist management in the deterrence of fraud by identifying the effectiveness required of the system of internal controls and by examining and evaluating its actual overall effectiveness and its appropriateness to defend against a given level of fraud risk. With the expanded role internal audit has to play in fraud prevention, the meaning of the word *compliance* has undergone a shift from simply meaning "conforming with the rules" and is now interpreted as "complying with the *intent* of the rules." The onus is placed on corporate management to be ahead of the game in creating an environment in which the prevention and detection of fraud and other corporate misdeeds is carried out proactively, prior to a fraud actually occurring.

The overall system of internal control has also undergone a metamorphosis. Previously, fraud prevention and detection were spin-off benefits of the real objective of internal control: to ensure the effectiveness, efficiency, and achievement of operational objectives. In today's environment, the safeguarding of assets has become the overriding priority for many organizations because of the impact of previous frauds and their particular industry. As mentioned, the reputational impact of a widely publicized fraud can extend far beyond monetary losses directly attributable to the fraud itself.

The group most affected by this shift in attitude and emphasis appears to be internal audit, as one of the three major antifraud bodies within the organization. Internal audit, with its reporting structure to the board of directors and the audit committee, represents the third element of the triumvirate tasked with ensuring that fraud threats are mitigated.

The internal auditor is involved in determining:

- Whether the total organizational culture promotes fraud awareness and control consciousness
- Whether written policies exist indicating activities and conflicts of interest that are prohibited, together with the formal reporting cycle of such irregularities and the appropriate action to be taken should such irregularities occur
- The resistance and appropriateness of an authorization architecture for decision making and the processing of transactions
- The adequacy of monitoring mechanisms and the feedback mechanisms used to convey information regarding wrongdoing to the appropriate level that is able and empowered to take effective action
- Whether risk probabilities or potential damage levels have escalated and whether the control structure is still appropriate to reduce the overall fraud risks to acceptable levels

For many internal audit functions, this change in emphasis means a fundamental shift both in their attitude to fraud risk as well as in the skills available to them. It is impossible to adequately evaluate the antifraud measures in place within the organization unless internal audit itself has sufficient knowledge of fraud risk and the design and structure of appropriate control mechanisms. In the past, identification of the perpetration of fraud or its concealment by manipulation of the financial records was commonly left to the independent external auditor who would sweep them up at the end of the year during the annual fiduciary audit.

With the stress now placed on the continuous monitoring of fraud risk as an intrinsic part of the system of internal controls, the certification of their effectiveness on an ongoing basis fall squarely on the shoulders of internal audit. External auditors were expected to provide the missing expertise at the end of the year; today the internal audit function must have the skills, tools, and techniques to monitor fraud risk on an ongoing basis.

Unfortunately, most internal audit functions do not have sufficient staff to identify fraud risk within the organization and provide the necessary assurance to senior executives and the audit committee. The skill mix in the area of fraud investigation is not necessarily the same skill mix that would be expected of an internal auditor five years ago. Many internal auditors have neither the experience nor the training to identify fraud schemes—despite executive management's reliance on internal audit's work in the area of fraud detection and particularly in the area of financial fraud risk assessment.

Current trends indicate that, perhaps due to the present economic cycle, the source of risk may be increasing in the area of disgruntled current and ex-employees. Internal fraud will become a major threat source that can be controlled only by adequate overall management of the system of internal control.

External Audit

In the past, external auditors primarily focused on considering the inherent and control risks of potential material misstatements that could occur themselves in financial accounts. With this focus, inherent risk can be seen as the susceptibility of a misstatement within an account balance or even a single transaction at a material level. Control risk then becomes a risk that the internal control structures would be inadequate to prevent, detect, or correct a material misstatement. The external auditor was not seen primarily as a fraud prevention consultant or a fraud detection auditor. As a result, when the external auditor was focusing on control risk, the control elements designed to prevent or detect a significant fraud were not necessarily the same controls that would be evaluated for a material misstatement in the records.

Where fraud is not seen to be the primary focus of the audit, auditors tend to assess the control risk as low. That is, they evaluate the controls against the objective of detecting material misstatements and the probability that they will be effective in this may be rated as high since there is no perceived intent to defeat the controls as there would be in a case of fraud. As a result, the quantity of evidence gathered may be lower and the testing less rigorous. Had the auditor evaluated the controls with the presumption that there was an intent to defraud, particularly by a person or persons in a position to influence or even bypass the controls, the reliability of those controls would have been more readily called into question and substantive audit testing probably would have increased significantly.

This belief can become a self-fulfilling prophecy: If the risk of fraud is assumed to be low, less testing will be done. If less testing is done, there is a lower probability that fraud will be detected. As a result of lower detection levels, the presumption is that the risk of fraud is low.

With the changed priorities set by new legislation worldwide, external auditors must revise earlier assumptions assessing the likelihood of significant risks to the financial accounts. By actively promoting the role of external auditors in fraud prevention and detection, legislators around the world have heightened the level of awareness of fraud required of the external auditors in presenting an opinion. As a result, testing has increased, and the amount of fraud detected has risen accordingly. It is unknown whether more attention must be paid to fraud because its incidence is increasing or whether detection is increasing because more attention is being paid to fraud.

In practice, the net effect is that, as with the internal audit, external auditors are more alert and aware of the potential for fraud within the financial areas audited. Accordingly, external audits now have a higher probability of detecting fraudulent entries within the financial accounts. Training in areas of potential fraud has raised the awareness and alertness of external auditors for indicators that could indicate the presence of fraud.

Legislation, notably in the United States, requires all members of audit teams to specifically determine how and where the entity's financial statements might be susceptible to material misstatement directly attributable to fraud. In addition, auditors must consider whether management could be in a position to perpetrate and conceal fraudulent financial reporting or misappropriation of corporate assets.

It is not yet been demonstrated, however, that the external auditor's role has extended to early detection of potential frauds where no current misstatement exists within the accounts. Such detection would normally fall within the remit of the fraud-consulting arms of external audit firms.

Fraud Examiners and Forensic Auditors

The role of the fraud auditor is subtly different to that of the forensic accountant, although some fraud examiners undertake both roles. Fraud auditors, both accountants and nonaccountants, have a primary focus on the internal control structures to prevent fraud and offer early detection. Their role commonly is to research how and why the organization is vulnerable to fraud and provide recommendations for management action to be taken to minimize the risk of fraudulent activity. This is a proactive role with work undertaken before there is any reason to suspect that fraud has taken place.

Forensic accountants carry out their work by actively seeking incidences of white-collar crimes, such as bankruptcy fraud, procurement and contract fraud, money laundering, and the full variety of potential frauds within an organization. They typically come from a financial accounting background and may work independently or with the assistance of fraud examiners.

Fraud examiners can be drawn from financial or nonfinancial backgrounds. They normally work in a reactive manner responding to allegations, tip, red flags, and other indicators suggesting that fraud may be a possibility. They carry out their work in anticipation of potential litigation. On occasion, forensic accountants may also operate in areas that are not fraud related but where the evidence they uncover may come under public scrutiny and debate.

The actual work involved in investigating a claim of fraud normally involves interviewing all parties involved or potentially involved in the execution or concealment of a fraud incident in order to gather and preserve evidence. Documentation may be examined, field surveillance carried out, and computer files examined. In addition, evidence may be sought from third-party sources external to the organization for corroboration for evidence already gathered. Interviews with third-party sources may fall within the local legislative restrictions on interrogation of individuals in order to ensure acceptability of evidence gathered in court. Examiners frequently have to carry out background checks, including employment records or medical records, subject to the restrictions of local laws. The ability to follow an electronic audit trail is of critical importance in modern investigations. The fraud investigation itself is covered in more detail in Chapter 9.

By the time the fraud examiner is called in to investigate an occupational fraud, it may have been carried on for years prior to detection. The longest fraud I personally have been involved in investigating had lasted 17 years before it was detected.

Fraud examiners are not normally law enforcement officers, although they may have such a background. Nevertheless, they must work with law enforcement to obtain search warrants and serve subpoenas if required.

To be certified as a fraud examiner, proficiency must be shown in the areas of:

- Fraud prevention and deterrence
- Fraudulent financial transactions
- Fraud investigation techniques
- Legal elements of fraud

A critical element in both forensic and fraud auditing is an understanding of the legal aspects of fraud and the production of forensically acceptable evidence (i.e., evidence that would be acceptable in a court). When fraud auditors are examining internal control structures and making recommendations to improve the effectiveness of both preventive and detective controls, the evidence they produce, particularly by detective controls, must be capable of standing up in court.

IT has dramatically affected the roles of all three types of auditors. Because a great deal of fraud is now committed using computers, all fraud prevention, detection, and investigation activities have to take place with the presumption that IT may play a significant role. Both fraud awareness and fraud examination require a heightened awareness of the opportunities within computer systems to commit fraud as well as the sources of evidence and its reliability during investigation. These roles are covered in more detail in Chapter 10.

WHISTLEBLOWING IN DETECTING FRAUD

Given the role that tips play in the detection of fraud, the role of the whistleblower has come under increasing corporate scrutiny as organizations seek to increase the frequency of such reports.

Whistleblowing involves the provision of information that the individual reasonably believes to be true regarding:

- Violation of any policies, plans, procedures, rules or regulations
- Waste of corporate assets
- Abuses of authority
- Bribery and corruption
- Sexual harassment
- Racism in the workplace
- Dangers to health and safety
- Damage to the environment
- Any other form of mismanagement or misdemeanor

Such information could relate to activities of employees, customers, suppliers, or the organization itself.

Reporting of such activities can create a dilemma for whistleblowers themselves as they must decide on a personal basis whether, when witnessing or being aware of unethical or illegal practices in the workplace, they believe it is their responsibility to report it. If they do report it, they may wonder: What will the consequences be to me personally? Will anything be done? Can anything be done? Who will know I reported this? If I don't report it and it's discovered, will I be held responsible for nonreporting? Will the company hold it against me if I do report? What if it's not true? Will I be seen as a snitch?

In addition, the organization may have a culture in which whistleblowing is seen a stabbing colleagues in the back or betraying their trust by informing.

All of these uncertainties can reduce the likelihood that information will be forthcoming from those who are aware of improper activities. It is the responsibility of the organization to set these fears at rest before an incident occurs causing the need for such a decision.

Staff members most commonly report wrongdoing by whistleblowing where they have genuine concerns about specific actions or transactions that they believe may be harmful to the organization and where there is no other procedure to be followed. This decision is influenced by the individual's ethical standards and unwillingness to stand by in the face of actions that are harmful to the organization or was carried out by the organization against the common good. Whistleblowing takes a degree of courage because whistleblowers cannot know what the ultimate results of their action will be. Laws and policies may exist to protect whistleblower, but no policy can force coworkers to like a person. Low-level retaliation is always a concern.

When wrongdoing is observed, generally staff members first seek remedies through the normal operating policies of the organization, such as:

- Grievance policies
- Prevention of fraud policies
- Disciplinary policies
- Health and safety policies
- Discrimination and harassment policies

Only when these conventional routes are exhausted will typical employees resort to unconventional means of communicating concerns. Organizations often are concerned that employees will externalize whistleblowing to newspapers and the likes to the detriment of the reputation of the company. In order to maintain confidentiality externally, there must be a known route within the organization whereby any stakeholder can report wrongdoing, knowing that the organization will treat all such reporting confidentially and seriously. Employees should understand their duty to report and at the same time maintain company confidentiality unless there is a legal obligation to report the matter to appropriate authorities. Where such information is already in the public domain, revealing it is not classed as whistleblowing since the employee is not revealing information of a confidential nature.

The desired message to be communicated to all employees, customers, vendors, and other interested parties is: "If in doubt, tell someone."

Many organizations have implemented whistleblowing awareness policies laying out the options and avenues for reporting in order to ease these fears. It is also common for organizations to indemnify staff against any subsequent claims or legal proceedings brought against them with regard to any whistleblowing activities, whether the wrongdoing is proven or not, as long the accusation was made in good faith and there has been no malicious intent and falsehood in the information provided.

The U.S. Sarbanes-Oxley Act extended whistleblower protection to employees in publicly traded companies by:

- Making it illegal to "discharge, demote, suspend, threaten, harass or in any manner discriminate against" whistleblowers
- Requiring board audit committees to establish procedures for hearing whistleblower complaints
- Establishing severe criminal penalties for executives who retaliate against whistleblowers
- Providing legal mechanisms for whistleblowers who have, in their opinion, been unjustly dealt with to seek redress against the organization

False accusations for malicious purposes are not protected under such laws and normally are dealt with severely when proven.

In the public sector, whistleblowing may pose a unique problem in that the disclosure of confidential government information may itself be a crime, resulting in the prosecution and imprisonment of the whistleblower even if the case is proven. If, however, the whistleblower has knowledge of an organization, person, or entity cheating or attempting to cheat the federal or state government in the United States, the False Claims Act provides "qui tam statutes" (*quid tam pro domino rege quam prose ipso in hac parte sequitur*: Who pursues this action on our Lord the King's behalf as well as his own). The statutes allow the whistleblower, or relator, to bring a case personally and seek damages on behalf of the government. The benefit to the relator of a successful prosecution can be anything from 15 to 30 percent of the government recovery, even if the government steps in to assist in the prosecution. In the case of multimillion-dollar frauds or malfeasance, such prosecutions have netted whistleblowers substantial cash settlements. This reward structure is a throwback to the old common law provision that existed in the United Kingdom prior to the enactment of the Common Informers Act in the early 1950s.

NOTE

1. Ernst & Young, "Driving Ethical Growth: New Markets, New Challenges," 2010, www.ey.com.

CHAPTER NINE

Investigating Fraud

As long as the world shall last there will be
wrongs, and if no man objected and no man
rebelled, those wrongs would last forever.

—*Clarence Darrow, Lawyer and Civil Libertarian*
(1857–1938)

After studying this chapter, the reader should be able to:

- Identify the red flags and indicators of fraud appropriate to triggering a fraud investigation.
- Identify the forensic techniques available and the resources and training required to implement an appropriate fraud investigation.
- Identify the requirements for establishing an internal investigation function and determine the appropriateness.
- Identify and evaluate the appropriate measures for tracing and recovering lost assets.

Incidents of private and public fraud are being reported daily in the media, and more and more prosecutions for this offense are being conducted in the various courts. This chapter examines the phenomenon in order to obtain a full appreciation of what exactly fraud investigation is and how such an investigation is triggered.

Fraud investigation is typically a reactive function triggered by internal or external recognition of a red flag indicating the potential presence of fraudulent activity. The investigator needs the ability to differentiate between red flags indicating operational ineffectiveness or inefficiencies and deliberate fraud. The more the awareness of management, employees, and other stakeholders of potential red flags is raised, the more likely it is that an investigation will be triggered in the appropriate areas based on the nature of the indicators observed.

In the United States, since 2008, a requirement has been laid on organizations to implement the Red Flags Rule. This rule is enforced by federal bank regulatory agencies, the National Credit Union Administration, and the Federal Trade Commission. It requires organizations falling under the authority of these agencies to implement a written Identity Theft Protection Program specifically designed to detect the red flags of identity theft in order to spot suspicious patterns when they arise. Although program is designed specifically for identity theft and applies specifically to financial institutions and creditors, the same process is appropriate for the detection of, and reaction to, any form of fraud. It involves a framework consisting of four steps.

1. Provision of reasonable policies and procedures to identify the red flags indicating the possibility of wrongdoing.
2. Detection of the identified red flags.
3. Policies and procedures spelling out the appropriate actions when red flags of detected.
4. Periodic reevaluations of the policies and procedures to ensure their appropriateness and currency.

RED FLAGS AND INDICATORS OF FRAUD

A red flag is an indicator or warning that something is not right leading to closer scrutiny by the manager or supervisor. On its own, a single red flag is not proof that a fraud has taken place. Where clusters of such indicators are found, the manager should be more alert for irregularities.

In many cases, investigation of fraud reveals an underlying failure of management supervision and poor execution of company policies and procedures. People tend to follow their role models, and studies have indicated that fraud is more likely to occur under management that is unethical or incompetent. Fraud should also be suspected when salaries within the organization are lower than those of competitors. Reward structures based on short-term goals, dictatorial management in a power-driven environment, and constant crisis management are breeding grounds for fraud. Where individuals are in position of power to award lucrative contracts or where they handle large amounts of cash without adequate supervision, fraud may also arise.

Managers who play one subordinate off against another and seek personal loyalty without giving it may create an environment in which fraud is probable. Such managers frequently prefer informal procedures to formal, established policies since they commonly feel exempt from the rules and override them with impunity.

Triggering Events

The reasons why a trusted employee begins a fraud vary, but most common is an emotional trauma somewhere in the individual's life involving home, work, marriage, or some other aspect. This trauma affects the person's behavior pattern and may well be noticed by colleagues. The person may assume responsibility for a single client or a specific task that he or she jealously guards as the fraud continues.

Where the change involves heavy drinking, gambling, expensive social life, or extramarital sexual activity, a pattern of lies and deceptions may emerge. Coworkers often believe such deceptions because of the length of trusted service of the individual before the fraud actually begins.

Most frauds are caused by the lack of internal controls. However, in many cases, the controls are there but are not being adhered to and management is not policing the internal controls.

Personal Red Flags

Individuals involved in frauds often display characteristics that indicate a willingness to commit frauds. These characteristics, when coupled with a corporate environment conducive to fraud, create a breeding ground for fraud. In behavior, indications such as refusal to take vacation or sick leave may appear unusual but when combined with other indicators may point to the possibility of a fraud. The presence of one or more of the following signs often indicates fraud:

- *Gambling.* Where managers are known to be frequent gamblers, care should be taken to ensure that the gambling is not being funded from corporate resources.
- *Unusual expenses.* A common way of covering up the existence of fraud is the posting of expense claims. *Unusual patterns or values of such claims should be treated as suspicious.*
- *Extravagant living standards.* The desire to live a lifestyle that is out of financial reach can be a powerful inducement to fraud. Fraud-prone managers frequently are conspicuous consumers. Financial success and its trappings are important to their own self-image. Impulsive by nature, they find it difficult to postpone gratification and wait for what they feel should be theirs now. Many fraudsters are hard workers who compensate their families with material things because of their hours away from home. Suspicions should be aroused in cases of individuals in positions of authority over the disposition of corporate funds who are known to lead extravagant lifestyles.
- *Sexual promiscuity.* Sexual promiscuity may be an expensive habit for individuals with known and fixed incomes. These individuals may fund such expenses out of corporate funds in order to conceal the activity.
- *Undesirable associates.* Someone outside the organization may encourage an employee to participate in a fraud. For example, a manager may be able to sign off on fraudulent documents submitted by the outside conspirator.
- *Poor social skills.* Many fraud-prone managers are self-centered in relationships both at work and home. This attitude may lead them to treat subordinates as objects to be exploited rather than as valued employees and leads to their being disliked by both business associates and competitors.
- *Extravagant with the truth.* Fraud-prone managers are often careless with facts and may boast of personal achievements while ignoring the contributions of others. Such managers commonly treat opposition as betrayal and react with hostility, which can ruin working relationships.
- *Substance abuse.* Fraudster managers may also be heavily involved with drugs and alcohol abuse. Such extravagances have to be paid for and may be beyond the manager's means without "assistance."

Fraud-prone managers are also generally conspicuous consumers. Financial success and its trappings are important to their self-image. Impulsive and impatient natures make it difficult for them to wait for what they feel should be theirs.

Profile of the Fraudster

The profile of the typical perpetrator of fraud, although not exactly a red flag, is important for auditors and management to understand and recognize. In their 2011 report, *Who Is the Typical Fraudster*, KPMG suggest the typical fraudster is [1]:

- Male (accounting for 87 percent of frauds)
- 36 to 45 years old (accounting for 41 percent of frauds)
- Commits fraud against own employer (accounting for 90 percent of frauds)
- Works in the finance function or in a related role (accounting for 32 percent of frauds)
- Is employed in a senior management position (accounting for 53 percent of frauds)
- Is a long-term employee employed for more than ten years (accounting for 33 percent of frauds)
- Is working in collusion with another perpetrator (accounting for 61 percent of frauds)

Obviously, this does not mean that all males in that age group who have been employed for more than ten years and who work in a senior financial position are fraudsters. It is important, however, to bear these figures in mind as red flags when internal fraud is suspected. In cases where fraud has been detected, the same report indicates that in 56 percent of the cases, one or more red flags existed prior to detection although only 6 percent of them were acted on. Given the repetitive nature of many frauds, such red flags tend to accumulate. Corporate awareness coupled with rapid investigative response can result in significant savings when viewed in terms of an ongoing, long-term fraud. (The average fraud now takes 3.4 years to detect.)

In his 1973 book, Donald Cressey set forth what became known as Cressey's hypothesis:

> Trusted persons become trust violators when they conceive of themselves as having a financial problem which is non-shareable, are aware this problem can be secretly resolved by violation of the position of financial trust, and are able to apply to their own conduct in that situation verbalizations which enable them to adjust their conceptions of

themselves as trusted persons with their conceptions of themselves as users of the entrusted funds or property. [2]

This was the basis for the fraud triangle seen in Chapter 1.
Fraudsters generally fall into three broad categories:

1. *Opportunistic fraudsters.* These fraudsters have carried out a single fraud in response to a single set of circumstances that presented itself. Due to a temporary failure of internal controls, an opportunity was seen to commit a fraud in a manner that was highly unlikely to be detected. The temptation was too much, and the fraudsters succumbed.
2. *Repeat fraudsters.* Where the temptation came in the form of the recognition of a lack of internal control in a specific area, potential fraudsters may realize that there is an opportunity to perpetrate an ongoing fraud with little chance of detection. Again, the opportunity proves too tempting, but this time the fraud was intended to recur for as long as the opportunity existed.
3. *Organized fraudsters.* Organized fraudsters deliberately manipulate the control environment in order to gain the opportunity to perpetrate a specific fraud. Some large-scale frauds involve the deliberate placing of individuals into specific positions within the organization to facilitate an organized fraud involving collusion across multiple operational areas.

Managerial-Level Red Flags

As previously pointed out, much of the high-value fraud experienced by organizations is carried out of the managerial level. Once again, alertness for common red flags may point to an area appropriate for further investigation. Red flags in this area could include:

▪ *Reluctance to provide information to auditors.* Taken on its own, such reluctance may simply indicate a manager's previous negative experience with the internal or external auditors. In combination with other indicators, however, it may point to a totally different scenario: a manager's awareness that evidence of his or her malpractice is available and that an investigation would lead to the uncovering of a fraud. In such circumstances, the intent of the reluctance to provide information could be to give the fraudster time to conceal such evidence. Where concealment is impossible and discovery is inevitable, the intent simply is to delay the ultimate detection.

- *Frequent changes in accounting environments.* Evidence that a manager has been involved in multiple changes of bank accounts or the appointment of new external auditors may point to attempts at concealment of activities, fraudulent or not.
- *Management domination of the group.* The presence of a strong and domineering managerial culture may have nothing to do with fraud or fraudulent intent. Many highly effective managers operate in such a manner. It does, however, give management the opportunity to take unilateral actions that will not be questioned by subordinates or other managerial-level staff. This in itself may be a temptation to fraud.

Other fraud indicators at the managerial or executive level could include that continuous rolling over of loans, the disposal of corporate assets below market values, high employee turnover rates associated with an individual manager, compensation programs out of proportion to an executive's contribution, or simply transactions authorized by the manager that do not make commercial or common sense.

CORPORATE FRAUD INDICATORS

Just as there are personal red flags that could indicate the presence of a fraud, corporate red flags exist that can indicate the areas of potential irregularity.

Reduced Cash Flow

Popular ways of fraudulently creating an appearance of corporate growth beyond actual growth are to book sales prior to payment, delay the recording of expenses to reduce expenses for research and development, or fail to record obsolete inventory as an expense. Typically, this manipulation will show up as an increase in net income of cash flow from operations while profit is reducing or not increasing in line with net income.

Overstated Assets

Overstated accounts receivable and inventory levels are common ways to hide corporate fraud. The ratios of accounts receivable to goods sold and inventory value to cost of goods sold should remain fairly constant over a period of time. Simple manipulation of the inventory levels can be used to cover losses as a result of fraud. Where these ratios move rapidly, it can be an indicator of fraud or simply an indicator that future problems will arise since either customers are not paying their debts or inventory is not turning over as it used to. In addition, inventory levels, accounts receivable, and sales typically move together. Sales figures should lead the way, with neither accounts receivable nor inventory levels growing at a faster rate. Another indication that there may be something wrong may come in the form of growth in accounts payable exceeding growth in inventory levels. There may be legitimate reasons for such movements, but management should investigate.

Decreases in Corporate Earnings

The trend of movement in operating income can be a highly visible red flag since it could indicate operating conditions in which fraud is more likely to occur.

Strange Entries in the Accounts

High-value account balances with no explanation or with convoluted definitions could indicate something abnormal of a creative nature. In addition, off-balance-sheet items may hide a multitude of sins. Accounts may also indicate potential frauds with excessive numbers of voids, returns, and/or discounts on journal entries. Discrepancies may exist between bank deposits and amounts posted into ledgers. The existence of unknown and unauthorized bank accounts should immediately set all alarm bells ringing.

Fraud at a lower value level can also be indicated by abnormal expense claims or employee reimbursements. Petty cash, although petty, is a highly liquid asset. Any excess movement within petty cash or utilization to cash employee checks should warrant further investigation.

Payroll Red Flags

Despite, or perhaps because of, the heavily computerized nature of modern payroll processing, many of the controls that existed in the manual environment have either disappeared or operate with severely reduced effectiveness. Indicators that should alert auditors and investigators as well as operational management to areas of potential fraud include items such as employees with duplicate bank accounts, identity or Social Security numbers, addresses, telephone numbers, or even names. Inconsistent overtime, overtime payments made to employees whose grade would not normally incur overtime payments, or employees with fewer deductions than expected are also warning signs.

Glaring Omissions in Controls

Standard controls, such as segregation of duties, are clearly understood and should be in place in all areas where assets are supposed to be controlled. The person responsible for the assets should not be the one responsible for recording the assets or reconciling the records. Unrestricted access to either assets or records can facilitate the bypassing of most controls for fraudulent purposes. These are basic controls and should be in place in all organizations. Lack of such controls or their ineffective implementation can be a major temptation to fraud and should be a red flag to management.

Procurement Red Flags

Depending on the nature of the organization, procurement may be one of the most significant areas of opportunity for fraud. Abnormalities within the vendor arena could include alerts such as:

- Vendors not present on an approved vendor list
- Excessive use of sole-source vendors
- Vendors with no physical address
- Vendors with information matching employee information, such as addresses, bank accounts, and the like
- Vendor payments that are collected in person rather than being mailed or sent electronically
- High volumes or values of purchases from new vendors

In addition to vendor-related procurement red flags, other indicators may relate to the handling of inventory after it has been received. Such indicators could include:

- Increased procurement volumes with no increase in business activity or inventory levels
- Increasing or unusual inventory shrinkage
- Excess levels of inventory particularly when combined with increased purchases from specific vendors
- High levels of slow-moving items in inventory

All of these red flags apply to organizations and individuals operating within any market sector. There are, however, specific red flags that may apply to specific industries or types of operations.

Mortgage Processing Red Flags

A specialized area involving high cash values is the processing of mortgage bonds, in both the residential and commercial markets. Once again, indicators may exist at the general level or in specific parts of the processing operations. Inconsistencies may not indicate the presence of a fraud but should be followed up to ensure that no fraud is present.

General Fraud Indicators

Red flags for mortgage processing fraud may indicate absence of controls or failure of controls that will have a pervasive effect on all processing carried out in connection with the mortgage. Irregularity in verifications, including dates of completion or address discrepancies, could indicate sloppy processing or the intent to defraud. Any indication that documentation has been amended or altered, including differing type styles as well as handwriting, should be cause for immediate investigation. Perhaps most critical information relating to an application for a mortgage is that which identifies the applicant. Any irregularities in identity numbers, Social Security numbers, tax numbers, company registration numbers, or personal information, such as names and addresses, should be immediately suspect.

Application Form Red Flags

Once again, it is irregularities that may trigger suspicion that all is not well. Personal information that the seller and buyer have in common, such as telephone numbers, or cases where the buyer currently resides in the property to be acquired may be unusual but not an indication of fraudulent intent. When combined with other red flags, however, suspicions may be aroused. Discrepancies in application forms, such as lack of dates or lack of signatures as well as significant or unusual changes from handwritten to typed applications, lack of sufficient employer information, or an individual without a known permanent residence seeking new funding for investment property may also signal potential fraud.

Contract Red Flags

Discrepancies on sales contracts may also indicate attempts to defraud the lending financial institution. Nevertheless, sometimes these are legitimate but unusual conditions for the sale. A seller could use a power of attorney for legitimate reasons, have agreed to a real estate commission that appears excessive, or even be the real estate broker or a relative of the broker without there being a fraudulent intent. Should these indicators be combined with others, such as a purchaser not being the applicant, or the owner reflected on the title deeds not being the current seller, fraud awareness should be heightened. Other red flags could include the presence of an undeclared first mortgage or anomalies in deposit monies. All of these issues highlight the risks of fraudulent provisions existing within the contract and need to be examined.

Income Documentation Anomalies

As mentioned in Chapter 4, documentation anomalies may be used to conceal borrower's inability of lack of intention to repay a debt. Use of a nonexistent employer as proof of income may show up when employers cannot be contacted or the address given cannot be traced. Errors in payment records can range from incorrect calculations of taxation or erroneous tax certificates through to irregularities in the employer identification. Other anomalies may be more directed toward the presumed lifestyle of the aspiring borrower. Where income reported is disproportionate to bank account details or lifestyle and where income is claimed to arise from investments or dividends that cannot be substantiated suspicions should be aroused. Common sense may also supply red flag indicators if income claimed is out of line with the nature of the employment indicated or with the applier's personal characteristics.

Anomalous Credit Information

In a mortgage loan application, an individual's previous credit history is checked to ensure that no prior indications of bad debt or fraud exist. An individual or organization with a dubious past performance on debt may have to falsify creditworthiness in order to acquire further indebtedness. In addition to the obvious red flag of a lack of credit history, any discrepancy between the credit check report and the application itself should trigger an alert. As with the income documentation, anomalies on credit reports should prompt further investigation. Where the length of established credit claim is inappropriate to the applicant's age or where pages or supplementary reports are missing, the trustworthiness of the credit information becomes suspect.

Other Anomalies

Other anomalies may exist in the areas of the applicant's assets, documentation of current domicile as well as irregularities regarding the property to be purchased. Its value and current ownership may be questionable.

The PMI Mortgage Insurance Company has provided a useful checklist for the detection of red flags for fraud in the mortgage industry.[3] Although it is geared to the U.S. market, it can be adapted to other national jurisdictions.

Red Flags in the Medical Field

Despite originally being included in the classification of "creditors" under the Red Flags Rule, the American Medical Association succeeded in having an amendment, the Red Flag Program Clarification Act of 2010, enacted such that physicians, lawyers, dentists, and other professionals were no longer classified under the Red Flags Rule. Despite this, the need for awareness of fraud indicators is critical in the medical environment simply because of the volume and values being processed.

In her book *Healthcare Fraud: Auditing and Detection Guide*, Rebecca Busch drew attention to the staggering figures of medical-related fraud in the United States, which in 2006 amounted to approximately $25 million per hour.[4] Busch gives detailed advice on the use of analytical techniques to identify fraud.

Health care frauds may be carried out against health insurance companies, personal injury insurance policies, commercial insurers of compensation claims, government social security benefits, and workers' compensation insurance for injury sustained in the workplace. Such frauds can be carried out by both service providers and patients themselves. Typical red flags of possible health care fraud could include indicators such as:

Provider Fraud
- Patient recollection of care is inconsistent with medical records.
- Patient has no knowledge of the medical ailments described in insurance claim forms.
- Medical records indicate treatment differing from that described in insurance claim forms.
- Medical records place the patient at two different treatment centers on the same date and at the same time.
- Medical treatment prescribed is inconsistent with the diagnosis.
- Nonmedical personnel are used to render treatment.
- Service providers' notes are identical for multiple patients exhibiting different conditions.
- Medical records indicate provision of nonapproved treatments.
- The cost claimed is higher than expected for the type of treatment and age, sex, and condition of the patient.

- Higher volumes of drugs prescribed than expected for the type of treatment and age, sex, and condition of the patient.
- There are repeated patterns of dubious provider insurance claims.
- There are frequent delays in replying to requests for substantiating documentation for claims.
- Claims are made for repeated treatments of patients living at extreme distances.
- Billing is made for services unlikely to have been performed on that particular patient for that particular treatment.
- Medical records change materially after the date of treatment.
- Date of treatment indicates a time when the service provider was unavailable.
- Utilization rates of providers exceed the norm or even exceed the time available.
- Providers charge for bundled treatments as independent line items.

Patient Fraud
- There are erasures and corrections on documents submitted for compensation claims.
- Patient occupation claimed is inconsistent with the nature of the employer's business.
- The injury is inconsistent with the claimed cause of injury.
- Date, time, and place of incident is unknown.
- Repeated claims are made for the same treatments, particularly surgical treatments.
- Patient can never be contacted since he or she is constantly "resting."
- Claims of treatment cannot be substantiated by medical providers.
- Claims are made for injury in the workplace at a time when the employee was elsewhere.
- The injured worker refuses to accede to diagnostic procedures intended to confirm claimed injuries.
- Workers who claim for permanent injury, with or without the collusion of service providers are later observed taking part in activities incompatible with the injuries claimed.
- There are no witnesses to accidents that patients claim to have occurred at work.
- Patients delay treatment for work-related accidents for extended times.
- Another red flag is that the patient is in line for early retirement or future layoff or retrenchment.

Part of the reason for the volume and value of the frauds perpetrated under the heading of health care fraud is the extreme difficulty in detecting such frauds without extensive and costly investigation. Data analytics can be a very effective tool in detection, but even with such tools, low-volume claims for treatments not performed can be difficult to identify. Prevention requires a level of integrity from all involved—patients, doctors, and other service providers. The occurrence rate of fraud seems to indicate that such integrity is not forthcoming.

Contract Fraud Red Flags

As mentioned in Chapter 4, frauds can occur at any stage of a contracting process. Bid proposals, contract pricing, amounts billed, and compliance with contractual terms are all areas where the potential for fraud exists. Three primary types of fraud may occur depending on the nature of the contracts:

1. Incurred-cost or cost-plus contracts
2. Acquisition fraud
3. Fixed-price contracts

Incurred-Cost or Cost-Plus Contracts

Incurred-cost or cost-plus contracts involve an agreed percentage of profit added to the incurred costs related to the particular contract. This type of contract could include both direct and indirect costs claimed by a contractor or service provider. Many view the very fact that a contract is an incurred cost contract as a primary red flag necessitating closer independent scrutiny and physical verification, particularly in the accounting for labor costs. Ensuring that the labor costs are being appropriately charged to the work actually being performed is fundamental to ensuring the accuracy and integrity of the costs on which the profit percentage is being applied.

Anomalies in this area could include disproportionate movements in direct and indirect labor costs with cost increases being applied differently in different types of contracts. Charges to indirect costs moving at disproportional rates to direct labor costs could also be problematic. An enormous red flag is the cost of labor applied to incurred-cost contracts rising while the cost of labor charged to fixed-price contracts remain static.

Overall red flags on labor charges to incurred-cost contracts include:

- Sudden shifts in charging patterns
- Decreases in charges made to contracts approaching their budgeted maximum
- Employee time charged against the contract when attendance records show an employee was elsewhere
- Contractor expenditure frequently just below budgeted maximums, never above
- Constant movements between direct and indirect charging of the same employee
- Generally poor controls over labor charging

In addition to labor costs, such contracts are also vulnerable to fraud in materials acquisition, utilization, and costing. In such contracts, the use of subcontractors may be classified as a cost of material, and such costs may be inflated to cover subcontractor expenditures in kickbacks to employees to obtain contracts.

Acquisition Fraud

Fraud types in the acquisition area include:

- Transfers of materials from incurred-cost contracts to fixed-price contracts, thus allowing the fixed-price contract to receive the materials "free" while the incurred-cost contract picks up the cost of materials it never received or utilized
- Transfers of materials from current contracts to be scheduled for delivery for use in future contracts
- Transfers of material at costs significantly different from the incurred cost

Red flags include:

- Poor segregation of duties within corporate procurement
- Purchasing staff have a standard of living beyond the means of their corporate income
- Poor contracting procedures for awarding subcontracts
- Poor documentation on contract awards
- Recent purchases of items previously written off as scrap
- Significant increases in scrap or rework

Where the contract involves the purchasing of services, no materials normally would be involved; however, red flags in such cases could include:

- Lack of formal signed contracts
- No documented support, such as detailed invoices
- Services paid for without clear evidence of the services provided

Fixed-Price Contracts

Even in the case of fixed-price contracts, procurement procedures may require the submission of pricing data in order to determine the appropriateness of prices charged. Where standard costing systems are used for material and labor costs, manipulation of these costs can make a quotation look reasonable while the costs actually are being used to inflate the price quoted. This type of fraud normally is easily detected by comparing standard costs used to historical actual costs, should such information be available. Fraud opportunities in such circumstances could include:

- Substitution of lower-quality material or personnel while maintaining cost charges
- Use of outdated standards for costing proposals
- No clear audit trail exists to verify the accuracy and integrity of direct charges
- Supplier ability to manipulate direct charges
- High usage variances

Red flags indicating the existence of such practices could include:

- Specific individuals named as key employees not used on the contract
- Significant differences between contracted and actual services provided with no change in the scope of the contract
- High-cost employees being charged against a contract with no evidence of their participation in the actual work done
- Original documentation consistently unavailable for inspection
- Original documentation contains amendments without proof of authorization

In all cases where such red flags are identified, the significance must be evaluated in order to determine the overall impact and any action required.

Where sufficient fraud indicators exist, a full investigation into the possibilities of full-scale fraud may be required.

CONDUCTING AN INVESTIGATION

As many organizations have implemented red flag alerts, investigations are now far more likely than in the past. However, the mere identification of red flags or the evaluation of an area as high risk cannot be relied on to prove fraud in individual cases. Knowing that people are in a position to commit a fraud, or that they maintain an extravagant lifestyle or have had previous accusations made against them is not adequate proof.

Overall, the fraud investigation is intended to resolve fraud allegations from inception to disposition. The investigation includes:

- Obtaining evidence
- Investigating fraud
- Taking statements
- Writing reports
- Testifying as to findings in detection and prevention of fraud

As such, it is critical that the investigation seek an early resolution regarding the probability that a fraud has in fact occurred in order to maintain cost effectiveness. In all fraud investigations, the direct causes of the losses as well as the financial and other damage incurred must be evaluated early in the process to determine the fraud probability as well as its priority in terms of investigation. This task involves *predication*, which means the examination of the totality of circumstances that would lead a reasonable, professionally trained, and prudent individual to believe that a fraud *has* occurred, *is* occurring, and/or *will* occur. Fraud examinations must be based on predication.

Before an investigation can begin, the investigator must be satisfied that no conflict of interest exists that would make it inappropriate for him or her to conduct the investigation. Conflict of interest could be presumed to exist where:

- There exists or existed a personal or professional relationship with the individual subject to the investigation.
- The investigator or an associate could be presumed to benefit by a positive or negative finding regarding the subject of the investigation.

- The investigator has now or has had in the past a financial interest with the individual subject to the investigation.
- The investigator knows of the existence of a personal or professional bias on his or her own part that could affect or be presumed to affect his or her impartiality in the execution of the investigation.

A common way of conducting an investigation is to utilize the fraud theory approach. This four-stage approach involves the analysis of available data, creation of a hypothesis regarding the method of carrying out the fraud, testing the hypothesis, and refining and amending the hypothesis.

In all cases of fraud investigation, four significant factors must be determined and proved: motivation, opportunity, means, and method.

Motivation

Most frauds involve some form of *economic* motivation—that is, financial gain—although not necessarily directly for the perpetrator. In some cases, where the individual committing the fraud feels badly done by, passed over for promotion, or not receiving the raise he or she feels entitled to, or when the person wishes to feel morally superior, a fraud can be committed for *ideological* reasons. Some frauds, in particular some computer frauds, are committed for *egocentric* reasons: Perpetrators wish to show off to peers how clever they are in being able to penetrate antifraud measures. In some cases, the same motivation drives frauds carried out for no financial gain but simply to keep the fraudsters' reputation of always hitting targets. In such cases, asset recovery efforts may achieve 100 percent as the money was never the motive; it was only a way of keeping score. *Psychotic* motivation for conducting fraud is rare and is a kind of motivation more readily associated with habitual criminals.

Opportunity

Opportunities to commit fraud come in a variety of forms. In some cases, inadequacies in system controls, such as accounting controls, permit authorized individuals to carry out unauthorized acts. Inadequacies in access controls may permit unauthorized individuals to gain access to assets, records of assets, and information systems.

Inadequacies in management controls, such as the reward system, the ethical climate, or even the climate for trust, can remove the focus from the prevention of fraud and the effectiveness of control to areas such as personal enrichment, beating the opposition internally, or covering up lack of integrity.

Means

For fraudsters to have the means to carry out a fraud, they may be able to operate within the internal control structures or to overrule the system of internal controls. Based on the fraudsters' position in the organization, they may be the person responsible for enforcing the system of internal controls. In any event, they must have the ability to commit the fraud with a reasonable chance of success and the ability to remain undetected.

Method

As has been discussed in earlier chapters, there are multiple methods by which a fraud can be committed. In the event of an investigation, the investigator seeks to prove motivation, opportunity, means, and method.

Starting the Investigation

When an allegation of fraud has been made, the procedure laid down in advance and approved by the board should be followed in order to ensure that the claim is properly considered and evaluated. A major element of the process is designating a specific person to conduct the initial investigation and determine the desired course of action. This designation may involve the acquisition of skills external to the organization in order to ensure the appearance of independence in the investigation process. Such acquisition may involve the bringing-in of an outsider on a contract or even a permanent basis.

The starting point in any investigation is a presumption of innocence of all people who potentially are involved. This is the only safe point at which to start. If the initial presumption is that a fraud has occurred, all evidence will appear to point directly to the fraud and possibly even to a specific fraudster. If the initial presumption is that there is an innocent explanation for what occurred, much of the evidence may point to a mistake, something overlooked, or a misinterpretation of the rules. In any event, should the case come to court, the defendant's legal team will offer such explanations. The prosecution must be in a position to show that these possibilities were considered but rejected because of the preponderance of evidence. If the defense is able to show that there was another possible explanation that the investigation did not consider, a reasonable doubt may have been introduced. Only when all potential innocent explanations have been considered and dismissed can the investigator conclude that a probable act of fraud has occurred. That being the case, the investigator must seek out supporting evidence to prove the contention.

Where the allegations involve senior executives, the board, or potential legal liability, other areas of the organization may need to be brought into the investigation. Depending on the nature of the organization and industry, external authorities have to be notified immediately that an investigation is about to start and the rationale behind it. Parties that must be notified can include regulators, legal authorities, corporate insurers, external auditors, or labor unions.

When fraud is alleged, sometimes management responds with an immediate knee-jerk reaction of trying to fix the problem immediately, as quickly and as cheaply as possible. Rushing the task without fully planning out the project will significantly decrease the probability of a successful outcome in terms of asset recovery or fraud prosecution. In addition, innocent employees may be wrongfully accused while guilty parties may emerge unscathed and with legal claims for damages against the organization.

From the inception of the investigation, the assumption must be that all evidence gathered, whether proving or disproving the existence of a fraud, will have to be presented in court as part of a civil or criminal proceeding, whether in prosecuting the accused perpetrator of the fraud or in a defensive action against improper accusations, should an allegation fail to be proven and an action be brought against the company for defamation of character.

The full investigation starts with the formulation of an action plan to determine the scope and extent of the alleged fraud. Primary objectives of the action plan would be to:

- Determine the probable extent and duration of the fraud, quantify potential loss, identify who could possibly be involved, identify the nature and sources of evidence available, and determine how the evidence will be preserved during the course of the investigation
- Determine the organization's goals, objectives, and priorities for the investigation, including defending against reputation risk, determining any third-party liability, evaluating legal liabilities, and determining the probability of asset recovery including the insurance implications
- Determining the optimal depth and cost benefit of the investigation, including skills requirement, sources of specialist skills, probable duration, and likely outcomes
- Ensure legal compliance with all applicable legislation regarding the acquisition and custody of evidence, including the interviewing witnesses
- Ensure external notifications to all interested third parties as detailed earlier

- Ensure the objectivity of the investigation team is maintained throughout the course of the investigation until final disposition
- Ensure completion of the investigation in an appropriate time span to mitigate losses or potential reputation risk

Business documentation and transaction records regarding the functional area within which the fraud has allegedly been performed will be examined, and individuals associated with the area under review will be identified and interviewed. Data evidence will then be gathered to be subjected to forensic examination. The gathering of evidence may require a multidisciplinary approach in order to ensure the availability of the appropriate knowledge skills and disciplines required to acquire and make sense of the evidence. Where the skills are not available in-house, outside experts may be required. A skilled forensic investigator, like a skilled tracker, will identify signs and patterns within the evidence that would be invisible to the layperson. Use of outside experts may also prove beneficial because of their experience of interpreting evidence and presenting it orally as well as in court.

At all times throughout investigations, both the information obtained and its source should be held confidential unless disclosure is essential to the ultimate proving of the case. From inception to final disposition, information should be made available purely on a need-to-know basis. In addition to maintaining confidentiality, this guards against possible information corruption or loss during the process.

TOOLS AND TECHNIQUES

Depending on the nature of the fraudulent activity, a variety of investigative techniques may be required. Only once the appropriate technique has been identified can the correct investigative tool be selected to match that technique. If the use of professional investigators is warranted, care should be taken over the use of covert investigation techniques, as their legality can vary from country to country. If evidence is mishandled at the start of the investigation, it cannot be put right of a later stage and may jeopardize the whole investigation.

Documentary Analysis

It is critical that all documentary evidence relevant to the investigation be identified, obtained, and secured before tampering is possible. Internal documents pertinent to the investigation may be gathered from a variety of sources, including:

- Financial records
- Transaction records
- Personnel records
- Items of public record
- Customer and vendor records
- Media records
- Surveillance records
- Previous investigative reports

Documents may be examined for confirmation of the existence of fraudulent activities as well as proof that the document has not been altered from its original form, that the document is itself an original, or that it contains a valid signature of an appropriate authorizer.

The investigator may also be searching documents to correlate against data entered into computer systems or simply because they are the primary source of evidence sought in the course of a fraud examination.

In order to determine the authenticity of a specific document, document examination may be carried out, usually by a specialized forensic document examiner. This process may be able to create an evidentiary linkage between the suspect and the fraud. Handwriting evaluation may be able to determine whether a signature is genuine or forged and who the author of a particular piece of writing is.

Printed documents may similarly be linked to an individual printer or typewriter. Many of today's printers print a concealed, encoded serial number during the normal printing process that can be traced back to a specific printer.

Document examination may also reveal alterations or erasures and may even be able to recover the original text as it was prior to alteration. In addition to the text itself, the ink used can be analyzed. It may be possible to reveal alterations by identifying the brand of ink used, the production batch number, and even the time interval between the writing of the original message and the amendment. This process may identify alterations after the document was created order to commit forgery. The paper itself can also be examined for time of production or the inclusion of watermarks.

In general, documents may be examined for handwriting used as well as the sequence of entries. Alterations, obliterations, and erasures may be detected and deciphered. Printers, typewriters, and copiers can be identified;

the authenticity of reproduction copies can be established; and original documents can be identified. Inks may be compared and dated, and specific pens or pencils used for writing can be differentiated.

Paper can be authenticated and dated. Even documents that have been burned or faded may be reconstructed.

Data Analysis

Using the power of computers, the examiner can inspect large quantities of data from a variety of sources in the course of an investigation. Data may come from external sources as well as internal ones and may take the form of computerized records or printouts that can be scanned into digital form for analysis. Digital data for subsequent interrogation and data mining may include:

- Transaction logs
- Access control records
- E-mail records
- Mobile phone records
- Corporate phone records

Care must be taken to ensure that all documentary and digital data is legally gathered and securely maintained and that the chain of custody remains unbroken and fully documented.

Data analysis tools have become considerably more sophisticated over the last few years and can be used to scan databases for specific red flags or supplementary evidence to support fraud possibility suggested by red flags.

Most of the generalized audit software (GAS) available is capable of handling multiple functions in common use by auditors and examiners. Among the more common of these are:

- Record selection and filtering
- Verification of corporate policies
- Duplicate searches
- Gap searches
- Ratio analysis
- Correlation analysis
- Regression analysis
- Transaction tracing
- Benford analysis

Record Selection and Filtering

Using the data mining packages currently available, it is easy to filter large volumes of data to seek anomalies. To take a payroll with 20,000 records and search for any records where the net pay exceeds the gross pay is a single line instruction. In the same way, to look at 200,000 inventory records seeking those items recorded within negative stock on hand is also one line instruction.

Verification of Corporate Policies

Using the same techniques used for record selection and filtering, corporate policies such as pricing policies, discount policies, employee loan policies, and the like can be used as the filtering criteria. Large quantities of data can be examined looking for records or transactions where the corporate policies have not been applied.

Duplicate Searches

One of the key control elements in data processing is the assurance that each transaction is processed once and once only. Anomalous duplicates in sequenced numbers may indicate erroneous double processing of transactions or fraudulent double processing. In either event, the duplicate requires a follow-up to determine the cause.

Gap Searches

Where business documents, such as purchase orders, invoices, or checks, run in a prenumbered sequence, gaps may indicate an abuse of a known structure in the numbering sequences or missing documents that may indicate the presence of a cover-up of fraudulent transactions. Again, this type of document omission may indicate errors or even a pattern of errors, or the documents may be missing intentionally as part of the cover-up of a fraud.

Ratio Analysis

Ratio analysis is commonly used in examination of financial figures to determine whether movements over time are as expected or not. *Horizontal ratio analysis* is used to observe trends in the values of an individual item on the financial statements over time. Vertical ratio analysis is used to analyze the relationship among multiple items in the financial accounts by expressing all individual line items as a percentage of the total. Again, movements in these ratios over a period of time can indicate where the value of one line item is moving at a disproportionate rate to the others. This movement could be caused by normal movements in a given line item or by fraudulent manipulation.

Correlation Analysis

Correlation analysis permits the examiner to evaluate the relationships among individual pieces of data to detect anomalies. For example, if sales increased by 20 percent, there should be an increase in cost of sales. While this will not being necessarily 20 percent, there should be some measurable and consistent relationship between the two values. The linear association is measured by the correlation coefficient, which will vary between −1 and +1. A −1 indicates a perfect negative relationship such that if one item is sold, quantity on hand will decrease by one. A +1 indicates a perfect positive relationship, which can be found if the value of sales and cost of sales both increased by the same percentage.

Correlation analysis is used in fraud analysis where a relationship is expected to occur (positive or negative) in order to determine whether the relationship appears to be in proportion as expected.

Regression Analysis

Regression analysis is also used to determine the relationship among data. In this case, it is used to predict the expected shift in one variable (the dependent variable) based on movements within one or more independent variables. For example, if cost of materials increases in a known way and cost of labor increases in a known way, overall costs should move in a predictable way. If this movement is not in line with predicted value, an anomaly exists that could be due to some form of fraudulent activity.

Transaction Tracing

Data mining software can be used to trace transactions as the progress through information technology systems. The impact of a given transaction on a file can be simulated by using the software to create a *parallel simulation* in which the live data are processed through the examiner's software to simulate calculations in live systems. The results of the simulation may then be compared to the live system to determine the accuracy and integrity of calculations within the normal processing of the system.

Benford Analysis

Benford's law states that the first digit in many types of data sets is distributed in a nonuniform way. For nonstatisticians, this may sound like gobbledygook. What it means in practice is that information extracted from a computer system can be analyzed to find abnormalities within the data by comparing the pattern of occurrence of data against predetermined frequencies.

In any given set of numbers, the number 1 will appear as the first digit about 30 percent of the time. The number 2 will appear about 18 percent of the time all the way down to the number 9, which appears in the first position only approximately 5 percent of the time.

Where Benford analysis comes into its own is the analysis of high volumes of data looking for fraudulent transactions. Individual fraudulent payments may appear genuine, but, unless fraudsters have designed their data to comply with Benford's law, the frequency distribution will not follow Benford's curve, making possible fraudulent manipulation of data easy to spot.

Where this analysis is used in fraud investigation, care should be taken to ensure that the data are appropriate for such analysis. Data sets need to be natural, such as amounts, rather than predetermined, such as identity numbers or account numbers. The results also will be inaccurate if this analysis is used on data specifically selected to fit within a range.

Prior to its inclusion in audit software packages, Benford's law was normally tested using nonparametric tests, such as the Komogorov-Smirnov test or the chi squared test for larger populations.

Interviewing

For an effective investigation, interviewing is a critical communications process. Often the interviewer is in a position of receiving critical information in an interview and therefore has a responsibility to listen carefully. This is not as easy as it sounds. When dealing with a series of interviews, it is difficult to maintain focus.

Listening, strange as it sounds, is an active function and an acquired skill. Most of us have a lifetime of bad habits to overcome. Poor listening habits include losing concentration by becoming impatient with speakers or simply allowing minor annoyances to distort the message. This usually results in the questioner interrupting the speaker to make the questioner's own point instead of listening as a good receiver should. Boredom can lead to scanning what is being said. Here the interviewer basically stops listening unless a key word is heard that is of interest. Distraction may also come in the form of personal priorities, prejudgment of anticipated information, or even dictation taking (i.e., writing down every word heard, without trying to understand what is being said).

It is difficult to develop good listening habits and, in particular, to maintain interest in an otherwise boring information transfer. Nevertheless, it is possible to learn to encourage the person you are speaking to with nonverbal support (nods of the head, paralinguistics, etc.). In addition to giving nonverbal support, you can also be alert to nonverbal behavior, such as body language, gestures, and so on. Summarizing and recapping what has just been said gives the speaker the message that you are listening and understand. It is important to learn to be sensitive to the clues in the message the speaker is broadcasting and to be noncritical when evaluating the information you are listening to.

No suspects or co-conspirators should be interviewed or confronted until the organization has carried out preliminary assessments and legal advice has been taken regarding subsequent interviews and actions to be taken. Interviews would normally start as remotely from the suspects as possible in terms of operations or business function. This is partly to prevent the conducting of unprofessional interviews before background information has been obtained, evaluated, and fully assimilated. A fraud interview can too easily turn into an unprofessional interrogation with interviews even being conducted illegally. Fraud interviews need to be structured and planned in advance as well as cleared through the organization's legal services in order to ensure that the evidence will be forensically acceptable. Structuring the interview ensures that critical information is not forgotten because the interviewer's attention is diverted by information already provided.

Potential witnesses should be questioned like any other interview where an interviewer is attempting to elicit facts.

The first phase of any interview is the introduction. During this phase, the interviewer should try to relax the interviewee by establishing a rapport and removing, as far as possible, any fears that the interviewee may have simply because it is known or suspected that this interview is part of a fraud investigation.

Once the interview is actually under way, the investigator should set the tone. During this phase, the interviewer may do most of the talking. The background, goals, and objectives of the investigation and interview need to be explained; however, this phase should not dominate the interview.

Questioning may be structured or unstructured. A structured interview may adopt the checklist approach, in which the interview follows the structure of what happens next. An alternative to sequential checklists is the less structured objective-based approach where questions are sequenced by business or control objectives. This method can keep the interview focused on the key issues from the fraud investigator's perspective but can be disjointed and fail to ensure that all stages of a process have been covered.

Often in everyday conversation we anticipate the answer to a question and start to formulate the next question before the first one is fully answered. In an extreme case, this approach can make it obvious to the interviewee that you are not listening. You must learn to listen, evaluate, and perhaps modify your approach based on the answers given. Paraphrasing or summarizing can leave the interviewee with the impression that you have listened and understood. General rules for asking questions include:

- Let the interviewee do the talking and keep the questions short.
- Avoid multiple-answer questions. If you offer a choice of A or B for the answer, you may get the truth, you may get a lie, you may get what the interviewer thinks you want to hear, or you may get a best guess based on the alternatives given.
- Avoid leading questions where the interviewer implies the correct answer within the question.
- Where possible, avoid closed questions. Yes/no questions are conversation stoppers. Open-ended questions, such as "Tell me how orders are placed" or "How do you know?" are more likely to elicit descriptions of control weaknesses that could have facilitated the fraud.
- Encourage the interviewee to continue talking using your own body language, such as nods, smiles, and so forth.
- Listen to the interviewee and adapt your approach based on what you are being told. Asking a question and ignoring the answer is a complete turn-off for interviewees who actually want to help you. Do not use your interview plan as a checklist simply to be ticked off as you go.
- Be careful with note taking and recording interviews, as this can cause even a willing interviewee to go silent. Take notes only of what you must (new knowledge, unexpected responses, and the like) during the course of the interview but record all salient points immediately afterward. For evidence to be produced in court, the timing of when notes were taken can be critical with less reliance placed on notes made after a significant passage of time.

In preparing for an interview, the investigator must clarify in his or her own mind the aims and objectives of the interview. The interview may be taking place for you to gain knowledge about a process or specific control event or to confirm facts.

The order in which to interview people depends on the objectives of the investigation and where the previously gathered evidence places the interviewee in the chain of events.

Neutral Third-Party Witnesses

Enquiries at this stage include discussions with suppliers, customers, and other third parties where there is no known vested interest. Whenever possible, the fact that a forensic investigation is in progress should not be made public knowledge. Even the knowledge that such an investigation is taking place could have a detrimental impact on the corporate reputation and give involved parties the opportunity to hide or destroy evidence. At this stage, questions are primarily focused on fact elucidation with no attempt to prove or disprove any allegations made.

Corroborative Witnesses

Once specific facts have been alleged by the neutral third-party witnesses, corroborating evidence from other independent witnesses may be sought. At this point, it is important not to directly confront the accused co-conspirators. The intent is simply to achieve independent corroboration of information received from neutral parties. The results of these interviews may affect the focus of subsequent interviews as well as further documentary evidence to be gathered and analyzed before additional interviewing.

Co-conspirators

Once the evidence gathered to date can clearly identify the probable fraudster and potential co-conspirators, a series of directed questions can be developed to be put to putative co-conspirators in order to determine the extent of the fraud, number of third parties involved, as well as who the mastermind and executors of the fraudulent activities were. Any sources of direct evidence can also be sought at this time for further analysis.

Fraudsters

Only once all other parties have been interviewed should the investigation phase move toward direct interviewing of the supposed fraudster. Bearing in mind the onus of proof, the intent of the questioning is to determine whether this person indeed is the perpetrator, who else may have been involved, how the fraud was executed, the duration of the fraud, where the assets are now, and how they can be recovered. It is highly unlikely that any interview will result in explicit admission of guilt, particularly from experienced fraudsters. Because they know that consistent outright denial of any knowledge of any intentional fraud is the hardest to disprove, their most likely response is repeated flat denials.

Lies, Lies, Lies

At all stages of interviewing, the person being interviewed may choose to lie. Lies can take several forms, and clues may be detected depending on the nature of the lie:

- *Lying by omission* is the most common form of deception. The interviewee does not actually lie but evades answering by omitting the information that he or she wants to conceal. If the omission is detected, the interviewee can always claim that he or she forgot or did not consider the matter important enough to mention. Since the person is not directly lying, the personal stress is limited.
- *Denial* of having participated in the fraud or having any knowledge of it is another common form of lying. While it avoids the stress of giving a false answer, it creates a mental conflict known as dissonance, as the liar attempts to balance the prohibitions against lying learned as part of his or her upbringing and the need to protect him- or herself from the consequences of being caught.
- *Making up a story* is the most difficult type of lie to attempt and maintain. The liar will require a good memory to remember what has already been said and must be a quick thinker to maintain consistency in the lie. Such fabrication generally is uncovered because of inconsistencies in the details of the lie or the sequence of events claimed. The starting point of the fabrication and the end point are normally genuine events and time periods. It is what happened in between and when that is fabricated and where the specific details can be forgotten.
- *Lying by minimization* downplays negative aspects of the interviewee's behavior or performance. Careful questioning and healthy skepticism on the part of the investigator normally can uncover the truth.
- *Exaggeration* may also be used as a lie and is frequently used when a suspect exaggerates the amount of work conducted or the degree of checking carried out. Once again, careful questioning may reveal the truth.

At certain critical points of an investigation, a polygraph (see next section) may be used during interviews in areas where this is a legal technique. In the absence of a polygraph, investigators observe the interviewee's behavior patterns to identify areas of possible concern.

Delays in responding to questions involving the simple recollection of facts may alert investigators to a possible attempt at deception. The liar has to consider his or her version of the facts to ensure consistency with what has already been said.

The use of qualifiers in answering questions also can indicate lying. Suspects can use expressions such as "as far as I can remember," "to the best of my knowledge," and "probably" to conceal deception. The terms may signify omissions and areas that interviewees wish to avoid.

Interviewees who are telling the truth normally answer questions promptly if they are simply recalling a memory. Care should be taken, however, to distinguish between the delay before a lie and the delay of a person taking sufficient time to ensure the question is answered accurately. Questions that require an answer based on the individual's judgment normally involve some form of delay. Delay over yes-or-no questions can indicate the weighing of the pros and cons of replying with a particular answer.

USE OF THE POLYGRAPH

A polygraph is a measuring device that makes a permanent recording of various physiological changes taking place within the subject's body as a result of psychological stimuli. The stimulus is brought about by maintaining a certain environmental and emotional climate during the polygraph examination and asking questions that have been structured and phrased in specific ways. The questions asked during the examination are developed beforehand with the subject; there are no surprise questions that can cause a false reading.

Two basic types of polygraph instruments are in current use: analog and computerized polygraphs. Both are state-of-the-art technology, which, if used by a professional polygraph examiner in a satisfactory environment, can very accurately distinguish between truth and deception.

During a preexamination interview, the examiner gathers details on both the case and the person to be tested. The examiner must establish a rapport with the examinee and allay his or her fears, suspicion, and general anxiety. The examinee then usually is questioned in a nonaccusatory interview about knowledge regarding the alleged incident, and the test questions are developed. The test questions are discussed with the examinee in advance. At no stage during the test would any surprise questions be put to the examinee. This technique is known as the Comparative Question Test. An alternative testing method is known as the Guilty Knowledge Test or Concealed Information Test. The tester questions the subject on the knowledge of the crime in part using information that could have been known only by the guilty party. The questions used are multiple choice, and subjects are evaluated based on how they react to the correct answer.

During the examination itself, pneumographs, galvanic skin response, and cardiograph sensors are attached to the examinee. The examinee is then asked each of the test questions at least twice, and the physiological responses are recorded.

The polygraph is not a lie detector. It is an instrument that uses the autonomic nervous system (i.e., that part of the nervous system that we cannot voluntarily control). There are two branches to the autonomic nervous system; one has to do with growth and development and the other is an emergency system. The emergency system becomes dominant only when there is some threat and the individual becomes fearful.

The polygraph test measures such a response. If the truth is told, the body functions at its normal level. If examinee is asked a question in response to which he or she intends to lie, he or she becomes afraid of being caught in that lie, and the body automatically shifts into the emergency system. All of the physiological changes will be recorded on the polygraph chart.

After the test, the examinee is questioned about the responses to the relevant questions, if any. A numerical scoring system is employed to analyze the examinee's polygraph charts to determine if there are any significant physiological responses to the relevant questions.

Arguments continue over the validity of polygraph tests. Many hundreds of test studies have been conducted which suggest that when an established testing procedure is used by a properly trained examiner, the accuracy of the decision made by polygraph examiners can be between 90 and 95 percent for specific issue investigations. Studies also indicate that although it may be possible for someone lying to be shown as truthful, it is highly unlikely that a person telling the truth will be evaluated as lying. In fraud investigations, the polygraph can be a useful aid but is not without its limitations. It cannot replace conventional investigation, since its focused approach cannot be used to examine more than one specific issue at any one time.

DOCUMENTING THE INVESTIGATIVE PROCESS

At all points throughout the investigative process, the law must be followed scrupulously. All activities, sources of information, questions and responses, data interrogation, interviews, denials, counterallegations, and admissions must be fully documented together with the names and contact details of other witnesses present during questioning or observation.

EVIDENCE ANALYSIS

Materiality, the traditional auditors' watchword, may be irrelevant since even a small error showing up, where an error should not exist, can be indicative of fraudulent intent. It is unfortunately true that in today's world, a low level of dishonesty, poor ethical standards, and theft are not only tolerated but expected in many organizations. When conducting analysis of evidence during an investigation, any level of dishonesty or unethical behavior becomes a smoking gun in the search for fraud. In the course of one of my first fraud investigations, I uncovered evidence that a new employee at a senior executive level had fraudulently increased his salary from $220,000 to $240,000 per annum. The loss to the company was a mere $20,000. The loss to the executive was $220,000 per annum, his reputation, his freedom, and his family. The risk to the company was that the executive controlled a budget of over $280 million per annum and an example was set to all employees.

Analysis of evidence gathered during a fraud investigation seeks unusual patterns of transactions or events, lifestyles, or behavior. Any anomaly, however small, can point to a fundamental dishonesty that, left unchecked, can escalate the organization's fraud risk profile to unacceptable levels.

INVESTIGATIVE ERRORS

Professional fraud investigations take time and can be expensive. Suspected fraudsters can use this fact to their own advantage by delaying the process with a series of legal maneuvers aimed at increasing the cost to the organization and wearing down management willingness to participate further. The process may further benefit fraudsters if they can wear down management far enough to pay the fraudsters cash settlements just to go away and keep their mouths shut. In some cases, this occurs because management is fearful of the effect of public disclosure on the organization's reputation. This fear can become a self-fulfilling prophecy if not appropriately handled to completion. In addition to the monetary losses, avoidance sends the wrong message to employees, customers, vendors, investors, and the general public.

It is known that all organizations may suffer from fraud from time to time. A clear and public prosecution of the individuals involved sends an incontestable message that the organization has integrity and will not accept illegal or improper activities conducted behind closed doors. When properly handled, this can result in positive coverage and an enhanced corporate reputation as well as an internal morale boost for employees who did not participate and who see that the guilty did not get away with anything.

Perhaps the most fundamental investigative error is failing to maintain an adequate chain of custody of evidence gathered. A simple act of permitting an investigation file to rest unattended in an unlocked office can be sufficient to destroy the integrity of everything in the file as far as evidential support in a court of law is concerned. Forensic auditors and investigators must maintain the chain of custody of any evidence that comes into their possession. Any break in the chain of custody may result in the item or document being inadmissible at trial. Evidence must be securely stored at all times with access controlled by an evidence custodian.

Securing the location can be as simple as keeping a door locked; however, from time to time, evidence must be transferred from the custody of one person to another, and the transfer must be documented. Any movement of evidence, including sending it to a crime laboratory, document examiner, or law enforcement, must be accounted for as well. The simplest way to do this is to create an evidence trail within the evidence register that lists each item by number and description. Any transfer of evidence is then noted in the evidence register by the person designated as the evidence custodian. In this way the chain of custody can be maintained and documented.

Poor documentation of the investigation plan, progress, activities, evidence gathered, time frames, and personnel involved in conducting the investigation can all invalidate the evidence gathered in the event of a prosecution.

Failure to follow legal procedures in the acquisition of evidence, illegal searches, and failure to treat individuals according to the mandates of labor legislation can result in the inadmissibility of evidence in court and can even lead to the defrauded organization being held legally liable in both criminal and civil actions.

AFTER THE EVENT

Once a fraud investigation has been completed and adequate proof of fraud or other malfeasance has been gathered, the decision has to be made regarding the actions to be taken. For internal fraud, the organization may opt to go with disciplinary action where the offense is seen as minor and the employee has a previous long record in good standing. In such cases, the burden of proof is normally on the balance of the evidence. The same level of proof is normally required in civil proceedings intended to recover assets lost.

Should the case become a criminal action, the burden of proof shifts to beyond a reasonable doubt, which requires a greater level of evidentiary support for any assertions.

Many organizations refused to prosecute on the basis that the cost of prosecution in terms of impact on the company's reputation as well as the direct financial cost exceed the amount of the fraud itself or the amount liable to be recovered.

In some cases, organizations may fear that a failed prosecution may give carte blanche to other would-be fraudsters to conduct similar frauds due to the publicity given the weaknesses within the internal controls.

Whether prosecution takes place or not, the failure or lack of internal controls has to be remedied to prevent repetition of the fraud. Doing this must be a management priority not only in the area where the fraud occurred, but also in other areas within the organization where similar control structures are relied on. Internal and external auditors should also be on heightened alert for evidence indicating similar frauds in other operational areas during the course of subsequent audits.

ESTABLISHING AN INVESTIGATIONS FUNCTION

Where patterns of fraud have occurred within an organization, it is not uncommon for the company to seek to establish its own forensic investigations function. The skills requirement in such a function is a combination of audit, information technology, and criminal investigation skills. The overall mission would be to provide objective and fair investigation of significant irregular incidents within an organization. In addition, the function would provide advisory and consulting services, including security scenario planning. Any irregular conduct would first be reported to this forensic investigations department, while allegations of criminal nature would be referred to law enforcement without delay.

Investigation departments normally assemble and research irregular conduct and practices in order to determine their unlawfulness as well as identify causes and vulnerabilities.

The scope of this department work normally includes investigations of alleged or suspected fraud, bribery, corruption, and other irregular activities of a sensitive or serious nature. From time to time, the function may be tasked with conducting special investigations and maintaining adequate records to facilitate the valuation and analysis of ongoing threats to the organization as a result of irregular activities.

TRACING AND RECOVERING ASSETS

While it can be personally satisfying to see fraudsters jailed for their offenses, it is even more satisfying from a corporate perspective to be able to recover the assets of which it has been defrauded. In today's world, with high-speed movement of funds internationally, retrieving assets can involve a variety of jurisdictions and legislation. Tracing the whereabouts of assets is only part of the solution. Perhaps the more critical component is the execution of effective recovery programs.

Following the preinvestigative phase of information gathering and the investigative phase itself comes the judicial phase in which the accused fraudster may be acquitted or convicted. If convicted, a decision is then made on asset recovery or confiscation. Unfortunately, in many fraud cases, this is where the activity ends. Despite being awarded damages or return of assets by the court, few of the assets ever end up back in the hands of the original owner. One major reason is the extended time interval between the offense taking place in the awarding of a judgment. The delay facilitates the fraudster's disposal of the assets by dissipation, transferring to other individuals, or removal offshore. Different jurisdictions handle the problem differently.

In the United States, criminal forfeiture statutes provide two potential methods for preserving assets subject to forfeiture pending the conclusion of the criminal trial:

1. The government may seize the property with a criminal seizure warrant.
2. The government may ask the court to restrain the property pursuant to a pretrial restraining order.

In both cases, the intent is to ensure that the property is not dissipated, alienated, or removed from the jurisdiction of the court prior to the time when the court may order the forfeiture of the property as part of the defendant's sentence. These statutes are under constant dispute in federal, state, and local courts.

In South Africa, the Asset Forfeiture Unit established in 1999 may seize assets that it believes were derived from criminal activities under the authority of a court order. The main objective of asset forfeiture is to take the profit out of crime by depriving the criminal of the benefits of the crime as well as a seizure of any property or assets used to commit the crime.

Four court orders can be sought: restraint (restraining the criminal from transferring or disposing of the asset) and confiscation (seizure of the asset by the state) orders as well as preservation and forfeiture orders. The first two orders, restraint and confiscation, require there to have been a successful prosecution and a guilty verdict. Preservation and forfeiture orders do not, however, depend on a prosecution. Some evidence of criminal activity linking the asset to the proceeds of a crime or as being instrumental in the committing of a crime is required for the orders to be granted. Such orders target specific high-value items, such as the house, car, or other property of the accused. This is known as an action *in rem* (see Glossary) (i.e., directly against a property not against the person). Should the case be successfully prosecuted, restraint and confiscation orders would follow. Should the prosecution be unsuccessful, the assets may be returned to the previously accused or may not if the acquittal is on a technicality. Successful seizures have included those sought by overseas jurisdictions, such as the U.S. Department of Homeland Security, since the act also applies to crimes committed elsewhere.

In the United Kingdom, a freezing order may be issued by a court to prevent the disposal of an asset, removal of an asset from the jurisdiction of the court, or any other dealings in the assets prior to final judgment being issued. If some of the assets are held overseas, a worldwide freezing order may be issued to avoid the necessity of starting multiple cases in multiple jurisdictions.

Whether assets are seized pretrial or not, the investigation itself is typically used to prove the case in court by means of a historical perspective describing what was done, how it was done, and who did it. It is then up to the court to decide if the case has been proved and award repayment or damages. Very rarely is there any focus post trial on what needs to happen in order to recover the assets in terms of subsequent seizure or ownership transfer. Even seeking a restraining order preventing further disposition of the allegedly stolen assets normally has jurisdiction on in the area in which it was granted. Funds or assets that have left the jurisdiction will not be covered by the restraining order.

The final phase is the disposal phase in which the asset is seized and either returned to its original owner or disposed of by the state as required by law. Asset confiscation undergoes a three-part process:

1. Identifying
2. Trace
3. Seize or freeze

Identifying the assets may be dependent on the nature of the assets stolen and the degree of transformation that has taken place. In the case of the fraudulent theft of money, the number of movements in the transaction trail, combining of assets, splitting of assets, and changing the currency of the assets can all seek to confuse the identification and tracing of origin back to the original assets stolen.

Under normal circumstances, fraud investigators, other than the legal authorities, have no authority to independently access:

▪ Credit information
▪ Bank accounts
▪ Investment accounts

Tracing movements of financial assets may require court orders or subpoenas to obtain information from closed sources. There is, however, an alternative that can be effective in tracing assets via publicly available sources. *Open source intelligence* is a form of information gathering and analysis involving the acquisition of information from publicly available sources and its analysis to trace asset movements and ownership. Use of the Internet as an information source can be highly effective, although care should be taken since much of the information available on the Internet can be erroneous, misleading, or prejudicial.

Within the United States, information can generally be collected from:

▪ Public records offices (liens and legal judgments)
▪ State secretaries of state (corporate filings)
▪ Securities and Exchange Commission (filings)
▪ FINRA (Financial Industry Regulatory Authority) and other regulators
▪ PACER (Public Access to Court Electronic Records)

- Certain government databases
- Third-party (chargeable) databases
- Universal Commercial Code (UCC) department judgments (enacted by individual states)
- Social networks

Information may be gained both on individuals and at an aggregate level. Information available on individuals, although publicly available, may still involve a breach of privacy if not properly secured by the investigator and may thus be inadmissible in court. Nevertheless, information gathering remains a powerful tool in gathering basic information on individuals and their assets. Information can be gathered on:

- Ownership of companies, properties, and other assets
- Secured and unsecured debt
- Current and previous bankruptcy status
- Use of assets for collateral
- Codebtors
- Divorce status
- Probate filings
- Trademarks and patents assigned (intangible assets that may be hidden)
- Aircraft, vehicles, and vessels owned
- Lifestyle, hobbies, employment history available from social networks

Information at the aggregate level may or may not be reliable, depending on how it has been gathered and stored. The investigator may have no way of determining how much reliance can be placed on it. Information searching goes substantially beyond the simple use of search engines and is generally considered a specialist area for investigation.

Information can also be retrieved from noncomputerized sources by conventional methods, such as surveillance, questioning business associates, Dumpster diving, and other legal information-gathering techniques.

Asset tracing and recovery normally require a documented asset movement transaction trail to prove that the seizure sought is against assets derived from the original fraud. This tracing could involve recovering property being held by a previous business partner or funds that have been moved offshore to a "secure" tax haven. In such cases, the old fraud maxim of "follow the money" becomes significantly problematic.

Overseas Asset Movements

Anti–money-laundering activities have grown to the extent that a joint initiative was formed between the United Nations Office on Drugs and Crime and the World Bank. The StAR (Stolen Assets Recovery) initiative was launched in 2007 to foster cooperation between the public and private sectors as well as between developing and developed countries with the objective of ensuring that stolen assets be returned to their rightful owners. Its primary emphasis is on the theft of public assets in areas with high levels of corruption and low levels of accountability and transparency. Within these environments, the primary mechanisms for moving assets derived illegally offshore include the use of offshore trusts, shell companies established in jurisdictions that maintain bank secrecy with deposits in the form of cash, wire transfers, or bearer instruments. This confusion of the audit trail can be compounded where bankers, lawyers, accountants, and other professionals fail in their due diligence obligations.

Such movements are facilitated by weak national monitoring frameworks and inadequacies in international legal frameworks. In such environments, asset recovery becomes complicated by the need to complete investigations in multiple jurisdictions and in areas where there are significant legal differences between civil law countries and those based on common law. Even when assets are traced and identifiable in the new location, seizure may be complicated by the international nature of the original crime.

Where it is believed that the proceeds of a fraud or corruption within the organization may have moved offshore, specialized forensic tracing and recovery firms are normally called on to assist.

 NOTES

1. KPMG, Analysis of Global Patterns of Fraud, "Who Is the Typical Fraudster," www.kpmg.com/US/en/IssuesAndInsights/ArticlesPublications/Pages/typical-fraudster.aspx.
2. Donald R. Cressey, *Other People's Money: A Study in the Social Psychology of Embezzlement* (Montclair, NJ: Patterson Smith, 1973), p 30.
3. PMI Mortgage Insurance Company, *Fraud Schemes Red Flag Checklist*, 2009, www.pmi-us.com/media/pdf/resourcecenter/toolkits/FraudSchemes Checklist.pdf.
4. Rebecca S. Busch, *Healthcare Fraud: Auditing and Detection Guide* (Hoboken, NJ: John Wiley & Sons, 2007).

Computer Fraud and Countermeasures

In the old days, people robbed stagecoaches and knocked off armored trucks. Now they're knocking off servers.

—Richard Power, Computer Security Expert and Author

After studying this chapter, the reader should be able to:

- Identify areas of vulnerability to fraudulent use of information systems and processing of fraudulent transactions.
- Design and implement appropriate measures to defend the digital assets of the organization.

Advances in the use of computers in our daily lives has put confidential information about all of us personally and about our organizations and our families in the public domain with easy access from anywhere in the world. As a result, we all are open to the potential for fraud on a massive scale.

Even five years ago, much of this information remained comparatively hidden, and computer software to retrieve such information has become a major threat. Such *malwear* (malicious software) and *spyware* (unauthorized software gathering personal or confidential information on a computer or its users) has had to become more sophisticated over the years because much of the information that used to be gathered surreptitiously is now publicly available.

Operational management bears primary responsibility for the prevention and detection of all frauds, including information technology (IT) frauds. Nevertheless, IT has a major role to play in assisting management in establishing a control environment in which fraud is unlikely to occur or, where it does occur, it will be quickly detected.

Because of the threats of unauthorized online access to mobile information, it is easy to forget that most computer fraud is not carried out by outsiders but by authorized insiders and even executive management. We address the threats in this area from the inside out, starting with the fraud risks and countermeasures at the computing core and working outward to threats from afar, including mobile computing and the cloud.

To prevent IT fraud, it is necessary to understand how such frauds can be carried out. To implement effective controls, it is necessary to understand the architecture surrounding computer systems.

In general terms, information processing is affected using an architecture similar to the one shown in Exhibit 10.1. At the heart of the computer, and the target of most fraudulent activities, is the raw data of the organization. If access to this information is obtained (legitimately or by stealth), the organization is immediately exposed to potential fraud. Legitimate users can process unauthorized transactions, and legitimate technical users may be able to manipulate the raw data directly without the need to process transactions by direct manipulation of the data contained in database. In order to ensure that only legitimate users can access the data, controls are implemented at the mainframe level to keep unauthorized outsiders out and insiders where they are supposed to be. Within the mainframe, the organization's application systems carry out the business functions as programmed, and built into them are the business controls such as segregation of duties, reconciliations, user authentication, and the array of antifraud controls that organizations have built up over the years. These controls will be dependent on the nature of the business and the types of fraud exposure faced. All of these application programs run under the control of the computer's operating system and other components of system software handling communications, access control, data manipulation, and the like on behalf of the operating system. Within each of these

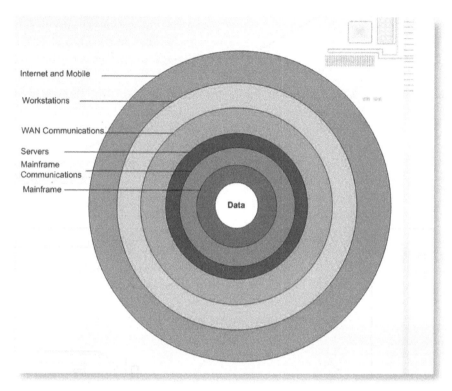

Internet and Mobile
Workstations
WAN Communications
Servers
Mainframe Communications
Mainframe
Data

EXHIBIT 10.1 IT Architecture

components, control opportunities exist that will be implemented or not at the discretion and under the control of the organization's IT function.

In the early days of computers, physical security controls were as far as technical controls needed to go. Since transactions had to be entered directly into mainframes through punch cards and paper tapes, integrity and antifraud controls rested within the user arena.

In today's environment, organizations typically operate in an online, real-time environment in which transactions are entered remotely and gain access to the data through a variety of intermediate steps. The next ring out from the mainframe itself is therefore mainframe communications, which permit intermediate processors and various types of servers to talk to the application systems running on the mainframe under the control of the mainframe operating system. Again, control opportunities exist at this level, which the IT function may select and implement. Many of these control opportunities have to do with system performance and availability rather than antifraud. The more controls that are introduced, the more operational overhead is placed on the running computer system and the more computing power is required to continue to operate an acceptable levels.

Servers themselves are computers that store information and run application systems. They also are potential entry points through which frauds can be introduced or even perpetrated, depending on the nature of the server.

From the servers, communication extends through wide area networks (WANs) out into the user environment to place computing power where it needs to be, in the hands of the end user.

Users can access the communications from workstations that are within the organization's physical environment and therefore directly under its physical control. Alternatively, they may connect via remote terminals where the organization has no direct physical control over who is sitting at the terminal. By connecting the WANs to external networks such as the Internet, access can potentially be achieved by anyone. With the advent of mobile computing, we have to add to from anything.

Next we look at each of these in turn to identify fraud potentials, the nature of controls in each environment, and the appropriateness of their use in fraud prevention and detection.

MAINFRAME ARCHITECTURES

Not all organizations make use of mainframes. Many use super mini-computers or even powerful servers instead. All computers continue to maintain similar architectures although the technical components may be different. In each case, the control objectives in terms of fraud prevention remain the same, although the controls implemented may be different.

As can be seen from Exhibit 10.2, multiple users use a computer system for multiple purposes.

In all cases, their communications must pass through the operating system to reach the network management system, which recognizes terminals, lines, and communication protocols. Once the communication has passed through the network management system, it will be passed on to whichever transaction processing monitor, editor, or tool is appropriate for that particular class of user. At this layer in the architecture, user ids and rights of access are checked. Where appropriate, conventional users are passed on to the application system to handle their transactions.

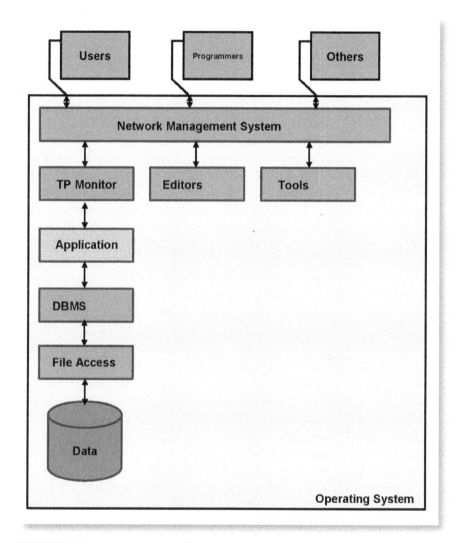

EXHIBIT 10.2 User Access Paths

Other users, such as programmers, network analysts, and systems engineers, are not passed to the application systems since they are not processing transactions. They utilize whichever tools they are authorized to use to fulfill the appropriate functions.

Conventional users have transactions passed on to the appropriate database management system and from there through a given file access system into the data themselves.

At every stage of processing, controls exist to ensure only recognized and authorized individuals may execute tasks to authorized parts of the system. Rights and access to data may be controlled by a user or by groups of users, including the right to access information and the authority to execute specific transactions on that data.

These controls exist in all modern operating systems, although they may or may not be used, at the discretion of the particular organization. In many cases, companies still operate a "go where you like, do what you want" architecture. This approach is not always intentional and may happen because the staff members responsible for implementing controls have neither the knowledge nor the ability to select which controls are appropriate in which area to achieve which objectives.

Many unauthorized accesses can be blamed on lack of training and lack of understanding of the fraud risk, should the control architecture not be robust. Even where access is well controlled with only authorized users able to process appropriate transactions, there is nothing within this architecture to prevent an authorized user from processing a transaction to their own benefit or the benefit of a third party. Thus, the controls within this environment can be used to enforce the controls at the *business level* to achieve the *business control objectives*. Where the controls are poorly designed or nonexistent within the business function, the internal controls within the computer system merely mimic the ineffectiveness of the *overall control structures* within the business.

In addition to straightforward transaction processing, the other authorized users such as programmers, network controllers, and systems engineers are not following the conventional route to data because they are not processing normal transactions. Instead, they may be writing programs, controlling networks, or modifying the operating environment itself. They are in a powerful position because of additional authorities they have been granted and the power of the tools they use. Potentially they can bypass the business antifraud controls programmed into the application systems and move directly to manipulation of data on the disk itself. In these cases, a higher level of technical control is required within the operating environment to limit the ability of these individuals to manipulate live data and to monitor all other activities they carry out.

This level is a very technical area in which to apply internal controls, but it is a critical one. All other antifraud controls within the IT environment rest on this foundation. If their integrity can in any way be compromised at this level, the whole computer environment is open to penetration. At this level, organizations typically call in specialists to examine the adequacy and effectiveness of the control environment to ensure that the rest of the controls on which the whole antifraud architecture depends is reliable on an ongoing basis.

MAINFRAME COMMUNICATIONS

Communications into and out of the mainframe operating environment can also serve as control points in which antifraud measures can be strengthened or weakened or even bypassed. At this control point, the organization is seeking to ensure that all communications are coming in from a known source and being returned to a known source and that the communications maintain their confidentiality and integrity. Encryption of information moving through networks is an essential weapon in the antifraud armory. When encryption is combined with advanced authentication techniques, the integrity and authenticity of messages can be established. A number of encryption techniques can be used at various points in computer processing. These techniques include symmetrical key cryptography, asymmetrical (public key) cryptography, and digital signatures.

Symmetrical key cryptography utilizes an algorithm to scramble information and render it unintelligible to any party who does not possess the key required to decrypt it and return it to understandable condition. The Data Encryption Standard (DES) was developed in the 1960s and is perhaps one of the best-known symmetrical key encryption techniques. Very few organizations use DES in its original form, but variations such as NewDES and 3DES continue to be popular.

Asymmetrical (public key) cryptography operates with two separate but related keys. One key is used for encrypting a message with a second key used to decrypt the message. The process can also be reversed with a second key being used to encrypt and the first key to decrypt. The asymmetry means that neither of the keys can encrypt and decrypt the same message. One key of the pair is normally designated the *public key* (disclosed to other computers or servers that are sending messages); the other is kept secret as a *private key* retained solely at the receiver's end. If messages are intercepted by a fraudster, they cannot be decrypted and understood without the fraudster's possession of the private key. Nor can the message be amended in an undetected manner. Any attempt to change the encrypted message will result in a failure when the legitimate receiver attempts to decrypt the message. In this way assurance can be gained that the message was not tampered with and that confidentiality has been maintained since only the authorized computer is in possession of the private key to decrypt a message. The degree of effectiveness of such communication encryption depends on the strength of the algorithm used and on the sizes of the keys. As we see when we look at encryption on the Internet, not all algorithms are created equal.

Encryption, itself, does not mean that a message which has a fraudulent content will necessarily be detected at this point. If the message originated from an authorized source and was correctly encrypted, it will be decrypted and acted on as if it were a genuine message from an authorized source.

Public key cryptography is also the basis for a sender's *electronic signature.* When sending a message using public key cryptography, the organization has gained assurance that only the authorized receiver can decrypt the message. It does not provide a guarantee that the originator of the message was an authorized sender since the public key is, by its nature, in the public domain and can be used by any message originator. An electronic signature, in effect, encrypts a message with the originator's private key, indicates who the message is from, and sends the message. When the message is received, the receiver can recognize who the message is from and look up the originator's public key to decrypt a message. Any fraudster intercepting the message can also obtain the public key and decrypt the message; however, only the authorized originator could have initiated the message since only he or she had access to the private key. Thus, although a fraudster may gain access to a message that has been sent and can read it, the fraudster cannot alter the message and send it on since he or she does not have the private key.

As we will see when we look at e-commerce, origination authentication is critical to the prevention of fraudulent transactions.

 ## CONTROL OF SERVERS

Servers may be classified as a type of software program providing a specific kind of service to client software running on the same computer or other computers within a network. Each server has its own particular control opportunities and must work within the ambit of the overall control architecture. A variation on servers is the use of server virtualization. In this scenario, the server administrator divides one physical server into multiple virtual environments using a software control application. These environments are known alternatively as virtual private servers, instances, emulations, guests, and containers. One of three approaches are common: virtual machine model, paravirtual machine model, or virtualization at the operating system level.

In either of the first two approaches, each guest runs on a virtual imitation of the hardware layer, allowing guest operating systems to run without modification. Multiple operating systems are possible since each guest is unaware that it is running in virtual mode, not on real hardware. Real computing resources are, however, required from the host. Where the virtualization is at the operating system level, a single operating system kernel is run on the host computer with functionality exported to each of the guests, which must use the same operating system as a host.

If this sounds complicated, from a technical standpoint it is. From an antifraud perspective, virtual environments can be made even more fraud resistant since applications processing sensitive business data can be isolated further than is possible on physical computers. Virtual machines on the same physical server can be isolated based on differing trust levels. Unfortunately, virtual servers also bring their own security problems. Administrators of the virtual environment may, in the nature of their duties, have access to restricted data with powerful virtualization management tools. Should unauthorized access be gained to these tools, data integrity may be compromised and fraud enabled.

Virtual machines, as opposed to physical boxes, are essentially files that can be combined to fit on removable storage media. This could enable unauthorized copying of confidential information.

Internal controls at the virtual level include the proper configuration of the virtual machines to restrict the existence of unauthorized devices. Changes to virtual machine files should be monitored independently as a detective control for unauthorized changes. Backups and replications of information need to be established in the security architecture to prohibits secure machines from being migrated to insecure storage. Overall, the control objectives and architectures of these virtual machines do not change and still remain as:

- Access authentication
- Segregation of duties
- Integrity controls
- Integration with nonvirtual environments
- Enforcement of existing antifraud policies
- Extensive logging of activity as a detective control

The interconnectivity and flexibility of the environment make it appear as if antifraud measures become too complicated to permit efficient management of a secure antifraud environment. When the control objectives are clearly defined, it is easier to identify the points of control and implement, on an ongoing basis, the appropriate control mechanisms.

At this level, unauthorized access prevention controls may commonly use demilitarized zones, firewalls, proxy servers, and the like.

 WAN COMMUNICATIONS

WAN communications represent the communication media from workstations to the server environment. The control objectives are the same as for mainframe network communications; however, the population of users and terminals connected via WANs is generally much larger. In addition to the sheer volume that is processed over WAN communications, generally the authentication of individual users and the administration of access rights is considerably more problematic.

In this area, once again, encryption is a major control mechanism in the prevention of unauthorized access to, loss of confidentiality of, and manipulation of the contents of messages. Encryption has no control influence over the accuracy, the authenticity, the validity, or even the existence of the message. Depending on the nature of the network and type of communications, encryption may not even be possible under some scenarios. For example, communications using the telnet protocol cannot be encrypted, so all messages including user ids and passwords are transmitted in clear text.

Other control mechanisms, such as secure socket layers and other security-enhancing protocols, may give additional assurance that fraud via unauthorized access is less likely.

 WORKSTATION SECURITY

At the workstation level, fraud prevention also rests in knowing for certain that the person using a workstation has been authenticated as the genuine user, operating from an authorized workstation, via the correct communication lines, and using the authorized communication protocol. In addition to these technical controls, at this point antifraud measures migrate back into the user environment to ensure that transactions input at the workstations are authorized, accurately captured, and complete.

Authentication at the workstation level involves gaining assurance that the user can be validated. This is the bedrock of antifraud mechanisms within the computer environment; the segregation of incompatible duties, the restriction of access rights, and the processing of authorized transactions relies on knowing for a fact that the user is who he or she claims to be. While no authentication method is 100 percent foolproof, users at workstations are commonly if indicated by:

- Something they know
- Something they have
- Something they are

At present, passwords remain the most common form of user authentication based on something people know. Although passwords have been popular for a long time, they suffer from some major drawbacks. Like their cousins, personal identification numbers (PINs), they are normally short and commonly written down. To be effective as authentication controls, passwords should be hard to guess although easy to remember, well guarded, and frequently changed.

Despite best efforts at user education, passwords and PINs normally are not changed unless the system enforces such changes. Requiring users to remember passwords commonly leads to user selection of easily guessed words, short words, names, and other such weaknesses dictated by human nature. If a longer or more complicated password is used, it is common to find that it has been written down and stored somewhere near the workstation. A fraudster merely has to gain physical access to the vicinity of the workstation and find the password in order to successfully impersonate the genuine user and gain access with all of that person's authorized access rights.

Perhaps one of the easiest ways to obtain the user's password is to simply ask for it. If phrased correctly—for example, as a request from the auditors—many users will happily divulge their passwords. The next most common technique is known as shoulder surfing, which, as it sounds, simply involves looking over a person's shoulder as he or she enters a password. In some "high-security" environments, inspection may show that the closed circuit cameras intended to improve security actually may point at keyboards and record all passwords entered.

Passwords often are passed around or shared; it is common to find that a senior executive shares the password with his or her assistant, who is normally the person who enters the computer on behalf of the executive. The same executive would not allow the assistant to sign a check with the executive's name but will readily allow impersonation by permitting his or her password to be used by a third party.

MOBILE COMPUTING AND THE INTERNET

Many forms of Internet fraud have been described in Chapters 3 and 4. In this section, we focus on the internal control structures that can obviate these threats.

Internet Fraud

As mentioned earlier, one of the biggest potential fraud areas on the Internet is identity theft. This is particularly true where Internet users, in their private or corporate capacity, utilize social networking and make publicly available a wide variety of confidential data. Names, birth dates, birthplaces, Social Security numbers in the United States, identity numbers, and credit card numbers are some of the most useful information that identity thieves can get their hands on.

Once this personal information is obtained, fraudsters can create a variety of forms of debt laid at the feet of the genuine person. In addition to the losses incurred by that fraud itself, the potential reputational damage from debt incurred and not repaid can be crippling in the individual's personal and business activities.

Obviously, other means are available to obtain such information than the Internet, but here we are looking specifically at that source of threat. Social media sites give users the opportunity to create privacy rules to prevent this kind of attack, but such rules often are either ignored or badly implemented. Many Web sites request a "secret question and answer" for password recovery purposes. This information is the type of personal information that people readily put on the social media sites. Having obtained this information from the individual's site, fraudsters can use it to gain access to a variety of sites as the legitimate user by claiming to have forgotten the password and providing the answer requested. A safer option when asked to give a "secret answer" is to choose a secondary password as a standard answer to any such question and ensure that does not appear on any social site. Ideally, the secondary password should be unique for each site visited. This can be achieved using the first two or three letters of the site name as a prefix.

In addition to identity theft, Chapters 3 and 4 discussed Internet scams, such as 4-1-9 frauds, Internet auction frauds, investment frauds, Internet business frauds, and the like.

For most of these frauds, the main internal controls are alertness and awareness coupled with the healthy skepticism when offered something for nothing or insider information that only the rich know. These are simply modern variations of the snake-oil scams prevalent in the nineteenth century. Many so-called investment newsletter subscription services utilize a free scare-mongering service designed to convince potential subscribers that the only way to avoid a national or international economic collapse is to subscribe to the newsletter, which then produces regurgitated information freely available on the Internet. In addition, the secondary sting is to convince the subscriber that the answer lies either in another subscription to a more "confidential" newsletter, which effectively becomes a sales pitch for further salable services.

There are legitimate versions of these services, but in all cases background searches should be carried out to ensure that they are legitimate. A good tip is to do a search for the name plus the word "scam."

Another common form of fraud via the Internet is known as friendly fraud. In this variety, an Internet purchase is made with the individual's own credit card and, after receipt of the goods and services, a delivery denial is made accompanied by a chargeback request to the individual's issuing bank or requests for delivery of a duplicate item. Chargebacks are intended to be a defense for the cardholder against dishonest merchants applying unauthorized charges against their account. In a friendly fraud, it is very difficult for the business to verify the authenticity of the charge, particularly when it applies to digital products where proof of delivery is problematic.

When it comes to mobile connectivity, the fraud possibilities are enormous. Recent estimates indicate that by the end of 2013, one eighth of all e-commerce transactions will take place from a mobile device. For such transactions to maintain their integrity, user authentication must be supplemented by more powerful and useful fraud detection tools. Context-aware security tools are now available for mobile devices with capabilities such as:

▪ *Device identification and location awareness.* This permits a vendor faced with a transaction from a mobile device to identify the geolocation of the device and the confirmed authentication of the device identity (device fingerprinting), which can then be compared to the normal device identity and geolocation of that particular user. Device identification can also be used to determine whether this particular device has, in the past, been associated with the fraudulent transaction.

▪ *Predictive risk analytics*. This method uses the history of transaction patterns to raise the level of authentication reliability in deciding whether to accept the new transaction.

In addition to frauds carried out by impersonating a legitimate mobile user, theft of mobile devices is reaching epidemic proportions. Even as recently as three or four years ago, the major such threat was theft of smartphones in which users had installed personal information, bank account numbers, credit card numbers, user ids, and passwords. Indications are that up to 40 percent of stolen mobile computing devices have no password protection. E-mail accounts and passwords are common on such devices, and many e-mails themselves contain confidential personal and corporate information. Answers to the security questions noted earlier are also stored on these devices; in some cases even PIN numbers can be found. Where such information exists on smartphones, particular care over their physical security must be taken. Any loss or theft should be looked on as a serious situation, not merely an inconvenience.

Even where there is no loss or theft of such devices, damage requiring technical repair can mean that an innocent user hands a device containing highly confidential personal and corporate information to a third party with little or no thought of protecting the information contained thereon. When a person leaves a job, he or she should wipe all personal information from a corporate phone before handing it over.

Over the last two or three years, the proliferation of tablet devices, iPads, and the like have made possible the theft of mobile devices that would pass device identification tests, at least for an hour or two until the theft is recognized and reported, at which point the mobile transaction capability can be frozen and the geolocation of the stolen unit identified. A successful fraud can be perpetrated in that short window of time using the legitimate device and authentication information stored within it; fraud from a geolocation close enough to be acceptable.

Users of such devices have to be aware of the dangers of storing confidential information on them, useful as it may seem, and of the need to provide physical protection to prevent their theft. In addition, a separate mechanism is required to speedily notify a service provider of the device's theft so it can be immediately immobilized.

CLOUD COMPUTING

Cloud computing originally evolved as an extension of the traditional client-server approach to computing in which a network-friendly client version of a particular application system was lodged on client computers. These versions utilized the client system's memory and central processing unit for processing, while the resulting data files were stored centrally on the corporate data servers. Multiple user licenses of an application had to be purchased for the many users on a network.

Cloud computing differs in that the application systems are provided from the server and executed and managed by the clients' Web browsers; there is no need for an installed client version of the application system. This form of application centralization gives the cloud service provider absolute control over the versions of an application system provided to clients, thus removing the need for license agreements on an individual client basis as well as easing software version control. This form of cloud computing is commonly known as SaaS. As a result of cloud computing, both hardware and software requirements on the user's side decrease, with the cloud's network taking the bulk of the load.

In terms of fraud risk, cloud computing exacerbates the risks to information security and privacy since the data as well as the applications are maintained within the cloud itself. System users and service providers can be exposed to potentially serious risks of data loss as well as fraud and cyberespionage. In addition, where the data reside in a country other than that of the cloud users, the users may be exposed to legal issues regarding future access to their own data in a fraud prosecution as well as issues regarding ownership of the intangible property under the terms of another country's legislation. A further complication arises should access to the cloud services be unavailable for any reason.

One critical management aspect in deciding on a cloud environment is the difficulty involved in migrating existing applications to a cloud platform. Selection of a cloud provider will inevitably complicate application architectures since the existing enterprise solutions typically will involve dissimilar architectures. Switching over from internal databases serving large user bases and involving highly variable access rights can prove a stumbling block to effective cloud migration. In many complex environments, an organization that adopts cloud computing typically ends up utilizing new applications. If this is the case, care must be taken to ensure that all antifraud measures previously existing within the application systems also get migrated to the cloud environment. Because of the nature of the cloud, additional controls, particularly on the monitoring side, may also be required.

Users of cloud services could be left in an untenable position where their ability to do business is severely restricted. Should a client then decide to migrate the data to another cloud provider, further complications may ensue due to the lack of porting standards.

To be migrated to the cloud, an application must be a Web application. This may seem like common sense, but it can trip up the unwary. It is important that, before migration, the organization understands the technological aspects of what is being transferred. Different cloud environments support different technologies, including the database management system as well as management and monitoring tools, all of which are essential to the effective control of fraud.

Ensuring that the application will run in an adequate security environment means that the organization must understand its own internal security requirements and determine the cloud provider's ability to deliver ongoing security against these criteria.

In choosing the specific cloud platform on which to run the application, transferability may become a significant determinant. If the application system requires modification to fit the specifications of a specific cloud platform, it may lock the organization into one specific architecture, thus potentially restricting its ability to implement company-appropriate antifraud measures.

Considerations for cloud computing applications ultimately depend on whether the organization intends to implement:

■ *Software as a Service (SaaS)*, where the intention is to use the provider's applications running on a cloud infrastructure. The applications are then accessed via various client devices through a thin client interface such as a Web browser.
■ *Business Process as a Service (BPaaS)*, where business-process services may be any business process delivered through the cloud service model via the Internet with access attained via Web-centric interfaces and exploiting Web-oriented cloud architecture.

A variation on Cloud usage is the concept of the private cloud, which involves a proprietary architecture leased or owned by an individual organization to provide hosted services to internal customers of the organization. This architecture is increasingly attracting large organizations; however, effective implementation requires that the corporate data center be capable of provisioning new environments, boosting computing power, and adding storage capacity at very short notice to facilitate the scalability of a cloud environment.

From a fraud prevention perspective, it is possible to implement a hybrid combining the scalability advantages of a standard cloud environment for lower-risk applications while maintaining a private cloud behind an adequate firewall for high-fraud-risk or sensitive systems.

COMPUTER AND INFORMATION FRAUD

Most economic crimes now have a cyberversion that promises larger payoffs for fewer risks. Payment systems can be compromised electronically with transfers available in the blink of an eye to transfer funds or launder money. Effective governance in an IT environment involves the implementation of adequate controls to protect the digital resources coupled with a monitoring process to alert management to any unexpected incidents in a timely fashion. Even with the best-designed internal control system in the world, breakdowns will still happen when the business risk outstrips the controls designed to mitigate against it or when operational priorities change to the extent that control effectiveness can be weakened.

As part of internal control, the internal auditor has a role to play in assisting management to establish a control environment in which fraud is unlikely to occur, but, where it does occur, it will be quickly detected. This is in contrast to the approach of the IT forensic auditor whose primary obligation is the resolution of IT fraud with sufficient evidence to prove or disprove allegations of fraud. IT forensic auditors must presume that all cases eventually will end up in litigation, and the quality of evidence gathered must take this into account.

Controls themselves can fail because of human error or poor initial design. At minimum, fraud prevention controls over computer systems should consist of general controls and effective monitoring.

General Controls

As mentioned, the most effective controls other than the technical controls mentioned earlier are user vigilance and awareness. There are, however, some internal controls that can be readily implemented in order to make computer fraud by outsider more difficult and easier to detect:

■ *Personal information* should not be disclosed, and care should be taken whenever a computer user is asked for sensitive information. Such information should never be disclosed electronically unless the user is fully satisfied that the requester has a right to know, such as legitimate law enforcement or taxation authorities.

- *Passwords* should be protected both at the user end and when on mobile devices. In addition, passwords should be changed regularly and should contain a mixture of characters, numbers, and special characters like exclamation marks, question marks, percent signs, and the like. Most passwords are case sensitive. Mixing upper- and lower-case characters can make it considerably more difficult for "brute force" attacks to succeed. People entering passwords should beware of shoulder surfers, particularly if they seem to be using a mobile phone at the time. The phone may in fact be videotaping the password entry.
- *Destruction of confidential scrap* is essential to prevent ID theft. Shredders, particularly cross-cut shredders, should be used for any paper product containing personal information, including the user's name. Modern shredders, not necessarily expensive ones, generally can shred credit cards and even DVDs. Where this facility is available, use it.
- *Doing business via computers* means that users have to be sure who they are dealing with electronically. When purchases are made, users must take care to check any agreements implicit within the transaction or policies being agreed to. If there is any doubt at all as to the authenticity or the acceptability of any terms and conditions, do business elsewhere. If businesses utilize free e-mail addresses, such as Hotmail, Yahoo, or the like, avoid them; it is too easy for them to disappear with whereabouts unknown and then reappear with a new identity mere seconds later.
- *Be wary of special offers*, unique bargains, pyramid schemes, Internet auctions, business opportunities, and the like. Some of these are legitimate, but many are not. As with all other too-good-to-be-true schemes, be wary and be aware.

Effective Monitoring

Monitoring to ensure the ongoing effectiveness of controls designed to ensure IT system integrity, confidentiality, and fraud resistance is commonly under-resourced or even ignored by the executives responsible for ensuring effective fraud risk management and good governance. Where resources are scarce or the skill to interpret the monitoring is not available in-house, using technology to monitor technology should be considered.

Besides performing the monitoring, technology can also assess the ongoing effectiveness of these controls themselves. As has been repeatedly stated, fraud is more likely to occur when the basic internal controls are known to be ineffective or easily circumvented. Effective monitoring on an ongoing basis is not only a detective control but also a deterrent control since the incidence of fraud is known to decrease where the expectation of being detected is higher. Continuous monitoring capabilities exist within many software packages, including generalized audit software, such as IDEA and ACL (see Appendix F). Use of continuous monitoring can help fraud detection by:

- Providing better access to real-time indicators of potentially fraudulent transactions by allowing improved speed and quality of detection and management response
- Reducing the business impact of frauds by reducing the length of time they go undetected
- Ensuring corporate compliance with relevant laws and regulations
- Giving early warning of reduced reliability of computerized antifraud controls

Continuous monitoring may be the only control possible in high-volume transaction processing systems. Where such systems use distributed networks or virtualized servers, computerized monitoring techniques may be the only way in which relevant, reliable, and timely information can be utilized to monitor transaction flow effectively. Using technology in this manner makes possible the 100 percent checking of every transaction against predetermined indicators of potential fraud, such as high-value transactions, unexpected patterns of transactions, transaction volumes, or values moving against normal trends.

To be effective in detecting fraud, monitoring controls must produce information that is relevant, reliable, and timely. Information produced may be direct substantiation of the effectiveness of the controls and business processes designed to mitigate fraud. Alternatively, they may provide a context or background information against which the direct information can be evaluated, such as performance of key risk indicators or operating and trend statistics.

For any monitoring to be effective, there must be a standard or baseline against which the results of the monitoring can be compared. Only then can observers detect deviations from the norm in order to assess the effectiveness of control operation. In addition, by understanding the existing operations of controls monitoring mechanisms may be designed and implemented in a more effective manner. Continuous observation monitoring is designed to ensure that controls function as intended during times of normal operation. This type of monitoring is not necessarily restricted to using computerized tools. There is a danger for management to assume that, once automated tools have been implemented, normal controls of supervision, reconciliations, and the like can be suspended. Continuous monitoring by automated tools, if effective, will give management early alert of potential defects within the control environment. Such a monitoring infrastructure must be designed to meet the needs identified during management's IT risk assessment.

As noted in Chapter 8, the starting point of effective use of internal controls to mitigate fraud risk is the understanding of the nature of fraud risk and the sources from which such risk derives. Only then can an effective system of internal controls be designed to mitigate risk. Once such a system has been implemented, continuous monitoring can be used to determine the ongoing effectiveness of such controls. It also can check the risk levels encountered in order to determine whether control design is still adequate.

It would be neither effective nor efficient to attempt to monitor each control individually. If the risk analysis has been done properly, the control objectives should have been prioritized together with the identification of the key controls designed to achieve those control objectives most effectively.

Designing the monitoring architecture is therefore a combination of:

- Identifying and prioritizing risks
- Identifying the key controls intended to mitigate the risk
- Identifying the key indicators that would show that the likelihood of achieving the control objectives is declining
- Implementing automated or manual monitoring of these indicators to identify as soon as possible any decrease in the adequacy of the internal control structures or their effectiveness in achieving the control objectives

Depending on the nature of the risk and the design of the controls, monitoring may be done of the controls themselves or of the degree to which the control objectives are being achieved or a combination of the two bearing in mind that it is the overall attainment of the control objectives that is essential, not the selection of individual controls. Monitoring against control objectives allows management to monitor the effectiveness of multiple controls, each of which contributes to the control objective in circumstances where it is not cost effective to monitor each individual control. This statement is particularly true in fraud-sensitive areas, where key indicators for early warning of fraud may facilitate management confidence regarding access controls, division of duties, and a variety of other control techniques without the need to monitor each one individually. The design of such monitoring mechanisms may, in itself, identify weaknesses in internal control structures where reliance has been placed purely on preventive controls. Many of these controls provide no evidence as to their ongoing effectiveness and must be supplemented by detective controls specifically designed to leave an evidence trail that can be monitored.

Unfortunately, when they were first designed, many operational computer systems did not have the internal control structures designed with continuous monitoring in mind. This has led to the implementation of control structures that may be highly effective in controlling risk or may not be, but may provide management with no information one way or the other. This is particularly true in legacy systems developed many years ago and still running, but it also can be found in some of the latest systems implemented. Because of the nature of modern systems—high speed, high volume, multiple entry points—the control focus typically has been on preventive controls because the opportunities for human intervention as a result of detected problems are minimal. Automated preventive controls are commonly used to implement control on an ongoing basis. Without an evidence trail, however, management is relying on the overall design adequacy of the system of controls rather than being in a position to assess the effectiveness of the control structure on an ongoing basis.

 ## MONITORING TOOLS

Automated monitoring tools come in a variety of forms and with a variety of primary purposes. Many were not designed with ongoing monitoring in mind; nevertheless, they can be readily adapted to this purpose. For example, change control is intended to ensure that, once a program has been put into a live environment, only authorized changes that have been fully tested can be implemented in an authorized manner. It can also monitor live systems for unauthorized changes and provide a continuous assurance of a fixed level of processing integrity.

Data analytical tools of the type used by auditors can be used to monitor transaction streams against known tolerance levels to determine whether a control designed to prevent certain types of fraud has been breached.

Error and exception reports can also be monitored electronically using the same tools to ensure that patterns which could indicate fraudulent intentions will be detected in a timely manner.

Access logs can be monitored on an ongoing basis to seek a pattern indicating invalid access attempts to sensitive areas of systems and transaction types that could potentially facilitate a fraud.

In all cases, such tools can be rendered ineffective when users ignore the information they provide. As mentioned, the tools may be worse than useless since they can lull management into a false state of security because it believes it has implemented continuous monitoring whereas all it may have implemented may be continuous recording. Management must also realize that continuous monitoring does not prove fraud. At its most effective, it can only indicate a heightened possibility that an event has fraudulent intent.

Continuous monitoring does not provide a comprehensive, enterprise-wide fraud risk management approach. It does, however, provide a key component in the fraud risk management process. Overemphasis on continuous monitoring at the expense of a comprehensive antifraud management approach can significantly reduce the effectiveness of the overall management of fraud risk.

To be effective, the antifraud strategy requires the active involvement of information system owners and the suppliers of common controls all operating within the overall mission and strategic objectives of the organization. Generically, continuous monitoring and continuous auditing can play a significant role in fraud prevention and detection and can ensure compliance with policies, plans, procedures, laws, and regulations and generally monitor both risk compliance and effective risk management. They therefore become significant factors in ensuring corporate risk oversight and transparency.

The two critical questions must be answered before such tools can be effectively implemented:

1. How much monitoring is required to provide acceptable levels of assurance?
2. At what level should the monitoring trigger an alarm that conditions may not be as desired?

Both of these questions should be addressed as part of the risk assessment process. They are responses to management's decision regarding its level of risk acceptance or risk tolerance, for example, if management decide that high levels of risk are unacceptable, the response must be to determine how much monitoring is necessary. In this case we refer specifically to fraud risk. The risk evaluation process should have identified areas where systems are most vulnerable to fraud and where assets can be moved most easily. Levels of significance for indicator movements should have been established as an integral part of control structure design since without these levels, the adequacy of the design of the system of internal controls cannot be determined.

When choosing the appropriate tool, in addition to the obvious requirement of cost effectiveness, care should be taken to select a package that is customizable to meet the organization's requirements and has a history of upgradeability to meet the organization's changing IT needs.

PREVENTING E-COMMERCE FRAUD

As with preventing many other forms of fraud, the starting point for preventing e-eommerce fraud is an understanding of the nature of the particular type of fraud and sources from which the risks originate. This is particularly true since it is now seen to be a critical part of sales and marketing to facilitate the organization's participation in the e-commerce business model making e-commerce almost compulsory. Different industry classes are entering this world with different objectives. Some seek to reduce costs and streamline business activities; others are reducing the overhead of having to maintain large, expensive premises. Some electronic traders even manage to remove the need for warehousing and now act as clearinghouses where transactions are routed directly to suppliers who supply directly to customers, with the electronic trader taking a commission.

Using e-commerce to gather information on customers' preferences and behavior enables organizations to direct their marketing efforts to targeted customers, allowing cost-effective market segmentation.

Online auctions have created a brand-new market. Physical auction houses were generally seen as a specialist consumer area, in some cases for hobbyists or collectors. With the advent of online auction sites, a new home industry has developed since, for minimal cost, anyone can become a retailer working from home with little overhead. Unfortunately, this is one of the hottest areas for consumer fraud with unscrupulous "sellers" advertising nonexistent products, collecting the payment, disappearing, and setting up anew under a different identity, with different e-mail addresses and telephone numbers. Substitution of inferior-quality goods for those advertised is simply an electronic version of the old bait-and-switch fraud. Online auction houses expend a great deal of effort to protect customers since one bad consumer experience, spread over the Web, can have a major impact on future trading in that site.

The sites are also becoming of high value to thieves who can sell stolen goods over the Internet for close to full value instead of having sell through a fence, where the fence makes the bulk of the profits.

Auction fraud is covered in more detail in Chapter 3.

For organizations dependent on the speed of transactions, such stock market trading, e-commerce has enabled customers to execute thorough research and then purchase or sell shares in any selected company, in any market in the world, at a fraction of the cost involved in dealing through a full-commission brokerage house.

Online banking offers customers the ability to monitor their accounts and transfer money among their accounts without having to queue at a branch, possibly even at multiple tellers. E-banking permits the payment of bills from home, and banks can give customers the option to receive statements electronically, reducing printing and mailing costs dramatically.

Multiple versions of e-commerce are possible, each with its own particular fraud opportunities. However, the primary control objectives remain the prevention of the theft of customer data and prevention of fraudulent transactions against that customer data. Both of these control objectives are achievable without excessive cost, although, again, the specific risk elements inherent in each type of e-commerce must be understood.

Business to Consumer

In the business-to-consumer (B2C) form of e-commerce, customers deal directly with an organization electronically. Advantages to the customer include potentially lower costs as well as a virtual guarantee that the goods are always in stock. Doing business in this manner, however, exposes consumers by forcing them to disclose confidential information. Identity theft is perhaps the most common route via which e-commerce fraud is committed in B2C, and the most common form of e-commerce fraud is credit card fraud.

Credit card fraud is as simple as the retrieval of a preapproved credit card from a mailbox before it is collected or using information gathered from a social networking Web site to apply for a new credit card in the victim's name. Individuals, even in today's more fraud-aware society, will give out credit card details to Web sites or via telephone or will hand over the credit card in a retail environment or restaurant and then ignore what is done with the card. Recording the details, making additional imprints, or even simply photographing both sides of the card can make the information available to fraudsters.

Even where the credit card information has been legitimately recorded within the corporate environment, details are vulnerable to attacks by insiders and outsiders. Examples of such attacks abound:

▪ In 2005, a dishonest insider within the Atlantis hotel compromised 55,000 credit card numbers and the holders' associated Social Security numbers, names and addresses, and/or bank account details.

- In 2007, Stop & Shop Supermarkets had credit and debit card account information as well as the accompanying PIN numbers stolen by modifying the self-swipe card readers in several shops. (The card readers were later made tamper-proof simply by bolting the PIN pad to its station.) In 2009, a hacker, Albert Gonzalez, was indicted for penetrating Heartland Payment Systems, which processed 100 million credit card transactions each month. Over a two-year period, he stole and resold more than 117 million card and automated teller machine numbers.

Private information on individuals and organizations can readily be bought from underground servers at a price, and not a particularly high one. It is now possible to scan the information from a magnetic stripe or a microchip on the card without the card ever leaving the cardholder's pocket.

Controls to prevent such frauds include:

- Ensure cards are signed as soon as they arrive.
- Carry cards separately in a metallic scan-proof wallet.
- If handing over the card to a third party, keep a close watch on the card as it is being processed.
- Open credit card bills promptly, reconcile the transactions against your own records, and report any questionable transactions directly to the card company.
- Void incorrect receipts immediately.
- Ensure cards are never lent to others or left lying around.

Many companies provide employees with company cards to be used when expenses are incurred on behalf of the organization. In addition to the previous controls, a careful check should be made to ensure that all charges are substantiated by original documentation and that all expenditures are for authorized purposes.

Denial of receipt involves an electronic purchaser repudiating a purchase by denying receiving the product or service, denying agreeing to the product or service, or even denying ordering the product or service. When goods and services are purchased via the Internet, many reputable retailers, in the name of good customer relations, will issue refunds or resend merchandise without proof of failure to deliver. The cost of investigating each such claim makes it prohibitive; companies are now requiring additional payment to cover the insurance cost of such frauds. In the same way, returns of items purchased electronically may also go astray, and e-commerce traders are now requiring that failure of proof of return delivery will be met with additional charges. Other internal controls in this area to prevent fraud include:

- Reviewing online orders manually. This is impractical for all orders in e-commerce. Again, continuous monitoring of order volumes and values in comparison to trigger points can flag suspicious orders for manual confirmation. This again means the person carrying out the confirmation has to be fully aware of fraud risk and diligent enough not to simply rubber-stamp queried transactions.
- Recording all known attempts to defraud and using continuous monitoring to seek matching identification parameters, such as delivery addresses, telephone numbers, and payment card numbers (particularly for customers with a high level of returns).
- Use of card issuers' transaction confirmation services, which can verify transactions prior to completion of order processing.
- Use of transaction/customer profile databases.
- Transaction verification/validation services.
- Rules-based filters.

In the event of an attempted or successful e-commerce fraud, the most critical part of any follow-up attempt to prosecute or recover assets is the availability and integrity of adequate documentation, whether manual or electronic. Given the fact that there may be some time delay before a fraud is recognized, electronic and clerical records should be retained in forensically acceptable manners (i.e., under lock and key with a chain of custody and a means to prove the integrity of the records).

Where goods and services have been delivered, shipping information and evidence regarding the individual who signed the receipt are critical. Use of local police services with knowledge of the area to which goods were delivered as well as jurisdiction over that area may be essential to succeed in apprehending and convicting fraudsters.

Business to Business

Business-to-business (B2B) e-commerce is conducted with a different set of objectives in mind. By connecting business partners and creating a virtual supply chain, it is possible to reduce costs while simultaneously reducing re-supply times. This form of e-commerce is growing exponentially. This type of e-commerce gives small businesses the ability to trade internationally. It offers an enormous temptation and has proven tremendously successful in enabling small company growth at rates previously unheard of. This opportunity applies not only to exporting to overseas markets but also to the establishing of supplier relationships with lower-cost geographical areas.

Fundamental in this e-commerce arena is the verification of suppliers, both in terms of quality and simple existence. Any Internet user can, comparatively cheaply, create a sophisticated-looking Web site offering heavily discounted component supplies and raw material supplies. Once payment is made, the site is closed and the fraudster moves on. There are a variety of supplier verification sites available on the Internet, some of which are themselves frauds. At a minimum, verification of the addresses, phone numbers, and e-mail addresses must be carried out. E-mail addresses themselves may prove nothing since it is cheap and easy to register a domain name with associated e-mail addresses, and the actual owner of the site may be almost untraceable in certain jurisdictions. Slightly more sophisticated fraudsters will clone the Web sites of genuine large companies with subtle changes to Web addresses and contact details so that potential trading partners carrying out cursory checks will believe they are doing business with a reliable supplier.

When making initial contact, look up the telephone number of the genuine supplier independently of any advertised telephone number and confirm that it is the same organization that you are considering doing business with.

If in doubt, use credit checks to determine which companies are real and which are fraudulent. Not only do such checks provide assurance that the company is real; they also can provide critical information on ownership, creditworthiness, legal status, financial status, and worldwide basis.

Once the identity of the trading partner has been confirmed, trading contracts must be examined closely in order to determine that all conditions of sale, payment methods, dispute arbitration, national or state laws governing transactions, and rights of inspection are covered. In addition, trading partners should remember that a signed contract sent electronically is of no more worth than a long-distance photocopy and would not stand up in court in many jurisdictions.

For larger companies doing B2B business, a favorite type of fraud is the accounts payable fraud whereby the fraudster, perhaps with the assistance of an insider, sends payment requests virtually identical to those of genuine trading partners but with minor changes to payment details.

Consumer to Consumer

Consumer-to-consumer (C2C) e-commerce is a form of e-commerce involving consumers selling directly to other consumers—for example, through an auction site such as eBay or through online sites such as Craigslist—where the site serves a conduit to enable C2C trading. The concept behind it is the formation of a virtual community, that is, people who come together via the Internet specifically to share items of common interest. From a consumer perspective, the reduction in costs enables individuals to communicate or conduct business with almost no overhead.

On the downside, C2C is perhaps the least safe and least reliable place to conduct business with problems ranging from frauds to, in an extreme case, the "Craigslist killer" who used a site as an access route to his victims. Not all such sites are equally vulnerable; some now require all buyers and sellers to register a membership for identification and authentication purposes.

E-Governance

E-governance relates to the use of Information and Communications Technology (ICT) delivery of government services to business, citizens and government. There are some subtle differences between e-Governance and e-Government, but in general use the two terms are used synonymously. Once again there are variations between:

- Government to Government (G2G)
- Citizens to Government (C2G)
- Government to Citizens (G2C)
- Government to Businesses (G2B)
- Government to Employees (G2E)

Common arguments against e-Government include the disparities among citizens regarding their access to the Internet and therefore to e-Government as well as the potential threat of the technology enabling a "Big Brother" scenario.

 ## E-COMMERCE CONTROL OPPORTUNITIES

Safeguarding confidential information is of paramount importance to any individual or organization involved in e-commerce. In addition to the legal consequences in certain countries and jurisdictions resulting from a breach of privacy, the impacts of such breaches on the business can be devastating. Confidentiality failures in e-commerce tend to make good newspaper headlines with significant reputational risks for even the largest organization. In the United States, the Payment Card Industry Data Security Standard (PCI-DSS) lays down standards that all organizations doing business using the various forms of payment cards must comply with. Achieving this certification is costly and is proving difficult for small organizations to implement due to the added costs. As a result, business is increasing for e-commerce and PCI consultants and service providers. One drawback in the implementation of PCI-DSS is its focus on preventing the compromise of stored data. If the data have already been compromised elsewhere, PCI-DSS compliance will not prevent the acceptance of a stolen or fraudulent card.

In situations where transactions take place without the physical presence of a payment card (known as card-not-present [CNP] transactions), liability for the education of card users identities rests with the e-commerce business and not with the bank which is the merchant account provider.

 ## E-PAYMENTS

When mobile devices are used for payments, currently the most commonly accepted payment method is via mobile Web browsers, although payment from mobile applications is starting to catch up. Among those organizations accepting payment via mobile devices, the most commonly observed fraud type remains ID theft.

 ## INTERNAL CONTROL BEST PRACTICES

In the e-commerce environment, best practices involve a combination of:

- Staff training, particularly regarding the risks of CNP transactions
- Implementation of end-to-end encryption
- Maintaining up-to-date records of fraud attempts in order to detect patterns, particularly of chargebacks, and switch management emphasis to fraud prevention in those areas
- Networking with other e-commerce service providers to exchange information on the nature of attempted frauds and the effectiveness of preventive and detective measures

- Implementing appropriate security measures depending on the nature of the e-commerce being carried out
- Seeking advice from payment processors on fraud detection and consumer behavior

NEWER FRAUD SCHEMES

Newer and more complicated fraud schemes are emerging that utilize technology itself to gain access to a user's authentication information:

- *Phishing attacks* involve sending out a blanket e-mail purporting to come from victims' financial institutions in order to collect passwords and authentication information. Many of these attacks take the form of warnings to victims that an attempt has been made to defraud them and that this message is designed to enhance their security. Most of these warnings are obviously fake since they come from financial institutions where the victims do not hold an account.
- *Spear phishing* is an attempt to make the e-mail fraud more credible by utilizing personalized information already gained from social networks and elsewhere. Recently there has been an increase in the targeting of corporate employees to gain access to corporate banking information, customer databases, and the like. Senior executives tend to be the target because of their rank and authority levels within targeted computer systems.
- *Business services phishing* goes beyond the targeting of employees. Recent attacks have included the targeting of businesses using IT services such as Google AdWords, Yahoo!, and the like. The organizations are then the targets of the phishing as they are the consumers such services rather than individual employees of the business. Again, confidential information, such as corporate credit card information or user ids and passwords, is typically sought.
- *Defensive phishing* plays on people's fears that they may already have been compromised and purports to come from the individuals' or organization's service provider, which is providing an early alert so that defensive action can be taken. Obviously, taking such action requires individuals to confirm their identity and authenticate it using their password before the enhanced protection can be put into effect. In some cases, users are then directed to a spoofed copy of the service provider's Web site and told they must download and implement "security-updated" software immediately. What actually is

downloaded is malware containing a keylogger. Unlike conventional keylogger malware, phishing-related keyloggers record specific actions to specific institutions, seeking the normal user ids, passwords, and account numbers.

- *Botnets* involve the use of a collection of compromised computers to run "bots," or Web robots (simple repetitive programs to carry out fraudulent or malicious activities, such as denial-of-service attacks or harvesting of e-mail addresses using *spambots* as well as other fraudulent techniques). Antibot software typically uses a graphically encoded word or phrase requiring human reading and input. This is a type of *Turing test* named after Alan Turing who, during World War II, was instrumental in the construction of Colossus, the world's first programmable computer used to crack the German Enigma encoder.
- *CVV* (card verification value) *cracking* involves reading the magnetic strip on the back of each card or the number printed flat on the back of the card. Once fraudsters obtain this number, they can use it in conjunction with the card number to make fraudulent purchases.

PROTECTING DIGITAL ASSETS

Companies are coming more and more to recognize the value held in their digital assets. Although these assets may not appear on the organization's asset register or balance sheet as such, for many organizations digital assets represent the most valuable asset of all: information.

The first stage of protecting the digital assets of the organization from fraud is the development of a framework to identify items to be protected and the nature of their vulnerability as well as the protection required. It can be as basic as:

Identity and Social Security numbers	Vulnerable to disclosure
Corporate financial information	Vulnerable to disclosure Vulnerable to manipulation
Passwords	Vulnerable to disclosure
Personal information	Vulnerable to disclosure
Encryption keys	Vulnerable to disclosure Vulnerable to destruction
Corporate planning information	Vulnerable to disclosure Vulnerable to destruction Vulnerable to manipulation

By categorizing the information in this manner, one can structure the appropriate internal controls to overcome the vulnerabilities for each category of information. For example, encryption keys that are vulnerable to both disclosure and destruction would require controls such as concealment and restriction of access to prevent disclosure and controls such as restriction of access and adequacy of backup to prevent destruction.

The design of the control systems themselves must fit the needs of both the asset class and vulnerability. In order to ensure the design adequacy and implementation effectiveness, the roles and responsibilities of the stakeholders must be clearly identified.

- *Owners of data* have the responsibility to identify who can access the information and what that individual is permitted to do to the information: create it, update it, copy, delete it, or simply use it.
- *Users* are responsible for keeping their identities and passwords confidential and not attempting to go beyond their level of authority. They are also responsible for maintaining confidentiality since as users of information they automatically have read access and, therefore, by association, copy access.
- *Security management* is not responsible for deciding the level of security required for a digital asset; that is the responsibility of the data owners, who are responsible for choosing the mechanisms by which the level of security is achieved. Where the owner of the data lacks the knowledge to control access, security management may act as internal consultants to the data owner.
- *Internal audit* is normally tasked with the responsibility of assessing the adequacy of the design of the system of internal controls intended to prevent fraud and to test the system's overall effectiveness and make recommendations regarding ineffective controls.

Techniques such as data encryption are now achievable within certain of the system software that accompanies the operating system; for example, Windows 7 has an Encrypting File System available in some versions, and its BitLocker Drive Encryption allows full disks containing confidential information to be encrypted with the encryption key stored on a flash drive. These methods are available only in the Ultimate and Enterprise versions of Windows 7. Where such security techniques are implemented, it is essential that users understand their limitations. Neither of these techniques will prevent files being deleted. With BitLocker, files remain encrypted only while they are stored in the encrypted dive. Copying to another drive or partition automatically decrypts the information.

When confidential information of value to a fraudster is to be sent via e-mail, encryption should definitely be used. Most e-mail software permits the attachment of an encrypted or digitally signed file. Users should recognize, however, that the messages sent internally are encrypted between the server and the client but are *not* encrypted in the user's inbox. In the inbox, messages are vulnerable to any user, such as a network administrator, who has access to the server on which the inbox resides. Given the fact that most fraud carried out on computers is internal fraud, this may be a problem that can be resolved by the acquisition of the appropriate software tool to provide an internal Public Key Infrastructure (PKI) to use the encryption structures discussed earlier in this chapter.

FOILING THE HACKERS

In terms of fraud, computer hacking is looked on as the electronic equivalent of breaking and entering. It involves a deliberate and unauthorized access to a computer system. Hacking is not synonymous with computer fraud since much hacking is done either through simple nosiness or to cause malicious damage. Some hackers have even argued that they provide a useful service by conducting unauthorized penetration studies of information systems and that they should be thanked rather than castigated. By this argument, housebreakers should be thanked for testing the alarm system.

Hacking is now becoming big business in terms of fraud perpetration. Some groups have developed a "hacker for hire" business approach. As previously discussed, it can be relatively simple to obtain the access privileges of a legitimate user if a high fraud awareness is not part of the corporate culture. Hackers have at their disposal a wide variety of tools, many of which were originally developed for the use by IT security personnel to test vulnerabilities in a system's online access. These tools include sniffers, password crackers, keyloggers, spoofers, and a variety of bots. Using these tools, hackers can easily exploit the built-in security weaknesses of many sites. These vulnerabilities include:

- Continued use of the passwords that were built in when the software was first installed. This is particularly problematic with passwords that are built into operating systems.

- Users failing to change their passwords at appropriate intervals depending on the risk levels of individual systems. "Change every 30 days" is still a common rule enforced by the computer systems themselves with no thought given as to whether 30 days is appropriate, inadequate, or overkill.
- Systems that require no password access whatsoever because they are deemed to be low risk but from where a hacker may be able to bridge over into a secured environment.
- Lack of corporate policies on the implementation of antifraud internal control architectures and therefore no user education as to their role in fraud prevention.
- Poor user fraud security awareness at all levels including executives and IT personnel.
- Poor personnel policies in which employees are hired without background checks and given unrestricted access to fraud-vulnerable areas of information systems.
- Poor antifraud operating environment within the company's IT division where the criteria on which they are measured is focused on systems availability and response times with little or no emphasis on achieving a robust antifraud environment.
- Lack of overall security enforcement. In some installations, physical security is high and even the mechanics of logical security is strongly enforced. However, if the user manager adopts the attitude "I trust my staff" as the number-one control priority, all of the technical control enforcements are unable to prevent or detect fraud.

In other words, most hackers gain entry into computer systems because of inefficient and ineffective internal controls, which themselves can be attributed to a failure to carry out fraud risk analysis.

 INVESTIGATING COMPUTER FRAUD

In any computer environment, activities consist primarily of three main elements: input, processing, and output. On that basis, IT fraud can be classified and investigated in a similar structure based on input frauds, processing frauds, and output frauds.

Input frauds normally appear as amended or forged transactions entered into the computer in such a way that, without disturbing normal systems processing, assets can be obtained without setting off alarm bells within antifraud controls. This form of fraud is most commonly conducted by legitimate and authorized users of the systems. Often a clear audit trail can be found, since the fraudster expects that no one will look at the trail unless something strange happens, such as the audit trail being missing. Where such frauds are perpetrated externally—for example, by a hacker—again the audit trail often is available since the hacker may have no knowledge of what transaction trails are retained, where they are kept, and how they can be adjusted without leaving a trace.

Throughput frauds typically involve modification of live systems or direct manipulation of information held on the computer disks. In some cases, these frauds involve alteration to the live systems coding. If the system was written in-house, access to the source code normally is required with a fairly high degree of computer expertise to modify it and convert it to executable code without leaving behind a trace. The fraudster will require access to the live source code (the program as the programmer wrote it), programming expertise in that particular programming language and the software required to convert it to machine-executable form. Where the systems are based on a purchased package, the package provider could turn out to be the source of a fraud or an external threat source with the provider's programmers having an even higher degree of computer expertise to modify the package and insert it into a live environment without leaving a trace.

An alternative form of throughput fraud can be introduced via viruses, back doors designed into systems from inception, or other malwear.

Output frauds occur when a correct invalid output is intercepted and amended prior to its use for a legitimate purpose. Such frauds may take the form of amended payment information or simple breaches of confidentiality.

When an IT fraud is suspected, the first task of the investigator is to confirm whether an incident actually occurred and, if so, whether an error was made or whether there was an intent to defraud. If the investigator believes that a fraud has either been perpetrated or attempted, the process becomes a fraud investigation. This potential transformation to a fraud investigation creates a need to ensure that evidence is accumulated in a lawful manner, handled in a way that ensures a fully documented chain of custody, and proves all the requisite elements of the case in terms of the means, opportunity, and method that was used to carry out the fraud.

While the investigation is going on, it is important to protect the privacy rights of both the organization that has been defrauded and the possible perpetrator. The damage that can be done to an organization's reputation when information is leaked about a possible fraud can be colossal. Even if, in the end, it is determined that no fraud took place or that the assets lost were of minimal value, the damage to the organization's reputation may be permanent and may result in greater losses than the fraud itself did or could have caused.

An important consideration that can erect barriers to an effective investigation is the need to minimize business disruption. The gathering of forensically acceptable evidence usually involves the isolation of the evidence source in order to avoid potential contamination of the evidence as a result of ongoing processing. In a computer system, this usually means taking a forensically acceptable backup of all digital media that could have affected or been affected by the alleged fraud. This must be done in a manner that will allow for legal recrimination.

An effective incident investigation methodology was proposed by Mandia and Prosise and comprised of an 11-stage process[1]:

1. Pre-incident preparation
2. Detection of incidents
3. Initial response
4. Response strategy formulation
5. Duplication and the preparation of forensic backups
6. Investigation
7. Security measure implementation
8. Network monitoring
9. Recovery
10. Reporting
11. Follow-up

Pre-incident Preparation

Pre-incident preparation involves the hardening of systems to ensure that preventive controls reduce the possibility of fraud occurring while detective controls exist to produce evidence such that, should a fraud occur, the organization will be able to determine precisely what happened, which systems were involved, and how the fraud was achieved. Evidence therefore is required regarding:

- How access was acquired
- Who was in a position to carry out the fraud
- What systems were involved
- What data were compromised
- Which files were modified

- Which programs were involved
- Who processed the suspect transactions
- How long the fraud has been running
- When it started
- Whether it is still running

In addition to evidence regarding the actual fraud itself, thought must be given at this point to how normal processing will be resumed and who should be informed of the incident.

To execute this, the fraud risk analysis should have determined which vital assets may be exposed together with the most likely source of the exposure. Individual servers containing those assets or exposed to those risks could then be prepared to detect incidents using techniques such as secure logging and maintaining cryptographic checksums of critical files.

Should the fraud threat arise as a result of a denial-of-service attack, frequent backups of critical data stored securely may mitigate the impact. The frequency required will depend on the risk exposure of that information. This would be a corrective control in the event of a successful attack. Preventive controls would primarily focus on access to block unauthorized incoming software applications from sources, including authorized internal users. Directive controls could include maintaining users' awareness of the risk of fraud and their role in its prevention.

Access via networks can be restricted by the use of effective firewalls, intrusion detection systems, and access control lists on routers. Authentication of users can be extended to biometric authentication. Authentication of other computers can be achieved by cryptographic handshakes or the use of digital certificates. Encryption of network traffic can prevent the introduction of spurious transactions in an undetected manner as can message authentication codes. Monitoring of network traffic can be an effective detective control in highlighting unusual communication patterns or sources.

In keeping with the maintenance of user awareness, policies can be prepared to outline the appropriate corporate response stance. Depending on the nature of the incident, this could range from ignoring the incident, simply defending against further attacks, or performing surveillance in order to gather data regarding the incident for future use or prosecution. In some high-security installations, it is felt that it is better to try to track and trap hackers than simply to reject the access attempt and leave them to try again. The installations therefore prepare a honeypot (a secured area containing data files and functionality that, it is thought, may be attractive to a hacker entering the site). Access into the honeypot would automatically trigger an alarm and set in motion automated tracking and forensic monitoring software, thus preparing the groundwork for future litigation.

From an investigative perspective, preparation would involve the creation of a *forensic response toolkit.* This toolkit normally consists of a hardware/software combination intended to demonstrate the forensic acceptability of evidence gathered. The hardware typically is a high-end processor with extensive memory and storage capability. The storage itself would normally be scrubbed clean electronically so that no potential contamination of evidence could occur. The exact nature of the hardware to be used depends on the nature of the system to be investigated. An uninterruptible power supply is essential to prove that no corruption occurred during data transfer or any other part of the investigation fees because of power outages. In addition to the computer equipment, other items in the forensic response toolkit include those a forensic investigator would use: folders and labels for evidence, lockable evidence storage containers, a printer and paper, a digital camera, computer connectivity and burn bags to enable secure disposal of evidence after approval has been given by legal counsel regarding its future need.

Software tools investigators normally include:

- Two or three native operating systems, depending on operating environment to be investigated
- Forensic duplication tools, which can make exact copies of digital media on a bit-by-bit basis
- All of the drivers required to access all platforms and systems
- A file viewer capable of handling a variety of file structures and formats
- Disk-write blocking software

An incident response team should be put together prior to a fraud occurring so that a potential fraud can be confirmed or dispelled in a time frame that can minimize the damage and scope. Should a fraud be confirmed, the team will collect and document all evidence and maintain a chain of custody for that evidence. At the same time, they will ensure the protection of corporate and individual confidentiality and privacy rights and be prepared to provide expert testimony should a prosecution follow.

Detection of Incidents

Fraud incidents may be detected in a variety of ways, ranging from tips to intrusion detection systems as well as via firewalls, suspicious activity within a system, or malfunctioning services. As part of the user education program, a detection protocol is essential to ensure that critical details are immediately noted, including:

- IT system involved
- Date and time of discovery
- Suspected date and time of the incident occurring
- Who/what software is reporting the incident
- The nature of the incident: intrusion, spurious transaction, out-of-balance conditions, error reports, and the like
- Hardware, data files, and software affected
- Contact information for involved personnel

Initial Response

When a suspected fraud incident is detected, the initial reaction of the response team should be directed toward establishing what appears to have happened and determining the most appropriate *response strategy*, bearing in mind the need to stay within the letter of the law.

Determining what probably has happened involves an examination of the local network topology, potential access routes, and figuring out the actual effectiveness of the preventive and detective measures in place. All this is done as part of preparing the groundwork for the full investigation by conducting interviews of personnel, management, IT systems administrators, network administrators, and end users. All actions taken by the investigator must follow the basic rules regarding interviewing and investigation in the jurisdiction within which the investigation will be carried out to ensure that any evidence, physical, documentary, or verbal, is not compromised during this phase.

Response Strategy Formulation

Not until this phase is complete should the investigator seek to forensically secure evidence from the computer itself. Acquiring evidence from the computer system initially involves securing the physical environment. Before anything is to start, photographic evidence should be gathered of the area around the workstation or server involved, including all papers and removable media, which should be collected and inventoried. Photographs should also be taken of the system, the monitor, and all cable connections.

The system should be shut down by unplugging it directly from the power supply. Under no circumstances should the keyboard or mouse be touched or the power switch used to power down the machine. If the machine is a laptop with its own battery power, this should be removed before disconnection. Shutting down the computer in a normal manner may trigger software specifically intended to encrypt or delete data regarding the fraud. At a minimum, a normal shutdown will alter the data held in temporary files on the disk.

Before the computer itself is moved, it needs to be sealed and all cables and connectors must be clearly labeled. Once the computer has been moved to the physical location where it is to be examined, the case may be opened and, once again, photographs should be taken of the inside of the machine, particularly of any connections, before anything is touched. All hard drives within the system should be isolated by disconnecting the power leads before any attempt is made to stop the system. At this stage, the computer can be plugged in and started so that the system date and time may be collected from the setup menu. This will be needed to compare date and time stamps retrieved from other evidence. It is normal at this point to change the BIOS, the Basic Input Output System containing the startup parameters for the system, on the motherboard to ensure the system boots only from an external source such as a CD drive, a floppy disk, or a USB thumb drive. At this point, the machine may be switched off again.

A forensically cleaned empty hard disk is then connected to the system to be the target drive for the forensic backup. This driver be designated drive 0 with the original desk switched to drive 1. Doing this may involve changing jumper settings on the physical drive. A bootable device, CD, thumb drive, or diskette containing the forensic copying software should be inserted in the appropriate drive and the system restarted.

The forensic copy of the hard disk will then be created, and all drives should be removed from the system, placed into antistatic banks, sealed, and labeled. The sealed disks can then be dated and signed and placed in a secure environment.

Making Forensic Backups

As a general rule, forensic examinations are always conducted on copies of original media. An exact clone is made of the original media, which is then stored securely. In cloning the media, care must be taken to ensure the verisimilitude of the copy. Most of the backup software in general use was not written with forensic replication in mind and seeks to optimize disk utilization during the copying process. Data that has been deleted on the original desk is not normally copied. Typically, only current files are copied and, where they are fragmented on the original disk, they are restructured into contiguous space on the copy. A copy like this would be unacceptable for forensic investigation. To be acceptable, the copy must be made on a bit-by-bit, sector-by-sector basis. This means that fragmented files stay fragmented and remain in the same place they were on the original desk. In addition, files that were deleted from the original desk but have not yet been overwritten will be copied as they are onto the replicated disk. Even fractions of files may contain forensically useful evidence, and they too will be copied. Temporary files will also be duplicated, and the slack space on existing files will be brought over bit by bit. Only cloning at this level of detail will result in a copy that can be investigated and whose results will stand up in court.

Forensic replication software also utilizes encryption technology so that the investigator can guarantee in court that, having made a clone of the original disk, the integrity of the copy was maintained throughout the investigation. This means that no other individual or piece of software could have changed the information on the disk without the investigator being aware of it. To achieve this, the media used to copy to must be forensically sterile. Even brand-new media can arrive with software on it or residue from the manufacturer's testing routines. The investigator normally uses scrubber software to overwrite the disk with random patterns to internationally accepted standards prior to use.

All examinations must take place in a manner that ensures that the evidence remains in its original state and is not in any way adulterated by the examination process. Even the act of looking at a data file on a computer will modify the file attributes of the file. Where such modification is unavoidable, the investigator must retain an investigation log detailing all accesses that took place, which files were accessed, when they were accessed, and what was done to them.

In line with all forensic examinations, the chain of custody must be maintained all times.

If the examination is not conducted to suitable standards, the evidence may be inadmissible in court. Common mistakes include failing to maintain adequate documentation throughout the examination process, which may result in a failure in the chain of custody or results that investigator cannot account for. Failure to notify decision makers within the organization under investigation may jeopardize the legality of the evidence-gathering process and invalidate it for litigation purposes. As with any other evidence to be presented in court, if digital evidence is not properly controlled and secured, its forensic acceptability may be challenged by the other side.

One of the more common mistakes in such investigations involves the underestimation of the scope or duration of the fraud. If the investigation is restricted to too narrow a focus, critical evidence showing the train of events leading up to the fraud may be omitted or even destroyed by the fraudster or by the investigator during the course of the investigation.

Technical errors include allowing date and time stamps on evidence media to be altered before recording them. This, together with failing to record the revised time and date stamps, can inadvertently destroy the forensic acceptability of the evidence. Failure to record the commands used in interrogation or use of untrustworthy software, including pirate copies, can also throw doubt on the validity of all evidence gathered. Even where the software is legitimate, incorrect installation can overwrite significant parts of the evidence and cast doubt on the integrity of what is left.

Where notification of authorities is a matter of law, failure to report in a timely manner may delay litigation and allow fraudsters sufficient time to defeat the ends of justice.

Investigation

Once a fully cloned copy of the data is available to work on, the investigator must decide what evidence will be sought in order to substantiate the accusation that a fraud was committed and the accused was the guilty party. Depending on the nature of the fraud, evidence regarding transactions processed, files accessed, e-mails sent and received, programs executed, and Internet sites visited may all be critical to the prosecution of the accused. In its simplest form, direct manipulation of the data on disk, investigators seeking evidence that the information on a file has been altered may have to look for a previous version of the file. If the previous version has been deleted, it may be possible to resurrect all or part of the previous version for comparison to the current version.

Critical elements of evidence may include log files showing who was online at the time of the fraud, transaction logs showing which transactions were entered by which user id and from which terminal, which programs were used to process the transactions, and who executed the programs. Modern operating systems have the capability to record which files were accessed, the date and time of access, network paths taken, and the programs executed at the time the fraud occurred. Even the overwriting of a computer program with a new, adulterated version, executing it, then returning the program to its original state is recorded within the registry on a Windows system and elsewhere in other operating environments. Unfortunately, although all systems have the capability to record and retain all of this information, not all systems do so.

Once again, the investigator may have to search for files that were deleted but where a residue still exists in fragmentary deleted files.

Security Measure Implementation

As can be seen, once an investigation has been completed it is essential to ensure that such an incident cannot recur by implementing the appropriate security mechanisms. In common with all IT security, such measures must encompass data confidentiality, integrity, and availability of resources. In the case of a fraud investigation, however, security measures must also be seen in the light of the results of the investigation determining the methodology used, resources accessed, and abuse of access rights or user privileges.

With this in mind, security measures must be tailored to specifically address these problem areas in such a manner that the recurrence of such a fraud attempt would be unlikely to succeed and detected early in the attempt.

Network Monitoring

Where the fraud is an ongoing one and insufficient monitoring has been carried out, the investigator may need to monitor traffic flow over the network using packet sniffers, which can detect all network movement from one address to another and copy it if necessary. This evidence may not, on its own, prove the case, but it is a detective technique intended to confirm or dispel suspicions. This information may be one of the indicators of the scope and duration of the fraud, which will dictate the nature and source of more convincing evidence regarding the execution of the fraud.

This type of evidence may also assist the investigator to categorically identify the parties involved and the time line of the fraud execution. At an extreme, it may identify other previously unknown individuals as parties to the fraud.

In the course of an ongoing investigation to a fraud in progress, covert installation of monitoring software on the suspect's computer can record all events on the computer itself as well as all communications to and from that address. Covert use involves running the software in stealth mode with the information gathered automatically sent to the investigator's machine for interrogation. Once again, care is required to ensure that the evidence is legally gathered, unchanged in transit, and stored in an acceptably secure manner both on the target's machine and the investigator's. Such evidence taken from the investigator's machine normally would be considered hearsay evidence but could point the investigator to the information and its location on the suspect's machine once it has been seized.

Recovery

The ultimate intention of any incident response is the restoration to normal operation of the organizational function affected and the computer systems utilized in the perpetration of the fraud.

In some cases the computer systems may require an overall restoration in order to shut down any loopholes in the original system which facilitated the fraud. In other cases recovery may involve a retraining of operational staff where the fraud was perpetrated as a result of weaknesses at the operational end.

If the data files have been affected by the fraudulent activities, a separate exercise may be required, under careful control, to repair damaged data structures and restore the integrity of databases. This kind of exercise may require direct manipulation of the database and must be viewed as a high-risk activity. The involvement of information technology resources, user management, and internal audit will be required throughout the process.

Reporting

As with any other fraud, IT incidents must be reported through the normal fraudulent activity reporting process. Depending on the individual organization, this may involve internal reporting, external reporting, or a combination of both.

Where the incident has been identified within the IT division, initial internal reporting will involve the notification of the user and owner of the system and data affected of the nature of the incident, time and duration, resources involved, impact on data integrity and assets affected.

With this addition, the reporting of fraud would follow the normal procedures as discussed in Chapter 6.

Follow-up

Part of the follow-up to any incident investigation involving fraud will involve ongoing follow-up monitoring to identify future occurrences of similar fraudulent attempts. This may require the introduction of additional monitoring controls within the user area or the computer systems themselves or a combination of the two.

Where the computer systems require amendment in order to introduce additional monitoring controls, the normal change control procedures and system testing requirements must be enforced.

 **COMPUTER LAW**

When computers first became popular as business tools, problems were encountered on a global basis since the laws under which businesses operated focused primarily on tangible properties. With the exception of copyrights, information was not normally seen as something that required protection. The advent of hackers and other forms of computer misdeeds created a requirement for different category of law to protect access to information as well as manipulation or even disclosure of such information.

Governments were particularly concerned about abuse of classified information and its disclosure to foreign nations. At one point in the early 1980s, I discussed with legal authorities in one country what hackers could be charged with under the existing laws. After much debate, we concluded that, if we were able to prove it, hackers could possibly be charged with theft of electricity—the amount of electricity the computer used to do unauthorized things as instructed by an outsider. We concluded that law enforcement was not going to get terribly excited about the theft of a few cents' worth of electricity.

In addition, computer evidence in cases of fraud or embezzlement led to problems in the definition of what was evidence.

In the past, evidence was generally taken to be something that was produced in court originating from a person. Since the computer was not recognized as a person, much of the evidence from it was looked on as hearsay; the only evidence that was acceptable in some courts was that derived from transaction logs and other computer information *that had not been computed.*

Obviously, this situation could not continue. Laws were enacted in jurisdictions around the world to recognize the existence of computed information as an evidence source, particularly where computer output is used in the normal course of business. Before the requirement of the court may be proof that the computer-generated evidence was derived from source that itself was protected and not subject to external tampering before it was produced in court. In addition, unauthorized access to computers, particularly with the intent to defraud, began to be seen as a crime in its own right. Once again, the initial emphasis was on access to government computers and information.

In the United States, laws were enacted in 1984 to ensure that unauthorized access to federal computers with intent to defraud and obtain anything of value, other than the simple unauthorized use of the computer, became a federal crime. Destruction or damage to information on federal computers, whether intentional or not, caused via unauthorized access also became a federal crime. Less significant crime categories were also created for simple unauthorized access to government computers by outsiders but not necessarily insiders.

By the 1990s, the advent of the Internet created new versions of old crimes, such as identity theft, copyright violations, creation of malicious software, cyberstalking, and the like. In efforts to keep up with computer criminals, generic prohibitions were drawn up to create categories within which prosecutions could take place. Wire fraud statutes enabled the prosecution of anyone who used communications media in international or interstate commerce in order to commit a fraud. The statutes were of limited use since not all computer crimes take place with intent to defraud and not all use international or interstate lines. In the United States, it was not until 1996 that an act was passed to make it illegal to even view information held on a computer without appropriate authorization.

Following the events of September 11, 2001, and the enactment of the Homeland Security Act, the Cyber Security Enhancement Act was passed. Powers of law enforcement officers were greatly increased, including the ability to obtain information from internet service providers without a warrant.

Penalties for unauthorized usage of or access to computers vary greatly on a country-by-country basis. Even in the United States, few computer criminals actually end up in jail with the longest sentence of 20 years imprisonment handed out going to Albert Gonzalez in 2010 for Credit Card theft and the selling of 170 million Credit Card and ATM numbers. In contrast, as early as 1995, in China, a computer hacker was executed after being found guilty of embezzling $200,000 from a national bank.

Worldwide legislation now covers such elements as:

- Cyberdefamation laws
- Data protection acts
- Online piracy acts
- Stored communication acts
- Uniform computer information transaction acts
- Digital copyright acts
- Digital evidence acts
- Computer fraud and abuse acts
- Antispam acts in over 30 countries
- A variety of child protection acts

Because many of the laws were enacted several years ago, the wording may seem to be out of date with current threats. There is continual pressure across the globe to make laws up to date with new risks inherent in today's mobile and social networked world. In all cases, investigators should be aware that, at any time, computer evidence may be challenged as to its relevancy, reliability, and admissibility.

The only thing that can be said for sure about computer law is that it will change on an ongoing basis.

 NOTE

1. Kevin Mandia and Chris Prosise, *Incident Response: Investigating Computer Crime*, Berkeley, California: Osborne/McGraw-Hill, 2001

CHAPTER ELEVEN

Legal Issues Surrounding Fraud

The more gross the fraud the more glibly will it go down, and the more greedily be swallowed, since folly will always find faith where impostors will find imprudence.

—*Charles Caleb Colton, British author and clergyman (1780–1832)*

After studying this chapter, the reader should be able to:

- Evaluate the current legislative framework for the country/countries within which the organization is operating and evaluate the effectiveness of the legal structures as a deterrent mechanism for fraud including electronic fraud of an international nature.

There are two primary legal systems under which a case of fraud may be made. These legal systems operate in different jurisdictions. *Common law* traces

275

its roots to the ancient laws of England under which the courts would rule based on precedence and the customs inherent in the particular society. These precedents were interpreted by courts and other judicial tribunals.

In England, these precedents were decided on by three different legal authorities: the Exchequer, the King's Bench, and the Court of Common Pleas. Before AD 1215, the king's word was law and all cases had to be brought before the king's court (*curia regis*). Following a revolt by nobles against the power of the king, the original Magna Carta (Great Charter) was established and forced on King John. This charter established the fundamental principle that no one, whether king, noble, or lawmaker, is above the law. (The text of the Magna Carta may be found at www.constitution .org/eng/magnacar.htm.)

After that time, the Court of Common Pleas permitted cases to be held before a magistrate as long as there were no royal interests involved. Criminal matters were heard before the King's Bench, which also heard appeals against decisions of the Court of Common Pleas.

Common law is the basis under which case law, which derives from judicial judgments rather than legislation, operates and predominates in the United Kingdom, the United States, and other countries previously colonized by the United Kingdom. Disputes under common law are settled using an adversarial exchange of evidence and arguments before a neutral arbitrator, judge, or jury. The evidence is evaluated, the appropriate laws are applied, and judgment is rendered. Either party may appeal the decision to a higher court, although, in a common law system, appellate courts may review findings only in terms of the law and its interpretation, not in terms of facts.

In many parts of Europe and in previous French and Spanish colonies, *civil law* predominates. Under civil law, which dates back to the days of the Romans, legislation is seen as the primary source of law, and court systems may act as inquisitors with precedents overturned based on the court's interpretation of the law. The laws themselves are laid out in comprehensive codifications that have been drawn up by legal scholars. Legislators in such countries use these codifications to structure the code under which all legal control cases are decided. In most countries operating under civil law, juries are not necessarily required, and appellate courts may make findings on both facts and interpretation of the law.

In the United States, the term *civil law* carries two meanings. The first relates to the European definition, as noted earlier, while the second relates to the body of laws governing disputes that do not fall under the heading of criminal law.

IMPACT OF A CONSTITUTION

The legal foundations of many countries are embedded in their constitutions, which set out the general frameworks of government. Many of these constitutions can trace their ancestry to the Magna Carta and operate under government principles of common law; others are drawn up to provide a framework for civil law.

Where a constitution forms the foundation underlying common law or civil law, interpretations of the law normally look to the constitution as a final arbiter of what is or is not legal.

In the state of Louisiana, historically influenced by both France and England influences, the state's constitution, administrative and criminal law, civil and criminal procedures, and rules of evidence are generally derived from common law, although Louisiana itself is normally referred to as a civil law state, and judges, unlike those in other states, are not bound by judicial precedent.

FRAUD AND THE LAWS OF EVIDENCE

When a case is prosecuted in court, judgment is normally made based on the quality and quantity of evidence presented to the court. Regardless of whether the case involves a criminal prosecution or a lawsuit claiming a civil fraud, the nature of the evidence will remain the same, although the burden of proof is heavier in criminal cases.

Evidence is taken to be any form of proof legally presented at trial to prove the truth or falsity of a fact. Evidence may be:

- *Direct evidence*, which is oral testimony with regard to information obtained from any of the witness's five senses called to prove a specific act (e.g., testimony by an eyewitness).
- *Real evidence*, which consists of tangible objects that prove or disprove guilt, such as physical evidence linking the suspect to the scene of the crime.
- *Documentary evidence*, which takes the form of printouts, business records, and the like presented to the court. Most computer evidence submitted takes the form of documentary evidence.
- *Demonstrative evidence*, which is presented to a jury to demonstrate how an event could have taken place or how the crime could have been

committed. Again, evidence submitted as proof in a computer fraud could include diagrams, charts, and illustrations, such as access opportunities, proving that a crime could have been done in a specific manner.

A key element in regard to evidence in a fraud case is that there is no such thing as accidental fraud. For an act to constitute fraud, *intent* must be proven. Intent is difficult to prove without direct evidence by an eyewitness that indicates the actions leading to the execution of the fraud were intentional. An order given to a subordinate to make fraudulent entries in the books of account may be presented as *best evidence*.

Real evidence, as defined earlier, may create an indirect connection between the fraud and the accused, which may, circumstantially, indicate intent. It is difficult to prove a whole case based on circumstantial evidence, which could easily be interpreted as evidence of an error.

Generally, evidence can be led in court in order to demonstrate that the individual had a *motive* to carry out of fraud. Even without proof that the individual was able to put funds generated by the fraud directly in the bank, fraud may still be provable. A motive may be shown, such as recording items fraudulently in order to improve sales-based compensation or to achieve performance targets that would otherwise not have been achieved.

Concealment is another indicator of intent. Although a case could be made that fear of management punishment for making errors was the reason for the concealment, it is normally taken that honest people have no necessity or motive to be reticent about their activities or seek to hide them.

Evidence that indicates *ongoing patterns* of behavior or transactions may indicate that, instead of a one-time error, there exists a trail indicating intent over an extended period of time.

In addition to intent, evidence would need to indicate that the accused had the *opportunity* to perpetrate fraud. Again, this evidence could be in the form of direct evidence by a witness, either to indicate a particular event occurred or that the normal manner in which accused carried out his or her duties would have given the accused the opportunity to commit the fraud. In the absence of direct evidence of a witness, documentary evidence showing levels of authority or job descriptions that indicate the ability of the accused to commit fraud in the manner in which it happened would also go a considerable way to indicate opportunity.

Even should there be proof of falsification with intent to deceive, this does not necessarily prove fraud unless it also can be shown that there was a victim of the fraud who *relied* on the falsification in order to make a business decision or suffer a loss.

Whether there was a financial loss or not, even a loss of reputation may be sufficient to prove *damage*, and a court may award actual damages, punitive damages, or both.

- *Actual damage* usually involves the amount of direct loss that can be shown in court.
- *Punitive damages* usually are assessed by the court based on other issues than provable cash losses and may, in some cases, be considerably higher than the amount of money directly attributable to the fraud itself. Loss of customer confidence or even embarrassment may be taken into consideration.

At any time, a court may exclude evidence on specific grounds. For example, in the United States, evidence gathered in a manner in violation of the constitutional rights of the accused may be ruled inadmissible in a criminal case. In such a case, the state is prevented from conducting illegal searches and seizures by the Fourth Amendment to the Constitution, which forms the basis for the exclusionary rule. The concern is not what the evidence proves but rather how the evidence was acquired.

Such evidence is commonly referred to as fruit of the poisonous tree. Exceptions do occur permitting such evidence to be admitted if the court decides, for example, that the information would inevitably have been discovered despite the violation or if it was uncovered partly from a second source, not in violation.

In a civil case, however, such exclusions normally fall away since they apply to criminal cases. Since the Fourth Amendment to the Constitution applies specifically to government officials, evidence obtained from the accused by a private person is normally admissible even if unlawfully gained, although this too is subject to debate.

 ## ASSET RECOVERY

In bringing an action to court, part of the intention is to attempt victim restitution in the form of asset recovery. As mentioned in Chapter 9, in certain cases asset forfeiture is used to deprive those engaged in fraud from the proceeds of their crime. The primary objective of asset forfeiture is to secure assets in order ultimately to restore them to the victims of crime. One problem is assessing which assets can be linked to the crime as proceeds and can be seized and which are merely assets of equal value, known as substitute or equivalent value assets, which can prove problematic in seeking a seizure order. Asset forfeiture targets specific assets, primarily those that can be proved to derive from criminal activities. Where redress is being sought in a civil action, asset forfeiture does not apply since a civil case is, by definition, not specifically attempting to prove criminality.

In addition, problems can arise where, in addition to the victims, money is owed to creditors and other third parties such as financial institutions who may seek a prior claim to the seized assets. In these cases, proving who has first claim on the defendants' assets may become a matter of contract. Victims and secured creditors normally are favored, and unsecured creditors are left without remedy.

In the cases where assets have been moved overseas, the problems multiply. The use of offshore trusts along with companies registered in foreign jurisdictions, offshore assets, and bank accounts make the identification, tracing, freezing, and seizure of such assets considerably more difficult. With the ability to move funds from country to country electronically, asset transfer can stay ahead of all seizure attempts. By the time a warrant is executed, the money may be long gone.

Identification and tracing the movement of such assets becomes critical, particularly in areas of public corruption and money laundering. This identification commonly means uncovering and identifying ownership interests where the interest in property and control over it has been deliberately disguised, frequently by changing the form of the ownership as well as its nature. Tracing generally is a first step in the development of an asset recovery process. Not only must the assets be located, but the relationship must be established between the asset itself and the criminal activity that led to its removal. Asset movements processed through conventional financial systems normally can be traced via the conventional audit trail. Such tracing can, however, be extremely complicated since fraudsters generally use multiple accounts to confuse the trail and multiple corporate entities may seem to be temporary owners of the asset. Where the assets are moved internationally, the trail may be even more complicated to follow because of national legislation and the nature of the local financial systems. In transactions that normally are cash based, conventional audit trails may fail, and assistance from local law enforcement agencies will probably be required.

Once assets are identified and a causal relationship with corruption, bribery, and simple crime is identified, steps must be taken to prevent asset removal beyond the reach of the investigator or legal authorities. A *freezing order* can prevent the disposal of assets or their removal from the jurisdiction of the court that is awarded the order. In order to obtain a freezing order, the applicant must demonstrate that there exists a good, arguable case that the assets are located within the court's jurisdiction. In addition, the applicant must demonstrate a serious risk that the assets will be dissipated in the absence of such an order. Such freezing of assets has its own drawbacks, however, since it immediately alerts perpetrators to the investigation. It may also prevent further evidence regarding other potential assets as yet uncovered from becoming apparent because of the secession of movement of the discovered asset. Where this disclosure of interest is seen to be a source of risk, legal steps can be taken to prevent financial institutions from informing the current "owner" of the assets of the existence of the investigation.

Seizure of assets uncovered, particularly in international cases, requires legal action, which may involve civil proceedings against an individual (*in personam*), criminal confiscation against an individual (*in personam*), or civil procedures specifically against property (*in rem*) in order to transfer ownership of the frozen assets back to the requestor of seizure. In countries where civil law applies, an *accion civil resarcitoria* (a civil action of restitution) may be used to separate the need for criminal conviction of a perpetrator from the award of monetary compensation for the asset. In such cases, a concurrent criminal investigation must make it all the way to a trial. At this point, the criminal prosecution separates from the civil action for restitution. It is possible that civil action will succeed despite the criminal prosecution failing.

Other court orders can be sought, including *third-party disclosure orders* requiring third parties who innocently became embroiled in the commission of the fraud to disclose information that assists in the location of either the accused fraudster or the missing assets. Such orders normally override duties of confidentiality of the third party toward the accused fraudster. Search orders can be granted where a case has been made and accepted by a court that the applicant faces serious actual or potential damage from the fraud and that there is clear evidence that incriminating documents or items exist in the possession of the subject of the search order.

International recovery of losses is an extremely complicated procedure with a range of obstacles. Depending on the value of the assets lost, an individual or organization must also consider the chances of a successful recovery before deciding to proceed. The nature of any insurance coverage may also dictate the approach required in attempting recovery. Where, for example, the insurance company has paid based on a valid claim, the ownership will normally revert to the insurance company itself, and the decision to attempt recovery must be made by the insurance company, not the original owner.

The time it takes to proceed with the case both locally and internationally can give the perpetrator additional ways to conceal the assets and compromise the investigation. In addition, the more complicated legal procedures required, the more substantial the legal costs will be to seek a judgment that ultimately may be too late to implement. Where the assets removed have been transferred and transmuted into other assets—for example, money into property—it may be difficult legally to prove that money stolen in one country is essentially the same asset as property owned in another country, particularly if it is owned by a third party.

Where there has been any impropriety in the original acquisition and ownership of the asset, attempts to recover legally may expose the original owner to legal liability in its own right. If victims of the fraud then seek to continue the case after an impropriety has been uncovered by changing the representations they originally made, an *estoppel judgment* may be made, effectively preventing the fraud victims from asserting a fact inconsistent with the position previously presented.

Piercing the veil may prove necessary where corporations have been established specifically to shield owners from any legal obligations by creating the corporation as a separate "legal person." This is a judicial doctrine that enables corporate shareholders to be held personally liable for damages or debts caused by a corporation under their control. In order to pierce the veil, it must be demonstrated that the shareholders have acted both intentionally and illegally or that the corporation is an alter ego of the shareholders established in order to defraud creditors.

In its 2009 document on asset recovery, the International Center for Asset Recovery present a practical approach to the investigative process and demonstrate the importance of information technology in tracing stolen assets.[1] It also demonstrates the use of the anti–money laundering framework as a way to trace assets.

 ## LABOR LEGISLATION AND FRAUD

In many countries, labor legislation is designed to ensure full-time workers are entitled to a range of benefits, including minimum wages, maximum working hours, and paid vacation time. In some jurisdictions, labor law also dictates the conditions under which employment can be terminated. Fraud can occur when an employer seeks to bypass such legislation in order to reduce costs and improve competitive ability at the expense of workers. At times of high unemployment, "unemployed" workers may collaborate with employers by accepting conditions below legal minimums for fear of job loss.

Workplace fraud exists when an employer misclassifies a worker as a non-employee in order to avoid paying unemployment insurance taxes, payroll taxes, worker's compensation insurance premiums, and the like. In most jurisdictions, failure to classify a worker as an employee is illegal since it denies the state the appropriate taxation revenues and denies the worker the appropriate rights and privileges. It may also exist when organizations are paying workers less than the legal minimum or have working conditions or hours of labor that exceed legal standards.

In some cases, companies knowingly seek to evade labor legislation by classifying workers as independent contractors rather than employees. In order to legally achieve such classification, an individual must be demonstrably:

- Free from day-to-day control and direction
- Customarily engaged in an independent business of the same nature as the work being undertaken for the present company
- Performing similar work for organizations other than the present company on a regular basis
- Performing tasks outside of the usual course of business of the company

Where companies cannot demonstrate such independence, an employer–employee relationship may be presumed to exist.

A common way of bypassing legislation is the use of temporary staffing; some organizations effectively outsource their workforce to agencies and bring their workers back into the organization as temporary agency staff. Such staff members may still be working on a temporary basis several years later but, because of their nonemployed status, many aspects of labor legislation do not apply to the contract in company. Labor legislation is also designed to protect employees from retaliation by an employer if a complaint is filed alleging corporate violation of that legislation.

Labor legislation does have other applications in fraud cases. When an employer has uncovered a fraud involving employee deception, the steps that can be taken against the employee are commonly laid down within the national labor legislation. Most such legislation contains clauses for disciplinary procedures or dismissal for a variety of offenses with an "express lane" where such offenses involve fraud. It is common within such legislation that the standard of proof is based on the balance of probabilities rather than the more rigorous beyond a reasonable doubt required in criminal cases. As a result, where employee fraud is detected, it is common for employers to seek redress under labor legislation with its less rigorous standard of proof rather than attempt to press criminal charges, where the burden of proof may require excessive cost of investigation or prosecution. This response can lead to fraudsters being detected and dismissed with no criminal charges and no blot on their record, which frees them to seek employment elsewhere and repeat the fraud.

 NOTE

1. Basel Institute on Governance, International Center for Asset Recovery, *Tracing Stolen Assets A Practitioners Handbook2* (Basel, Switzerland: Author, 2009).

CHAPTER TWELVE

Industry-Related Fraud Opportunities

The man who is admired for the ingenuity of his larceny is almost always rediscovering some earlier form of fraud. The basic forms are all known, have all been practiced. The manners of capitalism improve. The morals may not.

—*John Kenneth Galbraith, Canadian-American economist and author (1908–2006)*

After studying this chapter, the reader should be able to:

- Identify those fraud opportunities that are specific to individual industries as well as government institutions.
- Design effective control mechanisms specific to those industry risks to achieve optimized control effectiveness at minimized cost.

In addition to defrauding opportunities and indicators that have been discussed earlier in this book, fraud opportunities exist within specific industries that can be treated individually to structure internal controls in order to achieve optimum fraud risk reduction for minimum cost.

BANKING FRAUD

Banking fraud is a scheme intended to defraud a financial institution or to obtain the assets under the control of a financial institution by means of fraud. Multiple variations of bank fraud occur, including:

- Money laundering
- Card fraud
- Check fraud
- Wire fraud
- Online fraud

Money Laundering

As mentioned in Chapter 2, money laundering involves the processing of a financial transaction representing the proceeds of unlawful activity in such a manner to conceal the nature, source, or ownership of the proceeds or to avoid a legal requirement to report such a transaction.

This form of banking fraud differs in many ways from traditional banking fraud since the bank is not itself the target; nor are the bank's depositors. Rather it involves the use of the banking environment and infrastructure to carry out an illegal activity. The impact on financial institutions is primarily reputation with monetary exposure as part of a legal penalty. The risks to a financial institution include:

- Operational risk
- Compliance risk
- Reputation risk
- Legal risk

In order to fight money laundering, financial institutions often are required to maintain detailed records of any prescribed transactions with such information furnished to the appropriate authorities on request or as required.

They are also normally required to keep records showing the verification of the identity of banking clients. Depending on the jurisdiction, such records may require to be kept up to ten years after ceasing business with those particular clients. The overall objectives of anti–money laundering activities are:

- Prevention of the use of the financial institution or its infrastructure for money laundering purposes by criminal elements
- Implementation of appropriate internal controls specific to money laundering in order to detect activities defined as suspicious under the laws of a given jurisdiction
- Ensuring compliance by the financial institution with all applicable laws and regulations
- Improving the financial institution's knowledge of the financial dealings of its own customers in order to ensure the appropriate management of the financial institutions risks

Combating money laundering involves increased care in the area of data management. All transactions become subject to monitoring with automatic triggers for suspicious activity that fall within a legislative reporting requirement. In some jurisdictions, triggers for suspicious activity are laid down by legislation and can be automated within the information systems of the financial institution. In others, risk profiling may be required in order to identify suspicious patterns when compared against potential money laundering scenarios. When applied at a customer level, risk profiling is normally based on an analysis of transactional behavior, particularly those behaviors associated with high-risk or high-value transactions.

Banks may retain these profiles within a high-risk database structured alternatively by geographic movements, high-risk services or products, or customers on the watch list of law enforcement authorities in that particular jurisdiction. With the volume of transactions entered into via banking systems, only the application of continuous monitoring techniques using computerized resources can effectively carry out anti–money laundering scrutiny to an acceptable level. Such monitoring may be targeted toward transactions that appear abnormally large or are unusually complex as well as unusual patterns of transactions. Transactions that are outside the normal profiled activity of a customer may be flagged for attention as may large amounts or values of cash transactions. Any transaction that involves counterfeit or forged currency will obviously be given special attention. Most jurisdictions have a requirement that the appropriate authorities be notified in a timely manner of all significant transactions in terms of anti–money laundering legislation with significant penalties for a financial institution that fails to provide such notification.

One of the more critical controls involves a due diligence approach to customers. Confirmation of the authenticity of an identity claimed by a customer of a bank is legislated in many countries in an effort to stamp out money laundering under assumed names of individuals or companies prior to the opening of a bank account. Internal controls over customer identities include verification by:

- Documentary evidence of the legal status and address of individuals or organizations
- Ensuring and verifying the identity of any person authorized to act on the bank account
- For organizations: Recording the nature of business activity, financial status, as well as value and volume of turnover

Most financial institutions and most jurisdictions take the threat of money laundering very seriously. Nevertheless, there are still loopholes in the application of such legislation that can decrease its effectiveness and the overall effectiveness of counterterrorist financing regulations. Intensive employee education and occasionally a change in the internal culture of a bank is needed to overcome a historic attitude that the confidentiality of customers' accounts and transactions is sacrosanct and should not be disclosed to any of individual or authority without a direct instruction from a court of law. Many law-abiding customers find such monitoring and notification to be an unwarranted and unacceptable intrusion into the personal privacy of their financial dealings. Customer education then becomes a key component of effective implementation of anti–money laundering controls.

Card Fraud

There are three basic types of card fraud:

1. Credit card fraud
2. Debit card fraud
3. Automated teller machine (ATM) card fraud

Credit cards allow the delay of payment and the extension of credit while *debit cards* involve the automatic deduction from the cardholder's account at the time of transaction. In many countries, debit cards are used for ATM transactions; in others, separate *ATM cards* are issued by financial institutions. A major difference between credit cards and debit cards/ATM cards is the manner in which the cardholder is authenticated. For credit cards, this is based on recognition of the signature when compared to a record held of the authentic signature. This authentic signature is usually recorded on the white strip on the back of the card. Since their inception, credit cards have suffered from their use of this authentication method. If a card that has been signed is stolen, a would-be fraudster has a template of the authentic signature to practice copying. If it is not signed, the fraudster can simply add the name from the front of the card using his or her own handwriting. In many cases, the signature is irrelevant since no actual verification takes place when a card is used even in the presence of a checkout operator.

Where the card itself is not required, only the number (card not present [CNP] transaction)—for example, for purchases on the Internet—authentication must take place in another way.

Online authentication usually involves a request for some form of personal information, such as the address or postal code to which a bank statement is sent. Such information often is available on social networks, and all that is required is knowledge of the name on the card. In some cases, the three- or four-digit number on the back of the card known as the card security code (CSC) or credit card ID (CCID) plus the expiration date are all that is required. In the case of a stolen card, this is readily available.

Unfortunately, this is not the only way credit card fraud is carried out. Credit card information is commonly stored on computer systems and is vulnerable to theft in the event of a breach of such systems. Since 2005, over 265 million credit and debit card records have been stolen. Many thousands of new stolen credit card numbers are offered for sale on the Internet each day with prices ranging from under a dollar to over $30, depending on the type of card. Unless negligence or intent is proven, neither the consumers nor the merchants suffer the loss; it falls back on the financial institution. Credit card information also can be found on discarded statements, discarded receipts, or even carbon duplicates of transactions. A more sophisticated way of gathering information involves card skimming, where a dishonest employee captures credit card numbers as well as the information on the magnetic stripe using a device known as a skimmer after customers have handed over the card. Once again, this information can be used for CNP transactions, but it can also be used in the manufacturing of fake credit cards.

Debit and ATM cards authenticate purely by use of a personal identification number (PIN). Once, again this is vulnerable to skimming as well as obtaining the numbers from third-party sites.

Internal Controls Against Card Fraud

To counteract this in the United States, the Payment Card Industry (PCI) has created its own Data Security Standard (DSS). While the standard is not regulatory or statutory, compliance is a contractual obligation. As such, card associations can be selective regarding what services are provided to merchants, and merchants accept the services on a voluntary basis. Association rules place restrictions on participating banks requiring them to monitor merchants' compliance with the standards. The PCI-DSS standards themselves include requirements such that all parties to payment card processing including merchants, card issuers, processors, acquirers, and service providers must achieve a minimum standard of protection for cardholder data that includes:

- *Building and maintenance of a secure network* that includes the installation and maintenance of firewalls as well as the changing or removal of vendor-supplied default passwords and security parameters.
- *Protection of cardholder data*, both in a stored form as well as transmission across open networks when encryption is a requirement.
- *Maintenance of a vulnerability management program*, ensuring the use and updating of antivirus software and the development and maintenance of secure systems.
- *Implementation of strong access controls* in order to restrict access to cardholder data on a need-to-know basis. This requires unique computer access IDs as well as the restriction of physical access to cardholder data.
- *Network monitoring and testing* to ensure the tracking and monitoring of all accesses both to networks and cardholder data accessible via the networks, with security systems and processes requiring to be tested regularly.
- *Maintenance of an information security policy* covering security for all personnel.

The full standard requirements and security assessment procedures is downloadable from the PCI Security Standards Council Web site at www.pcisecuritystandards.org.

Once a fraudster has obtained the appropriate information regarding the credit or debit card, it can be used wherever a CNP transaction can occur.

The Internet is an obvious target for frauds of this nature with goods and services purchased based on stolen information.

Credit card numbers themselves have a built-in check digit that can be used to verify whether the number itself is valid. Verification using this number is known as a Luhn check, after the German computer scientist who invented it. In essence, the final digit of a credit card number is a check digit. Credit card number validity may be authenticated by recalculating this check digit.

For example, on a 16-digit credit card number, the check digit may be verified by:

- Working backward from the check digit, every second digit is doubled, eight digits in total.
- If this doubling results in a two-digit number, the digits are added together to get a single-digit number.
- These numbers are then used to replace the original numbers that were doubled on the original credit card number.
- All of the digits in this "new" credit card number are added together. If the number is exactly divisible by 10, the credit card number is valid.
- In the case of a 15-digit credit card number, the principle is the same but only seven digits require doubling.

The Luhn check does not prove that a number is a genuine, issued credit card number, only that the number itself complies with the rules for verifying the check digit.

In addition to CNP transactions, fraudsters can manufacture fake credit cards that appear to be legitimate, including the correct graphic, hologram, and magnetic strip information on the reverse. Even smart chips can be added to fake cards. The process requires special equipment but is neither complicated nor overly expensive. Such equipment is obtainable via the Internet.

The current direction for card authentication is the incorporation of biometric authentication techniques. Biometrics is a technique based on the underlying assumption that individuals have unique physical characteristics that cannot be reproduced, such as fingerprints, handprints, voice prints, retinas, or facial recognition geometry. In many cases, such technology is not 100 percent foolproof but it does raise the barrier on the degree of sophistication required of a card fraudster. There are already smartphones that double as debit and credit cards with transactions authorized by fingerprints. An alternative that is currently being developed in the United Kingdom is VoicePay, which allows users to make online or cell phone purchases with authentication achieved using voice recognition. Even signatures can be digitally recorded on a card and compared with a signature entered using a magnetic pen. One major problem in the use of biometrics is that, should a breach occur, legitimate users cannot change, for example, their thumbprint.

In addition to technical controls covering authentication of cards and card users, it is important that traditional controls are not neglected on the assumption that the technical controls are all that is required. Traditional controls to prevent card fraud include:

- Signing the back of the card in permanent ink as soon as it has received.
- Recording all card numbers and keeping them securely stored for ease of cancellation in the event of a card loss or theft of a purse or wallet.
- Never carry all cards at once. In the event of a theft or loss, canceling one or two cards is considerably less inconvenient than having to cancel all cards.
- Review statements to ensure the validity of transactions as soon as the statements are received. If possible, it is even better to perform frequent online reviews of card transactions.
- Be aware of when statements are due and alert the card issuer if statements are late.
- Shred all documents containing identification information before disposal.
- Never divulge the credit card number to an unknown Web site even if they ask for it.
- Never write a PIN number on the card or download it to any third party.
- Store PIN numbers separately from the cards.
- Never lend cards, even to close friends or family. The cardholder remains responsible for all charges.
- Be aware of the possibility of skimming or someone using a cell phone in the near vicinity that could photograph the card or make a video of the PIN entry.
- When the card is used for a purchase and returned, ensure it is the same card.
- Notify the credit card company in advance if large purchases are to be made or if the card will be used out of your normal area.
- Never allow a merchant or service provider to retain your card details on file if requested. Penetration of their system would give your credit card details to potential fraudsters.

Once again, none of these controls is individually effective in card fraud prevention; in combination, however, they can have a significant impact on reducing card fraud risk.

Internal Controls Against Card Fraud: Merchants

From the merchant's perspective, card fraud becomes a significant problem in CNP sales. Where a physical card is presented to the merchant and a transaction is authorized, the liability for fraud rests with the card issuer as long as the merchant conforms to the regulations. If so, the merchant will receive its payment.

In the case of a CNP sale, whether by the Internet, mail order, or telephone, the liability rests with the merchant. Most commonly this type of fraud results in a chargeback when the legitimate card owner disputes the payment. This is true even when a bank has authorized the transaction. The bank simply verifies that the number is a valid one that has not been reported stolen and that the account has funds sufficient for the transaction; the onus of the acceptability of the transaction rests with merchant. As a double impact on the merchant, credit card processors may raise their prices because of increased risk. If a merchant's fraud rate becomes too high, its account with the card company may be suspended. Other internal controls at the merchant level include:

- *Address verification systems.* In the United States and some European countries, the cardholder's address or zip code may be confirmed by the bank that issued the card. This is not foolproof since fraudsters, once they have the genuine card information, can look up address information to match the card from social sites on the Internet.
- *Payer authentication programs.* This software uses personal passwords to confirm the identity of the card user in a CNP online transaction. Where this program is used by merchants, some of the costs of online fraud may be attributable to the card issuer of many cards. Users may, however, run pop-up blocking software that will block such authentication requests.
- *Card verification methods.* This refers to the use of the security codes imprinted on the card although not encrypted in the magnetic stripe (CID American Express: CVV2 VISA: CVC2 MasterCard). Where credit card numbers have been stolen, it is less likely that fraudster will have access to these security codes. If the card itself has been stolen or a merchant's employee has recorded the security code from the back of the card, this control is ineffectual. Nevertheless, requesting this number online or telephonically can deter fraudsters who only have access to the card number itself.
- *Bank Identification Number(BIN) checks.* The first six digits of each card identify the issuing bank for the credit card. The name of the issuing bank can

be checked at: http://all-nettools.com/toolbox, financial, which provides the bank name, the funding type, the card type, contact details, and the country of origin.

■ *Card pattern recognition.* For online purchases, a fraudulent pattern may emerge of multiple purchases to be shipped to the same address using different credit cards. If these purchases are made from the same Internet Protocol (IP) address, there is a strong possibility that a stolen list of credit card numbers is being used. In the same way, where the same card is used with a variety of expiration dates, the fraudster may have access only to the card number and may simply be giving expiration dates until one works.

■ *Beware free e-mail accounts.* Where purchases are made from free e-mail services, the ability to trace the originator of the e-mail is severely limited. Although many legitimate customers may use such e-mail addresses, virtually all fraudsters use them in order to remain anonymous. Customers who claim to be businesses rarely use free e-mail accounts.

Once again, these controls are not foolproof. Depending on the nature of the transaction and the value involved, it may or may not be cost effective to implement such controls. Where the risk is high, these controls may be seen as a minimum level to assist in the detection of possible attempts at card fraud.

Check Fraud

Check fraud remains popular among the fraudsters due to the lack of sophistication required to commit such fraud. Utilizing the simplest of computer technology, unsuspecting and unsophisticated victims can easily fall prey to such frauds. Counterfeiting of checks normally involves the use of special papers and inks. It can be countered using the controls described in Chapter 2 in the section titled "Document Fraud."

Check fraud within the organization most commonly takes place when an employee issues a check without proper authorization. Often fraudsters issue corporate checks without proper authorization for an extended period before detection. Such fraud also, however, can take place when an incoming check is stolen, endorsed, and presented for payment at either a bank or retail establishment. A variation on check fraud involves the issuing of checks on accounts that have already been closed or where there is no intention of providing funds to cover the amount. This technique is known as *paperhanging.*

Check kiting involves utilizing accounts at multiple financial institutions to create apparently legitimate balances. A check is drawn on an account with insufficient funds in bank A and deposited into bank B. A second check, this time drawn on the account in bank B, is deposited into bank A, apparently to cover the amount withdrawn on the original check from bank A. This type of fraud utilizes the banking *float*. The float represents the money present in the banking system during the interval between time the original deposit is made into bank B and the time the money is deducted from bank A. Once a check has been deposited into bank B, it will be credited immediately to the depositor's account on the assumption that bank A ultimately will send the funds to bank B. By depositing the second fake check from bank B (which now thinks the depositor has the funds) into bank A, bank A is now under the impression that the funds are available to cover the original check and will pass the payment on to bank B, which will, in turn, order the check to be deposited into bank A. While this may seem a waste of time since the same money is flowing backward and forward, the creditworthiness of the depositor is being increased in both banks. Over a period of time, the value of the checks will increase significantly until eventually the apparent funds actually are withdrawn. This type of scheme may involve multiple people using multiple bank accounts in a circular manner, making detection considerably more difficult. Where depositors appear to be businesses, the value of such checks and therefore the ultimate losses to the banks can increase dramatically.

Counterfeiting generally takes two forms: use of chemicals and solvents to modify the information written or printed on a check, or the complete fabrication of a fraudulent check, typically using today's computer technology and high-quality scanners and printers.

Check fraud as a whole is generally taken to be a breach of criminal law. In the United States, check kiting is a federal offense while paperhanging is taken to be a breach of state law. The Check Clearing for the 21st Century Act or Check 21 Act of 2004 permits financial institutions to utilize digital images of the original check (front and back) in place of the paper document. This has made check fraud more difficult since legitimate signatures on canceled checks may no longer be available, having been replaced by the digital image. It has also substantially reduced the clearing time for checks since there is no longer the requirement to physically move paper from one side of the country to the other and money transfer can now take place electronically.

Once again, a critical component of the control structures preventing check fraud from occurring are employees' knowledge, awareness, and alertness. Internal controls, such as maintaining the physical security of checks and deposit slips, are critical. Segregation of duties between check writers and the account reconciliation function can go a long way toward early detection as well as prevention of check fraud. The fewer personnel authorized to sign checks, the lower the chances of check fraud being attempted. Ensuring that the checks themselves are printed on paper that uses high-security features to prevent simple document fraud will make counterfeiting more difficult.

If an organization is shown to have inadequate controls to prevent and detect check fraud, it may be held to be partially liable for any losses due to such frauds.

Check security at the corporate end involve controls such as:

- Ensuring there have been recent background and credit checks on all employees handling the processing of payments.
- Ensuring vacation policies are enforced, since it is during vacations that check fraud often comes to light.
- Ensuring all supplies of checks and other banking documents are stored under lock and key at all times.
- Limiting the number of authorized signatories.
- Requiring more than one signature on large-value checks and notifying the bank of this.
- Ensuring segregation of duties exists between the check writing, signature, and reconciliation functions.
- Ensuring all accounts are reconciled promptly and frequently.
- Limiting the value of checks that can be drawn on specific accounts with additional controls placed on accounts authorized for the processing of high-value checks.
- Using Positive Pay, which warns banks of checks being issued including check numbers, dates, bank information, and amounts.
- Using Reverse Positive Pay in which the bank sends the organization a list of the day's presented checks to be matched against the company's own checks-issued database. Dubious checks can then be viewed online and then paid or returned as appropriate.
- Reviewing returned checks to ensure no counterfeits have been processed against corporate bank accounts. Counterfeits may be detected through variations in paper, color, perforation, check size, check style, or corporate logo.

Wire Fraud

Wire transfers involve the transfer of money and securities via electronic media with almost instantaneous transfer taking place. Wire fraud or wire transfer frauds occur when transfer is made to an account that is not intended as the recipient by someone other than an authorized individual. Because of the speed of transfer, funds transferred fraudulently or as the result of a hoax can be moved on in seconds, leaving a cold audit trail. In addition to the execution of a fraudulent transfer, con artists have enormous opportunities to persuade a target with legitimate access to electronic funds to transfer them to another's custody, from where they can be retransferred instantaneously. Many such cons have already been described in Chapter 2.

In practice, wire transfer frauds tend to occur more in business and government accounts than in consumer accounts because the funds available to be transferred are larger. Where payments are due and the intention is for the payee to pay them into a corporate bank account, information must be provided to facilitate the payment. This includes the bank, clearing codes, bank address, and bank account number. Armed with this information, a fraudster is in a position to commit check fraud or wire fraud against this account. Where payments are made to an organization electronically, a special account should be set up to receive such payments with the bank informed that this should be nondispersing account (i.e., an account into which money can be paid but not withdrawn). All funds transferred in should then be automatically transferred by the bank solely to the organization's own accounts. In this way, money can be received by wire with full disclosure of the account details without fear that money will be withdrawn.

In the United States, payments via an Automated Clearing House (ACH) debit enables a merchant to accept an authorized debit from a customer's checking account. Such debits may be:

- One-time debits
- Recurring debits
- Business-to-business (B2B) debits
- B2B recurring debits

Genuine B2B debits typically are used for invoiced payments to suppliers or wholesalers as well as for the supply of business services. The request to the bank for such a debit must come from account holders themselves but may come via the Internet, in person, or by telephone. Despite their undoubted convenience, there are some drawbacks in the use of ACH debits. These include:

- The need to hand over information regarding bank account details as well as access to a bank account to a third party.

- Accidental overbilling may be noticed and challenged only after payment has taken place.
- Accounts maybe overdrawn accidentally if overbilling occurs or if insufficient funds are available at the exact time of processing the debit.
- Automatic payments discourage the checking of invoices to ensure their validity prior to payment.
- Fraudulent overbilling may not be noticed if no independent authorization is required prior to payment.

In addition to attacks directly on consumers by individuals purporting to be an account holder with sufficient identifying information to satisfy the financial institution, corporations may also be hit.

The starting point for such a scam is the individual's or organization's account information, which is readily available on any check. Fraudsters targeting a specific company have been known to work for the organization for a single day and then quit in order to receive a paycheck with the company's account number and routing number. Unlike checks that require specified signatories and may require two signatories for high-value checks, direct debits often are not subject to such dual control or senior-level authorization. The individual responsible for reconciliation of bank accounts, while not an authorized signatory on check, still may be in a position to authorize an ACH debit against the account he or she is responsible for reconciling, thus removing independent reconciliation as a control.

Should such fraudulent activity be detected, the account holder may be able to seek restitution from the bank, but there are time limitations of 60 days for consumer accounts and only 2 days for corporate accounts.

Where organizations intend to use ACH as a method of payment, internal control structures can be implemented to minimize the risk of fraud. These include:

- Placing debit blocks on all accounts except one specifically set up to process ACH debits.
- Notifying the organization's bank directly of those suppliers who are authorized to debit from that account.
- Reconciling all accounts, blocked and unblocked, on a daily basis. Blocked accounts that have been erroneously debited by the bank can be refunded relatively easily. Unblocked accounts debited fraudulently or erroneously must have the transaction challenged within two days for recovery purposes.

Since all funds have to end up in a bank account, ACH fraud is far easier where the recipient banks have been negligent in the implementation of know your customers.

Online Fraud

There has been an enormous increase in online banking due to its convenience and the lower costs associated with such transactions. A matching increase in the numbers and value of online banking fraud has arisen.

Using a variety of techniques, online fraudsters will steal identities and online credentials to target individuals and organizations using the Internet to process financial transactions from home or work. Among the techniques used to gain such information are several that have already been discussed, including:

- *Shoulder surfing.* As previously discussed, this technique involves simple observation of the data entry of personal information into a computer system in order to gain access to Internet banking. Obviously, use of this technique requires the presence of the fraudster or an accomplice near where the target is using the computer. This techniques includes the use of computers in public places, such as hotel business centers, airport lounges, or even within bank premises where such facilities are offered as a convenience to customers. Individuals using public computers should, wherever possible, avoid access to computer systems containing confidential or valuable information. In some cases, microcameras have been placed near such computers by fraudsters to gain log-on information. In addition, users have no idea whether software has been installed to record such access information and transmit to a third party. This can be done using a variety of keystroke loggers.
- *Keystroke loggers.* A keystroke logger may reside on public computers but may also install itself on an individual's own computer via fraudulent e-mails or applets inadvertently downloaded from Web sites visited. These applets install themselves, capture the information required, and then pass it on to a Web site from which the would-be fraudsters can download it at their leisure. Such malware is used not only to record keystrokes but can to record screen images and mouse clicks on screen images. The malware allows fraudsters to capture information even when the user clicks on an on-screen numeric keypad rather than entering keystrokes themselves.

- *Use of malware.* Malware comes in a variety of forms. One sophisticated is man-in-the-middle software, where the malware inserts itself in the middle of the user's transaction in order to steal the account information and debit money from an account. If the user views his or her transactions online, the malware conceals the transactions it has processed and artificially alters the values of transactions processed and balance totals presented to the user. In other words, the user is not seeing the bank's computer image but an altered version presented on the screen by the malware. As a result, the user can remain ignorant of the fraudulent transactions until either the bank account becomes overdrawn and the user's own transactions start to be rejected or until the user checks an official printed version of the bank statement that will reveal the false transactions. Many online banking users have opted not to receive such printed information.
- *Phishing schemes.* As mentioned earlier, phishing schemes commonly use e-mails that appear to originate from within customers' own bank prompting, for various reasons, users to log in to the bank in order to, for example, receive urgent information, authorize a pending transaction, or even confirm their identity and "change" their password because of a suspected attack on their account. Most financial institutions have spent time and effort to educate customers regarding the dangers of phishing and how to protect against it.
- *Pharming.* Pharming is a technique involving the redirection of a Web site's traffic to an alternative bogus site. The danger inherent in this technique is that the attack is not directed at the user's computer but at the domain name system (DNS) servers that are the intermediary computers that resolve Internet site names into actual Web addresses. Because the user's own computer is not being targeted, antivirus software and antimalware software will not detect such attacks. More sophisticated antipharming techniques are required to defend against this form of attack. Since most DNS servers use high-quality software to resist such attacks, an alternative form of pharming is gaining momentum, particularly in the world of home wireless networks. Most commercial low-cost routers have built-in abilities to maintain their own firmware. It is possible for unauthorized access to happen if a fraudster can gain access to the router using the administrator's password. Just as users often omit password protection on their computers, people often leave the original default password or an easily guessed password as a router password. These routers are also vulnerable to brute-force password attacks with software guessing every possible combination of characters and numbers to try to crack the password.

This is possible since routers for home use do not use blockages based on number of invalid tents to guess the password. With everything else left unchanged, the router is then redirected to a DNS under the control of the fraudster, where the banking Web site accessed is a fraudulent clone of the real bank's Web site.

- *Web site impersonation.* In some jurisdictions, the impersonation of legitimate Web sites is against the law. However, in others, no such legislation exists. It is comparatively easy for fraudsters to copy the code required to make a screen look like the legitimate Web site of a bank. The first such page is typically the log-in page requiring the user id and password. Once such information has been entered, users commonly get the bank's standard password error screen as if they had accidentally entered the wrong password. They are then directed to the bank's legitimate log-in screen, where they will reenter the correct password and assume they have had finger trouble. In reality, of course, they have just handed over the access information to fraudsters.

- *Use of botnets.* Also known as a zombie armies, botnets are computers attached to the Internet that, unknown to their legitimate users, have had malware installed to forward transmissions such as viruses or spams to other computers on the Internet. At present, the most common use of botnets is to attack a designated computer using a distributed denial of service attack. Botnets also can be a means of spreading malware to a wide variety of computers. Should a trace be performed, the malware can be traced back only to the computer on that the bot is executing.

- *Fast flux.* A fast flux is where botnets are used to deliver phishing and malware, ultimately the source of the bots may be traced the fraudster. Fast flux DNS is a technique used by fraudsters to prevent law enforcement officials from tracing back through network connections. It utilizes a weakness in the load balancing of DNS that enables the registration of a number of IP addresses using a single host name so that the load can be balanced among multiple servers. By swapping associated IP addresses in and out at high speed, the actual Web address of the fraudster can be concealed.

Online Banking Weaknesses and Controls

Although it is impossible to completely eliminate the possibility of being a victim of online banking fraud, individuals and organizations can use certain basic precautions that to minimize the risk. Using a three-layered approach to ensure strong preventive controls, early detective controls, and rapid response can make a significant impact to reduce the risk inherent in online banking.

Preventive Controls

◾ *Use of secure sockets layer (SSL) and transport secured layer (TSL) protocols.* These are methods of securing transactions based on public key cryptography while transferring data. This may sound complicated, but in reality accessing an e-commerce Web site automatically causes the Web browser to connect using a secure connection. Encryption is based on a certificate that provides the browser with the identity of the Web site and the owner or company as well as the information required to make a secure connection. The user can use such a certificate to authenticate the identity of the Web site prior to providing personal or financial information. In Internet Explorer, accessing such a site causes a padlock to appear next to the address. This indicates that encrypted communications are being used. Clicking on the padlock will display the identity of the site owner. Similarly, other browsers display symbols other than a padlock to provide proof of encryption. These are normally to be found beside the Web address.

These protocols include proof of identification and message integrity in that they come from the expected server and they have not been tampered with in transit. They also provide proof that confidentiality has been maintained throughout the transmission in both directions.

If an e-commerce site does not provide encryption capability, users or organizations should consider carefully the risk inherent in proceeding with the transaction.

◾ *Wireless network control.* When a wireless network is provided for the use of customers or guests, it must be kept separate from the normal corporate network so that no traffic can enter the organization's internal systems via this route.
◾ *Internal wireless networks.* Where organizations utilize internal wireless networks for low-risk activities, such as library systems, prevention of users connecting to both wireless and wired networks simultaneously must be enforced at a technical level.
◾ *Wireless encryption.* Most commercially available routers offer a choice of the level of encryption to be provided. Only Wi-Fi Protected Access

2 (WPA2) or later should be used. Earlier versions can be penetrated comparatively easily.

▪ *One-time password devices.* As already mentioned, conventional password authentication can be extremely weak. In the absence of biometric authentication, an alternative is to use a one-time password. It operates in addition to knowledge-based authentication in as much as the user must possess a token, smartcard, or mobile application with special software for generating passwords. To activate the application, users must enter their original password (knowledge-based authentication). The device or software then provides a password that is usable for one single transaction. Any would-be fraudster who captures this password will find it unusable on a second attempt.

▪ *ACH and wire payments.* Where wire transfer payments are being made, ensure that two separate individuals, operating from two different computers, must participate in the transaction. One individual enters the transaction, and another approves it independently. Obviously the risk of collusion still exists.

▪ *Access review.* User access rights should be audited frequently, particularly for users who process banking transactions.

▪ *Single-use computers.* In the corporate environment, all online banking activities should be initiated from a separate computer dedicated to this purpose. No other communications, such as e-mail, are enabled.

▪ *Firewalls.* Ensure corporate firewalls are kept up to date with the latest patches recommended by the vendor.

▪ *Antivirus and antimalware.* Ensure antivirus and antimalware software is installed and active on all computers and that virus and malware definitions are kept up to date.

▪ *Restrict access.* In the corporate environment, the safest option is to block all Internet access except where required for specific corporate purposes. In those cases, access should be restricted to specific sites.

Detective Controls

▪ *Alert services.* If wire transfers are being used, organizations can subscribe to various notification services that raising an alert whenever an electronic debit or credit is processed against an account. Remember, it may be possible to process a credit for a negative amount, depending on the system. Although not recognized as a debit, the transaction will have the same effect.

▪ *ACH fraud filters.* Banks provide a variety of blocking and filtering options in order to deter ACH fraud. These methods include filters, debit blocks, and the use of proxy account numbers to maintain the anonymity of customers' account numbers.

▪ *Reconciliations.* Where online banking is concerned, even daily reconciliations may not be frequent enough. High-value transactions and accounts with permission rights for the processing of high-value transactions should be monitored on an ongoing basis as they occur whenever possible.

All of these techniques are powerful and reduce the risk of fraud. However, the number-one control available to individuals and organizations is an understanding of the risks, coupled with the knowledge of what to do and whom to alert should the possibility of a fraud be discovered.

MONEY LAUNDERING

As discussed in Chapter 3, money laundering involves changing the appearance of the proceeds of illegal activities to make them seem as if they were produced by legitimate means. That is to say, it involves changing dirty money into clean money. Using the three-step method described in Chapter 3, money is *placed* into the legitimate financial, moved around within the system to confuse its source and value by *layering* the money through multiple accounts until it is ultimately *integrated* back into the financial system as legitimate funds from a legitimate source.

Numerous forms of legislation have, over the years, been introduced around the world to make the process of money laundering more difficult and to make its discovery easier by enforcing measures to identify sources of funds. Some of the laws enacted in the United States, for example, are:

▪ *Bank Secrecy Act of 1970.* This act laid down standards for the records that must be retained regarding movement of funds and monetary instruments by financial institutions as well as private individuals. It also required banks to report large cash transactions to the appropriate authorities.
▪ *Money Laundering Control Act of 1986.* This was the first legislation to establish money laundering as a federal crime.
▪ *Anti-Drug Abuse Act of 1988.* This act expanded the range of commercial activities that must report on transactions involving large amounts of cash to include real estate dealers and car dealers.
▪ *Annunzio-Wiley Anti-Money Laundering Act of 1992.* This act tightened the requirements for the reporting of suspicious activities and included a verification record-keeping requirement for wire transfers.

- *Money Laundering Suppression Act of 1994.* This act was designed to improve the detection abilities of banking agencies and required the registration of all money service businesses.
- *Money Laundering and Financial Crimes Strategy Act of 1998.* This act set in place a requirement that all examiners employed by banking agencies must be trained in anti–money laundering techniques. It also made the development of a National Money Laundering Strategy a requirement within a variety of government agencies and initiated the High Intensity Money Laundering and Related Financial Crime Area task forces to operate where money laundering is believed to be common.
- USA PATRIOT Act of 2001. This act has, as one of its subtitles, the International Money Laundering Abatement and Financial Anti-Terrorism Act. It is intended to restrict, intercept, and obstruct the funding of terrorism via money laundering techniques. It tightens controls on U.S. financial institutions in order to prevent the intentional or inadvertent conduct of business with foreign shell banks. Financial institutions must execute acceptable due diligence procedures and expand their anti–money laundering programs.
- Intelligence Reform and Terrorism Prevention Act of 2004. This act gives the secretary of the Treasury the rights and obligation to require the reporting of cross-border electronic funds transmittal.
- *Dodd-Frank Wall Street Reform and Consumer Protection Act of 2010.* This act contains provisions regarding the participation of the Consumer Financial Protection Bureau in the Federal Financial Institutions Examination Council.

One of the main control components in the prevention money laundering is the implementation of an effective anti–money laundering (AML) program. Such programs consist of:

- Internal controls, policies, and procedures to ensure compliance with the Bank Secrecy Act and subsequent legislation
- The appointment of a compliance officer to ensure the effectiveness of the AML program covering the everyday operations of the organization
- Implementation of an ongoing training program covering all employees involved in areas where money laundering could occur
- The execution of an independent audit ensuring the adequacy and effective implementation of the AML program

The internal controls, policies, and procedures are intended to ensure that the financial institution can confirm the identity of each of its customers.

This confirmation includes verification of information used to identify the customer, comparison of customer information with lists of known or suspected money laundering individuals or organizations as supplied by the government, the maintenance of appropriate records, and notification to customers of their role in AML.

In 2005, the United Nations Office on Drugs and Crime (UNODC), in conjunction with the International Monetary Fund (IMF), established a model law covering the financing of terrorism using money laundering.[1] This law listed the legal measures that could be incorporated in domestic law within member countries in order to prevent and detect money laundering and the financing of terrorism as well as to effectively sanction organizations found to be participating in such activities. The model law includes sections on:

- Definitions
- Prevention of money laundering and financing of terrorism
- Detection of money laundering and financing of terrorism
- Investigation and secrecy provisions
- Penal and provisional measures
- International cooperation

In 2007, the UNODC issued an overview on a variety of international standards regarding money laundering.[2] This document covers the essential aspects of customer identification; record-keeping requirements; reporting requirements, both internal and external; as well as the appropriate training and supervision requirements for anti–money laundering.

Following this, and in line with the model law, the Commonwealth Secretariat based in London, in 2009, issued Model Provisions on Money Laundering, Terrorist Financing, Preventive Measures, and Proceeds of Crime for common law legal systems.[3] This document identifies the offenses and obligations of financial institutions to detect and report such criminal activities and also details the preventive measures required in terms of customer identification, record keeping, internal programs, due diligence, and ongoing monitoring requirements. It also goes into detail regarding the structuring and establishment of financial intelligence units as well as provisions for confiscation and benefit recovery, civil forfeiture, and establishment of recovered asset funds.

For organizations operating within the securities industry, the U.S. Financial Industry Regulatory Authority has issued guidelines in the form of a template in MS Word format to assist in the formation of an appropriate compliance program as laid down in the U.S. Bank Secrecy Act. (The template is downloadable from its Web site at: www.finra.org/Industry/Issues/AML /p006340). It contains examples of rules, text, and Web sites containing other resources for AML implementation for small firms. In addition, many computer financial systems now come complete with built-in AML guidance, record-keeping, and reporting modules.

The full details of anti–money laundering programs are beyond the scope of this book. Many excellent textbooks cover this subject on a worldwide basis and give a full breakdown on the policies, procedures, and programs required within local jurisdictions to combat money laundering.[4]

 ## HEALTH CARE FRAUD

Health care fraud encompasses a variety of techniques adopted in order to defraud those entities who provide the funding for health care. The frauds may be at the governmental level or private health insurance companies and may be conducted by patients or the medical profession.

Cost of Fraud

In the United States, estimates of the cost of health care fraud vary depending on the method of statistical calculation used and the period covered. In 2010, it was estimated that health care fraud was costing America in the region of $100 billion a year, with health care identity theft most common means of carrying out such frauds. With the help of insiders with legitimate access to patient information, organized criminals are able to target the government Medicare system which, with a budget of over $450 billion and over 40 million beneficiaries, is seen as a major cash cow for fraudsters. Medicare also suffers a large drawback compared to smaller private insurers since it is required by law to send out payments within a very short time period. This gives the criminal the opportunity to falsely claim, take the money, and run, leaving Medicare to chase after attempting to:

- Find the criminal
- Prove that this was the individual making a false claims
- Seek restitution

The timing element means that Medicare is not in a position to check the legitimacy of all bills before payment is made. Thus, Medicare is forced into a reactive mode, responding to tips and allegations rather than being in a position to proactively establish antifraud measures.

Frauds can range from the selling of personal information to individuals who have no Medicare coverage so that they can obtain treatment using an assumed identity. Not only does this cost money, but it also leaves the genuine individual with a potential medical record for conditions and treatments belonging to someone else. In an emergency medical situation, this false information could be damaging or even life threatening to the genuine patient. Equally, it can be medically dangerous for the person assuming the false identity. When patient records are checked prior to treatment, it may be found that the genuine Medicare beneficiary may have an allergy to treatment or may not have allergy to treatment where the false patient may have the opposite condition.

On a larger scale, using the identification information of legitimate Medicare beneficiaries, bills can be charged for treatments that were never prescribed, equipment that was never used, and drugs that were never issued. In these frauds, bills are normally issued by shell companies created specifically for that purpose. These companies quietly disappear before an investigation can take place, reemerging under a different name and with different addresses in different cities. Once again, such false claims can create a false record of treatment for an individual that could, for example, indicate that specific drugs had been prescribed with no negative medical impact. If the real patient then developed a similar condition, drugs could be administered that could be ineffectual, trigger an allergic reaction, or even put a patient into life-threatening anaphylactic shock. In addition to the dangers of drug misuse, misdiagnosis may occur because a patient's record indicates that certain tests had been carried out with no condition found. These may be the very tests required by the patient's condition, and because of the false record of previous treatment, they may not be carried out

In some respects, Medicare fraud is a regional problem since it is most easily hidden where there is a large population requiring frequent medical attention, often because of age. Where a region's population is particularly young on average, false claims for pediatric care may not be readily noticed. Similarly, in a region popular with the elderly, geriatric care is more common and frequently more expensive, and false claims can disappear in among the many legitimate care claims. With the significant cost of health care in the United States, such frauds are highly lucrative and can net high dollar paybacks, with bills, particularly for diagnostic tests, quickly running into tens of thousands of dollars. In 2009, some $47 billion was claimed for questionable medical treatments alone.

In Europe, a 2010 study indicated that out of the €1 trillion spent annually on health care, €56 billion is lost as a result of fraud: an estimated rate of 3 to 8 percent of total costs.[5] Much of this research was based on older information, and no attempt was made to bring the costs forward to present-day values. In the report, fraud losses were noted in the areas of:

- Fraudulent provision of sickness certificates
- Prescription fraud by pharmacists
- Prescription fraud by patients
- Fraud and error concerning capitation payments to general practitioners
- Fraud and error concerning payments made to doctors to manage a patient's medical care
- Falsification of dental charges by patients
- Fraud and error by opticians concerning the provision of sight tests
- Fraud and error concerning employees of health care organizations
- Fraud and error concerning payments for in-patient hospital services
- Fraud and error concerning long-term care

Nature of Health Care Fraud

Most common forms of health care fraud involve:

- Offering and receiving kickbacks and shared fees for referring patients for diagnostic or medical treatments.
- Billing for services that were never rendered either using genuine patient information to create fictitious claims or, more simply, by padding claims with charges for services or medical procedures that were never carried out during the treatment of a genuine patient.
- Conducting tests, clinical procedures, or even surgeries that were not medically necessary.
- Conducting unnecessary diagnostic tests in order to justify increased insurance claims.
- Representing treatments as medical necessities in order to ensure insurance cover for treatments not generally covered in terms of the insurance policy.
- "Upcoding" the treatment actually provided to a patient to claim for a more expensive procedure. This is usually accompanied by changing the diagnosis code of the patient to a more serious condition justifying the additional services.

- Billing a patient an amount greater than the contribution required by the insurance or even billing the patient for services already paid in terms of insurance contract.
- Overbilling the insurance carrier to cover the amount due to be recovered from the patient when the patient claims poverty.

In order to combat these fraud events, controls are required to ensure that all billings use the correct coding in order to avoid improper claims and payments. Such claims often are identifiable where coding combinations are inappropriate or mutually exclusive. *Mutually exclusive codes* could, for example, involve claims for two or more medical procedures that are clinically similar and would not normally be seen together, where a claim would be either procedure A or procedure B but not both simultaneously. In addition, codes may be claimed that are *comprehensive and component* codes. These codes involve procedures that are considered to be an integral part of a more extensive procedure separately coded and that would not normally happen to the same patient in a procedure carried out by the same physician on the same date.

In the case of Medicaid and Medicare frauds, because both agencies are government controlled, frauds can be prosecuted under the False Claims Act, which, as its name suggests, is intended to protect against government fraud in the form of false claims. Where individuals or organizations knowingly submitted false claims to the government and were reimbursed, such payments can be recovered by the government department concerned. Interestingly, in this act, the expressions "knowing" and "knowingly" indicate that an accused person:

- Has knowledge of the information
- Acts in reckless disregard of whether the information is false or true
- Acts in deliberate victims of whether the information is false or true

This means that, under the False Claims Act, intent to defraud does not have to be proven in order for a person or organization to be found guilty.

Other laws governing government health care programs include the prohibition of the receiving of, or offering of kickbacks in, for services or items covered by federal health care programs. The Anti-Kickback Statute prohibits bribery and kickbacks in any form whether directly or indirectly offered or received for providing services or items or for referral of patients to providers of services. Kickbacks may be monetary or the granting of discounts, special concessions, or provision of gifts. In this case, however, the intent to break the law is a factor that must be proven.

In an effort to prevent the referral of patients or procedures for unnecessary health services at clinics or laboratories in which the physician or an immediate family member of the physician has a financial interest, the Stark Laws were passed in 1989 and 1993. Despite amendments in later years, exceptions can still occur, such as the provision of free or discounted health care to the physician, the physician's family, or members of the physician's office staff. Where breaches of these laws occur, intent to defraud is not required to be proved and any violation of the provisions, intentional or accidental, may be chargeable.

Although Stark and Anti-Kickback laws applied primarily to health plans that are government run, the False Claims Act and code of use are applicable in all cases of health insurance fraud.

Controls around Health Care Fraud

In order to avoid the possibility of deliberate or accidental breaches of the laws protecting health care programs, the implementation of an effective compliance plan can not only prevent intentional fraud but can demonstrate an intention of complying with the law in the event of an unintentional breach. The Office of the Inspector General issued guidelines for such a plan to include:

- Conducting of internal monitoring and auditing
- Implementation of compliance and practice standards
- Designation of a compliance officer
- Conducting of appropriate staff education and training
- Developing a response plan and implementing a corrective action plan
- Ensuring open lines of communication
- Enforcement of disciplinary standards for breaches of the guidelines

The Healthcare Fraud Prevention and Enforcement Action Team (HEAT) was created in 2009 with the intention of enhancing collaboration between the Department of Justice, the Department of Human Services, and the Department of Health. The objectives of Project HEAT were to:

- Expose systemic vulnerabilities commonly exploited by fraudsters
- Identify those geographic locations most vulnerable to federal health care fraud
- Enact appropriate fraud prevention programs
- Increase the recovery rates for fraudulent transactions under the False Claims Act and other legislative initiatives

- Detect patterns of fraud
- Strengthen the partnerships between public and private health care sectors
- Improve data sharing
- Break down bureaucratic silos between agencies

As part of this initiative, multidisciplinary teams—strike force teams—have been established in multiple U.S. locations to identify, investigate, and ultimately prosecute Medicare frauds.

Controls at the Individual Level

At the individual level, awareness and alertness are the primary elements of control activities to prevent health care fraud including:

- Treating health care insurance information with the same degree of care used for maintaining the confidentiality of credit card information. Carelessness with this information is an invitation to commit fraud. In the same way that credit card information is protected, health insurance information should not be disclosed telephonically or over the Internet. Where an insurance ID card is lost or stolen, the insurance company should be contacted immediately.
- Offers abound on the Internet and via e-mail for free health tests or treatments and the provision of a variety of health care services. While there are genuine and generous free treatments and services available, in many cases these are fraudulent offers designed to obtain an individual's health care information in order to defraud the insurance company a later date. In addition to the damage this can do to the individual's health care costs, such fraudulent bills can affect the individual's health record and may result in future mistreatment of a serious condition.
- As with credit cards, examination of transaction records and reconciliation of accounts to the patient's recollection or records of treatment received are critical. Where such transactions are expected, the patient's record should be checked. Where they are unexpected or untimely, the insurance company should be notified immediately of the possibility of a fraudulent transaction.
- When bills are received or benefit statements arrive, it is the insured's responsibility to compare these records to their own memory of treatment received or records kept in order to ensure the treatment matches, the dates match, the number of visits match, and no duplicate transactions are being

processed. On occasion, this may mean checking previous statements to ensure the transaction was not processed already two or three months ago.

■ All suspected fraudulent bills and transactions should be passed on to the insurance company immediately. Most companies now provide fraud hot lines as well as the ability to report via the Internet.

 ## INSURANCE FRAUD

Any insurance policy is a legal agreement between the insurer and the insured based on the concept of utmost good faith. This means that each party is obliged by law to reveal to the other party any information that might have a bearing or influence on the contract between them, whether it is specifically requested or not. This concept relies on integrity and honesty on the part of the two parties. Because of the ease with which a client can obtain a policy, insurance companies are placed under pressure to validate information supplied in order to maintain the concept of utmost good faith.

The degree of faith that the customer hold with regard to the insurance company is largely based on their reputation in the marketplace, equitable settlement of claims, and efficiency in their processing of claims. This faith poses a major reputation risk for insurance companies when a fraud is uncovered. Many such companies are reluctant to admit the scale of fraud they face even to shareholders and policyholders. It can also result in the insurance company believing claims to be fraudulent but nevertheless settling them in order to avoid negative publicity. With this in mind, a fraudster may see little downside to making a false claim since the most probable outcome if the fraud is detected is that the claim will simply be denied. This is a false assumption; insurance companies go to great efforts to detect claims that are fraudulent, particularly where there is a pattern of multiple high-value claims made.

Insurance fraud takes a multiplicity of forms that may generally be categorized as internal or external fraud. *Internal frauds* are those executed by employees, agents, or even executive management against the interests of the policyholder or insurance company. *External frauds* are schemes perpetrated by policyholders, vendors, beneficiaries, medical providers, or even career fraudsters.

Internal frauds include such activities as:

■ The issuing of fake policies, insurance identification cards, or insurance certificates in order to fraudulently collect premiums without actually providing insurance cover the "policyholder" expects

- The falsification of information on insurance records, including the creation of records of fictitious policies and supporting documentation for onward processing to reinsurance companies

External frauds take a wider variety of forms and may include schemes such as:

- Property fraud schemes, where multiple insurance policies are purchased for coverage of a single vehicle or property that is subsequently stolen or destroyed so that multiple claims can be made. A variation on this scheme is arson for profit, when an individual is hired to burn a vehicle, business, or home at a time when the owners and policyholders have witnesses to place them elsewhere.
- In the event of damage to property or vehicles, the repairer may, in collusion with a policyholder, bill the insurance company for repairs to damages beyond those actually incurred, either to split the additional monies claimed or simply to have additional work over and above the repair of the actual damages.
- False claims of personal injury based on intentional "accidents" in commercial premises where customer injury insurance may be expected to exist. In some cases, for example, retail customers have been known to intentionally spill slippery liquids so that an accomplice can slip and fall in an area believed to be under closed circuit camera scrutiny. Obviously, if the perpetrator slipped himself, fraud would be suspected and no successful claim would be made. Where the "injured" party is an apparently unrelated individual, the chances of a successful claim may actually be high.
- Other fraudulent claims schemes against corporate insurance include claims of foreign bodies being found in food or drink, faked burglaries or vehicle theft, and even fraudulent death benefit claims.
- Retrospective insurance schemes take place when a genuine loss or injury takes place in an uninsured condition. The loss or injury is concealed until insurance coverage is obtained, and then the loss or injury is reported. For a claim to be successful, the insurance coverage must have been in place at the time the incident occurred. This type of fraud is common where policies have deductibles requiring the insured to pay proportion of the damages or loss. Under these circumstances, a claim may be delayed while the policyholder increases the damage in order to take it over the deductible limit. This type of fraud has even been carried out in medical claims with injuries being exaggerated in order to push up the amount claimable.

- Car owners should be wary of insurance fraudsters who use a variety of techniques to enable claims for fake injuries against a driver's insurance policy. A typical such technique is the swoop and squat in which a suspect vehicle swoops in front and brakes suddenly, causing a rear-end collision. The car hit will often have rear-seat passengers. The squat car is frequently an older one with the victim's car being new (well insured) or even rented. Initially, the driver of the squat car will suggest that, since no one is injured and minimal damage was done, neither the police nor the insurance company need be involved. Contact information is exchanged. A few days later, a lawyer's letter informs the victim that the damage was considerably worse than thought. The passengers are claiming painful or disabling neck and back injuries that are then claimed against the driver's insurance policy. In a variation on this technique, three cars are used. One car is driven in front of the target's car. The second car swoops in front the confederate's car, causing him to break hard, or squat, resulting in the victim's car hitting it from the rear. On the highway, a third car may be used to box in the target, preventing it from changing lanes to avoid collision. In all these multicar cases, the swoop car drives off, leaving the victim having hit the squat car.
- Other varieties of this fraud include the drive down in which the fraudster slows down to allow the victim to merge into traffic, waves him forward, then denies waving the victim into the traffic, a denial substantiated by his passenger, who was "injured." The sideswipe takes place where two lanes are turning together. Any drifting by the victim driver will be dealt with by a deliberate sideswipe, resulting in "painful injury" to the fraudster. Since the lane change was the victim's fault, it is very hard to prove that the sideswipe was intentional on the part of the fraudster. These frauds generally require some medical complicity regarding the fraudsters' injuries.
- Medical frauds of all kinds abound and have been covered in the section on health care frauds.

The variety of insurance claim frauds is limited only by the fraudster's imagination.

Fraud Prevention Initiatives

Insurance companies are not taking such fraudulent activities lying down and simply passing on the costs to consumers. Insurance companies have substantially increased their expenditure on antifraud measures in recent years, including the establishment of claims investigation units, customer education on the red flags or potential frauds, and the provision of hotlines for reporting fraud.

In-house staff members as well as independent insurance agents commonly receive extensive and ongoing training on how to spot fraud indicators. Companies are also overcoming previous concerns regarding the sharing of information, and fraud conviction rates are rising due to an increased willingness to prosecute.

In fighting the fraudster's use of fake insurance companies, regulators are taking a closer look at the finances and market practices of insurance companies. These regulations are also assisting in the fiscal discipline and good governance of insurance companies, making it less likely that a company will simply declare bankruptcy to avoid payment of high-value claims.

Insurance Fraud Detection

The front line of fraud detection in most insurance companies is the staff members who deal with the initial claims handling process. Unfortunately, often these are inexperienced personnel with inadequate training in fraud detection, and a high percentage of attempted frauds pass this first scrutiny. To overcome this weakness, some companies provide claims handlers with lists of fraud indicators that incoming claims can be matched against. These lists have, in the past, been company-unique with companies reluctant to share such information in the face of heavy competition and the need to maintain commercial confidentiality. In addition, should such indicators enter the public domain and potential fraudsters become aware of them, their effectiveness as predictors of possible fraud could be severely diminished. Where matches are found against these indicators, claims may be referred for further investigation.

Traditional insurance fraud investigation techniques commonly involve the use of a claims investigation unit based on a field adjuster's recommendation. Claims are then evaluated against a number of criteria, including the insured's claim history, length of time as a customer, and other indicators that may cause a subjective evaluation that there is a possibility of a fraud event.

In the case of, for example, a claim for injury as a result of a motor accident, a common detection method is the use of an independent medical examination in which an independent assessment of the injured claimant is conducted by a doctor selected by the insurer to verify the level of injury and treatment claimed. An alternative technique for this type of investigation is a medical audit in which the medical expenses claimed are reviewed by a specialist seeking to identify any unusual factors appearing within the claim.

Certified insurance fraud investigators are professionals who are trained in the appropriate methodology is to investigate suspected insurance fraud. Certification is granted by the International Association of Special Investigation Units based on experience as well as an examination. This certification adds to their credibility in bringing a case to court as an expert witness.

Obviously, tips from law enforcement, neighbors, and even family can point the way to detection of fraudulent claims. Insurance companies also seek to use the data accumulated to try to predict areas of potential vulnerability. In the past, this approach involved attempts to understand the characteristics of fraud by means of surveys and sampling of known fraudulent claims. This has not always proved successful, partly due to the volumes and varieties of successful frauds that were excluded from the samples.

Faced with escalating volumes and sophistication of fraud, the insurance industry has responded with aggressive use of analysis software to identify events of potential frauds. With the ability to search multiple databases with large volumes of data in order to find discrepancies in adjudicated claims, insurance companies are utilizing techniques such as *predictive modeling* in a proactive manner to deter fraud rather than simply detect it after the event.

Use of data mining techniques can detect patterns within text material as well as identification of abnormal patterns of claims. Analysis techniques include:

- ▪ *Database searches.* A variety of database search services are available through which subscribers can submit abbreviated data of claims that have already been adjudicated. This gives them access to similar data submitted by other service users, which facilitates the analysis of claims across multiple insurance companies to identify patterns of similar claims to multiple companies as well as patterns of acceptance and denial of claims. One drawback of this technique its inability to indicate intent. When a match is found, a human interpretation is still required to determine the likelihood of fraudulent intent. Failure to find a match does not necessarily indicate the lack of a fraud, only that no fraudulent pattern was uncovered.
- ▪ *Online analytical processing (OLAP).* This technique, when employed by a skilled analyst, facilitates profiling models of the behavior of individuals or peer groups of individuals as well as *clustering* of behavior patterns in order to identify anomalies in comparison to the typical group profile.

Once again, an anomaly may or may not indicate the presence of a fraud or a potential fraud, but it can raise levels of risk awareness and monitoring.

▪ *Rules-based testing.* This technique evaluates each transaction against a predefined rules base in order to calculate an aggregate score that can be compared to threshold values so that any claim that exceeds the threshold can be treated as suspicious. Thresholds may be based on value of claim, nature of claim, frequency of claims, or failure to disclose previous claims. The advantage of this type of system is that, once a rules base has been computerized, continuous monitoring of transactions is rapid and low cost. Disadvantages include a high number of false positives that can indicate potential frauds that then require expensive and laborious follow-ups as well as the inherent disadvantage of a historical-based system that cannot predict the new fraud techniques.

▪ *Predictive modeling.* This technique combines attributes of both OLAP and rules-based testing in order to build fraud propensity scores using data mining tools. When combined with wide database searches, this technique may be highly effective in reducing the number of false positives and narrowing the investigation requirements. Once again, a limitation is the need to keep the models current as new patterns of fraud emerge.

▪ *Network analysis.* This technique uses a different form of computerized analysis in order to identify network patterns of interrelated relationships. Again, this method can be automated as a continuous monitoring process to identify transactional commonality from related parties.

▪ *Text mining.* Computer software can be used to analyze unstructured text, such as claimant interviews or customer service calls. Where, in the past, an analyst may have to review multiple files or witness statements of an accident to seek commonality, text mining software can parse unstructured text looking for both commonality and abnormality, either of which could indicate a need for further investigation.

▪ *Logistic regression analysis.* This analytical technique uses information from known fraudulent claims as well as legitimate claims to identify independent variables. These could include the number of years the insured has been a customer, whether the insured is a new customer, the claims history, the number of claims per year, or whether the policy is a known high-risk policy. Using this information, a correlation analysis can be conducted to determine whether the variables have a measurable relationship to fraudulent claims for this particular type of policy. Based on this logistics model, claims can be analyzed to identify, with a predictable probability, those claims that may indicate a fraudulent intent.

Detection of Fraud Against the Consumer

Where consumers are in a situation where insurance fraud may be perpetrated against them by, for example, a fraudulent or unlicensed insurance company, preventive controls would include:

- Verification with the local insurance regulatory authorities that the company or agent offering the insurance coverage is legitimate, registered, and licensed to sell such insurance.
- Being alert for any abnormalities, such as late delivery of a policy, which could indicate fraud on the part of the agent or an employee of the insurance company where premiums are collected but no insurance coverage is in fact issued.
- Early reporting of any suspicious activities to the local regulator. Again, this is possible via insurance hotlines or online reporting.

As the global economy changes, so the nature of insurance fraud is also changing. Use of fake insurers coupled with money-laundering schemes can move fraudulent funds overseas using Internet techniques. The aging population of Baby Boomers is increasing the frequency and cost of health insurance fraud.

One of the biggest target groups for insurance scams remain the elderly. Investment scams include sales of fake promissory notes guaranteed by nonexistent insurance companies and sales of nonexistent policies reaping large benefits for the fraudsters.

As in all fraud detection, the most critical antifraud measures involve staying alert, being aware, maintaining a healthy skepticism, asking questions, and always remembering "There ain't no such thing as a free lunch."

TAX FRAUD

To many people, tax fraud is not a real crime but a minor peccadillo, comparable to drinking alcohol in the days of Prohibition. Over the years, it has become part of the global culture to see tax evasion as a minor offense and tax avoidance as every citizen's civic duty. *Tax evasion* involves the failure to declare income classified by the local legislation as taxable and is against the law. *Tax avoidance* involves structuring economic activity to take advantage of any legal avenue to reduce the level of taxable income. Since tax avoidance is using legal avenues, it is not against the law. As tax legislation changes over time, new opportunities arise where the differences between evasion and avoidance become blurred. This can create opportunities where a new tax avoidance scheme may be implemented that will remain legal until a court decides that the law has been wrongfully interpreted and the continuation of such activity would be tax evasion.

Governments, however, regard tackling taxation fraud as a major imperative in order to protect:

- Revenue income required for investment in public services
- Honest, taxpaying organizations from criminal or unfair competition
- Social objectives underlying taxation levels and specific items
- Against organized crime that benefits from the financial advantages of tax evasion

The reduction of the taxable portion of income has become a major concern to individuals and corporations. At the individual level, this can be seen in the spread of secondary jobs, payable in cash and thus concealed from taxation authorities. As long as the primary employment provides sufficient income to satisfy the authorities regarding the taxpayer's standard of living, the second employment may fall through the net. Such after-hours or moonlighting activities also makes it attractive to offer a discount for payments made in cash for the provision of services. The most common explanation for such discounts is that payment in cash makes concealment of income easier and therefore reduces the need to declare the income to tax authorities.

Use of Tax Shelters

A tax shelter is intended to reduce tax due to be paid to a government by reducing the taxable income declared. Many tax shelters are legitimate, and their intended use is for tax avoidance. Such shelters could include retirement accounts and other investments or deposits that are not heavily taxed. Charitable donations also lower the taxable income and are classified as legitimate tax shelters. Other such legitimate tax shelters may include:

- Investment in pension plans
- Employer-funded education
- Employer-funded health insurance
- Employer-funded life insurance

- Investment in real estate
- Retirement annuities

Determining the actual state of tax evasion is a complex exercise, and the most common method involves calculating a probable tax by comparing the population income and expenditure against those taxpayers whose income is derived in a manner that cannot avoid the declaration and payment of tax such as a pay-as-you-earn system. Based on that, the extent of tax evasion can be generally inferred if the total economic activity can be estimated and declared income deducted. This allows the derivation of the value of the so-called shadow economy. A common method for determining the total economic activity is the use of the published estimate of the gross domestic product (GDP) of the country. The World Bank has recently reported data on the extent of shadow economies across the world.[6] Using this form of analysis, the shadow economy is, by definition, non–tax paying. By calculating the percentage of tax actually paid and applying it to the shadow economy, the amount of tax evasion can be estimated.

A recent survey by the Tax Justice Network, an independent organization established in the United Kingdom in 2003, estimates the size of the average shadow economy worldwide to be 18 percent of the total GDP.[7] The shadow economy is largest in developing countries, where the percentage rises to over 34 percent and peaks at nearly 37 percent in South America. A potential tax evasion loss of over $3 trillion on a worldwide basis has been calculated. Although the percentage losses are higher in developing countries, the actual amounts are lower because of the lower GDP. For example, in Africa, the tax revenue losses are estimated at $79 billion based on 34.8 percent of GDP. This compares to estimated losses of $1.5 trillion in Europe based on 20.5 percent of GDP and losses of $453 million in North America based on a shadow economy amounting to only 10.8 percent of GDP.

Indirect Tax Fraud

Indirect taxes, such as value added tax (VAT), are also vulnerable to fraud. When a business charges indirect taxes the consumer, the taxable portion must be remitted to the appropriate taxation authorities within the country. In the case of VAT, businesses are normally permitted to offset VAT paid for specific goods or services against their VAT collected, and the net amount is then paid to the taxation authority. Depending on the nature of the VAT system implemented, tax due may be calculated at the time of invoice or at the time of payment. This, itself, can give rise to fraud where tax refunds are claimed for items invoiced where no payment has as yet been made.

A common fraud in such an environment is the collection of VAT by organizations that are not registered for such collections and the failure to remit the tax income to the taxation authority. An alternative method of fraud for a VAT-registered business is simply to underdeclare the amount of VAT collected. Common red flags for this type of fraud include:

- Requests for payment to be made in cash and failure to provide an invoice
- Offering of discounts for cash payments
- Reluctance to accept payment by check or credit card
- Request that payments be made to someone other than the registered business
- The offering of goods or services for sale at rates substantially below market value
- Processing the sale without recording it

In these ways, the organization can collect the taxation and retain it within the business without declaration to the taxation authorities.

A third common method of conducting a VAT fraud is to claim back the VAT for goods and services not received. Such claims can be substantiated by the production of fraudulent invoices from genuine registered suppliers or organizations using any of the techniques for document fraud discussed earlier in the book. As long as these fraudulent invoices do not become excessive or are spread over a wide variety of suppliers, there is a strong possibility that an organization conducting such a fraud may remain undetected for an extended period.

In one African country that converted from a general sales tax (GST) to a VAT basis, a tax refund was offered during the conversion period for deductible goods and services on which GST had already been paid. This resulted in fraudsters registering dummy companies with the taxation authorities and then claiming nonexistent GST payments based on fraudulent invoices. Once the tax refund had been received, the companies disappeared forever.

Within the European Community, another form of VAT fraud is made possible by the varying tax rates within member countries. This is known as a *missing trader intracommunity* fraud. In one variety, an *acquisition fraud* occurs when goods and services are purchased within a European Union member state in which those particular goods or services are zero rated for VAT purposes and then sold in another member state for the standard rate. The importer then fails to account for the VAT due for the items sold.

In a variation of this form of fraud, the goods are purchased overseas at zero rate, brought into the country without payment of the importation VAT, and reexported to a zero-rate member state with a refund claimed locally for the tax that was supposedly originally paid as import VAT. This fraud can be repeated over and over with the same goods, leading to its name of *carousel fraud*.

Such fraud is detectable using appropriate analytic techniques even though it is often concealed by means of contra trading in which the perpetrator participates in both a tax-loss chain (purchasing with a tax liability and selling overseas at zero rate, creating a tax credit) while simultaneously participating in a contra chain that goods are acquired from a member state and then sold, creating an output tax liability from the local sale. In this manner, the organization will have input tax credit to offset against the output tax liability.

In 2009, a study was conducted within the European Community to determine the gap between the accrued VAT receipts and the calculated theoretical net VAT liability.[8] While this was not intended as a direct measurement of VAT fraud, since it included tax not paid as a result of legitimate tax avoidance, it gives some indication of the extent to which fraud may be impacting the collection of indirect taxes. The study indicates that indirect taxes collected averaged 12 percent less than their theoretical maximum in 2006. This represents a gap of over €100 billion, a proportion of which may be attributable to direct fraud. Although this study is not intended to quantify indirect taxation fraud, a U.K. study in 2011 estimated the U.K. VAT tax lost to fraud at between £0.5 billion and £1.5 billion.[9]

Other forms of indirect taxation fraud include the avoidance of excise duty on commodities such as fuel, tobacco, and alcohol. Revenues from these indirect taxes represent a significant portion of the taxation income of all governments, and tax evasion in these areas is seen as a significant threat.

Use of Tax Shelters

A tax shelter is intended to reduce tax due to be paid to a government by reducing the taxable income declared. Tax shelters may take the form of investments in accounts, such as retirement accounts, which attract lower tax rates. A common difference between legitimate tax shelters and those used for concealment of income is normally the financial benefit of the shelter. Legitimate shelters usually are seen as income earners in their own right. Legitimate tax shelters include:

- Investment in pension plans
- Investment in retirement annuities

- Employer-funded education
- Employer-funded life insurance
- Employer-funded health coverage
- Investments in real estate
- Investment in side businesses

Real estate investment is a particularly popular form of tax shelter since not only does it facilitate capital growth, but it also allows taxable deductions for mortgage interest, insurance, and property taxes, depending on the legislative area within which the investment has been made. In some jurisdictions, primary income may be used to fund a secondary business, thus reducing taxable income from the primary source. The tax regulator typically requires proof that the side business is intended, ultimately, to make a profit, which would then be taxed.

Nonlegitimate or abusive tax shelters involve mechanisms designed simply to reduce the amount of tax legitimately owed to the government. A common mechanism for such tax evasion is the use of multilayered transactions processed through multiple entities to mask the genuine ownership of the funds. Common among these abuse of tax shelters are:

- Use of international business corporation transactions
- Lease in/lease out transactions
- Stock compensation transactions
- Use of foreign trusts
- Use of variable prepaid forward contracts
- Use of offshore tax havens

Offshore Tax Havens

Offshore tax havens may be identified by specific characteristics, including:

- No taxation or nominal taxation on the relevant income (not in itself sufficient to justify classification as a tax haven)
- Lack of transparency
- Lack of effective exchange of information
- Lack of substantial activities towards remedying other defects

For a country to be classified as a tax haven, it has to meet the listed characteristics. By committing to the internationally agreed tax standards, since 2009 no countries remain on the Organisation for Economic Co-operation and Development list of uncooperative tax havens, although not all countries worldwide have fully implemented the exchange of information and high standards of transparency.

The exchange of information involves removal of restrictions on exchange caused by bank secrecy or domestic tax interest requirements. Such information must be available on request where it can be seen to be "foreseeable relevant" to the administration and enforcement of the domestic laws of a treaty partner. Within this requirement, assurances are maintained of strict confidentiality of information exchanged as well as the respect for taxpayers' rights. Bank secrecy continues to be maintained an individual countries, but, under specific and well-defined circumstances, it can be lifted so that domestic tax laws and international treaty partner requests can be responded to. Requests for such information by a treaty partner can be denied for a variety of reasons by the receiving country.

SOCIAL SECURITY FRAUD

In the United States, the Social Security number (SSN) has been, since 1936, the fundamental method of identifying individuals. Its original use was intended to be a mechanism whereby the federal government could track earnings in order to credit the appropriate amount of Social Security taxes to the specific taxpayer. Recently, the SSN has come to be the standard identifier used by both government agencies and the private sector as an unofficial national identifier. With the SSN, a fraudster is able to:

- Access financial accounts
- Obtain credit cards
- Commit bank fraud
- Falsely obtain employment
- Falsely obtain government benefits
- Obtain commercial credit
- Obtain false drivers' licenses
- Obtain false green cards
- Obtain false Social Security cards

The obtaining of false drivers' licenses by use of false SSNs is of particular concern in the United States since these licenses are the most commonly used mechanism for authenticating the identity of an individual in nongovernmental areas. Driver's licenses are commonly used at airports for passenger identification and authentication when entering secured areas, as a means of authentication when applying for firearm licenses, and even for crossing borders.

It is one of the most critical elements in identity theft within the United States which led Congress to enact the Privacy Act in 1974 in order to place express restrictions on the use of the SSN. This act also made it unlawful for any agency to deny any right, benefit, or privilege to any individual because of their refusal to disclose the SSN.

By 2004, identity theft had become such a scourge that the Identity Theft Penalty Enhancement Act (ITPEA) was signed into law in the USA, requiring mandatory imprisonment for anyone convicted of knowingly possessing, transferring, or using, without lawful authority, a means of identification of another person. This included information obtained by phishing. Previous acts had made it illegal to transfer such information, but the ITPEA enabled the prosecution of possessors of such information with the intent to commit, aid, or abet a crime.

Should a SSN fall into the hands of an identity thief, the individual's privacy, identity, and personal history become available for fraudulent purposes. Identity theft is taken to occur when an individual steals another individual's identification information and uses it for fraudulent purposes. In the majority of cases of identity thefts, fraudsters gain access to the personal information of another by taking advantage of an existing relationship with the SSN holder. In some cases, fraudsters then sell the information to a third party who becomes the perpetrator of fraudulent activities.

In many cases of Social Security fraud, it has been found that the SSN was obtained through Internet sites within both public and private domains as well as via theft of the information from mailboxes, wallets, and purses.

Identity theft is taken so seriously in the United States that it is not always necessary to prove that an accused intended to use a Social Security card or number for deceptive purposes. Simple possession of such a card or number not belonging to the accused may, under certain circumstances, be sufficient to support the belief that there was an intent to deceive.

Identity theft has been further complicated in terms of false claims for Social Security benefits with the advent of the use of "alternative signatures" as noted below in 2004. Since that time, the Social Security Administration (SSA) has permitted three alternatives to signatures in applying for Social Security benefits.

Attestation is used when an in-person interview occurs either at an SSA field office or via telephone. In this technique, an SSA employee electronically records, or attests to, the applicant's intent to sign. This process removes the need for retention of the paper applications that previously held a "wet" signature.

Click and sign is a mechanism whereby applicants via the Internet are no longer required to print and signed a completed application form and return it for processing. Applicants can now review the entries online and agree to sign the electronic application by pressing a "sign now" button on the screen. The application is considered signed when the applicant submits it.

Witnessed signature involves an electronic entry by an SSA employee when an applicant has submitted a "wet" signature application form, either in person or by mail. As with attestation, this method removes the need for the retention of supporting paper records.

If the process ended there, it would leave the government open to Social Security fraud by electronic means. To prevent this, the applicant is still required, as a final stage, to provide knowledge-based information to be matched against the applicant's information held within SSA databases as well as documentary evidence, although it will not be retained in paper form.

The system is not foolproof. It is still possible for a fraudulent claimant, for example, to lie telephonically on an application regarding income, attest to the truth of the false information, and agreed to inform the SSA of any inaccuracies on receipt of the mailed summary sheet. Should the lie be discovered at a later date, the onus would be on the SSA to prove that the applicant had received the summary and failed to correct the erroneous information. If the applicant denies making a false statement regarding income, blames the false information on the SSA interviewer inaccurately recording the information, and claims not to have received a summary sheet, he or she may be able to point to his at the station of the accuracy at the time of his interview as proof that the error was not at his end but was made by the SSA. This muddying of the water regarding the reliability of the SSA evidence may be sufficient to cause a prosecution to fail.

■ FRAUD AFTER DEATH

When an individual dies, the SSA records the fact on the Death Master File. This file contains over 87 million records created from SSA payments. Information recorded include the SSN, name, date of birth, date of death, state or country of residence, and zip code of last residence. Although not all deaths are recorded, estimations are that the records are over 95 percent accurate.

This file is available for inquiry on a subscription basis of and can even be accessed via iPhone or Android. The information is made available as a death verification tool, but it can also be used against the interests of the spouse or parent of the recently departed. Care should be taken to ensure that, when a recent bereavement has taken place, all personal financial contracts of the deceased are informed immediately so that when the information is published, it is valueless to a fraudster.

 ## CONSTRUCTION FRAUD

Construction fraud occurs in a variety of forms and may be directed against the individual property owner and construction companies or their clients.

Fraud at a Personal Level

In today's economic downturn, a growth industry for fraudsters has been in the construction sector. One of the more common low-level frauds in this arena involves organized groups who travel from area to area posing as contractors. Door-to-door solicitation is common with professionally produced leaflets and fliers offered to the householder. If the solicitation is fraudulent, workers frequently require a cash-up-front payment or a cash check to cover "materials and expenses." Once paid, they disappear. If the work is actually carried out, it may prove substandard and without guarantee. Frauds within this sector include:

- *Roof repair frauds.* Frauds in this area typically involve the insertion of a few new tiles or shingles, a lot of hammering, and spraying a liquid, even water, on part of the roof to make it look as if it has been repaired.
- *Paving frauds.* These frauds frequently involve the execution of substandard work where no ground preparation is carried out and a thin layer of tar and sand is laid down, only to disintegrate after a short period of traffic.
- *Sealant frauds.* In areas of severe weather conditions, it is common to reseal roofing, fencing, building sidewalls, and even driveways as weather protection. Frauds in these areas involve the use of substandard materials that generally have very little sealant effect.

Senior citizens are most vulnerable to this type of fraud since they commonly have limited incomes and cannot afford professional repairs. A common tactic is to suggest that they have a deficiency in their property that the fraudster just noticed when passing by. As a good Samaritan, the fraudster wanted to point it out before the condition became irreparable. The elderly may also be vulnerable since they may also have physical limitations, making it difficult to check any work that is actually undertaken.

A common entry for construction frauds is the use of the "free inspection" offer. The inspection could be for anything from heating to water leakage, electrical, or any area of construction where a repair would normally be seen as urgent. Typically, such inspections find some defect requiring urgent attention that can be done fairly cheaply by the fraudster since "we are already here." This technique is also used by professional burglars to case a home for future robbery.

Fraud within Construction Companies

As with any other companies, construction companies are open to the possibility of fraud through the normal mechanisms of cash disbursements, payroll disbursements, or worker compensation schemes. In some respects, such companies may be more vulnerable to fraud through skimming of inventory and other assets. Opportunities for corruption through bribery and kickbacks possibly combined with bid rigging abound.

With the impact of a struggling economy, pressure in the form of tightened bank credit and lower profit margins coupled with the risk of customer or supplier bankruptcy inevitably leads to an increase in the potential for fraud occurring. Construction funding can come from a variety of sources, including aid, grants, and subsidies from international or national donors and may involve subsidized costs or even nonrepayable grants. Some projects may be funded using equity investment by the shareholders or associated contractors or operators. Use of loans from governments or financial institutions and lease finance provided for the purchase of capital assets may be unobtainable with reduced economic activity and an increased requirement for financial guarantees and default insurance may be evident when loans are applied for. Even at this early stage of projects, corruption can creep in with bribes paid or equity offered in return for funding. Fraud can also occur where, for example, land required for construction may be acquired by an insider and resold at a profit to the fraudster. Bribes can also be paid to ensure that the acquired land is recommended for construction by concealing adverse social, environmental, or site data with regard to the proposed construction project.

Providing kickbacks and bribes to ensure the acceptance of higher-priced quotes increases the fraudster's ability to pay higher kickbacks and bribes. This becomes a self-fulfilling prophecy, where the more bribes are paid, the greater the cost must be to sustain both the bribes and profit. The more corruption, the more the fraudsters stand to gain. A situation in which collusion and corruption become systemic and deeply ingrained can arise.

Risk factors and indicators for fraud within construction include items specific to the nature of the industry, such as:

- Inadequate segregation of duties
- Inflation of billable hours
- Lack of mandatory vacations
- Rapid turnover of employees
- Use of significant bonuses for project completions
- Absentee owners
- Employment of underqualified personnel
- Involvement in contracts subject to regulatory restrictions or oversight
- Reputation within the construction industry
- Disregard for regulatory compliance
- Frequent changes in the appointment of external auditors
- Restrictions on information provided to auditors
- Failures of safety programs
- Pressures to meet loan covenants
- Impact on construction market of the economy

All of these fraud risk factors and indicators exist within other market sectors but are commonly seen at a greater level within the construction industry. Such frauds are most commonly detected as a result of tips or complaints from employees, customers, or vendors or by accident. In many cases in the construction industry, internal controls appear to be ineffective in preventing fraud. Opportunities arise where internal controls are known to be weak or poorly implemented either through ignorance or apathy on the part of local supervisors. In many construction projects, the operation priority is completion to a specific time frame while maintaining safety levels. Prevention of fraud then becomes relegated to a minor position in the overall risk scale. As with many other industries, small businesses frequently have lower levels of internal controls simply due to the lack of available personnel.

Frauds within these organizations are more likely to be detected by accident or tips.

Red flags for fraud include those related to fraudsters and those related to transactions. Fraudster-related indicators may include gift takers, rule-breakers, big spenders, and other indicators of bribe takers or embezzlers. Red flags that may indicate external fraudsters could include a record of successful bidding by an outside contractor, poor delivery of products and services, or the offering of gifts.

Red flags for transactional fraud typically include repeated use of the same vendors, ignoring purchasing policies, or abnormal pricing trends from a specific supplier. Construction fraud can also occur at the bidding stage; red flags here would include bidding sign-offs by unauthorized individuals, bypassing a big review procedures, abnormal variations in specifications or contracts, improper contact with the bidder, acceptance of late bids or backdating of bids, and general unusual patterns in bid awards.

In addition to direct financial losses, bribery or fraud during a construction project execution can result in an end product that is environmentally destructive, defective, or dangerous. From a funder's perspective, the additional dangers can include contractual liability as well as criminal liability and reputation risk.

Again, from a funder's perspective, adequate due diligence over key employees and participants in the construction project as well as agents and intermediaries is essential.

Prevention and detection methods typically are those for any large organization but with the inclusion of:

- Control over usage of small tools
- Securing large items of construction equipment overnight and at weekends
- Periodic inspection of inventory
- Ongoing inspection of additions and deletions to asset listings
- Rotation of major purchasing responsibilities
- Use of competitive bidding practices
- Ongoing verification of contractor performance and inventory delivery

The most effective fraud preventive measures in construction have been shown to be:

- Use a strong internal controls effectively implemented and appropriately monitored

- Background checks on new employees, including temporary workers
- Use of regular fraud audits to seek indicators of weakening of internal control structures
- Establishment and enforcement of appropriate fraud policies, including a willingness to prosecute where fraud is uncovered
- Ethics training for employees
- Provision of a fraud hotline or other fraud reporting mechanisms
- Adequate workplace surveillance

In terms of internal controls, implementation effectiveness is directed by the attitude of the top of the organization. Maintenance of a good ethics program and ensuring compliance with all organization procedures go a long way toward reducing the likelihood or incidence of fraud. Effective screening of suppliers and subcontractors, not only when they are first used but also on an ongoing basis, can minimize the opportunity for supplier-driven fraud. While preventing fraud and corruption during the execution of a construction project can be seen as everyone's responsibility, in many cases this responsibility falls to the consulting engineer, who typically is to approve payment requests and change orders and ensure that construction is to specification and that all appropriate controls are fully implemented.

NOTES

1. United Nations Office on Drugs and Crimes and International Monetary Fund, *Model Legislation on Money Laundering and Financing of Terrorism*, 2005, www.imolin.org/pdf/imolin/ModelLaw-February2007.pdf.
2. *An Overview of the UN Conventions and Other International Standards Concerning Anti-Money Laundering and Countering the Financing of Terrorism*, 2007, www.imolin.org/pdf/imolin/Overview Update_0107.pdf.
3. United Nations Office on Drugs and Crimes, Commonwealth Secretariat, and International Monetary Fund, *Model Provisions on Money Laundering, Terrorist Financing, Preventive Measures and Proceeds of Crime (for common law legal systems)*, 2009, www.imolin.org/pdf/imolin/Model_Provisions_Final.pdf.
4. Peter Lilley, *Dirty Dealing: The Untold Truth about Global Money Laundering, International Crime and Terrorism*, Kogan Page, London; 3 edition (3 May 2006) Peter Reuter and Edwin M. Truman, *Chasing Dirty Money: The Fight Against Money Laundering*, Peterson Institute, Washinton, CD, 2004.
   John Madinger *Money Laundering: a Guide for Criminal Investigators, Third Edition* CRC Press, Boca Raton, FL, 2011.

Wouter H. Muller, Christian H. Kalin, John G. Goldsworth, *Anti-Money Laundering: International Law And Practice*, John Wiley & Sons, 2007.

5. Jim Gee and Mark Button, *The Financial Cost of Healthcare Fraud*, 2010, MacIntyre Hudson, in conjunction with European Healthcare Fraud and Corruption Network and the Centre for Counter Fraud Services at Britain's Portsmouth University. www.ehfcn.org/media/documents/The-Financial-Cost-of-Healthcare-Fraud-Report-2011.pdf.

6. Claudio E. Montenegro, Friedrich Schneider, Andreas Buehn, *Shadow Economies All over the World, elibrary.worldbank.org/docserver/download/5356.pdf.*

7. Tax Justice Network, *The Cost of Tax Abuse: The Cost of Tax, A Briefing Paper on the Cost of Tax Evasion Worldwide* (London: Author, 2011).

8. Reckon LLP, *Study to Quantify and Analyse the VAT Gap in the EU-25 Member States*, http://ec.europa.eu/taxation_customs/resources/documents/taxation /tax_cooperation/combating_tax_fraud/reckon_report_sep2009.pdf.

9. HM Revenue and Customs, *Measuring Tax Gaps 2011*, www.hmrc.gov.uk/stats /mtg-2011.pdf.

A

Audit Committee Charter

1. **Purpose**. To assist the (fill in the organization name) in fulfilling the oversight responsibilities for the financial reporting process, the system of internal control over financial reporting, the audit process, the organization's process for monitoring compliance with laws and regulations, and the code of conduct.
2. **Mission.** To provide professional advice to assist the Accounting Officer and Executive Management to secure transparency; accountability; and sound management of revenue, expenditure, assets, and liabilities of the organization.
3. **Composition.** The Audit Committee will consist of at least three external and two internal members, with alternatives where necessary.

   The Executive Committee will appoint members and the Audit Committee will elect its own Committee Chair.

4. **Authority**. The audit committee has authority to conduct or authorize investigation into any matters within its scope of responsibility with

complete and unrestricted access to all books, records, documents, facilities, and personnel of the organization. It is empowered to:

- Retain outside counsel, accountants, or others to advise the committee or assist in the conduct of its responsibilities.
- Seek any information it requires from employees—all of whom are directed to cooperate with the committee's requests—or from external parties.
- Meet with company officers, external auditors, or outside counsel, as necessary.

5. **Meetings.** The committee will meet at least four times a year, with the authority to convene additional meetings as circumstances require. The committee will invite members of management, auditors, or others to attend meetings and provide pertinent information as necessary. It will hold private meetings with the Head of Internal Audit.

Meeting agendas will be prepared and provided in advance to members, along with appropriate briefing materials. Minutes will be prepared.

6. **Responsibilities.** The committee will carry out the following responsibilities:

Financial Statements

- Review interim financial reports with management and the external auditors before filing with regulators and consider whether they are complete and consistent with the information known to committee members.

Internal Control

- Consider the effectiveness of the organization's internal control over annual and interim financial reporting, including information technology security and control.
- Understand the scope of internal and external auditors' review of internal control over financial and operational reporting and obtain reports on significant findings and recommendations, together with management's responses.

Internal Audit

- Review with management and the chief audit executive the charter, plans, activities, staffing, and organizational structure of the internal audit activity.
- Ensure there are no unjustified restrictions or limitations, and review and concur in the appointment, replacement, or dismissal of the internal chief audit executive.

- Review the effectiveness of the internal audit activity, including compliance with the Institute of Internal Auditors' Standards for the Professional Practice of Internal Auditing.
- On a regular basis, meet separately with the chief audit executive to discuss any matters that the committee or internal audit believes should be discussed privately.

External Audit

- On a regular basis, meet separately with the external auditors to discuss any matters that the committee or auditors believe should be discussed privately.

Compliance

- Review the effectiveness of the system for monitoring compliance with laws and regulations and the results of management's investigation and follow-up (including disciplinary action) of any instances of noncompliance.
- Review the findings of any examinations by regulatory agencies, and any auditor observations.
- Review the process for communicating the code of conduct to the organization's personnel, and for monitoring compliance therewith.
- Obtain regular updates from management and the organization's legal counsel regarding compliance matters.

Fraud Detection and Prevention

- Be alert to factors that could be indicative of management fraud, including changes in lifestyle.
- Identify and assess the propriety of related party relationships and transactions at all levels.
- Request the review of management expenses.
- Review significant and unusual financial transactions, particularly near month-ends and year-ends.
- Monitor management's programs to ensure compliance with the organization's general code of conduct and conflict-of-interest policies.
- Monitor the adequacy of the organization's information management system and other physical security measures required to protect the entity from fraud and abuse.
- Ensure that all parties are aware that the committee is the contact point for reporting suspected fraud or abuse and that whistleblower protection is active.

- Liaise with external auditors regarding the assessment of fraud risks, the entity's responses to those risks, and any suspected or actual fraud and abuse reported to the audit committee during the year.
- Ensure the investigation of suspected fraud and abuse take place in a speedy manner, including communicating appropriate matters to legal counsel and law enforcement authorities.
- Ensure the review of the adequacy of insurance coverage associated with fraud.

7. **Other Responsibilities**
   - Perform other activities related to this charter as requested by the Management Board.
   - Institute and oversee special investigations as needed.
   - Review and assess the adequacy of the committee charter annually, requesting board approval for proposed changes.
   - Confirm annually that all responsibilities outlined in this charter have been carried out.
   - Evaluate the committee's and individual members' performance on a regular basis.

_____   _____

Chairperson: Audit Committee   Date

_____   _____

CEO/CFO or Accounting Officer   Date

Corporate Fraud Policy

THIS POLICY DEFINES THE RESPONSIBILITIES of management and staff of the organization with regard to the establishment and maintenance of an effective system of internal controls and defines responsibilities when impropriety, including fraud, is suspected or detected.

 POLICY

It is the policy of the board of directors that:

- Management officers and supervisors will develop and maintain an appropriate system of antifraud measures and will integrate adequate internal controls into organizational processes to protect the corporate assets and resources for which they are responsible. The system should ensure that all transactions are appropriately authorized and properly recorded, that assets are properly safeguarded, and that actions can be accurately traced with originators identified
- Management officers and supervisors will be responsible for evaluating and testing antifraud controls on a periodic basis and will develop the policies,

guidelines, and procedures appropriate to ensure the implementation of an effective system of internal control.

▪ Management officers, supervisors, and staff will maintain an understanding of the risks of irregularities or violations of internal controls and will be alert for any indicators of the potential existence of fraud.

▪ Management officers, supervisors, and staff will escalate and report any suspected employee or contractual party fraud directly to the appropriate corporate authorities.

▪ As part of this policy, any allegations of fraud will be investigated objectively, fairly, and promptly.

BACKGROUND AND IMPLEMENTATION

Antifraud controls exist as processes implemented within the company to ensure that risks are reduced that could lead to loss of resources or assets by the processing of transactions which are unauthorized or improperly recorded or which cannot be traced back to the originator. These controls are required to ensure the appropriate authorization, accurate, and complete recording and processing and accountability for all transactions.

In order to ensure the design of an effective system of antifraud controls, a full risk assessment must be conducted in order to identify the degree of threat posed by each fraud opportunity against the interests of the organization. Only at that stage can internal control structures be designed to address specific threats and assure the adequacy of preventive, detective, and corrective controls. The implementation of these controls will be directed by the corporate policies and procedures and guidelines together with the managerial control responsibilities assigned.

In general, fraud prevention and detection is a fundamental management responsibility. Fraud itself may be defined as the intentional deceit or misrepresentation of a material fact in order to gain an unfair advantage over another or to prejudice their legal right in order to secure such advantage. Frauds may be conducted against the interests of an organization as well as to the "benefit" of the organization which may, ultimately, be equally detrimental.

Frauds perpetrated to the detriment of the organization generally take the form of embezzlement of the organization's money or assets, including the falsification of records to conceal such embezzlement, intentional misrepresentation of financial and nonfinancial information, solicitation or acceptance of bribes or kickbacks, as well as the agreement to inappropriate terms of discounts on corporate transactions.

Frauds apparently to the benefit of the organization may or may not lead to direct benefits for the perpetrator but normally involve the gaining of an unfair or dishonest advantage over a third party, including such activities as improper valuations of assets, offering of bribes and kickbacks, failure to disclose significant information during the negotiation of contracts, and failure to uphold guarantees or to abide with negotiated terms of contracts.

It is the duty of management to ensure that all employees, suppliers, and customers are aware of the organization's attitude to fraud and that all stakeholders are encouraged to report known or suspected incidences of fraudulent behavior. Specifically, all employees are required to report to the appropriate authorities within the organization any:

- Suspected or actual fraudulent activities conducted by an employee or third party to the detriment or for the benefit of the organization.
- Violations of laws, regulations, policies, plans, and procedures.
- Misrepresentation of information in correspondence to or from clients, suppliers, or third parties.
- Acceptance of, or solicitation of, bribes, kickbacks, or other gratuities in contravention of corporate policy.

Once reported to the appropriate authorities within the organization, no further action should be taken by employees to investigate suspicious behavior. Such action could have a detrimental effect on subsequent investigations as well as potentially place the employee in danger. Suspicions should be reported by the authorized route and should not be externalized unless failure to do so would place the employee in breach of the law themselves.

When the allegations are made for the appropriate channels, the authorized member of management, normally the chief audit executive, will conduct an internal investigation in order to determine whether sufficient evidence exists to indicate that a fraud, crime, or other activity to the detriment of the organization has occurred or is occurring. Investigation may involve the examination of documentation and business records, conducting of interviews both internally and externally, and, if required, conducting of lifestyle reviews including credit checks on staff members who have fallen under suspicion.

Where the evidence is deemed factual, adequate, and convincing, the evidence will be appropriately preserved and a recommendation made to executive level as to whether the alleged offense involves a criminal breach and should be handed over to the appropriate legal authorities or whether it should be handled internally using corporate disciplinary procedures.

Disciplinary procedures may be instituted against employees who:

- Have committed, assisted in the commission of, or assisted in the conceal-ment of fraudulent activities.
- Made false statements in connection with investigations of fraudulent activities.
- Retaliated against another employee for reporting fraudulent activities in line with procedures outlined under this policy.

The results of all such investigations will be copied to the audit committee as well as the board of directors

 ## FRAUD AWARENESS TRAINING

Fraud awareness training may be conducted internally or utilizing outside resources in order to ensure all management and employees are aware of the provisions of this policy as well as red flags that may indicate the presence of fraud or fraud opportunities.

As part of management's ongoing risk management activities, fraud risk evaluation will be carried out on an ongoing basis at appropriate management and supervisory levels.

APPENDIX

Whistleblowing Policy

W HERE FRAUD HAS BEEN UNCOVERED, it frequently becomes evident that staff members realized that there may have been something wrong within the organization but did not express their concerns, either through fear of harassment and victimization or a misplaced sense of loyalty to their colleagues who are, in fact, the fraudsters. Other barriers to the reporting of wrongdoing have, in the past, involved:

- A lack of trust in the internal system whereby such allegations are investigated
- A belief that management will not be held accountable to the same standards as other employees
- An unwillingness to be seen as a corporate informer
- Fear of retaliation
- Fear of ostracism by other employees

This policy is intended to convey the organization's belief in openness and honesty combined with a commitment to the highest standards of accountability. We encourage staff members to raise serious concerns within the organization rather than ignoring a problem or externalizing it.

This policy is intended to bring to the attention of employees:

▪ Their duty to report areas of serious concern and the mechanism through which such concerns can be reported.
▪ The protection which the organization will offer against possible reprisals or victimization for the reporting of such concerns in the reasonable belief that the disclosure was made in good faith.

This Whistleblowing Policy covers major concerns including but not limited to:

▪ Possible fraud, corruption, and other forms of financial the regularity
▪ Unauthorized use of corporate funds
▪ Any conduct involving a breach of the law
▪ Unethical conduct on behalf of any employee or any level of management
▪ Sexual, or any other form of, harassment in the workplace
▪ Breaches of the corporate code of conduct or other unethical behavior

Where such conduct is reported, a zero tolerance approach will be taken to any attempts at harassment or victimization of the individual who made the report, and every effort will be made to conceal the reporter's identity if requested. This does not, however, preclude the need for the whistleblower to appear as a witness if a criminal prosecution is brought by the legal authorities. At all times, the reporter has the option to report anonymously. Anonymous allegations will be considered at the discretion of management taking into consideration the credibility of the concern expressed, the seriousness of the allegations made and the probability of being able to confirm the allegations from an independent source.

Should an allegation that is made in good faith be proved inaccurate by an investigation, no action will be taken against the reporter. Where the investigation indicates that the allegation was made maliciously or for personal gain, disciplinary action may be taken against the reporter. In this manner the organization seeks to protect its employees from being unjustly accused for frivolous or malicious reasons.

 REPORTING AND INVESTIGATION

Reporting may take place verbally, via the corporate hotline, by e-mail, or in writing. It should be noted by all that there is no onus on the reporter to prove the truth of any allegation beyond any doubt; however, there is a need to show reasonable grounds for having made the allegation in the first place.

All such allegations will be investigated by the appropriate authorities within the company and, where the whistleblower has given an avenue of response, feedback will be given on the conclusion of the investigation. The appropriate authorities within the organization may be management, internal audit, independent investigators, or legal authorities, depending on the severity of the allegations and at the discretion of management.

The Board Audit Committee will ensure procedures are established for the confidential hearing whistleblower complaints and all employees will be notified individually of the reporting mechanisms, including the use of the corporate hotlines and mailboxes.

Signed: _____   Chief Executive Officer

Signed: _____   Chairperson of the Audit Committee

Fraud Prevention Checklist

F OR THE PURPOSES OF THE EVALUATION of the organization's current fraud position, this fraud prevention checklist is intended as an aid to determining the antifraud posture of the organization and its ability to withstand fraudulent attacks. It is suggested that this checklist be used as an aid by both internal audit and the audit committee.

1. Is ongoing antifraud training provided to all employees of the organization?
   - Do employees understand what constitutes fraud?
   - Have the costs of fraud to the company and everyone in it—including lost profits, adverse publicity, job loss, and decreased morale and productivity—been made clear to employees?
   - Do employees know where to seek advice when faced with uncertain ethical decisions, and do they believe that they can speak freely?
   - Has a policy of zero tolerance for fraud been communicated to employees through words and actions?

2. Is an effective fraud reporting mechanism in place?
   ■ Have employees been taught how to communicate concerns about known or potential wrongdoing?
   ■ Is there an anonymous reporting channel available to employees, such as a third-party hotline?
   ■ Do employees trust that they can report suspicious activity anonymously and/or confidentially and without fear of reprisal?
   ■ Has it been made clear to employees that reports of suspicious activity will be promptly and thoroughly evaluated?

3. To increase employees' perception of detection, are the following proactive measures taken and publicized to employees?
   ■ Is possible fraudulent conduct aggressively sought out rather than dealt with passively?
   ■ Does the organization send the message that it actively seeks out fraudulent conduct through fraud assessment questioning by auditors?
   ■ Are surprise fraud audits performed in addition to regularly scheduled fraud audits?
   ■ Is continuous auditing software used to detect fraud and, if so, has the use of such software been made known throughout the organization?

4. Is the management climate/tone at the top one of honesty and integrity?
   ■ Are employees surveyed to determine the extent to which they believe management acts with honesty and integrity?
   ■ Are performance goals realistic?
   ■ Have fraud prevention goals been incorporated into the performance measures against which managers are evaluated and which are used to determine performance-related compensation?
   ■ Has the organization established, implemented, and tested a process for oversight of fraud risks by the board of directors or others charged with governance (e.g., the audit committee)?

5. Are fraud risk assessments performed to proactively identify and mitigate the company's vulnerabilities to internal and external fraud?

6. Are strong antifraud controls in place and operating effectively, including the following?
   ■ Proper separation of duties
   ■ Use of authorizations
   ■ Physical safeguards
   ■ Job rotations
   ■ Mandatory vacations

7. Does the internal audit department, if one exists, have adequate resources and authority to operate effectively and without undue influence from senior management?
8. Does the hiring policy include the following (where permitted by law)?
   - Past employment verification
   - Criminal and civil background checks
   - Credit checks
   - Drug screening
   - Education verification
   - References check
9. Are employee support programs in place to assist employees struggling with addictions, mental/emotional health, family, or financial problems?
10. Is an open-door policy in place that allows employees to speak freely about pressures, providing management the opportunity to alleviate such pressures before they become acute?
11. Are anonymous surveys conducted to assess employee morale?

Fraud Risk Questionnaire Sample

Company		
PREPARED BY		**DATE:**

Please **assign a rating value in the box provided below**. The rating should be from 0 to 5, with 0 indicating the lowest level of risk or no risk and 5 being the highest level or maximum risk. These risk categories are rated based on the evaluation factors below. At this stage, no presumption is made as to the likelihood of fraud or significance should a fraud occur. Nor is any consideration taken of existing antifraud measures.

ASSIGNED RISK CATEGORY	EVALUATION FACTOR	NO.	RATING
Financial Risk Areas	Account Balance Size	1	
	Transaction Values	2	
	Value in Suspense Accounts	3	
	Value of Suspense Account Trans.	4	
	Cash Values on hand	5	
	Value of Journal Entries	6	
	Value of Current Assets	7	

(continued)

ASSIGNED RISK CATEGORY	EVALUATION FACTOR	NO.	RATING
	Value of Current Asset Movements	8	
	Value of Accounts Payable	9	
	Value of Accounts Payable Trans.	10	
	Value of Accounts Receivable	11	
	Value of Accounts Receivable Trans.	12	
Human Resources	Value of Payroll	13	
	Number of Employees	14	
Information Systems	Impact of Technology	15	
	Significance of Information	16	
Procurement	Value of Stores Inventory	17	
	Purchasing Value	18	
Administration	Cost of Professional Services	19	
	Fixed Asset Value	20	
	Fixed Asset Movements	21	

At this stage, risk should be evaluated assuming no controls exist. In other words, it is an evaluation of the maximum *inherent* risk faced in each of the areas but taking into account the estimated likelihood and significance.

This evaluation normally would be followed by a questionnaire in order to evaluate the control environment, such as:

Concerns	Risk Factors	Yes/No	Tested
Level of fraud awareness	Is there a written code of ethics business conduct?		
	Is ongoing fraud awareness training carried out?		
	Are new employees made aware of the organization's position on fraud?		
	Does management set an example and enforce a zero tolerance approach on fraud issues?		
	Is there a corporate mission statement?		
	Does the corporate culture support ethical behavior in the workplace as well as in dealings with customers and vendors?		
	Do hiring policies involve background checks and credit checks for new appointments?		

Concerns	Risk Factors	Yes/No	Tested
	Is screening carried out for placement of employees in business areas particularly sensitive to fraud possibilities?		
	Is counselling available for employees with financial, substance abuse, or other problems?		
	Are compensation policies fair, equitable, and in line with the rest of the industry?		
	Do employees, suppliers, and customers know how to report a suspected incidence of fraud?		
	Are exit interviews conducted with departing employees?		
Internal control structures	Is fraud considered in the design and implementation of internal control structures?		
	Are adequate monitoring controls in place and effective to identify red flags for fraud, should they occur?		
	Is physical control in the workplace appropriate to the level of fraud potential, including access to corporate assets, records, and files?		
	Is there appropriate use of electronic access control, closed-circuit television, electronic surveillance, and so on?		
	Is segregation of duties appropriate to prevent fraud?		
	Do particularly critical or sensitive activities required two levels of authority?		
	Is logical access control appropriate and enforced within computer systems with appropriate identification and authentication controls in place?		
	Are employee access levels appropriate to the job duties undertaken?		
	Do written job descriptions exist for all employees?		
	Are job descriptions up to date and in line with functions undertaken?		
	Do job descriptions take into consideration the potential for fraud in defining authority levels?		
	Is there a requirement that employees take minimum numbers of sequential days of vacation time?		

(continued)

Concerns	Risk Factors	Yes/No	Tested
	Is there a policy for instant dismissal for commission of fraud?		
	Is there a policy for reporting all frauds to legal authorities and pressing charges?		
Management and supervision	Are management and supervisory staff alert for fraud opportunities and indicators?		
	Our appropriate monitoring controls enforced by management and supervisors?		
	When supervisory override occurs to control structures, how is it independently monitored?		
	How do management and supervisors ensure division of duties continues to be effective?		
	Do managers review customer and supplier complaints on an ongoing basis?		
Financial accounts	Are all bank accounts reconciled on regular basis?		
	Are all accounts payable reconciled?		
	Are all accounts receivable reconciled?		
	Are all subsidiary ledgers reconciled to the main general ledger?		
	Are all subsidiary ledgers compared on a trend analysis?		
Asset control	Are corporate assets easily convertible to cash?		
	Is employee access to assets appropriately controlled and subject to appropriate division of duties?		
Internal audit	Is there an internal audit function within the organization?		
	Does internal audit evaluate the effectiveness of antifraud measures on an ongoing basis?		
	Does internal audit liaise with external audit to ensure fraud risks are adequately audited?		
	Is there a fraud hotline and does internal audit have access to reported instances?		
Governance issues	Is the audit committee appropriately structured to ensure its independence?		
	Is the audit committee alert to fraud opportunities within the organization?		

Concerns	Risk Factors	Yes/No	Tested
	Do all fraud occurrences get reported to the audit committee as a matter of course?		
	Is the audit committee involved in allegations of fraud made by employees and third parties?		
	Does the audit committee take responsibility for monitoring fraud opportunities at board and executive level?		
	How often is the audit committee audited?		
Financial reporting	Are pressures on management to achieve revenue benchmark excessive?		
	Is management remuneration dependent on achieving earning expectations?		
	Do values of assets recorded on the balance sheets depend on subjective estimates by management?		
	Do the financial accounts reflect large numbers of complex subsidiaries?		
	Have there been recent changes to the accounting procedures within the organization?		

Fraud Risk Analysis

R ISK AND RISK ANALYSIS are large and complex subjects. Only the risk specifically of fraud is addressed here. The principal foundations for fraud risk analysis involve an understanding of the fraud threats, assets, external environment, and the organization itself.

Risks themselves may be seen as potential events that may threaten the business in terms of both its financial health and also its image and reputation.

Generically, risk management involves:

- The identification of risk areas
- Developing an understanding and assessment of the scale of risk
- Development of a risk response strategy
- Allocation of responsibilities and implementation of the strategy
- Implementation and monitoring of controls
- Reviewing and refining the overall process

In identifying fraud risk areas, it must be understood that fraud is only one component of an organization's operational risk. The major difference with fraud is that the risk occurs by intent and deliberate act designed normally to benefit the perpetrator.

In many cases, generic risk analysis tends to focus on a limited number of risk factors and most frequently on outsider risk. When conducting a fraud risk assessment, the emphasis needs to be on the activities and processes within the business and the assets affected by such processes.

Fraud risk assessment relates to management examining the organization's exposure to potential fraudulent schemes or internal and external corruption so that controls to mitigate and monitor the effectiveness of internal controls protecting mechanisms can be maintained. Such an assessment must be tailored to the organization's industry and to its position within the industry as well as the impact of pressures opportunities and rationalization, which are drivers toward fraudulent activities. Given these variables, it must be clearly understood that one size does not fit all and that the risk assessment must be tailored to the needs of the organization. Fraud risk assessment involves a process of:

- Fraud risk identification
- Assessment of inherent fraud risk
- Identification of the internal control structures intended to mitigate such risk
- Evaluation of the adequacy of such control structures
- Identification of the critical control components within those structures
- Testing and evaluation of the effectiveness of those critical control components

Normally, the internal controls to prevent and detect fraud involve a combination of manual and automated preventive and detective techniques. As in all cases, the cost of control should not exceed the benefit to the organization produced by such control, although this can be difficult to quantify in terms of benefits such as avoidance of reputational risk.

Most organizations realize that total elimination of risk is neither desirable nor cost effective. The objective is to reduce the risk to levels that management can tolerate. This approach can prove unacceptable to management since it involves the acknowledgment that the risk of fraud exists within the organization and will continue to do so despite management's best efforts. With this in mind, it has become a common practice for management to outsource their fraud risk assessment since it may be politically inexpedient for internal resources, such as risk management or internal audit, to be seen to evaluate an area as having a high risk of fraud.

Many organizations require that fraud risk be assessed by line managers on an ongoing basis based on some form of assessment of likelihood and impact.

Such a methodology normally involves an assessment of the probability of a fraud occurring within a particular time frame, such as within one year or within ten years. For such a methodology to be effective, the organization depends on the availability of historical evidence to support the frequency estimation. In an organization such as a bank, which may have access to historical information regarding, for example, credit card fraud, such risks can indeed be quantified over a period. Unfortunately, this information is not normally available to line managers, and their assessments of risk probability can vary greatly.

In part, this is because the probability of a fraud occurring depends on an individual having the motivation to commit a fraud, not solely on weaknesses within the internal control structures. When line managers assess probability of fraud, they tend to evaluate the control structures assuming they will function as intended. Where weaknesses and potential vulnerabilities exist, line managers may be reluctant to admit the possibility of fraud in the area under their control.

A more reliable method of assessing fraud probability is to consider where the operational area is vulnerable, assuming both an area of high dependency on the effectiveness of controls and the possibility that sufficient dishonesty may exist within individuals, internally or externally, to be willing to compromise the controls.

Effectively this reverses the process from considering the likelihood of a fraud to considering the degree of fraud resistance, should an attempt be made. It also makes it possible to target specific individuals who, by the nature of their job function or authority level, are in a position to perpetrate a fraud solely or in collusion.

In organizations where this approach has been taken, the fraud risk that previously had been evaluated as low was now evaluated as medium to high. The most effective way of developing fraud scenarios is to look at those that actually have been used by successful fraudsters in other organizations.

The process of conducting a fraud risk analysis involves techniques such as:

- The review and analysis of business process documentation
- Conducting interviews internally with management and employees regarding the procedures undertaken and the controls relied on
- Conducting interviews externally with customers and vendors to establish both their degrees of satisfaction with corporate internal control mechanisms as well as areas of weakness from their perspective
- The development of fraud scenarios based on weaknesses identified in the previous processes

- Conducting data analysis (with or without computer-assisted audit tools and techniques) as appropriate to establish the operational effectiveness of the controls relied on by management

Having conducted such a risk analysis, senior executives are in a position to evaluate the consequences not only of asset loss but the impact on reputation, regulatory impact, and loss of market share. A more accurate evaluation is then possible using a grid allowing multiple corporate risks from fraud to be factored in.

Risk Level	Fraud Method	Probability	Worst-Case Financial Loss	Reputational Impact	Regulatory Impact
Severe	Chief financial officer (CFO) creates offshore accounts to conceal high-value transactions	High	$100 million	Severe	Severe
High	Employee creates phony invoices for a fictitious creditor	High	$2 million	Medium	Low

Use of such a grid does not imply that the CFO is dishonest, only that, should he or she decide to commit such a fraud, the opportunity is there with the current internal control structure and that the impacts could be significant. Evaluating risk in this manner can point the organization directly toward areas where current internal control structures would allow the execution of a fraud with minimal chance of prevention or detection. This assessment enables the design and implementation of additional controls specifically to address the areas of vulnerability identified. The extent and nature of these controls are dependent on the risk appetite of the organization as well as the cost and the degree to which such controls may change fundamentals of the way the organization does business. The most significant fraud risks may require significant capital expenditure to address or major initiatives to adopt new working practices.

When an organization adopts such a risk approach, it is critical that it be maintained to reflect any significant changes in processes or structures of the organization.

APPENDIX

Fraud CAATs

N TODAY'S HIGH-TECH ENVIRONMENT, the search for evidence of fraud inevitably leads to the use of computer-assisted audit tools and techniques (CAATs). These tools and techniques facilitate information retrieval and analysis using automated procedures. Such programs can organize, combine, extract, and analyze information in a variety of forms and from a variety of sources in such a manner as would be acceptable to a court of law.

 ## TECHNIQUES

Before selecting the appropriate tool for the investigation in hand, the fraud examiner must decide what evidence is sought and where, in the course of this particular investigation, such evidence will be found. Should the information be available in documentation, the standard investigative techniques for examining such documentation and evaluation of the contents would come into play. Should the information exist in the knowledge of an individual, interviewing and interrogation may be the appropriate techniques. When the evidence regarding the effectiveness of the controls in preventing or detecting fraud, or evidence regarding the fraud itself exist within computer systems, the evaluator or investigator must decide where the evidence resides and what the appropriate technique would be to obtain and evaluate such evidence.

Source Code Review

The source code review involves the examination of program source code as it has been written by the programmers. With the sheer size of computer application systems and their integrated nature, such reviews may be impractical. However, should an investigator wish to evaluate the appropriateness of controls built into computer systems, examination of that part of the program that includes the antifraud tests and controls may be appropriate.

Problems with this technique include the need for the investigator to have the appropriate information technology (IT) skills in the particular language used to write programs as well as the difficulties in establishing that the source code reviewed actually matches the current version of the executable program. In addition, such examination must always take into consideration that the fact that appropriate controls exist within program code is no guarantee that the code will be executed. It is possible that an earlier stage of processing may include code to bypass the control section.

Use of Test Data

When the object of the exercise is to determine the effectiveness of internal controls in deterring fraud, monitoring fraud opportunities, or identifying evidence that fraud is actually occurring, one techniques available to the investigator is the use of test data. This technique involves using a copy of the live computer system through which a series of transactions is passed in order to produce predetermined results. This method allows the investigator to determine whether controls designed to prevent abnormal transactions or unauthorized transactions exist and continue to work effectively. Detective controls that will not prevent the processing of such transactions but will alert the organization to the existence of suspicious transactions may also be tested in combination with checks on the clerical procedures for handling such notification of abnormalities.

The drawbacks in the use of test data are that the system being tested is a copy of the live system and not the true system as it routinely operates. In addition, volumes of test data are normally limited, and not all possible routes through systems can be tested. Systems that generate internal transactions may also escape detection using test data methods.

Integrated Test Facility

The integrated test facility (ITF) technique, while similar in nature to test data, is effected by creation within the live database of a dummy entity (department, warehouse, etc.) and the processing of test data against the dummy entity *through the live system, together with the live data.* This technique has the advantage of testing the system as it routinely operates in order to ensure that potentially fraudulent transactions are either prevented or detected at an early stage. It also tests both the live computer system as well as the clerical procedures associated with the prevention and detection of such transactions.

Once again, there are disadvantages to the ITF technique. It must always be borne in mind that transactions are being processed against the *live* database. Where the ITF technique is used, all test transactions must be removed from that database before they affect live totals, postings, or the production of negotiable documents, such as checks. In some application systems, this may not be possible. Test transactions may be reversible but not removable, which may complicate future analyses of the live database. In addition, the investigator must always be aware that processing is being conducted through the live system against a live database. This technique should be used only to examine *how* the system operates, not *if* the system operates. A failure could involve bringing the whole live application system to its knees in the course of testing controls.

System Collection Audit Review Files

In application systems where audit trails may exist only as computer records (i.e., not printed) and then only for a short time or discontinuously, it may be necessary to have an built-in facility to collect and retain selected information to serve as an audit trail for subsequent antifraud examination. This obviously would make the system collection audit review files target for destruction or manipulation to conceal a fraud. Where such a facility exists, the integrity and completeness of the information must be assured.

Parallel Simulation

Parallel simulation involves the use of independently developed software to simulate the functional capability of parts of the live system in which fraudulent processing could occur. The live data are then processed through the simulating program in parallel with the live system, and the outputs are compared. This technique is especially useful in ensuring that calculations, discount rates, interest rates, and the like are being appropriately and accurately applied. The independence of software development is critical to ensure that, where a fraud has been built in to an application system, the same coding is not applied within the parallel software.

 TOOLS

Different varieties of such CAAT include:

- Applications software
- Online inquiry
- Information retrieval software
- Standard utilities
- Industry-related software
- Customized audit software
- Generalized audit software

All of these tools are designed to handle high volumes of data. They can be used in combination by a fraud investigator to uncover patterns of fraud and other evidence relevant to the proof that a fraud occurred and that a specific individual was responsible.

Application Software

Virtually all software designed to conduct business applications have interrogation capability allowing an investigator or auditor the ability to look at the data as they are seen in everyday processing by the business application system. Output may be in the form of printouts, screen-based information, or secondary files for onward comparison. The software was not originally written for the purposes of forensic examination. Should that be the intended use, the integrity of the software itself must be ensured. Where the software has come from a third-party producer, the accuracy and completeness of its processing should be covered in the software services contract. Fraud examiners still must satisfy themselves that the software is operating in the manner intended by the manufacturer and in a controlled manner. Where such software is developed in house, the examiner is faced with a choice. Using this particular software for forensic purposes will require a full-blown investigation into the development process, implementation, operating procedures, and change control under which the application system operates. In many cases, this exercise may take longer than the fraud investigation itself, and the investigator may decide to use an alternative approach.

Information Retrieval Software

Standard information retrieval programs, such as report writers and query languages, can perform many of the processes investigators require. Although not specifically developed for either audit or fraud investigation purposes, these tools can be effective in extracting information that would be forensically acceptable for production in court. Included in this category of software are standard report writers, program generators, and fourth-generation languages.

Online Inquiry

Interactive interrogation can provide comparative data for investigative purposes as well as confirmation of control processes. Effective use does not normally require high levels of IT skills but an understanding of the nature and structure of the information examined is essential. Armed with the appropriate access authorities, investigators may be able to obtain adequate forensic evidence to meet their requirements. It is, however, critical that examiners are certain about what they are looking at since it is comparatively easy to draw completely the wrong conclusions based on inappropriate interrogation.

Standard Utilities

Standard utilities are general-purpose pieces of software normally supplied with the computer's operating system or database management system. They are independent of the application systems and normally come from a trusted source. Once again, they were not initially designed as forensic tools but may prove effective in this role, depending on how the investigator utilizes them. Utilities can perform standard tasks, such as copying data; backing up systems; sorting data; extracting, merging, or even editing data; as well as printing. Since this software bypasses the normal processing mechanisms of the application system, it sees data as they actually exist and not as they are interpreted by the application system. For this reason, in certain circumstances, the outputs more reliable.

In their own right, standard utilities are extremely powerful. Inappropriate use by an inexperienced investigator actually can corrupt the evidence prior to a case ever coming to court. Where investigators do not have IT skills themselves, it is expedient to use the IT department to execute the utilities on the investigators' behalf. Obviously, where the IT area is suspected of involvement in the fraud, an independent third-party expert would be required. Where the evidence is not going to be used directly, this in-house gathered evidence may be all the investigator requires to point to specific areas for further investigation.

Industry-Related Software

Industry-related software is available for specific industries, such as insurance, health care, and financial services. Once again, such software is designed to perform standard tasks applicable to those industries, not specifically for forensic purposes. Many of these packages require standard file formats, which means that the data supplied from the client machine must be converted prior to processing. In essence, this means that the information the investigator is looking at is not the original information but has been further processed to make it acceptable to the industry-related package. The investigator may require a degree of IT skill to evaluate the conversion process and determine how much reliance can be placed on the information drawn from the converted data. Nevertheless, it can be useful for investigators who do not intend to use the information derived from this analysis directly in court but are seeking information pointing to a more forensically acceptable source of evidence.

Customized Audit Software

Customized audit software is designed to be run by auditors and investigators in unique circumstances and to perform unique tests. Where the computer system itself uses nonstandard data structures, interrogation software may need to be written specifically to address those eccentricities built into the applications. This type of software is normally expensive to acquire or develop. It also requires a high level of IT skill to use effectively and to interpret the results accurately. Where such software has already been developed for internal or external audit purposes, investigators must ensure that the answers provided by the outputs actually address the questions they wish answered. The software was written to answer specific audit questions in a specific manner and may not be relevant or appropriate in a fraud investigation.

Generalized Audit Software

Generalized audit software (GAS) is software that has been designed specifically for auditors in order to provide a user-friendly investigative tool to carry out a variety of standard tasks, including:

- Examination of records
- Testing of calculations
- Making computations
- Evaluation of control adequacy
- Evaluation of control effectiveness

Selecting, analyzing, and reporting on statistical samples are techniques that can significantly improve the quality of the investigation by allowing the quantification of sampling risk (risk that the sample may not adequately represent the population). In today's high-volume systems, such techniques can facilitate the effectiveness of investigation of suspected fraudulent activity and the seeking of evidence to a standard that would be acceptable in court. In a cloud environment, forensic investigation commonly involves the need to handle data presented in a nonstandard format where the software must be capable of automatic conversion to analyzable information.

While GAS cannot resolve all of an investigator's problems, it can help in many of the common problem areas since it is specifically designed for handling of large volumes of data by a non-IT specialist. The investigator can then focus on the evidence sought and the information required and pay less attention to the ongoing evaluation of tools for obtaining and interpreting such information. Because the outputs can be used for further computer processing, investigations can be linked over a period of time, as can the evaluation of the internal control environment.

Analytical Techniques Using CAATs

Common techniques for the detection of fraud indicators to the analysis of information using CAATs include:

- Joining information from different sources to identify common information where commonality should not occur; for example, matching names, addresses, telephone numbers, and bank account numbers on a creditor file against the payroll file.
- Calculation of operational statistics, such as high/low values or volumes, moving averages, or standard deviations of populations in order to conduct either trend analysis or to analyze population abnormalities that could indicate the presence of a fraud.
- Data analysis using Benford's Law to identify unexpected occurrences of digits in data sets that are naturally occurring and where such abnormalities could again indicate potential fraudulent activity.

- Duplication testing to identify move to duplicate payments, expense claims, health care claims, and other transactions that should be unique.
- Gap testing to identify missing transactions or values in data that should be sequential and contain no gaps.
- Verification of transaction dates to identify transactions processed at inappropriate times, for example, expenses incurred in connection with an event processed before such expenses are even possible.
- Classification of data in order to seek patterns or abnormalities within patterns.

When analyzing data, one problem likely to be encountered is the codification of information in data files. In order to improve efficiencies of processing files were frequently coded, for example, using short department codes rather than department names, in order to save space and processing time. As a result, it may be necessary to take information from multiple files and combine them in order to make sense from an investigative perspective. In implementing such coding structures, it is common to concatenate individual pieces of information, each of which has a specific meaning, into one single field. For example, the first six digits of the South African identification number is the date of birth. One such information is understood, anomalies such as an individual claiming a date of birth that does not match his or her identification number should immediately stand out in any analysis.

Any analytical technique relies on the integrity and reliability of the information analyzed, and that quality must be established prior to the conduct of the analytical review. This evaluation can be achieved by comparing numbers of records, total values, and the like to information sources known to be accurate. Where such reliable information is unavailable, reasonableness tests may provide sufficient confidence prior to analysis. For example, if there are 1,000 creditors, each paid monthly, it is reasonable to believe that payments over the year should involve approximately 12,000 transactions. The appearance of 20,000 transactions would be a red flag of something wrong, although the appearance of 12,010 transactions may prove nothing.

When an examination indicates the data as unreliable, that may be a sufficient indicator of potential fraud to warrant further investigation. Depending on the nature of the unreliability, the use of CAATs may have to be forgone and other investigative techniques undertaken instead.

Regardless of the apparent reliability of information, it must be borne in mind that data analysis is not direct evidence. Where anomalies are found, independent verification and double checking will be required.

 CONTINUOUS MONITORING

Using CAATs as a monitoring tool in order to ensure the ongoing effectiveness of antifraud measures is becoming a corporate imperative in the face of high-volume, low-value fraudulent activities. It is in this type of fraud that the conventional preventive controls may become ineffective as the individual value of each fraud drops below a tolerance horizon. Monitoring technology can deliver a powerful punch in the implementation of antifraud measures before the event rather than retrospectively, after fraud has occurred. Depending on the nature of transactions and their vulnerability to fraudulent activity, monitoring may take place and be reported on a weekly basis, daily, or even real time in a higher-risk environment.

This type of monitoring overcomes the traditional problems inherent in sampling by using the computer itself to do 100 percent of surveys of data while in transactions are in process. When monitoring systems were first introduced, the traditional approach was to use field-level comparisons of data to spot abnormalities, such as duplicate order numbers or payments. This comparison was normally implemented as part of the control mechanisms within application systems and was used most commonly to detect errors rather than fraud.

In a modern integrated continuous monitoring system, the objective is to identify overall *similarities* with corresponding *matches* at the detailed level. Once unusual transactions have been identified, the software can then evaluate against known patterns of transaction processing from specific users to differentiate between erroneous transactions and those exhibiting patterns associated with potential fraudulent activity. For example:

> *Fraud chains* are made up of sets of debit/credit pairs that appear normal but, when connected, can net out as a fraudulent transaction. When such transactions are split and hidden among multiple valid entries, the "chaining" may go undetected through normal methods. Only by implementing analysis using advanced fraud chain analytics can such transactions be detected.

Continuous monitoring of transactions also can detect inconsistencies in details, such as revenue recognition where, for example, inventory transfers may be booked as sales or goods may be shipped without invoicing or invoiced without shipping.

Most modern audit software enables statistical evaluation of populations as well as structural approaches and similarity comparisons to enable effective forensic monitoring.

Glossary

Accion civil resarcitoria   A civil action taking place in step with a concurrent criminal investigation but that separates the need for criminal conviction and may award money for compensation independently of individual criminal conviction.

Advance-fee fraud   Any fraud requesting a fee in advance in order to release a large amount of money. Also known as 4-1-9 fraud.

Affidavit   A sworn statement.

Agency fraud   Occurs when a third party involved in a financial transaction commits a fraudulent act or encourages a consumer to falsify information when acting on his or her behalf.

Animus nocendi   The subjective state of mind of the criminal, with reference to the exact knowledge of illegal content of behavior and of its possible consequences.

Anti–money laundering   The legal controls requiring regulated or financial institutions to prevent, detect, or report transactions or activities suspected of being used to launder money.

Back door   An unauthorized entry point to a computer system.

Bait and switch   Advertising a low-cost item and then steering the customer to a higher-priced item, claiming the low-priced item was sold out.

Best evidence   The most reliable evidence that the nature of a given case will allow so that secondary evidence, such as a copy of a document, perhaps with amendments, cannot be used to contradict primary evidence such as the original document itself.

Bid rigging   A scheme that gives the appearance of competitive bids but is actually not competitive, because the participants decide on the winner before the bids are submitted and other bids are placed with higher rates or unacceptable conditions to give the "winner" the best opportunity.

Bid rotation   A variation on bid rigging in which bidders for contracts collude to distribute work among themselves by deciding who among them will win particular bids.

Card not present (CNP)   The transaction type where the card is not present at the time of a purchase, such as for telephone, mail, or Internet purchases.

Caveat emptor   Let the buyer beware.

Caveat venditor   Let the seller beware.

Chargeback   The reversal of a credit card transaction after a sale has been settled. If a cardholder disputes a transaction, the issuer would then bill the transaction back to the merchant effectively charging him back for the reversed transaction.

Chain of custody   The record of possession of evidence from original discovery until its production at trial.

Check fraud   A term used to describe fraud related to checks, including counterfeiting, forgery, kiting, and paperhanging.

Civil law   A system under which legislation is seen as the primary source of law with the laws laid out in codifications and with judgments made both on fact and on interpretation of the law.

Common law   The system under which courts rule based on precedents and customs interpreted by courts and other judicial tribunals.

Computer hacker   A person who attacks another's computer and seeks to gain unauthorized access by defeating the computer's logical security system.

Confidence game   A fraud scheme in which the fraudster gains the confidence of the victim in order to defraud him or her in some way.

Conflict of interest   May be deemed to exist when an employee has some personal kinship, friendship, or financial interest in the transaction that may put his or her duty to the employer in jeopardy.

Conspiracy   Two or more persons coming together for the purpose of committing a fraud.

Contra ius commune   Against common law.

Corpus delicti   The body of the offense.

Corrigenda   Things to be corrected.

Credit card generators   Computer programs used to generate credit card numbers that are valid in terms of the numbering conventions but have not actually been issued.

Curia regis   Originally a council that advised the king of England on legislative matters. Ultimately it became the Parliament of the United Kingdom.

CVC   The generic term for card verification code tied to a debit or credit card and appearing on the card only in a nonembossed format.

Cybercrime   Frauds perpetrated on the Internet or through the use of computers.

De bonis asportatis   Carrying goods away—the traditional name for larceny.

De facto   Concerning fact—in practice but not necessarily ordained by law.

Defalcation   Embezzlement or acts that change a particular debt so it cannot be discharged in bankruptcy.

Demonstrative evidence   Evidence that demonstrates how an event could have taken place or a fraud have been committed.

Deposition   A pretrial legal proceeding in which an individual is questioned under oath by an attorney, usually witnessed and recorded, in order to induce the person to make statements of knowledge or fact that can be used at trial or to uncover evidence that may be used later at trial.

Direct evidence   Generally taken to be oral evidence with regard to information obtained from any of the witness's five senses.

Documentary evidence   Evidence in the form of business records, computer evidence, reports, and printouts.

Dumpster diving   Rummaging through corporate or an individual's trash in order to obtain personal information used to commit identity theft.

Embezzlement   Theft of money from an employer by an employee while using false entries in accounting records to cover up the existence or extent of the crime.

Entrapment   The unlawfully luring of an individual into a crime by an officer of the law.

Estoppel   An impediment preventing one party from asserting a fact inconsistent with facts previously presented by that party, particularly if the original assertion has been acted on by others.

Fiduciary   Someone who acts for and on behalf of another person in a particular matter in circumstances that give rise to a relationship of trust and confidence.

Firewall   A piece of software acting as a one-way mirror helping to protect a computer from online attacks.

Flagrante delicto   Caught in the act of committing an offense.

Forensic   Suitable for use in court proceedings or public inquiry.

Ghost terminal   A skimming device involving a fake automated teller machine (ATM) touchpad and reader, placed over a legitimate ATM, in order to obtain card information and personal identification number.

Hearsay evidence   Evidence that is not personally and directly known to a witness.

Identity theft   Theft of personal or financial details used to impersonate individuals, obtain credit, open bank accounts, or even set up companies.

In curia   The hearing of a case before a court sitting in public.

In personam   Directed toward a particular person.

In re   In the matter of.

In rem   Directed against a thing or piece of property.

Insider trading   Use of business information not released to the public in order to reap profits by trading in financial markets.

Intra vires   Within the jurisdiction of the court.

Kickback   A payment by a vendor to an employee in order for the vendor to receive favorable treatment.

Kiting   Using multiple bank accounts in multiple banks, by making deposits and writing checks against the accounts before the deposit checks clear the banking system, thus using the lag in time while checks clear to create a "float" of money.

Lapping   A fraud technique that involves theft of a customer's payment and then using a subsequent customer payment to cover the previous customer's account.

Lowballing   Placing an abnormally low bid in order to win the contract, with the intent to inflate the price later by means of extras or change orders.

Magna Carta or Magna Carta Libertatum   The Great Charter forced on King John at Runnymede in 1215. It is generally looked on as an uncodified constitution and the foundation or inspiration for many national constitutions.

Money laundering   The process of concealing the source of money gained by illegal means.

Money mule   A fraud in which individuals are offered payment in exchange for allowing their accounts to be used to "launder" the proceeds of crime.

Negative invoicing   Exploiting weaknesses in a computer system that may allow an invoice to be processed for a negative amount in order to cover a theft of a customer payment, since negative invoices normally are subject to less stringent controls than credit memoranda.

Nulla bona   No effects—the defendant has no goods of any value to remove.

Paperhanging   A type of check fraud in which checks are written on closed accounts.

Phishing   A type of social engineering fraud in which a fraudster makes use of e-mails that appear to come from legitimate sources and are designed to persuade the recipient to release confidential information, such as passwords or Social Security numbers.

Piercing the veil   A legal decision to remove the treatment of a corporation as a separate legal person and treat its rights and duties as the rights or liabilities of its shareholders. This treatment is normally used where a court has been convinced that the corporation has been created specifically to shield the shareholders from the law.

Ponzi scheme   A fraud in which a high rate of return is promised on investments with the first few investors actually receiving the high rate of return from part of the investments of later victims.

Prima facie   First sight: *Prima facie* evidence is considered enough/sufficient to prove a case unless disproved or rejected.

Quid tam pro domino rege quam prose ipso in hac parte sequitur (qui tam)   Who pursues this action on our lord the king's behalf as well as his own.

Real evidence   Consists of tangible objects that prove or disprove guilt, such as physical evidence linking a suspect to the scene of the crime.

Salami technique   A fraud typically found in high-volume transaction systems involving the theft of low-value items, such as fractions of cents in calculations, and moving them to a single account.

Sine qua non   A condition without which it could not be or without which there is nothing.

Skimming   A method used by fraudsters to obtain payment card information by using a device to read the magnetic stripe at an automated teller machine or a location where the transaction is processed out of sight of the cardholder.

Spyware   Concealed software transmitted, perhaps concealed in an email attachment, to a recipient in order to secretly gather confidential, personal information and pass it on to a third party.

Trojan horse   Unauthorized computer coding that is inserted into a live system and remains dormant until triggered by an external event to manipulate data, disrupt computer operations, or permit unauthorized access.

Ultra vires   Beyond the powers of the court.

About the Author

RICHARD E. CASCARINO, MBA, CIA, CISM, CFE, is well known in international auditing circles as one of the most knowledgeable practitioners in the field. He is a principal of Richard Cascarino & Associates with over 27 years' experience in audit training and consultancy. He is a regular speaker at national and international conferences and has presented courses throughout Africa, Europe, the Middle East, and the United States. Richard is a past president of the Institute of Internal Auditors in South Africa, was the founding regional director of the Southern African Region of the IIA-Inc, and is a member of ISACA and the Association of Certified Fraud Examiners.

Richard has been involved in the development of courses in both internal auditing and IP security for the School of Accountancy, University of the Witwatersrand, Johannesburg, where he continues to act as an external examiner. He has provided consultancy and professional development services to clients throughout the United States, Africa, Europe, and the Middle East. His clients include some of the largest corporations, government departments, auditors general, professional bodies, and financial institutions in their respective countries.

He is also a visiting lecturer at the University of the Witwatersrand, lead author of the book *Internal Auditing: An Integrated Approach* (Juta Publishing) as well as the author of the *Auditor's Guide to IT Auditing* (John Wiley & Sons). These books are extensively used as university textbooks worldwide.

About the Web Site

AS PART OF YOUR PURCHASE OF THIS BOOK, you have been given an education version of IDEA—Data Analysis Software. This software can improve your audit performance and extend your capabilities with IDEA's powerful functionality. With IDEA, you can lower your cost of analysis, add more quality to your work, and meet the new professional requirements regarding fraud and internal control.

IDEA can read, display, analyze, manipulate, sample, or extract from data files from almost any source—from SAP to QuickBooks—including reports printed to a file. IDEA adds depth and productivity to audits and helps users meet the requirements of SAS 99 and Sarbanes-Oxley 404. Examples of how IDEA can be used to meet audit objectives include: accuracy—checking totals and calculations; analytical review—comparisons, profiling, stratifying; validity—duplicates, exceptions, statistical samples; cut-off-date and number sequence analysis; valuation—A/R and inventory provisions analysis.

Included with this version is a combination of extensive HTML-based Help, Informative User Guide with tutorial, "IDEAssistants"—wizards for key functions, Windows-standard features like right-click and drag and drop, plus a carefully designed user interface make learning and using a breeze.

IDEA is a registered trademark of CaseWare International Inc.

The link to this software can be found at: www.wiley.com/go /corporatefraud.

The password is: cascarino.

Index